BEYOND VISION

Beyond Vision

Going Blind, Inner Seeing, and the Nature of the Self

ALLAN JONES

McGill-Queen's University Press

Montreal & Kingston • London • Chicago

© McGill-Queen's University Press 2018

ISBN 978-0-7735-5285-2 (cloth)
ISBN 978-0-7735-5379-8 (ePDF)
ISBN 978-0-7735-5380-4 (ePUB)

Legal deposit second quarter 2018
Bibliothèque nationale du Québec

Printed in Canada on acid-free paper that is 100% ancient forest free
(100% post-consumer recycled), processed chlorine free

This book has been published with the help of a grant from the
Eric T. Webster Foundation.

We acknowledge the support of the Canada Council for the Arts, which
last year invested $153 million to bring the arts to Canadians throughout
the country.

Nous remercions le Conseil des arts du Canada de son soutien. L'an dernier,
le Conseil a investi 153 millions de dollars pour mettre de l'art dans la vie
des Canadiennes et des Canadiens de tout le pays.

Library and Archives Canada Cataloguing in Publication

Jones, Allan, 1943–, author
Beyond vision: going blind, inner seeing, and the nature of the self /
Allan Jones.

Includes bibliographical references.
Issued in print and electronic formats.
ISBN 978-0-7735-5285-2 (hardcover). – ISBN 978-0-7735-5379-8 (ePDF). –
ISBN 978-0-7735-5380-4 (ePUB)

1. Jones, Allan, 1943–. 2. Vedanta. 3. Advaita. 4. Self-realization –
Religious aspects – Hinduism. 5. Self (Philosophy). 6. Vision – Philosophy.
7. Diplomats – Canada – Biography. 8. Blind – Canada – Biography.
I. Title.

B132.V3J66 2018   181'.482   C2018-901017-7
                                                   C2018-901018-5

This book was typeset by Marquis Interscript in 10.5/13 Sabon.

To Pressi and Evan,
and for those who would search out
the reality that lies beneath appearance.

Contents

Acknowledgments   xi

INTRODUCTION   CLAIMING THE TERRAIN   3

1 Can the Self Go Blind?   3

2 Finding a Path   10

3 Making Sense of the Pathfinder   12

4 Where We Are Heading   16

CHAPTER ONE   A SHEER WHITE CLIFF FACE   22

1 How Things Began to Go Missing   22

2 The Flight from the Truth   28

3 Inner Acknowledgment   32

4 Taking My Prognosis on Tour   37

CHAPTER TWO   THE FUNCTIONARY AND HIS MASK   51

1 Eyeing the Foreign Service and Angling for Tokyo   51

2 Down from the Plateau   62

3 Three Faces of the RP Identity   70

4 Trying to Catch Hold of Myself   77

CHAPTER THREE   INDIA, THE VISUAL CONUNDRUM,
AND LETTING GO   82

1 The New Delhi Sensorium   82

2 Disentanglement from Images   94

3 A Set of Mogul Pictures   98

4 Regarding Facelessness   108

CHAPTER FOUR   VEDANTA, THE EGO, AND THE FLESH   113

1 Re-enter Shiva   113

2 The Coils of the Ego   121

3 Factor X: The Centripetal Pull of the Body   126

CHAPTER FIVE   INTO THE PRE-VISUAL CENTRE   133

1 Skirting the Edge   133

2 Just by Walking   139

3 Factor Y: The Return of the Repressed   147

4 A Burst of Openness   157

5 Looking for My Others   165

CHAPTER SIX   VISION, SCIENCE,
AND THE WORLD-ILLUSION   172

1 Three Unconventional Perspectives on Seeing   172

2 Inside the Mall: Reality or Appearance?   181

3 The Great Light of Consciousness   192

CHAPTER SEVEN   LEARNING TO LIVE AN ANCIENT
TEACHING   202

1 Taking It in and Letting It Work   202

2 Spiritual Practice as Stress Management   213

3 The Subtle Arts of Equimindedness   223

CHAPTER EIGHT   THE CHALLENGE OF INTEGRATION   237

1 Factor Z, at Long Last   237

2 Interzone, Phantasmagoria, Ownership   246

3 Ordinary Life as I Find It   264

CHAPTER NINE   OPENING UP   279

1 A Humane Transition   279

2 A Final Affirmation of the Sensory World   287

Notes   305

ACKNOWLEDGMENTS

Listening Hard and Writing Out Loud

The Jorge Luis Borges epigraph that begins this book is taken from *In Praise of Darkness*, translated by Norman Thomas Di Giovanni (New York: E.P. Dutton and Company, 1974). I discovered Borges only after losing my reading vision. He profoundly influenced me, not only through the magic of his poetry and prose but because of the sheer, simple fact that he too had been a blind writer. I found myself acknowledging Borges, James Joyce, Milton, and Homer as models of a kind, all of them blind or visually impaired and all famously productive, as I was slowly grinding my way through my own lone book.

I would like to thank the Eric Webster Foundation, the CNIB Foundation, and Harvey Clarke for the generous financial support that helped McGill-Queen's University Press produce this book and find for it a readership. It is due to the acumen and skill of my acquisitions editor, Mark Abley, that the huge chunk of text I dropped thuddingly onto his desk was eventually transformed into a tightly integrated book, with all my overheated adverbs and adjectives swept away. Mark addressed the substance and philosophical implications of *Beyond Vision* with great intensity and commitment. When our views on this or that issue seemed at first to be at odds the rewrites always found the right course. I think that Mark would disclaim titles such as midwife or mentor, but as far as I am concerned he was both. In particular he showed me how challenging material need not be presented in a sharply challenging way. Thank you, Mark, for a most insightful and exhilarating ride.

I would like to thank copy-editor Anne Marie Todkill for correcting my many bloopers and non-standard usages, for teaching me the

McGill/Chicago style, and for her patience and cheerfulness in the teeth of my compulsive rewrites. I would also like to thank managing editor Ryan Van Huijstee for keeping me on track and explaining to this complete novice how the production system works. As to the finished product – the actual book – I am especially indebted to Kate Edgar, executive director, Oliver Sacks Foundation; Sharon Colle, executive director, Foundation Fighting Blindness (Canada); and Debra Hulley, director of administration, Professional Association of Foreign Service Officers, for their generous help in publicizing *Beyond Vision*.

If it takes a whole village to raise a child, it takes a village-sized, sprawling network to raise up, counsel, and logistically support a would-be blind writer. In learning how to write and work up the nerve to address a large, challenging subject, I was encouraged by the writerly advice of John Metcalf, Allan Peterkin, Howard Engel, and Sonia Tilson. As I got into *Beyond Vision* I was enormously influenced by Oliver Sacks, Dennis Lee, and Jon Kabat-Zinn. Oliver Sacks introduced me to ideas bearing upon the interrelationship of science, sensory experience, and selfhood that I could not possibly ignore. Dennis Lee introduced me to the via negativa, a philosophical tradition that penetrated Judaism, Christianity, and Islam, even as it seemed to reflect certain features of Advaita Vedanta, Buddhism, and classical Taoism. Jon Kabat-Zinn – the founder of mindfulness-based stress reduction (MBSR) – showed me through his engrossing books and meditation programs how the minutiae of daily life could actually open up rather than obscure the life of the spirit. The influence of these three writers, taken together, deeply informs the text of *Beyond Vision*. The upshot is that this book admits of no sharp divisions between physical science, social science, and spirituality.

Oliver Sacks died in 2015, three years before the publication of *Beyond Vision*. The endorsement by Dr Sacks that appears on the back cover of *Beyond Vision* was drawn from the correspondence that he and I maintained over a period of six years (2009–15). In those exchanges Dr Sacks expressed enthusiasm regarding my work-in-progress, commented on the manuscript at length, and urged me to press ahead to its completion. This was extraordinary support for a journeyman writer who is still finding his way. I am very grateful to Mark Abley and Kate Edgar for an exchange of emails in July 2017 in which they chose, from Dr Sacks's letters to me, the observations that comprise his endorsement.

Because my book project is influenced both by Advaita Vedanta and Buddhism, I am immensely grateful to Dr Nalini Devdas for helping me better understand the similarities and differences of those two traditions, within the broad context of Indian spirituality. Our conversations, together with her comments on the successive drafts of my text, proved to be both a great resource and a tonic. With her colleague Dr Richard Mann, Dr Devdas helped me to develop an extensive glossary of Advaita-related Sanskrit terms. This was an invaluable reference for understanding the nuances of Advaitic teaching. Dr Devdas also provisioned me with a useful, simplified approach to Sanskrit Romanization. Thank you, Nalini – for your broad perspective, for your precision, and above all for your friendship.

My fascination with India began in 1970 when I went backpacking through the country, a journey I never could have ventured without the white cane mobility training I received from the Canadian National Institute for the Blind (CNIB). Among the CNIB mobility instructors who attended me in Edmonton, Toronto, and Ottawa, I especially acknowledge the late Jay Wadsworth as a remarkably intuitive and resourceful white cane trainer. As my mobility improved I was able to meet, learn from, and share experiences with other people who, like me, were diagnosed with retinitis pigmentosa: Ivy Blakeney, Irene Ward, Joe Foster, Richard Marsolais, and Elizabeth Hurdman.

During my years as a foreign service officer I learned coping strategies from other blind professionals, Canadian and American. In 1980 the CNIB together with the Department of External Affairs arranged for me to meet with blind professionals in Toronto, Ottawa, and Washington, DC. My helpful new contacts in Ottawa included Jerry Neufeld – an absolute whiz as a computer user, professor, and author. In the Department of External Affairs I had the backup support, both abroad and at headquarters, of designated reader/secretaries. These high-spirited angels (that's how I thought of them) included Ann Johnson, Karen Reid, Gail Gow, and Caroline Pearson. It is here that I must acknowledge the efforts of Shirley Boles, External Affairs' persuasive and energetic equal opportunities coordinator. It was Shirley who made my novel and successful support system possible.

Yet the most important support system I was to experience was the one I had to innovate in order to research and write this book, under deteriorating physical circumstances. From 1990 onward I became multiply handicapped due to the long-term effects of a spinal injury, complicated by a rare metabolic disorder that expressed itself through neuropathy and a generalized ataxia. By degrees, walking and manual work (including keyboarding) became more and more difficult. These circumstances called for considerable assistance, but the first problem I urgently addressed was how to recruit volunteer readers. Once again I turned to the CNIB, making the novel suggestion that we advertise in the *Ottawa Citizen* for readers with an academic background and an interest in Indian philosophy.

Thus my most remarkable stroke of good fortune at this time was my recruiting of three wonderful readers – Dana Mullen, Sonia Tilson, and the late John Rogers – who for years on end tape-recorded volume after volume of the Vedantic and Buddhist material I required. Their involvement was invaluable, and we became lifelong friends. Their cassettes initiated my transition into listening hard and writing out loud: listening intently, memorizing key passages, and dictating remarks onto a second tape recorder. At first this was just for note-taking, but eventually it would serve for book-creating. As my capacity for keyboarding diminished, I arranged for other volunteers to enter material onto my computer. There were also volunteers who came to the house to read magazines to me or to drive me to medical appointments. These arrangements were made by a succession of efficient and enthusiastic CNIB volunteer coordinators: Pam Byrtus, Ann Ranson, and Perpetua Quigley. Over the years my volunteers might switch from oral reading and keyboarding to driving, or vice versa, depending on their preferences and my circumstances. They were great pinch-hitters. Here, then, are their names, in no particular order: Mary VanBuskirk, Ken Pearson, Mary Egerton, Ken Fowler, Tom Joseph, Bill Gayner, Ghinwa Karouni, David Morrow, Chris Seifried, Isha Tan, Bryan Wonnop, Art King, Herb Bergen, the late Michael Webber, and Cornelius Von Baeyer.

I want to make special mention of Herb Bergen and Art King for all the many trips they made driving me, and sometimes my wife Pressi as well, to our doctor in remote Kanata. It was a long stretch there and back, and I can never thank these two friends adequately for all their time and trouble. And then there is Ken Pearson, who is in a class by himself. Ken's patience over a period of years, typing draft after draft of my book and my steady output of emails, has been nothing short of heroic. The method we finally adopted was for me to listen through headphones to my most recently tape-recorded text, while dictating this material to Ken over the telephone. One listens and speaks almost simultaneously. This is not easy work: either one of us can make a mistake that will not be caught until the next round, and the exasperating speaker phones tend to cut off the first word or two of a sentence. Thank you, Ken. Without your involvement *Beyond Vision* would simply not exist.

Finally, I must pay tribute to the doctors and other health care professionals who helped me stay in one piece, and remain more or less functional, during the two decades of research and writing. At the top of the list is our former family doctor, Susan Dawson, who for twenty-two years helped us find our way through some challenging circumstances. She always responded to the problem at hand with a clear explanation together with an action plan, fortified by candour and humour and compassion. The other doctors who have kept me going include my very supportive neurologist, Elizabeth Pringle, who carefully monitored my neurological changes, kept my spirits up, and in 2006 diagnosed the metabolic disorder referred to above; my equally supportive and empathic physiatrist Sue Dojeiji, who coached me in the art of not falling down and helped me make the difficult transition to a walker; my cardiologist Sanjeev Chander; and Kirsty Boyd, a highly reputed surgeon who is looking after my hands and wrists. In addition I would like to thank our ingenious long-term physiotherapist Daniel Gagné, and our top-notch massage therapist Arlene Cybulskie, for their key contributions to my pain management program. But, above all else, it has been the practical help and great moral support of Pressi that makes it possible for me to get things done.

I live among vague whitish shapes that are not darkness yet. To think
Democritus tore out his eyes: time has been my Democritus. This growing
dark is slow and brings no pain. It flows along an easy slope, and is kin to
eternity. My friends are faceless; one street corner is taken for another; on the
pages of books there are no letters. Of the many generations of books on earth
I have read only a few, the few that in my mind I go on reading still, reading
and changing. I reach my center, my algebra and my key, my mirror. Soon
I shall know who I am.

Jorge Luis Borges, *In Praise of Darkness*
Norman Thomas di Giovanni, translator

That which sees not with the eyes but is aware of the act of seeing, learn that
that alone is Brahman.

The Kena Upanishad

The conditions of blindness and keen vision belong to the eye but not to the
Atman, the knower or true self. This Atman is the supreme being, the ancient
Brahman, always the same, the universal light of consciousness.

Viveka-Chudamani (The Crest Jewel of Wisdom)

The eye through which I see God is the same eye through which God sees me.

Meister Eckhart, *Sermons*

Claiming the Terrain

1 CAN THE SELF GO BLIND?

What is the self? How can we come to fully know it? Or rather how can we come to fully *be* it, inhabiting our true nature authentically and consistently without any further doubts about who or what we are? The subtle and seemingly veiled presence to which these questions refer – the true self or "I" – is the principal subject of this book. We all assume that we are, or have, a self. But few of us care to look into those particular findings of contemporary science that, taken together, knock most of our conventional notions of selfhood into a cocked hat. It is against this background of our own protective conventionality, and the radical discoveries of modern science, that *Beyond Vision* describes the twistings and transformations of false identity, and the means to genuine self-realization offered by one of the great Asian spiritual traditions: Advaita Vedanta. As a frank autobiography and medical memoir, this book documents how my absorption and application of the basic insights of Advaita profoundly changed my life, and transformed my experience of self.

I have written this memoir with three kinds of reader in mind. The first is the curious general reader who is interested in the elusive concepts of self and self-realization, and in the ways our selfhood can be seemingly entrapped by disease or liberated from it. The second is the reader who is living with the prospect of serious vision loss, or has a friend or relative in that situation, or who simply wants to get the feel of what it would be like to deal with such a challenge. The third is the kind of reader who would welcome an opportunity to look into a possibly unfamiliar, non-theistic or beyond-theistic spiritual tradition. I hope to give these various readers an inside view into an all-too-common problem – that of losing one's self-purchase, or even one's sense of identity, when medical circumstances bear down brutally upon the sensory body.

The specific instance described here is that of total vision loss, a condition or affliction that people fear at a deep, instinctual level. It was in part to expose the irrational sources of that fear, sources that really have nothing to do with the practical difficulties posed by blindness, that I undertook this work. *Beyond Vision* shows both the reader who has had no direct experience of vision loss, and the one who is now grappling with it, what it is like to penetrate beneath the fear of blindness and fully take in an alternative, parallel domain of sensory experience. On a more personal level, this memoir shows how self-enquiry led a young man with failing vision to overcome a pathological family background, and enter into a full life that coupled spiritual exploration with a career in the foreign service.

My narrative describes a particular way of going blind – not all at once as the result of a sudden trauma, but very, very slowly. It depicts this process from its experiential core, inhabiting it inwardly rather than observing its outward effects in the way a doctor or medical technician tries to do. This is the patient's-eye point of view, a subjective view that can never be captured in the objectifying language of the clinician.

The sighted general reader who takes up this viewpoint begins vicariously to enter into a different sensory world, the one permanently inhabited by persons with retinitis pigmentosa (RP). RP is a progressive eye disease that in most cases attacks the retina from its periphery inward, slowly but steadily reducing the visual field to a narrow zone of strained and constricted perception. The long-term result may be legal blindness (10 per cent normal field vision or less), or total blindness including loss of all light perception. Research into the fundamental causes and dynamics of RP has opened up exciting possibilities for treating this disease, but so far at least it has remained incurable.

Whatever the immediate future may hold for treating RP – and beyond that for achieving a definitive cure – this book is all about coping and affirmation. It does *not* belong to that genre of literature sometimes referred to as "pathography," which portrays mainly suffering and loss. On the contrary, *Beyond Vision* is about living in wholeness. I affirm from my own experience that it is possible to learn how to live with this disease – live with it not merely passively as a victim but actively, as a kind of explorer. One can do this right here and now, even as emergent lines of RP research are developed, tested out, and eventually implemented as effective treatment.

The key to dealing with RP, or for that matter any other serious disease, is to find the ways in which it gratuitously attaches itself to our sense of identity. That attachment can then be broken through a remarkable form of insight, one that can be shared and taught, an insight that taps into the autonomy and resilience of the deep self. Letting go of the false identity to discover our fundamental nature is a life-altering change, one that has far more significance than either the presence or absence of eyesight.

This kind of realization can be sought by any patient with any serious malady who is prepared to look beneath the surface of his or her experience, learn how the disease in question presents itself as a "personal" menace, and then radically reconsider what the word "person" actually refers to. As we familiarize ourselves with RP, our case in point, we will see that the sense of personal threat that it inculcates tends much of the time to be repressed, especially in adolescence and early adulthood. If the perceived threat could be dredged up to the surface of the patient's mind and put into the language of thoughtful but conventional selfhood, it would go something like this: As the self I am now, I am of course a seer. As this seer, this inherently sighted self, am I really going to go blind? What then would I be, deep down? Would I still be "me," or a reduced version or remnant of "me"?

This apprehension regarding a gathering threat to one's selfhood slowly intensifies as RP destabilizes the triangular relationship linking eyes, visible world, and mind. The effect may be likened to a protracted, paranoid dream in which one is trapped within a tunnel that is visibly closing up. As the symptoms of RP gradually become more intrusive, the tunnel mouth slowly contracts in a way that is almost impossible to describe. Above, below, and on either side of the unstable tunnel mouth, there is absolutely no sense of a surrounding darkness or blankness. There is no "there" there at all. What lies beyond the contracting perimeter of vision is simply the absence of visual object-consciousness. Inside the perimeter, the visual array gradually destabilizes and comes apart. The ordinary objects seen through the tunnel mouth require more and more illumination to keep them from blurring into incoherent fragments or dissolving completely. Even during childhood the inhabitant of the RP tunnel may be subject to night blindness, because moonlight and street lighting fail to adequately illuminate the scene as viewed through R P.

If I were to ask you to imagine what it is like to live in the R P visual world, your inner eye would try to conjure up its objects of perception. But can you imagine yourself as their perceiver? Our habitual experience is such that perceiver and perceived, self and world, are intimately conjoined in the act of perception. The "normal" or conventional sense of self, and the sense of its enfolding visual world, balance and mutually support each other. What happens to that normal experience of selfhood when the world to which it stands in dependent apposition slowly disappears? In this melting and increasingly empty space, what becomes of the seer?

That is what we are about to discover. We are going to take a journey of the mind and heart that begins with a visual pathology, as sketched above, and work our way by degrees down through the protective reactions of the ego toward the true self, which the ego in its adaptive conservatism generally manages to obscure. The objective of this journey is to dissolve the tight, strained nexus between the ego-based sense of self and the disintegrating visual world, so that we can occupy the deeper and more secure selfhood that does not have to batten itself on images. There is nothing esoteric about this goal: what it amounts to is bringing to light the foundational "I" that we have always actually been.

To propose the kind of reorientation described above – an inner movement away from pathology toward a more authentic and resilient sense of identity – is to propose that disease and the true self are separable enough that there can be a distinct shift of attention from the one to the other. The skeptic may challenge this at the outset. He may insist that serious disease can utterly overwhelm our sense of who we are, permeating us with malaise. Disease strikes the body and the senses; how can we deny that in so doing it strikes against our self?

One might respond that spiritual preceptors as seemingly diverse as Socrates, the Buddha, the masters of Vedanta, Jesus, and the adepts of the Neoplatonic *via negativa* or "negative way," all insisted that our true nature or ultimate identity is a reality quite distinct from the sensory body. If this is true, how do we account for the fact that people identify so intensely with their bodies and sense faculties? And how can the conventional experience of self that has become bound through habit to the sensory body be released or transformed, when the body or one of its sense faculties comes under serious attack? These are some of the questions that this book will not only ask but answer, to the extent that one man's experience can serve to indicate the direction in which the answers seem to lie.

I am totally blind, having reached the age of seventy-four and passed through all the stages of my particular kind of RP. I base this book on my direct knowledge of early onset RP, my years of practical adaptation as Canada's first blind diplomat, and my experience as a student and journeyman practitioner of Advaita Vedanta. Among the six classical schools of orthodox Indian philosophy, Advaita Vedanta has long had the reputation of being the most challenging when it comes to the question of our ultimate identity. The particular goal of Advaita is to clarify the nature of the largely hidden self, the transpersonal self that we all have in common, by exposing and stripping away the layers of false identity that seem to cling to it.

This project of exposure and refutation reveals Advaita's kinship with the other major iterations of the negative way. The Eastern wing of this perennial tradition includes Mahayana Buddhism and classical Taoism as well as Advaita Vedanta. The Western negative way, which is informed by the Neoplatonic philosophy of Plotinus and his heirs, has given rise to the most searching and iconoclastic interpretations of Judaism, Christianity, and Islam.

The real self that Advaita brings to light is deeper than the sensory body-mind, deeper and more enduring than either the adaptive ego or the personality, deeper by far than our fears and disabilities, and transpersonal in the sense that it is our shared essence. It is not individual – it is not, for example, an individual "soul." One might begin to think of the real self in terms of a common humanity, as reflected through empathy, fellow-feeling, and ethical behaviour; yet according to Advaita and its sister traditions it is more than that.

This deep and normally hidden reality is both self-knowing and the stable ground of all our shifting, unstable self-representations. Its gradual disclosure reveals it to be nothing less than the transpersonal, unabridged "I Am." It is not just *a* self but *the* self, a subtle but wholly affirmative presence that for all people everywhere stands quite apart from any personal attributes. Its nature is that of inner "light," the transparent, unobjectifiable, luminous subjectivity that registers the existence of the objective sensory world, and the ever-changing contents of the mind. We habitually look through this bottomless inner

luminosity as though it were not there. Its realization does not eliminate the individual ego and personality, but it does allow for a more
compassionate perspective on those pseudo-entities.

This unconventional and perhaps startling assertion about what
we most fundamentally are does not come out of the blue. It is
grounded in a 2,500-year-old, stubbornly resilient transcultural philosophy, which the reader need not have encountered up to now. And
indeed, *Beyond Vision* is not a treatise on Advaita Vedanta but an
autobiography, the story of inner change that was somehow informed
by Advaitic teaching even when I had only a partial grasp of Advaitic
premises. The chapters that follow render an account of how I gradually opened up into a mode of immediate experience that I can characterize only as spiritual. This is a much-abused and overused word,
and I employ it only rarely and with some care. What it applies to is
a self-validating experience that cannot be reduced to the physical,
the ideational, or the psychological. Its nature is metaphysical – a
category or domain inseparable from the foundational self, the universal "I Am."

The most significant and shareable good news that this narrative
offers to the person facing vision loss – and this is not to be accepted
on faith, but tested out through the resources that I will describe – can
be summed up like this: the self in its true fullness and depth does
not go blind. The deep, universal self is so whole and entirely self-
possessed, and yet so open and receptive, that it can accept the advent
of blindness and deal with it effectively without in any way being
diminished by it. This self is inherently autonomous: it is free from
all our usual structures of identity, whether physical, sensory, ideational, or psychological. These features may be thought of simply as
adjuncts of the self. Yet the self is in no sense alienated from its
adjuncts, for it grounds and bathes them in the light of acceptance.
In its constancy and pure sentience, this foundational self registers
the change from sightedness to blindness from the depths of its own
changelessness and luminosity. This kind of stabilizing experience can
be ours even during the most challenging stages of the vision loss
process, to the extent that we can align our sense of identity with the
sentient light that is our essence.

The general reader who is not visually impaired can take this investigation of RP false selfing as a kind of test case, and apply its broad
implications to his or her own circumstances – regardless of whether
these involve a medical problem. Here, then, is the good news for the

normally sighted: the self that you most fundamentally are cannot be diminished by any of the ills of the sensory body-mind, either now or in the future. The deep self can take in the travails and reductions of the senses, body, and mind-stream as though from a strategic inner distance, without being helplessly bound to or sucked into them. This is possible to the extent that you learn how to shift your sense of identity away from those physical and mental adjuncts that you conventionally take to be yourself, into the light of sentience that illumines them all. No matter how marked the phenomenal changes may prove to be in those adjuncts, the light of the deeper self can continue to affirm its wholeness of being, its stability, and its simplicity.

Simplicity? Does this sound too simple by half, too good to be true? Well, it is not – except insofar as we are bound to acknowledge two large caveats. The first is that, as stated earlier, the ideas and resources introduced here have to be tested out; after that, they are to be deployed as a matter of habit. Thus there is necessarily a two-stage process calling for experimentation followed by a degree of constancy, and it is of course easier to be lax than constant. This I have learned in spades from my own choppy experience.

The second caveat is that even if the deep self is in fact refreshingly simple and self-sufficient, as claimed above, the ego-based mode of mind we normally occupy is apparently not set up to register that fact. Egos as centres of reference are evidently unaware of, and thus unconcerned with, the deep self. Traditions such as Advaita take this fully into account, however. They do not attack the ego, but invoke through various means a growing sense of the foundational self that underlies all egos. This new sense of identity becomes by degrees a more stable and subtle center of reference.

In section 2 of this introduction I will try to set the context for the kind of transition sketched above, starting with some observations about how blindness is actually experienced and socially received. As a domain of existence, blindness connects with the "normal" sense-world imperfectly and at awkward angles. As a problematic, blindness is a condition that can be hard to address with full clarity from the inside, at least at first, even as it is all too easily judged or misjudged from the outside by the innocently prejudiced sighted observer. In section 3, I will then refer the problem of vision loss and identity to the deeper puzzle of the self, which as conventionally framed is rife with contradiction. This will lead us to consider how Indian spiritual philosophy addresses the self – that most subjective of subjects.

2 FINDING A PATH

RP may be considered as a life-path, or more strategically as a set of alternative, contrasting life-paths. Many of these are pitted and rocky; others lead to practical adjustment, yet others to the possibility of a different and deeper experience of self. Such an experience, that of our inner potential, reaches far beyond the practical adjustment that it incidentally reinforces.

In many cases the real odyssey of the youngster with RP begins when the cumulative symptoms of the disease start to get in the way, leading to confusion, resistance, and denial. This is the emergence of a new and unwelcome identity, one that is intimately entangled with RP. It is quite natural for a young person diagnosed with RP to resist that new identity and reject the practical adjustments that have finally become necessary. Those adjustments have to do with night blindness, situational blindness when interior lighting is dim, vision problems related to part-time work and participation in sports, and the complications that RP imposes on social and family life.

Underlying all four of these areas is the difficulty of explaining one's disability to others. This problem of self-representation is grounded in the fact that one can be visually helpless in some environments and fully competent in others. These daily or hourly lurches in identity may seem small in themselves, but they have a cumulative wearing effect. Against this gathering tension, the ego comes to identify compulsively with the faculty of vision, taking on the role of a protective but harried "seer." In consequence, this experience of personal tension tends to mount as one's visual capacity continues to decline.

It is an unfortunate fact of life that young people with progressive vision loss who remain unreconciled to their current degree of impairment, and cling tenaciously to their unexamined notions of selfhood, become deeply vulnerable to popular stereotypes of blindness. Readers with normal vision may be unaware of these stereotypes, or may presume that they are outmoded if not extinct. Yet such readers may discover in these pages that they have half-consciously subscribed to false assumptions regarding the blind. There are two stereotypes that apply to total functional blindness, the ultimate condition to which many cases of RP lead. They seem to pull in opposite directions, but impose on the person with RP the same burden of doubt.

There is on the one hand the widespread and fuzzy notion that the blind possess remarkable powers of memory and sensory compensation, the latter taking the form of super-acute hearing and touch. The youngster with RP who has just cracked his shin on some unnoticed obstacle feels sure that he could never develop such faculties. On the other hand, and this is the more deeply rooted stereotype, blindness is subtly conflated with stupid or wilful incomprehension and general incompetence. One who prefers not to "see" an uncomfortable truth is said to be "blind" to it. A fool is "blind" to his own interests; the lover is "blinded," meaning besotted, by his infatuation. Jesus referred to the spiritually unregenerate and their followers as the blind leading the blind. The blind person bearing a white cane may be addressed very loudly, as though he were also deaf or simple, or not addressed at all.

I have lost track of the number of times I have walked into a store or restaurant with cane in hand and a companion on my opposite arm, and greeted the clerk or server with an intelligible hello or a simple question, only to elicit a counter-question aimed not at me but at my companion: "What does he want?" "Can he see anything at all?" "What size does he take?" Or in a restaurant, "Where does he want to sit?" "Can he walk over there?" And once even, "Can he use a knife and fork?" What lies behind this silliness is the unexamined conviction that blindness is a sunken condition of abject, infantilizing dependency. It is of course this stark image of total dependency that the half-blind person with RP fears above all else.

Television and the popular press are less likely today than in previous decades to represent blindness as pitiful, but this is not because attitudes toward vision loss have genuinely changed. It is rather that the public display of those attitudes has become politically incorrect. The negative, fearful image of blindness continues to lurk in the unreflective mind. And indeed it still finds free expression in serious or literary writing, where both of the opposed conventional stereotypes remain fair game. There is for example the deadly and almost superhuman competence of the title character in Margaret Atwood's *The Blind Assassin*, and the exquisite tactile and aural sensibilities of the privileged, upper-class blind youth in Henry Green's *Blindness*. Who on earth could measure up to such models? At the opposite but equally marketable extreme is the unrelieved horror of José Saramago's *Blindness*. Here the Nobel prize–winning Portuguese novelist graphically portrays a mass epidemic of blindness that leads to psychological breakdown, social collapse, and violent anarchy. It is meant as allegory, of course, which makes one wonder what on earth was going on in Portugal.

If unrealistic representations of total blindness are one kind of problem for the person with RP, another is the complete absence of any representation of his current condition. This condition can best be characterized as situational blindness. It does not lend itself to stereo-typing because it simply draws a blank with the uninformed onlooker. Anyone can understand that a sighted person might have less than perfect vision, and everyone knows or thinks he knows what blindness is. But someone with RP might appear to be wholly sighted in daylight and wholly blind in dim interior lighting. This radical instability seems to run afoul of the human propensity to classify people and qualities according to neat bipolar categories. We like the definitiveness of good versus bad, white versus black, the light side of life versus the dark, and – by extension – sightedness versus blindness. The man or woman who transits back and forth between these last two categories is something of a puzzle to the literal-minded observer.

In short, the situationally blind person who is trying to cope with RP is in a kind of vacuum. Our culture provides him or her with no clear, custom-made path to practical adjustment, no positive role-models, not even a definite misrepresentation of RP against which he or she could rebel. There is just the blank incomprehension on the face of the passerby who has witnessed the person with RP commit some kind of gaffe, and farther down the RP life-path those crude and unprocessed myths of total blindness that occlude the sojourner's view of the future.

Given these circumstances, it is natural that the person with RP should have doubts about him or herself, doubts about basic present-ability and capacities. This uncertainty can not only limit self-affir-mation, in the practical sense of unnecessarily paring back life options, but can actually falsify the nature of the self. It is because the issue of the self is not consciously addressed that many young people with RP shrink from learning adaptive skills – most notably the skilful deployment of a white cane, the perfect resource to fall back on when the lighting is dim. To take up the white cane and be seen to use it may be felt as a virtual shift of identity, an abrupt fall into the social category of "the blind." It is this superstitious, identity-based fear of adjustment that most strongly marks the character of unreflective and unreconciled RP experience. The resulting maladjustment is both tragic and unnecessary.

3 MAKING SENSE OF THE PATHFINDER

The surest way for people with RP or any other challenging illness to avoid the trap of maladaptation is to really look into their condition, instead of just reacting to it. But we cannot even begin to do this if we are looking in the wrong direction. The right direction turns out to be straight inward, into our own minds. If we think of a serious malady as mainly or exclusively a problem of the afflicted body systems, or of the genes that control those systems, we "externalize" it in a way that puts it beyond our direct, intimate engagement. All we can do is wait for medical deliverance.

Yet the truth is that maladies such as RP, as they are actually lived, are hardly inaccessible: in each case the disease in question is right here, right now, as immediate experience. To find one's own path through RP is to enter deliberately into that experience – that is, into one's own visual-emotional-bodily consciousness. It is within the mind and nowhere else that we experience the world as seen through RP – as a flow of aberrant visual images, as emotional and somatic reactions that impress their tone upon those images, and as strong ideas about the acceptability or otherwise of what we see. It is this private interior terrain that we are called upon to claim, to scrutinize rather than avoid. And how could we really avoid it, and why would we even want to do so? Turning inward in a spirit of enquiry is in the end a turning toward the real self, our more-than-personal reservoir of strength and adaptation.

But what exactly *is* the self? In India they actually ask this embarrassingly obvious but annoyingly refractory question – the kind of question a child would ask – keeping it alive and current over the centuries. The question kept coming up because the standard answers seemed so obviously inadequate. The kind of ancient Hindu sage known as a *rishi* could see that the body-mind as we normally experience it does not add up to a real, stable, internally consistent and self-possessed identity. The body-mind is simply the domain or forum in which the problem of identity or selfhood has to be worked out. And when it is worked out, the old composite pseudo-self can be grounded in a far greater and more secure sense of reality.

Advaita Vedanta applies to our internal mental terrain the external topographical term *kshetrya*, a Sanskrit word for "field." Used metaphorically, kshetrya refers to the field of our total somatic, sensory, and psychological experience. This is the field of gross and subtle objects, as distinct from the partially veiled subject or true self that registers their presence. In Advaitic primers as well as the Bhagavad-Gita, the best-known Indian spiritual text both within India and outside it, the virtual definition of the human being – especially the human being who has entered the path of self-enquiry – is "knower of the field" (*kshetrya-jna*). It is only when we really know this field that we begin to discover what a scramble we regularly make of our sense of self.

At a certain level, we already know that we do not know the self. If we were truly self-possessed there would be no need for the huge pop psych industry that offers to put us in touch, for a price, with our inner whatchamacallit. We cannot even decide on our own which of our predominant characteristics is the real core around which our identity is organized. It is as though we carry a whole pack of ID cards, constantly sifting through them in our minds as a set of variant, situational identities. The result is inconsistency and even internal contradiction. Just consider the following examples:

In France, a country where under some circumstances adopted children might have difficulty determining the identity of their birth parents, a gifted and successful young woman confides to friends that she feels hollow and incomplete. Unable to learn anything about who her parents were or are, she admits that she lacks a firm identity. And yet it is clear that she identifies in many ways with her adoptive parents. When this is pointed out to her, she replies that it only adds to her confusion.

The dilemma of a mixed-race person in a racially divided environment is that he must tread two paths simultaneously: our example here is a Canadian boy whose father and mother are, respectively, white and Cree. His Winnipeg school is divided along racial fault lines, white versus Aboriginal. The boy tries to find hooks on either side onto which he can hang the trappings of identity. But he says that he feels "split."

An American girl born of conservative Muslim immigrants feels that she is defined in one way by her parents, extended family, and religion, all combining to articulate a single definite model of what a woman ought to be, and in quite another way by her Western acculturation and personal ambitions. How is she to arbitrate between these two disparate identities? And just who or what is it, deep down, that does the adjudicating?

Marla Runyan, an outstanding middle-distance runner, qualified for the US Olympic team in spite of her severe visual handicap.

Stargardt macular dystrophy had completely destroyed her central or straight-ahead vision, but still she ran. In the following
passage from her autobiography *No Finish Line*, Marla considers
what life would be like if medical science could someday restore
her vision: "These were teasing thoughts, almost taunting ones.
I had never really considered such things before. Now that I did,
the possibilities frightened me as much as they intrigued me.
How would they redefine who I was? My disability had become
such a part of me that in many ways it created me and determined who I was. If I erased it, who would I be and what
would I become? There were no answers to these questions."[1]

Although each of these examples has its own particularities, taken
together they illustrate the universal quandary in which we are all
caught up. In our need to be something definite we are drawn irresist-
ibly to cling to the forms of our physical, sensory, mental, and emotional experience. By binding ourselves tightly and indiscriminately
to such identifiers, we construct our provisional and sometimes con-
flicting representations of ourselves.

Uncertainty over these representations can lead us to change our
appearance, our career, our religious faith, our life partner, or our
citizenship or homeland, so that we might "find" ourselves. We may
spend years making zigzag excursions into identity politics in the
hope that some movement or group ethos will synthesize in us a stable
sense of self. From all these experiments and temporary transformations there sometimes arises an unvoiced, intuitive fear that all these
shifting identities are unreal precisely because they shift, one cancelling
out another only to be cancelled out in turn, as we go on to the next
option. What we are far less aware of, and would find jarring if we
could see it with full attention, is the way our ersatz identity radically
alters from one instant to the next.

With all people everywhere, the sense of "I" skitters, moment to
moment, from our visible outer form to internal body-feelings to a
strong identification with the external senses; from the turbulent
mind-stream to the bare, basic sense of self that hovers within that
stream; from a recurrent feeling of doubt regarding our adequacy to
some favourite idea we have about who we really are. And so it goes,
back and forth and back again, like the pea that is switched about in
the proverbial shell game. Which of these is the *real* I? Or is each of
us a succession of partial identities? Or are we something even less
than that – a succession of bits and pieces that don't add up at all?

To the busy modern Westerner, "theoretical" questions like these may seem abstruse or even irrelevant to practical life. But they quickly lose their abstract character when they are applied to a life as it is actually lived, as in the case of one who says "I am going blind." Which version of "I" is doing the speaking, and which version – if any – can be said to "go blind"? If you have RP or any other eye disease that can lead to blindness, you implicitly confront this riddle every time you gaze into the bathroom mirror while brushing your hair. Your eyes meet the eyes in the mirror and you wonder apprehensively if you – the "you" conceived of at that moment in intensely visual terms – will always be able to see yourself in this way.

What is at issue here is whether blindness afflicts the real self at all. The answer depends on whether the real self consists of the sensory body-mind as we already know it, or lies somehow deeper down. There is a world of difference between receiving trauma or loss of function squarely in your selfhood, or what you take to be your selfhood, and receiving it in some structure of body or mind that you know to be peripheral to your selfhood. The former kind of experience is devastating; the latter may be hard, but it can certainly be borne.

There is no getting around the fact that the ordinary, unreflective language that typifies or misrepresents the RP experience does not have an encouraging ring to it. It is no accident that the person with late-stage RP does not say, "my retinas are going blind," or "my eyes are going blind," but rather "*I* am going blind." This amounts to a declaration that the RP-infested visual apparatus is a critical part of the self, so much so that the disease is eroding the self from within. But there is absolutely no good reason for RP to be received in this way. It is equally possible to view RP or any other chronic medical condition as a problem that is intimately present to the self but still external to it, as something for the self to manage. I offer this possibility as a genuine and fruitful alternative because I have lived it out myself. It "works."

4 WHERE WE ARE HEADING

So far I have tried to shed some light on the themes, concerns, and sensory deficits against which a book like this gets written. I have had relatively little to say about myself, or about what might be called the plot line of the nine chapters that follow. Quite apart from the fundamental questions that *Beyond Vision* engages, it is above all else a particular life story. I can only hope that it conveys some of the intensity, uncertainty, and stickiness of real life. To fulfil these purposes, I necessarily describe aberrant visual experiences, vision-related fears and conflicts, sexual issues, and openings into an alternative sense of reality. These scenes may prove uncomfortable to some readers with RP, and to others who are fully sighted. I could just say "Don't worry," for the narrative does work its way to safe and habitable ground. But by way of a heads-up or advance notice I think it best that I say a little here regarding some of the things we are going to "see," chapter by chapter.

The big practical question that simmered away throughout my first three decades was how I could integrate progressive vision loss into the rest of my experience without either identifying with it or hating it as an enemy. Through trial and plenty of error I eventually found that the best way to live with RP was to open myself to it unconditionally: this, like nothing else, had the effect of neutralizing the toxic psychological effects of the disease. But getting myself to the point where I could remain consistently open was a long journey, one that began with the claustrophobically personal and moved by degrees toward the transpersonal or universal – toward something bigger than "me." In tracing this movement I present myself not as a model but as one who found himself pulled into the role of test case, a living instance of what can happen when certain teachings about the self are experimentally lived out.

I start off by describing my early entanglement with RP, my dawning knowledge of what it held in store for me, and the massive, reactive denial that snared me in five years of brittle maladjustment. I try to explain or at least document how I suddenly and unexpectedly broke through the denial, and came to terms with RP in sufficient measure to open up my life-options (chapter 1). This eventually led to my becoming a diplomat in the Canadian foreign service, after frankly and fully apprising the recruitment team of my ophthalmic condition.

As time passed, however, I found that the further deterioration of my remaining vision was instilling within me an obscure kind of self-doubt (chapter 2). This included competing versions of identity and a strong tendency toward workaholic overcompensation. I depict this state of affairs as it began to develop toward the end of my exhilarating five-year posting to Japan, thickening and becoming more oppressive during my subsequent term at headquarters in Ottawa. It was only during my subsequent posting to India (chapters 3 and 4) that

I came to terms with the problem underlying much of my growing tension – my as-yet-unresolved fear of the total blindness that awaited me in the future.

The resolution of this fear occurred as a direct consequence of my coming upon the teachings on the self developed by early Advaita Vedanta, as exemplified in the fascinating and seemingly exotic texts known as the Upanishads. This intense encounter with a new view of reality transformed and depressurized my relationship with vision; the larger effect of this inner change was a far more open experience of my whole sensorium. From this point on I document as clearly as I can how the visible world slowly transformed itself out of all recognition, with me as its fascinated witness and cautious, cane-wielding explorer.

In the second half of the book I describe the avocation of spiritual study that continued somehow to open up for me, after significant physical issues other than RP brought my diplomatic career to a premature end. This new life (chapter 5) involved a great deal of physiotherapy, certain restrictions on physical activity because of spinal problems, and the working-out by trial and error of a home pain-management regime. Later on, there would be progressive ataxia (loss of muscle coordination), increasing leg and foot neuropathy, and chronic dizziness related to vestibular problems, the combined effects of which would sometimes make it difficult to walk. Yet it was during these years that I got to know Douglas Harding, an independent-minded spiritual explorer and teacher who introduced me to a radically simple experience of introverted attention or "inner seeing." This was really a mode of self-awareness – a way of opening up to the vivid light of consciousness. Such an opening seemed to fit somehow into the Advaita Vedanta that I had begun to explore.

From the mid-1990s onward I broadened the ambit of my studies to include those aspects of Western science that have particular significance for the question of human identity (chapter 6). I was learning how certain basic findings in the fields of developmental psychology, evolutionary biology and modern physics, considered together, implicitly challenge our most cherished presumptions regarding the nature of the self, not to mention the nature of the world in which the self seems to be embedded. These findings do not in themselves buttress the truth-claims of any religious or spiritual tradition. But they are fully consonant with the deconstruction of the conventional self and materialist world view that was enacted more than twelve hundred years ago by classical Advaita Vedanta. I offer a personal account of why I found these discoveries, which are in essence starkly, breathtakingly simple, to be equally, breathtakingly liberating.

It is in part through this process of questioning and correction, coupled with a growing attentiveness to the actual presence and depth of consciousness, that the purely personal story of the earlier chapters opens out into a view of reality that is still biographical in form, but transpersonal in its reference. The resultant theme of universality or non-duality or oneness, the principal theme of this book, gradually comes to light in the successive sections of chapters 6 through 9.

Of course my engagement with a transpersonal perspective did not magically "disappear" my physical and other problems. In these same chapters I show how Advaita Vedanta helped me to manage chronic pain and deal with the later stages of going blind (see especially chapter 7, sections 2 through 4, and chapter 8, section 2). This process of adaptation involved learning and applying specific forms of practice that made possible a more relaxed and detached reception of aversive or garbled sensory experience. One such practice, mindfulness-based stress reduction (MBSR), was invaluable in preserving my white cane mobility skills as the last of my vision faded away.

One aspect of my life that Advaita helped me to address in a starkly direct way had to do with intimate and deeply repressed personal issues. In 1994 the Advaitic perspective on the self, with its quality of compassionate detachment, had been a key factor in resolving a sexual conundrum that had baffled me for years (chapter 5, sections 3 through 5); in 2001, I was finally able to come to terms with the closely related early trauma that had remained more or less suppressed throughout my adult life (chapter 8, section 1). Advaita's contribution to the trauma work was to help me to stay engaged and focused during sessions of an intense and pointed form of memory-recovery therapy. I describe this process in order to show the reader how in following a spiritual path the seeker is sometimes required to tear down the internal barriers he or she has erected against the self, and fully absorb what had once seemed poisonous and unassimilable. In my own case, this difficult work led not only to relief but also an enhanced capacity for simple happiness, and real joy.

What followed in the succeeding years by way of "visual" experience was a class of phenomena that proved to be entirely internal, with no extrosensory input at all. Like many other people who go totally blind, I began to experience intricate visual hallucinations,

confined entirely to my mind's eye. Such phenomena are the product
of a brain that remains healthy and active, despite the fact that it is
cut off from all external visual input. After a short period of adjustment I made friends with these mobile, streaming, hallucinatory forms,
which had become as ordinary to me as stationary home and office
furniture is to the sighted reader. It is against the backdrop of these
ethereal and rather exotic phenomena that I offer a valuation – a
positive one – of my blindness and the inner openings it has made
possible (chapter 8, section 2).

I then go on to document how, more recently, I was compelled to
reexamine my understanding of and commitment to Advaitic philosophy (chapter 9). This crisis, which forced upon me a full recognition of my hesitancy and defensiveness, opened me up at last to the
power of Advaitic logic and revelation. The result at first was like
free-fall, but this eventually ushered me into an experience of apprehended unity that was beyond anything I had known before. I knew
that this was only a glimpse or first taste of the way things really are,
but it made me feel that I was starting afresh – starting again with a
clean slate. Ironically, but such is life, all this came about at a time of
marked physical decline.

I would like to close this introduction by having a final word, first,
with my fellow explorers of the RP world, and all other readers with
failing vision. Everybody else please listen in. I unequivocally assure
every one of you that if current research does not halt the deterioration of your vision and restore that portion of it that you have already
lost, you absolutely do have the capacity to accept blindness or permanent partial-sightedness. I mean really accept it, with no permanent
residue of grievance or bitterness. This book is designed to help you
do that, and go on to a sensible practical adjustment. But you may
also find that it is possible to penetrate the world of blindness or
visual impairment in something more than a practical way, seeing
how its apparent poverty or dearth of visual images can unexpectedly
clear the way to a deeper engagement with reality.

The possibility that blindness could actually open up into an unsus-
pected depth of being lies implicit in the cautionary remarks on the
senses that are scattered throughout the Eastern spiritual literature,
and in the writings of Western negative way intuitives. According to
some of the ancient sources, an unfiltered overreliance on the external
sense-faculties can obscure the inner sense of what is ultimately real.

And it is eyesight above all other sensory and mental faculties that falsifies our sense of what the world is in itself, and reinforces the notion that each of us is nothing but a material thing dropped into the midst of countless other such things. This belief is really an image-mediated form of self-objectification and bondage, and it subtly afflicts the great majority of humankind.

Yet in the absence of eyesight – and in the presence of real acceptance of a non-visible or barely visible world – it is possible to find our supposedly limited and material selves subtly de-objectified or "unthinged." There are various ways of inviting this change, and Advaita Vedanta is only one of them. And yes, I do understand that within the perspective of shrinking and embattled tunnel vision, the claim that it is possible to finally accept blindness may strike readers who are living with R P as utterly outrageous. That is an entirely natural reaction. Please just wait and see, as I make my case step by step in all that follows.

As for the generality of readers who can take this journey unencumbered by any serious eye disease, you find yourself in a rather different position. You are not being called upon to accept anything outrageous – except perhaps to eventually give up some cherished convictions about your identity, in exchange for what must seem at first to be curiously insubstantial and indeterminate. But it is the substantial and determinate misrepresentations of self, those based entirely on refutable materialist illusions, that shrink and harden our sense of identity and impede our fulfillment. The chapters that follow illustrate an alternative to that kind of constriction. And here I can only say, once again, please wait and see.

There is no point in getting ahead of ourselves and in fact no way of doing so. The best place to begin this kind of journey is with storytelling, an entirely familiar medium that tells us what's going on, and sometimes even what to make of it. In chapter 1, after a few preliminaries, the story begins with the first visual manifestations of an obscure genetic quirk, as experienced by one small boy.

1

A Sheer White Cliff Face

1 HOW THINGS BEGAN TO GO MISSING

The medical phenomenon that threads its way through this memoir – an ambiguous phenomenon that plays the dual roles of destroyer and uninvited teacher – is the insidious eye disease known as retinitis pigmentosa (RP). The basic facts about RP are outlined at the beginning of the introduction. The phenomenality of this disease, and its remarkable significance for decoding the nature of the phenomenal world, are examined objectively later in this book. But in the first few chapters that follow I do not even try to be objective. I write with as much frankness as I can muster about my direct, subjective experience as a young person with RP. To be diagnosed with RP in the 1950s and 1960s was to be fully aware that there was as yet absolutely no prospect of effectively treating this disease. It was this single stark fact that made the RP experience destabilizing, not only in the obvious sense of progressively eroding the capacity to see, but in the more subtle sense of undermining self-possession.

For those of you who have not read the introduction, and in the course of writing this book and sharing my early drafts I learned to my horror that there are some people who *never* read introductions, I will bring you up to speed by boiling down all the previous pages into the single compound term that appears at the end of the previous paragraph: self-possession. Each of us believes in the existence of the self and more or less feels it as our own presence. But we have trouble putting it into words: somehow the self eludes the normal categories of language. It is quite real, we think, and it has to be right "here" front and centre. And yet it is hard to define or pin down as an object, except (or so they believe) by the most rock-ribbed of materialists. And in times of crisis or protracted stress, our self may seem increasingly opaque and indeterminate. It is this elusiveness of the self, its mercurial or ambiguous quality, that makes the experience of living with RP so hard to put into words. Nevertheless the self stands at the dead centre of our visual experience, as its experiencer.

Much of the time the presence of the self is only implicit. But for those of us who have RP, the self – or, rather, our muddled and emotion-laden conception of the self – is eventually brought to the fore, to stand as the defendant in an unavoidable test or trial. What is to be tested under the threat of blindness is nothing more or less than the validity and integrity of our self-concept. Such at least was my experience. I lived through this test for years, and not very skilfully, before I could even begin to articulate it.

In what follows below I deliberately pass over whole chunks of life not directly related to my purpose. My main intent throughout is to highlight one particular thing: how the experience of seeing less and less well was connected to my evolving experience of identity. I feel that the best way to present this material is not through the slow grind of a long and detailed documentary but through widely spaced steps, in a series of still shots or short scenes that may be separated by months or even years. The images are drawn from my dwindling but surprisingly tenacious stock of visual memories.

The ego does not like this disconnected approach, for it loves above all else the smooth sense of its own continuity. But the ego is not the self. So we will ignore its presumptions and proceed, at least through the first three decades, in deliberate jumps. The reader will notice that there is virtually nothing about the family into which I was born, or about interactions among members of the household. The reason for this deliberate omission will become clear in later chapters. It is enough to say here that as I began to experience puzzling difficulties in seeing, it was as though I was facing this situation in complete isolation.

I am gazing into a dark, vast, and secretive tunnel. It is 1946, in Edmonton, Alberta. I am in the poorly lighted hallway, an absolutely cavernous space by the standards of a poorly seeing three-year-old, that runs through the basement of our apartment building. I am big enough to reach the doorknob, to steal out of our flat on stockinged feet and walk slowly down that dark corridor, scared but fascinated by the echoless space that I can feel but not see.

As a prefiguring of the vision loss I would undergo in later life this little scene is just too pat, too obvious, the kind of gimmicky contrivance that any good film director would want to delete from the script. Yet the hall was real, and I experienced it in just that way. More than fifty years later, when I had lost all my object vision and most of my light perception, I would have recurrent dreams of that old dark place, my personal primal tunnel. The dreams were not at all frightening. On the contrary, they captured the mysterious and evocative tone of the original experience, in which a still and seemingly boundless space draws the walker onward and lifts him out of himself.

Now we jump to an image of a long blackboard covered with great big printed letters and diagrams. This is grade one, my first day at school. I am a late arrival; it is not September but well on into December. In the summer an ophthalmologist had warned my parents that my eyes were not good enough for me to cope with a regular school; I should be held back and placed in a special institution sometime later. Then in November a second ophthalmologist told them I should be able to manage. So, here I am. I am sitting right at the front of the class, the teacher having moved the kid who belongs in this seat so I can get a good, close view of the board. I stare at it, trying to decode its messages as I feel the many eyes boring into the back of my head. Besides being a latecomer I am gawkily taller than all the others, and the only one wearing thick Coke-bottle glasses. I need these because of my extreme nearsightedness. I am just different, a singleton. But because I am intrigued by the blackboard and already like the teacher, Mrs Bond, I decide I am going to like school.

Later that day I find myself on the stage in the auditorium with all the other grade ones, trying to dance. This is the dress rehearsal for the Christmas concert, for which everyone has been practising for months. We are supposed to be little Dutch children. The boys wear billowing, light-blue smocks, and the star of the show – a girl – taps about in wooden shoes. The children are weaving in and out in a pattern I find impossible to follow, especially after the arts teacher orders me to take off my glasses so I will not "stick out." That evening at supper when I am asked what I learned at school, I report that Dutch girls have clunky wooden boats on their feet and the boys wear dumb girly blouses and when they try to walk around together they get all mixed up. They are stupid.

Next there is a set of linked images from later childhood and adolescence. The common feature that makes them a set is their depiction of me in retreat, either walking away from something or withdrawing inwardly from a situation I cannot physically leave. The first shows me trudging home from the playground late in the evening, in the summer between grades three and four. I am guided by the high white stabs of the streetlights at the end of every long block. Back in the playground the boys are still immersed in the kind of rough-and-tumble play I like best, but in the gathering dusk I can hardly see them. I had blundered into everybody and messed things up. Baffled and angry, I left before I could be banished. But angry at whom? I must be angry at myself, for I don't blame the boys. Without meaning to I had whacked and bloodied the nose of one of the smaller ones.

A similar mental snapshot, this one from grade six, shows me walking away from the batter's box and throwing my bat down in disgust, having struck out once again. Up until the previous year I had been a competent batter and even in good stretches a heavy hitter, despite my thick glasses. I don't understand it: something is going terribly wrong. I am starting to have trouble with all ball games and most other sports – except for running, which I have taken to doing alone.

Then in grade nine there is that awful scene at the end-of-term dance in the school gym, my first dance ever, where I stand motionless with my back pressed against a wall. I gaze helplessly into what seems to my eyes to be a totally dark but obscurely seething mass. I am immobilized with embarrassment and the fear of collision. Over the following three years of high school I will avoid all the dances, but cannot help but be drawn into the evening activities of our church teen group. I can still picture myself on my first hay ride, which was also my last. Unable to see anything at all during our long, slow progress through the countryside, I stand frozen in place clutching one of the slats of the hay wagon. Fear of poking my hand or knee into somebody's face keeps me from venturing into the hay. So I just stand there, an animate oxymoron, a blind sentinel. I have no memory of how I justified my odd behaviour to the rest of the group. What was really extreme caution on my part would have looked downright oddball to them, and years later I confirmed with one of my old friends that they had no idea of how profoundly night-blind I actually was.

In a mercifully short sequence from my nightmarish high school phys. ed. movie, I am trying to dribble a basketball without losing it or running into anyone. I fix my eyes urgently on my hand, since I cannot see the moving ball, but it is no good. I always lose the damn thing on the fifth or sixth bounce. My floundering attempts are greeted at first with wisecracks, and then with jeers. The sports that had lost their appeal in junior high are now a source of open humiliation. Unable even to see where the ball has rolled to, I walk dejectedly back to the start line. From my flushed skin inward my whole physical being is permeated with shame. It is a good thing that phys. ed. happens only twice a week, for once I leave the gym it takes me an hour or so to reclaim my body.

The next bit of mind's-eye retrospective presents me as a sixteen-year-old slumped on a stool in a dimly lit room, staring dully at an illuminated eye chart. There is more eye-testing equipment to my left. To the right of the chart, two heavy-bellied minor functionaries of the provincial drivers' licensing bureau stand grinning at me with their hands in their pockets, each as lumpy and shovel-faced as the other, the two of them looking like a pair of overgrown garden gnomes. The one who gave me the standard test found the results so funny that he brought in his buddy from down the hall, and did the whole thing over again. The rerun was enough to make the second man laugh out loud. "Jeez, kid," he had said, "with eyes like that you couldn't get a licence to drive a kiddy car." As I get slowly to my feet, it is this man who stands directly between me and the door. I walk toward him, my hands balling into fists, aware that I am close to losing control. "Hey, hey," he protests as he gets out of my way, "I didn't mean nothing."

Another scene from this same year, 1959, finds me looking at a painting in a downtown art gallery. This may be the first time I have ever seen an original oil painting, and certainly the first time I have seen one of substantial size. My eyes are motionless; they have only just now stopped flicking repeatedly back and forth. This moment does not seem to signify much – an ordinary kid staring at an unremarkable painting. But it would take dozens of freeze-frames to show how I actually saw the canvas, as a succession of narrow and entirely separate partial views that changed with each small flick of the eye. As I tried to make sense of the partial views, each one disappearing as it was replaced by the next, I felt oddly disarticulated inside. During the previous summer I had come across an art book that contained good colour reproductions of the Flemish masters, and suddenly a portal I'd never known was closed swung open into brilliant light. I gazed in fascination at the details of those still lifes, bowls of fruit and musical instruments that glowed with an extraordinary and seemingly inner radiance. I copied the forms in charcoal sketches, wondering how the colours and luminosity were achieved. I knew I had some little talent for small-scale freehand sketching. Could I learn to become an artist?

I got more art books from the library. I learned from these that there was something called composition, which involved for example the distribution and balance of masses, and the strategic placement of particular persons and objects in ways that would suggest an underlying meaning or relationship. This would create an overall effect when grasped as a whole. But what I find that day at the art gallery is that I cannot grasp any whole, and only with difficulty the parts. That is, when I stand back at the maximum distance that allows me to recognize at least some of the fuzzy forms, my field vision can take in only a small portion of the painting. Rapid eye movements and immediate memory give me some notion of the general scene, but it seems that this must be a very pale facsimile of the real composition. For me there was no "composition" at all, no whole composed of interrelated elements.

So after that I turned away from painting. I did this without emotion and seemingly without intent, hardly noticing that it was happening. There was no conscious sense of defeat or disappointment: I simply cancelled something inside me. The resulting blank replaced the pained and inarticulate feeling that had crept over me while I was in the gallery. Evidently blankness was better than pain.

Although many other examples could be presented from this early set of images, they are not meant to suggest even in aggregate that my life had been overwhelmed by limited vision. Most or at least much of the time I could pass as "normal." As I explained in the introduction, the visual deficit imposed by RP is at first situational, confined to occasions that reveal deficiencies in dark-adaptation, side vision, and capacity to track rapidly moving objects. By the time I got to high school I had been conspiring with myself for years to avoid just such situations, and so live as unobstructedly as possible.

My real problem was in trying to understand what was happening to me. I did not know that I had RP, and indeed had never heard of the disease. Dr Grose, the gentle and protective ophthalmologist who had attended me for years, assured me (untruthfully and unwisely) that I had nothing worse than a mildly progressive myopia or near-sightedness. He may have taken the same line with my parents, but in any event my visual problems were never discussed at home. I knew what myopia was, but the more I stewed over it the more I felt that mere nearsightedness could not account for my increasingly patchy and puzzling visual experience.

That experience was resounding within me more and more as a jarring or destabilizing of the sense of being a perceiver. The real issue during those early years was this: to address the world in the primary role of perceiver or seer, and then to find increasingly that the seer cannot see what is really there, is to feel subtly subverted within. This sense of subversion was the key feature in all the incidents described above, and it is because of that shared quality that I remember them as a series. The significance of other elements – the occasional sense of humiliation, the unhelpfulness or lack of understanding on the part of others – has pretty well drained away. Of course I was incapable of describing this dilemma. We are not taught how to articulate our experience of self, let alone how to critically examine it.

In presenting these mind's-eye memory scenes I identified their common subject as retreat or withdrawal. It would be more accurate to say that they were only attempts at withdrawal, for I was coming to feel that the problem from which I was trying to escape was inside me. If my eye disease was nothing worse than myopia, then perhaps my real problem was not visual. Maybe I was essentially a klutz, or chronically inattentive, or incompetent in some basic way that I could feel but not understand. One would think that my experiences on the basketball court, at the vehicle licence bureau, and in the art gallery should have made it crystal clear to me that the basic problem was visual. But the resulting sense of lack attached itself not to the seeing, as an impersonal function of the eyes, but to the seer, as person. The feeling that enveloped me as I stood before that painting was of being less than whole. The interpenetration of sensory function and identity was beginning to cast cold water over every personal aspiration that was bound up with eyesight.

2 THE FLIGHT FROM THE TRUTH

When I was seventeen I finally asked Dr Grose if there wasn't something wrong with me other than myopia. I mentioned my failure to obtain a motor vehicle learner's permit, and his face tightened. For the first time, then, he mentioned retinitis pigmentosa but offered no details. He immediately changed the subject to diet alternatives, urging me at length to get more vitamin A. I just tuned out, remaining silent but reiterating inwardly the alien Latinate name of my disease.

It was knowing the name that would propel me, some days later, into the culminating scene of this series. It consists of a single still image.

It is a strange image, because it is almost not there at all. It is a pale, bleached-out impression of two hands, my hands viewed through my eyes, holding a large open book whose pages are blurred. There is in addition the remembered smell of the book, the musty, discouraged smell of a technical volume that is rarely taken down from its library shelf. That is all I have been able to retrieve; I do not know if it was the public or the university library I visited that day, let alone the name of the old ophthalmological manual that told me I could expect to lose all my eyesight.

This revelation put me into immediate shock, then into a massive and continuing denial. I "forgot" the entire incident – the prognosis, the book, the fact of having visited the library. It was only years later that I was able to recall just enough to know that the emergent memory was based on a real event.

How could I have buried the truth like that? Perhaps because I was acting alone and unobserved. It was I who dug up the news in solitude, not some authority figure who imposed it on me. I may have felt in some deeply irrational way that, working in secret, I could plunge the revelation back into oblivion. I would have taken this as an act of self-preservation.

I will largely pass over the subsequent five years of numbing denial, as the psychological mechanism of RP denial is examined elsewhere in this book. Here I present only two scenes: the first is that of a girl's head and her two forearms manifesting out of the darkness as three unconnected objects. Her body, which must have been darkly clad, is not visibly present. Her face and forearms are present only because they are weakly illuminated by a small table lamp, which I will presently knock over. We are in a dark subterranean bar frequented mainly by university students.

"You know," she says, "you looked so funny walking over here. You sort of shuffle across the room with your arms half out moving real slowly, like a ghost or a sleepwalker. Then when you sit down you sort of quickly touch everything on the table twice, the first time like you were finding out where things are, and then again to figure out what they are. Did you know that you do that?" I say nothing. "Are you stoned, or what?" I take a pull on my beer, turning myself off inside. Then I move my left arm abstractedly and knock over the table lamp.

The second freeze-frame comes from my final undergraduate year. It shows a large orange, brilliantly illuminated in my startled gaze by a shaft of sunlight pouring in through the window of the shabby graduate student office. I am holding the orange at lap level, having managed somehow to trap it by feel rather than sight after it struck me in the chest and bounced downward. A moment before, I had heard the word "Catch!" but could not see what was coming at me. Now I look up at the graduate student who had playfully or not so playfully lobbed it. "Jesus," he says, staring at me with amused contempt, "it's true. They told me you were half-blind."

I look down again at the glowing orange and then suddenly hurl it at his head as hard as I can. He jerks aside and it splats against the wall. "Fuck!" He opens his mouth to say more and steps forward, then changes his mind. I am not glaring or even staring at him but just watching, suddenly drained of feeling. Uncertain how to interpret my deadpan he hesitates, curses again, and stalks out of the room.

Once in high school I had to deal with a bully who, together with his pals, began to single me out for special attention in an unlit hall that I had to pass through on my way to chemistry class. He knew I couldn't see very well, at least not there. This continued for several days until I caught him alone outside the school and confronted him. He backed down and that solved the problem. The little incident in the office at the university was somehow more disturbing because of the context, which was in a twisted sort of way political or ideological.

The grad student and I were alone there taking a break from a long afternoon of running subjects in the improvised behavioural psychology lab just next door. The experiment was based on a particularly mindless kind of stimulus-response model. The subjects were freshmen and sophomores, sullen draftees who had been inveigled by one means or another into going through this. I had been grumbling for months about the pointlessness of this kind of research – and the dehumanizing model of the mind that lay behind it.

In those days fundamentalist behaviourism held full sway in the field of academic psychology. Its view of the human being was absurdly reductionist and materialistic, and often degradingly manipulative in its applications. Its chief apostle was B.F. Skinner, designer of the wretched Skinner Box in which captive rats were subjected to the operant conditioning that supposedly reveal deep truths about humans as well as rats. In another few years Skinner would publish a behaviourist social gospel titled, unsurprisingly, *Beyond Freedom and Dignity*. I had found that students attracted to this stuff tended toward hard right-wing opinions, xenophobia, or outright racism, and a swaggering contempt for any kind of perceived human weakness. Several of them were enthusiastic readers of Ayn Rand, the cult novelist who championed the idea of the unsocialized and pitiless Superman. These people, the ones I had been arguing with, had discovered in an evening setting that I had poor eyesight. And of course I was just a rather mouthy undergraduate doing some desultory work on the side – fair pickings.

Thus the airborne orange, and the triumphalist expression on the grad student's ruddy face, and the rasping tone of his voice when he said the word "blind." I got the point. Apparently my RP belonged with all those other physical, mental, and social markers that defined the *Untermenschen*. That's right – Untermenschen, the Nazi term for "sub-humans." As a kind of joke the Uber-behaviourist students made it a point to use this expression among themselves. I knew they were a bunch of jerks, and I had shown the orange-lobber what I thought of him. Nevertheless, he had managed to get my number. This slight but unsavoury incident just added more weight and resonance to the whole issue of failing vision. Because I couldn't really process any of this I slipped by degrees deeper into the old familiar lock-down.

Like other young people with RP I managed somehow to muddle along. Fortunately, I could still read without difficulty. I studied in a desultory sort of way, changing my major every year – from pre-law to honours English to casual English to psychology – cramming for exams and eventually earning my degree. Along the way I got into the usual undergraduate scrapes, joined clubs, and made friends. Most importantly, I joined the university male chorus and enjoyed four years of boisterous yet sometimes surprisingly beautiful singing, unfailing bonhomie, and beer by the kegful.

With three fellow-choristers I lived in a pleasant rental house not far from campus. My house-mates included Dennis Foth, an exuberant rake, succeeded a year later by Bob Decker, an intense conservative who was in the throes of converting to Catholicism in preparation for his forthcoming marriage. Agnostic though I was, I sang the solos at Bob and Marie's cathedral wedding in Saskatoon. My other two house-mates were the Nikolai brothers Helmuth and Ulrich, popularly known as Nick and Rick. On Sundays I often joined them for big family dinners out in the country. This was my first

introduction to truly functional and free-flowing family life, and I
didn't mind that much of the repartee was in German.

Yet I experienced all of this in a mind and body that were never
entirely free of tension. In situations that forced me beyond my visual
capacity I always ended up anaesthetizing myself. But there was a
bigger, deeper problem that was far more significant in its effects than
the chagrin or deadening provoked by RP situational embarrassments.
By wilfully suppressing my prognosis I had become inwardly divided
against myself, and this mental breach made any kind of real self-
knowledge difficult to achieve.

There were other issues in my life at this time that urgently required
my attention. But the habit of denial, once established, had slowly
spread out within me. American novelist Saul Bellow neatly captured
the dynamics of this process in the following words: "Everybody
knows there is no fineness or accuracy of suppression; if you hold
down one thing you hold down the adjoining."[1] It was during the
years of RP denial that I was intensively reading Bellow, and I find it
extraordinary that I came upon and mentally squirrelled away that
particular epigram without ever consciously applying it to myself.
Such a state of inner division could not go on indefinitely, and eventually my path led me to the meeting that completely changed my life.

3 INNER ACKNOWLEDGMENT

To this day, I can still inwardly "see" the basic layout of that room,
despite the slow decay of so many other visual memories. The setting
is the University Hospital in Edmonton. I am in a doctor's office,
where the two of us sit facing each other across his desk. His name
escapes me now, irritatingly, as so many other names have leaked
away over the last few years. And yet in this visual memory his form
is sharply outlined against the large window behind him, and beyond
the glass it is twenty below zero. It is only 4:30 in the afternoon but
already the northern light is failing. This is early December 1965.
I am twenty-two.

The room is silent; we just sit there with our eyes locked. He stares
at me round-eyed and unblinking like a baby gazing at its rattle, or
an owl sizing up a field mouse. I stare back in a kind of paralysis,
struck dumb by what he has just told me. His words ought to have
frozen the air between us. But nothing has changed except that my
mind has stopped and will not start up again.

For some months I had been experiencing anxiety and depression, and I could not seem to find a direction for my life. I finally presented myself to a harried intake nurse at Student Health Services and in consequence wound up with this doctor. During our second or third meeting the doctor asked me what was the matter with my eyes, for clearly there was a problem. I mumbled something about retinitis pigmentosa and tried to change the subject. He then asked how I knew I had RP, and how much I understood about its implications. I replied that five years earlier my ophthalmologist had told me the name of the disease without offering any information about it. Of course I did not mention my subsequent visit to the library, because I did not remember it. The doctor considered for a long moment, eyeing me appraisingly, then told me that he wanted me to see another ophthalmologist. Would I go? I said with a reluctance that must have been evident to him that I would.

He arranged the appointment with great dispatch, and it was only a few days later that I was able to see the specialist. He examined me closely and put me through several tests, his manner remaining dour and taciturn throughout. This took a long time. When he was finished he said only that he would forward the results to the referring doctor. And that was that.

So here I am with the doctor, frozen in his gaze, the test results spread out upon his desk. The silence stretches on. "I said," he finally intones, slowly and carefully as though I may have misunderstood him the first time, "that you are going blind. You may as well get used to the idea." After a few moments my eyes slide to the window, but I am not looking at anything out there. It is as though I were becoming inwardly aware of an enormous dead-white eminence, something like the sheer face of a great chalk cliff, one that I am going to have to climb. It looms within, massive but not frightening or even surprising. It has really been there all along – though somehow unobserved or unacknowledged. I find that what I am actually feeling is relief, a letting-go of the muscles around my chest, with an easing or opening-up of the mind to fully take in that white blank.

That evening when I tell my housemates what has happened they are horrified, both by the news itself and by the circumstances of its delivery. "How could he do this to you," demands Nick, "when you only went to him for help?"

"No, no," I say, "it's really okay. He did the right thing. It's all true." And then, confusedly, "It actually helps." At this they can say nothing.

A few evenings later we go out for a couple of beers, and on our way back home we make a detour to view the displays of Christmas lights on the big showplace houses along Saskatchewan Drive. I drink in those lights as though I had never seen such things before and would never see them again. I had as yet learned nothing about the typical course of RP, and for all I knew I might be blind by next Christmas. But there is no fear and no grief. All I feel is an undefended immersion in the vibrancy of those colours, seeing them as though through the eyes of a small child. In one part of my mind I am turning over the question of how under present circumstances I could be so at peace, and so open to what I see.

Looked at in terms of the popular psychology of the day, the explanation seemed to be obvious. I had let go of denial and this in itself lowered the pressure. But why should letting go have so positive an effect? Dropping the shield of denial meant that I was now facing the unobscured and looming menace of living without eyesight, and without as yet having formulated a strategy. But against all the odds, and seemingly against common sense itself, I was certain I would prevail. I felt that accession to the truth about myself left me free to succeed at whatever I should reasonably choose to do.

During the spring of 1966, in the wake of accepting my prognosis, I took a few necessary steps. First, I quit the master's program in psychology that I had begun the previous autumn, in the vain hope that I might be able to buck the system, with all its lousy Skinnerians, and do some meaningful research. This was a pipe dream, an expression of the obscure need to remain in the cocoon of university life. Second, accordingly, I joined the world of work downtown and got myself a stop-gap job in the reference section of the public library. Third, I began a course of mobility training at the local branch of the Canadian National Institute for the Blind (CNIB) that I hoped would make me functional and self-reliant, under conditions of poor illumination. This was the real beginning of my adult life.

By the end of May, I was ready to take my first experimental night walk. This clip from my memory bank is clear and vivid. I am standing at one end of an unlit and unfamiliar street in West Edmonton, not far from my cousin Nola's house. This stretch of darkness is where I intend to make my first solo sortie, having completed my white-cane orientation course just the day before. I stand there uncertainly, balancing the cane in my hand. I had vowed, not to some deity but to myself, that I would learn to wield the cane well enough to get along – despite my being congenitally fumble-fingered, undexterous. At my stage of RP I could function without much difficulty in a well-lit environment, despite my tunnel vision, but I was uncertain about my capacity to cope with night blindness. Here was my new white cane: now there could be no more avoidance or excuses.

The dodging of situations in which I would be virtually blind had become not just habitual but reflexive, a long-standing defensive strategy imposed by what might be called my RP persona. I am using the word "persona" here in its old meaning of theatrical mask, a false face that covers up the true. To abandon the maladaptive strategy of avoidance was hard at first, despite my recent gain in confidence. I was beginning to sense that my RP persona was a kind of cover-up, yet I had come willy-nilly to identify with it. The mask had to a great extent become my face. The act of ripping it away was bound to feel denuding, far more so than stripping down to the skin. So as I take my first step, intensely conscious of the white stick that from now on will publicly label me as visually maimed, I feel for a moment ridiculously exposed and vulnerable.

But soon I am walking briskly down the sidewalk, tapping the long cane to the left and right in accordance with the standard two-point touch technique. I had been practising this with more zeal than skill. One swings the cane out to the side opposite to the foot that is striding forward, so that it can locate any obstacle that might lie directly in front of the foot that will take the next step. This coordination of cane arc and stride makes good sense and works well once the rhythm becomes habitual. In my case, the rhythm was still vulnerable to disruption by my distractible mind.

As I bowl along through the darkness and stretch out my stride to the length that feels right for my 6' 4" of height, gearing myself up into a power walk, I feel more and more exultant. It seems natural that the sense of self or "I" should be pouring into the body, which is revelling (however prematurely) in its new competency. I feel the tension so long associated with darkness beginning to fall away, as though it is rolling off my shoulders and swinging arms. But then the sense of "I" begins to shift into the busy mind, as I start thinking of all the things I can do now that I am facing up to the future. I would launch myself into a program of deliberate job-hopping and world travel. By now all my attention has leaked away from my cane-taps and even from my muscles, pooling in my chattering mind. Europe first and then Asia, I am thinking, with one of those cool-looking aluminum frame packsacks –

Then I slam into the pole. It is a steel pole, and I have hit it with my right shoulder with so much force that I am knocked clean off my feet. My clever cane, apparently opting for a less subservient way of life, takes off like a projectile and skitters away deceitfully down the pavement. I cuss blue murder – at the cane, at the pole, at my wool-gathering mind. Then I pick myself up. After some awkward searching with my feet and more profanity I locate my errant stick. As neither it nor my shoulder prove to be broken, I carry on along my intended route. Now my sense of identity has receded right down into the wary consciousness that monitors what the body is doing. The mind, embarrassed as hell at itself, is temporarily quiet. I keep walking in this new way for some time, and then proceed to my cousin's house for a celebratory drink and a ride back home.

That evening did prove to be the beginning of something, but it had as much to do with taking one step at a time as with big aspirations. The lesson – to be rammed home tens of thousands of times in the coming years – was to keep the attention steady and clear. Everything else apparently depended on that. This basic fact, so strongly reinforced in the consciousness of active blind people, stood in marked and curious contrast to the normally scattered character of sighted mobility. The sighted could move about in a state of absent-mindedness; the blind could not. It would be many years before I learned that this requirement of extra attentiveness, imposed on the blind as an apparent burden, could actually be cultivated as a useful means for maintaining inner clarity.

My misadventure was enough to convince me that the rambling mind was no place for the blind pedestrian to park his sense of "I." As I worked at being more careful, the sense of self-presence sometimes receded inward to a deep vantage point where the external environment, the body, and the mind-stream, could be closely monitored. When this happened, both the observing and the walking went smoothly. But this was an unstable experience: it was often hard to keep the sense of "I" from getting sucked right into the moving body. When the body became egoized or personified in this way it soon grew tense, carving its way with effort through the occluded world of night. This state of affairs continued for a long, long time.

4 TAKING MY PROGNOSIS ON TOUR

Over the next decade I took advantage of my remaining functional vision to follow a course of deliberate exploration, working at many things and travelling widely. It was that golden time – the mid-1960s through the early 1970s – when economic conditions and social attitudes made it possible for young people to experiment with one vocational option after another, in a succession of fresh starts, and to travel abroad on remarkably little money. I had the good fortune to be on a plateau of relative visual stability throughout this restless period. In both my work experiences and my travels I learned by degrees to be frank but relaxed with people concerning my RP, explaining its peculiarities as circumstances required.

My first substantial job after leaving university, following two months of scut-work at the public library, was as a trainee at a private-sector family counselling agency. To an extent I could not have anticipated, this experience would challenge my sense of identity as a person facing vision loss. The arrangement was for me to work for a year or so under supervision, and then decide whether I really wanted a career in family counselling. If I did choose that option, I would go off to secure a master's degree in social work and then return to the agency. I approached all this with enthusiasm, seeing it as a great learning opportunity. During the hiring process I gave a brief account of my RP, and mentioned in passing that most people with this condition would find the lighting rather dim in the office that was to be assigned to me.

When I arrived for my first day of work I was surprised to find that the low-wattage incandescent bulb in my windowless office had been replaced by a large double panel of fluorescent lights. The effect was garish, even when seen from outside my office. Standing at the end of the pokey little hall onto which most of the counsellors' offices opened, I saw a not unpleasant passageway of subdued light broken abruptly by an exclamatory burst of white light on the wall just opposite my open doorway, where the fluorescence flooded out. Walking down that hall into my office was like going down a dim side street at dusk and turning into the dazzle of a video arcade. To sit in the office with a client, as I quickly discovered, was to have both of us intensely on display.

I found it curious that the alteration would have been made without checking with me in advance. All I had really needed was an ordinary goose-necked lamp on my desk to help me read. When I said as much to my immediate supervisor, he replied solemnly that if I wanted to be a good counsellor I had to be able to pick up every little nuance of facial expression and body-language. Getting the right kind of experience now while I was at least partially sighted would enable me to compensate somehow when I lost all my vision later on – or so one could hope. All of this struck me as wrong. I didn't like subjecting my clients to third-degree lighting, and I was pretty sure that the obvious means of compensation – careful attention to voice tone – could serve me just as well now as in the future.

But the director of the agency went out of his way to undercut this assumption, and more generally to drive home the idea that my visual deficit made of me a second-class man. A real man, as he made clear to me, was physically tough, an athlete, a warrior, this last being an obvious reference to his own wartime service as an ordinary navy seaman. I must have looked skeptical at first, for over the months he kept returning to the subject of a purely physical, athletic masculinity. Now and then he would make the point, seemingly as a joke, that I wouldn't be up to the challenge of defending hearth and home. After all, the half-blind could not be expected to shoot straight. On one occasion when he was teasing me about my unathleticism and awkwardness, which he said seemed to be as congenital as my eye disease, I mentioned that I could still at least throw a football with accuracy. "But can you catch one?" "Well, no." "Then you can't be a real player," he said, with one of his affable smiles.

The definitive expression of the asymmetry that in the eyes of the director defined our relationship was bluntly and publicly articulated early one afternoon, when he emerged from the elevator on our floor as I was waiting to go down. He was obviously returning from one of his more salubrious liquid lunches – you could tell by the smell, and the expansive bonhomie. "Allan!" he cried, all smiles. He gripped me by my tie with his left hand, while with his right he seized my left forearm just below the wrist, holding it aloft so that the hand stuck up uselessly. This was a simple, seemingly trivial means of asserting dominance and control, one that makes its recipient feel awkward and silly, one that he had used before. "It's men like me," he said in a stagy, carrying voice, "who go to war to protect men like you." There were several people within earshot, and I could feel their eyes on me.

It was hard for me to even begin to understand why he was doing all this. But there was the plain fact, which I finally settled on, that I was bookish and articulate and occasionally questioned his judgment, while he was dogmatic, intolerant of criticism, and permanently embittered by having flunked out of his doctoral program in social work. In that sense we were a bad fit. In little ways, apparently, I didn't know my place. When for example he ordered me one day to read *Sons and Lovers*, the D.H. Lawrence novel that explores an unhealthy relationship between a mother and her grown son, I said "I've already read it. Why did *you* read it?" His face hardened and he stalked out of my office without answering.

Apart from my occasional uppitiness there was another issue that hung between us, one that will be identified in a later chapter. It had to do with the way he would come in close and stare into my eyes. For that, at least, my vision was evidently sufficient. That stare, and the way he gently laid his hands on me, made me very uncomfortable. At the same time, having extracted from me some key information regarding the distorted nature of my upbringing, he had managed to insinuate himself into the position of a pseudo-father.

This highly charismatic and forceful man manipulated and misused people under the guise of helping them, instilling and exploiting dependency to maintain his own psychological predominance. In my case he had zeroed in on my visual limitation, working subtly and not so subtly to amplify in my mind its supposed negative implications for my independence and self-development. I had accepted R P, but now I began to feel uncertain about what the disease really made of me. The glaring ceiling fixture was there all the time to show any observer that my personal space had to be artificially enhanced. But as I slowly discovered, it wasn't just me who was being "helped"; the director had his hooks into almost everyone there. Nothing at that agency was as it seemed.

I quit after fifteen months. It would take time to rid myself of the uncertainty that the director had somehow managed to instill in me, and to suss out the issues that had both tied and divided us. Although this man has been dead now these many years, I am not identifying him or his long-defunct agency by name. Doing so could cause unnecessary discomfort to members of his family, and other people who are still very much alive. As things turned out, the director got embroiled in a nasty contretemps involving contending lawsuits; the point at issue was whether he had inappropriately touched a female client. This unfortunate mess was reported in the local press. Eventually the director resigned from the agency to establish himself in private practice, and left his wife and children to take up with a younger woman. The counsellors who had worked for him, relieved of his immediate presence and control and feeling the slow dissolution of the personality cult in which they had been steeped, eventually went through the inevitable reaction. One of them expressed to me many years later the lingering bitterness of having been gulled.

There is a little postscript to the account set out above. A former colleague whom I managed to track down during the course of writing this book revealed – and this was news to me – that the director had gone to great lengths (or rather had driven his minions to great lengths) to support the enlarged-print needs of a visually impaired member of the agency's board of directors. This, my former colleague continued, was a strategy for securing the board member's ongoing strategic support. What I as a visually impaired employee had to offer, by contrast, was the ready opportunity for a seemingly casual abuse.

It didn't feel casual, though. It finally struck me after talking to my former colleague that the director's abuse was a projection of his own fear and hatred – hatred of a condition which, if he had been compelled to experience it himself, would have totally undone his sense of hyper-physicalized masculinity. Within his full view I was dealing effectively from day to day with a condition that he could not have tolerated for a single minute. Once when I tried to hand him my white cane, offering to show him how to use it, he wouldn't touch it. He literally shrank away from the thing as though it were radioactive, backing out of my office without a word and disappearing.

I have focused on this man to show how, at one time long ago when I was young and very green, an expert manipulator managed to impose a morbid twist onto my reception of vision loss. The eyes of the one going blind can sometimes be like mirrors, reflecting back to a certain kind of predatory sighted observer the latter's gratuitous sense of superiority, and validating his appetite for control. Secreted deep behind the eyes of that observer, there may lurk the unacknowledged fear that drives the whole distorted process. Such people, thank goodness, are relatively rare. As one who had been under the gaze of such a man I began to learn how visual impairment could be falsely and demeaningly conflated with inner smallness.

After my time at the agency I worked in a purely administrative capacity at the University of Alberta, as assistant admissions officer. I supervised a dozen admissions clerks and reported to the associate registrar, the amiable Doug Burns. For many years Doug would re-employ me at intervals as I bounced around between Edmonton and working or travelling abroad. In my first stint at Admissions I found it to be a pleasant, low-key environment, and after the tension that characterized the agency I enjoyed the decompression. My visual impairment was not a significant factor for the kind of work I was doing now, and I assumed, hoped, or trusted that it would not be an obstacle to the plans I was beginning to make for the future. After a few months on the job I had privately decided to set off at last on my extended travels at the end of the year; I would give Doug plenty of notice to find a replacement. My current work entailed boning up on foreign educational systems and interviewing foreign applicants for admission to the university – including an increasing number of Asians. The idea of going first to Asia, specifically to Japan, began to gather in my mind. The more I read about Japan the more alluring it seemed.

Toward the end of my stint in admissions I secured a teaching contract in Japan, and in late 1968 I set out for San Francisco to board my Mitsui line passenger/freighter to Yokohama. In what was emerging as a consistent pattern, the teaching contract like the Admissions job was for a single year. My intention was to give each new experience one year and one year only of my remaining vision: beyond that I had no long-term plan for the future.

My sojourn in Japan was like an extended, idyllic vacation. The school was in Kofu, Yamanashi-ken, in the steep and verdant foothills of the Minami Alps, and my little tatami mat apartment had a view of hillside peach orchards and grape arbours. Yet Kofu as a prefectural capital was big enough and various enough to put me in touch with all the principal elements of Japanese culture and society. In those days, before the Japanese government developed programs for bringing in whole cadres of foreign English teachers, the few foreigners teaching at local private schools got invited everywhere. They weren't expected to know anything or do anything, apart from accepting hospitality and expressing thanks.

This was my first experience living as an expatriate in a very alien culture. Once I learned the rudimentary conventions of Japanese social life, and the ways in which foreigners were exempted from most of the rules they would find tedious and restrictive, I began to understand why the long-term Canadian and American teachers I had met were so attached to the country. Their privileged if artificial positions allowed them to sample and delve into a complex and fascinating culture without being enmeshed in it or responsible for it.

But even I in my inexperience could see how quickly the culture was changing. The neighbourhood communal life in which I floated as an almost weightless visitor was giving way to something bigger and more impersonal. Three or four times a week I trekked from my bathless apartment down to the *sento*, or public bathhouse, to wash myself and then soak in the communal hot tub with my male neighbours. The women were partitioned off on the other side. One old man who spoke a little English told me that I was the first and probably the last foreigner who would ever be able to learn Japanese in so easy a way, relaxing in the hot water with "the real Japanese." Redevelopment would soon eliminate the little wooden houses and walk-up apartments and the old sento that served them.

In Japan as in Canada, RP bifurcated my life into two distinct halves, that of daylight (uncaned) and evening or night time (caned). At school in the full light of day, my students seemed not to notice my visual problem, or were too circumspect to let on that they did. Finally I brought my white cane to class one day for show and tell, which of course created a sensation. I explained to the grade sevens how the cane was used for restricted fields and then gave them a demonstration, much to their delight and alarm, by marching up and down between their desks swinging the cane while peering through a rolled paper tube that I had prepared for the occasion. They were all agog. After I answered all their questions and they had settled down a bit, I steered them back into our regular class work. It was as though nothing had happened.

By now I was completely habituated to using a white cane at night, and before long I even got used to the goggle-eyed stares I attracted from the locals whenever I was out and about in the evening, wielding the big stick. I could pick up these stares when, for example, there was a streetlight or theatre marquee nearby. At this stage of my RP the contraction of my daytime vision was slowly becoming more significant in its practical effect, as my restricted fields obliged me to scan and mentally compose in order to get any sense of panorama. I assumed that a greater challenge to my diurnal and nocturnal visual capacity lay in store for me the following year, when I was to leave Japan to go backpacking alone through Asia.

As things turned out I had a fair amount of company during those travels. At that time there were so many Australian, European, and North American backpackers moving through Southeast Asia and India that it was easy to link up with temporary buddies. I found that the more psychedelically minded or downright stoned among my fellow-travellers were intrigued by my cane. "What a trip," they would say, or words to that effect, staring at the thing. Some of them liked to touch it, as though it were a talisman. I felt that behind this spontaneous or compulsive little ritual gesture there may have been a fair degree of discomfort.

At those times when I was travelling alone by bus or train and wound up after dark in some strange city or town where I did not speak the language, I did have to operate within pretty narrow constraints. But there were no major problems, except for one night in Bangkok when I was stupid enough to set my usual caution aside and ingest a mind-altering recreational substance. This led to my leaving that all-important cane behind in a taxi I suddenly had to abandon, in a temporary fit of bad-trip paranoia. So there I was at two in the morning somewhere in Bangkok, on a sidewalk I couldn't even see, stoned, night-blind, caneless, lost, and not knowing a single word of Thai. My extra folding cane was safely stowed in my backpack at the little Chinese hotel where I was staying, but that was no good to me now.

I have absolutely no memory of how I made it back to the hotel. I managed it somehow, for I woke up the next morning in my room. This was probably the single most idiotic thing I ever did in my long coexistence with RP. Apart from that one lapse – or even to some extent because of it, for it fed my sense of youthful invulnerability – I was developing a growing confidence in my capacity to navigate solo, anywhere. Of course I knew I had huge advantages that the fully blind did not: in the daylight I still possessed narrow but very useable central vision. Even so I began to take a certain pride in my dim-light mobility skills, and this proved to be the beginning of a rather complicated new persona.

I carried no camera with me during my year of teaching and subsequent travels. Why take photos that in a few short years I would not be able to see? I assumed that anything I encountered that had a lasting meaning for me would remain registered within, if not as a visual memory then in some other way. This proved to be true, and I find that the three images from those years that have stayed with me most clearly are from Japan and India. The first is of the raked sand and rock gardens at Daisen-in temple in the Daitoku-ji temple complex in Kyoto; the second is of a magnificent seven-foot bronze Nataraja that dominated a guest bedroom in a large and imposing house in Madras. The third image – the strangest and most perplexing of the three, and the one that has left the deepest impression – is of the view that opened to me when I looked out from an observation point high on the facade of Mahabalipuram Temple near Madras.

I went to Kyoto and to Daitoku-ji as often as I could during breaks in my teaching duties in Kofu. In Daisen-in I would position myself on the porch that surrounded the sand garden in such a way that my narrow sightline ran down the long axis of the garden. This allowed my visual field to compass the austerely simple pattern of the raked sand, a masterpiece of Zen art. I stayed at the garden for hours at a time, just resting my eyes on that microcosm and remaining quiet. This was in effect a kind of meditation, although at that time I would not have claimed it as such. I would have said that my preliminary exploration of Zen was just through reading, mainly the works of Daisetsu Suzuki. But this alone had been enough to convince me that Buddhism was about something real and important.

In the following year as I travelled through India I was introduced in a vividly direct way to its religious tradition. This part of my journey would culminate in my encounter with the Nataraja in Madras and my visit to Mahabalipuram Temple. But first I had to deal with a lingering illness, an unresolved bronchitis or some other kind of lung infection that had been a parting gift from the cold Japanese winter.

Throughout my travels in Southeast Asia the lung infection kept coming back. The thing resisted antibiotics, and for months it would resurface whenever I pushed myself too hard. It returned with a vengeance in Thailand just as I was preparing to leave for India. On the flight from Bangkok to Calcutta I hacked up quantities of discoloured phlegm into the airsick bag. When we landed in Calcutta I walked down the ramp into the steaming heat of West Bengal, absurdly coughing and shivering.

I stayed in a cheap but clean little hotel that I had heard about from other backpackers, situated in its own walled compound in a run-down neighbourhood with broken pavements and flooded gutters. There I tried to rest up. I also tried to get used to what I saw whenever I left the compound – the homeless. The indoor or housed population of this quarter seemed to be vastly outnumbered by the street people who lived and slept on the pavements. I could neither rationalize nor open myself to their wretchedness. I learned that their ranks had recently been swollen by destitute refugees from flooded areas of West Bengal. The more permanent residents of the streets were low-caste locals who seemed never to have had anything: the hotel manager told me that many of them were descendants of earlier generations of street people.

I spent some days in the compound alternately sleeping and coughing myself raw, trying to rest up for my planned journey down to Madras in the far south. I was continually aware of what lay beyond the compound walls. Early one morning when I felt strong enough to go into the city centre I left the hotel and headed for a cross-street where I had been told I could find little motorized three-wheelers, a local form of taxi. I threaded my way among the prostrate forms on the sidewalk and their sorry little bundles, not wanting to see any of this. At one point I found that the body around which I was edging seemed to be a corpse. I lurched away and almost fell over a woman who was sitting up nearby, stopping just in time. I stared down at the bowed figure wrapped in a greyish rag that once might have been a sari. Then she raised her face, and we were looking directly into each other's eyes.

Years earlier I had the experience one day of unexpectedly coming upon a black bear in a wood. The moment we saw each other our eyes just locked. What is most startling about such an encounter is the sudden presence of an alert consciousness shining out at you through the eyes, registering your own consciousness and drawing you in. In those first moments there is no thought of teeth or claws or anything else: there is just consciousness, reciprocally registering consciousness. It is like looking into a mirror, except that you do not so much "see" this interpenetration as feel it. Something similar to this but intensely more gratifying can occur when lovers look deeply into one another's eyes, each becoming "lost" in the other. It is as though the barrier between two subjects who normally see each other as objects temporarily dissolves, so that they seem fleetingly to fuse into a single subjectivity.

Something like this happened for a brief few moments when that woman and I gazed at each other amid the squalor that surrounded us. Startled into undefendedness, we could not at first break eye contact. But "contact" is too shallow a word. Although I cannot speak for her, I think that each of us saw our conscious essence in the other. I know that I saw mine in her. But then the immediate context came rushing back in, those wretched pavements and the fact of her homelessness, and I was no longer gazing into a pool of awareness that was both hers and mine. Her eyes somehow changed without turning

away, and I was looking straight into a soul that was lost again in
despair. It was as though I was seeing all my own capacity for suffering enormously amplified in her.

I could not bear it. I ran from her into the street and was nearly hit
by a scooter. I pounded through the puddles and the muck until she
was well behind me, and when I spotted the first available trishaw I
clambered into it and sat panting and coughing, trying to remember
where I had intended to go that morning. I realized that I had not
even thought to offer the woman the rupees I had in my pocket, and
felt a wave of shame. Then I rationalized that if I had done so in full
view of the watchful young men who were sitting apart from her, they
surely would have had those rupees in the end. It would be a few
years more before I grew the tougher skin required for more or less
inuring myself to such scenes.

Over the next week I took in some of the more salubrious sights
in Calcutta, but I couldn't seem to put the pavement dwellers out of
my mind. So I went to the railway office and got my ticket out, successfully using a phony international student ID card I had bought
for a pittance at the Hogg Bazaar. I had intended all along to learn
something about Hinduism, and it was mainly this that shaped my
itinerary. But I had no illusions about finding anything within that
tradition that could justify what I had seen in Calcutta, or explain
away the viciousness of the caste system.

In the Hindi heartland of North India I visited many temples, both
famous and obscure, joined exuberant processions, and marvelled
at how people could be so publicly yet unselfconsciously absorbed
in their prayers, oblations, and rituals. I found these many forms of
religious expression touching but exotic. They seemed at that time to
lie completely outside the ambit of my own religious aspirations, such
as they were.

Eventually I journeyed by third-class rail down to Madras, which
I intended to use as a base for a series of temple visits in the South.
But a bad relapse of my bronchitis, or whatever it was, compelled me
to rest there to recover my strength. Because of the non-delivery of
telegrams from the Tokyo office of the Experiment in International
Living, a cultural exchange organization that was supposed to arrange
home stays for me in Madras, I found myself billeted at short notice
in a virtual mansion. It was as splendidly furnished as I was shabbily
dressed, and this contrast somehow drew my thoughts back confusedly
to the street people. But whenever I entered the large bedroom to

which I had been assigned, all my attention was drawn to the massive Nataraja that stood against one wall.

The Nataraja or Dancing God (the Lord Shiva) is one of the most widely recognized forms of Indian religious art. Its posture and gestures are a beautiful instantiation of Hindu philosophy, a teaching tradition about which I then knew nothing. Yet I was strongly drawn to the compelling bronze figure. This attraction was in part an expression of my rekindled appreciation of the visual arts, which had been given fresh stimulus by my year in Japan. Yet my interest in the Nataraja was tinged with awe and even a little fear. I had never before been so close, in the literal physical sense, to a powerful psychological archetype.

Every evening after a late supper with my hosts I would plead fatigue and excuse myself, retiring to the bedroom. There I would lie gazing at the great four-armed Shiva dancing ecstatically within his circle of cosmic fire. I ran my eyes slowly over limbs and face and emblematic objects, which I could not see all at once, repeating the process until I could build up a faint but gleaming picture of the whole in my mind's eye. Then I would go back to just gazing at the face. Although the eyes of the Shiva were not directed at me, the dancing figure seemed to invite me somehow to join with it. It was this pull or magnetism that prompted something within me to dig in its heels and resist. Yet I could not help looking at the statue. The last thing I saw every night and the first thing I saw every morning was Shiva, mythological destroyer of the manifest, visible world.

The Nataraja and the sand garden were iconic works whose symbolism I understood only in the most rudimentary way. But I knew that both of them had something to do with the imperative that had broken into my life in 1965, that of finding inner freedom in the face of a physical fate I could not control. Eventually I would turn to the two traditions that had inspired these works of art, Hindu religious philosophy and Mahayana Buddhism, as objects of study.

The experience at Mahabalipuram Temple, which is located a few hours' drive from Madras, was quite another matter. It was not informed by any previous experience or by anything I had ever read. It was something raw and unmediated, and for a long time I could neither name it nor connect it with anything else I knew. What I saw was just the immediate surroundings and more distant lands that stretched out in front of the temple. The singularity of the scene had nothing to do with the land itself, which was unremarkable enough, and everything to do with the sense of sheer insubstantiality that permeated the whole display. There was no premonition or lead-up to this experience: it just came out of nowhere.

The day I set out for Mahabalipuram I was feeling much restored; it seemed that I had finally put the chest problem behind me. I was eager to begin exploring the district around Madras, and my host had kindly provided me with a car and driver. We reached the temple in the early afternoon. The driver indicated with a sweeping, dismissive gesture that he had seen all this before, and went off somewhere with the car. I entered the temple alone and climbed up to a place that opened out onto a kind of rampart or parapet that commanded a wide-angle view of the prospect. I was learning how to build up a composed sense of the panorama by shifting my gaze back and forth, as I did with the Nataraja. Far beyond the temple precincts at the outer rim of vision, the atmosphere shimmered with heat over baked agricultural land. Travelling through there on the way to the temple, I had seen the lower-caste or casteless farmers who worked in fields they would never own, their emaciated black bodies almost naked, their crude implements seemingly as old as agriculture itself. To be black and pinned down at the bottom of the caste structure in the India of 1970 meant that these men had no prospects. I wondered if they ever had the opportunity and desire to come to this temple – if indeed they could even gain admission.

Immediately below me now I could see the scattered figures of priests, prosperous-looking pilgrims, hawkers of religious mementos, and different sorts of beggars, some of whose leprous faces and amputation stumps I had seen earlier at closer range. It seemed to me that what I was looking at was life stripped of its usual palliatives and camouflage, a tangle of exuberant or desperate striving and suffering that apparently had no inherent meaning.

I stayed out there for a long time, just standing and looking. Eventually it came to me that everything spread before me was a kind of dream. None of it was real. I did not think this or even feel it but *saw* it, with complete certainty. I do not mean that the experience was like one of those lucid night-dreams, in which you realize that what you are seeing will soon dissolve into the world of waking-state consciousness. It was more like being wide awake in a cinema and watching visual images that you know to be nothing but projections – except that the projections I was seeing now were the things that make up the material world itself.

Yet this was not an experience of nihilism. The insubstantial images or projections did not manifest in a nothing or a nowhere, but appeared against a background that was intensely, almost palpably, real. Although this background was not visible I could feel it as a conscious presence that included everything within itself. This presence seemed to be primary and self-effulgent, not contingent on anything else. But the forms seen within it were nothing but contingent; in their unreality they had no inherent staying-power at all. Each little figure was wide open to dissolution and would be replaced by others like itself in endless succession. If these figures were all that mattered, all would indeed be meaningless. But the space-like consciousness against or within which they were seen somehow dissipated the sense of futility. Whatever this presence was, it was apparently inviolable.

The emotional tone of the experience is hard to describe. My attention was drawn mainly to the human images, to their vulnerability and the almost transparent thinness of their being. You could not see this without feeling some sense of pity. Yet even the pity seemed somehow unreal or thinned out against the presence of that great background consciousness. What it evoked in me was not so much an emotion as the recognition that it was beyond all judgment or questioning. It was absolutely magisterial. I had come upon something that I did not understand at all, and yet I felt that I was seeing clearly for the first time in my life. I was sure that I would never, ever forget this, not even after I had lost the last of my eyesight. What I could not then know was that decades later, when I could no longer read, I would nonetheless come upon intensely evocative accounts of that consciousness while listening to tape recordings of the Indian spiritual texts known as the Upanishads.

Over the next few months I thought a lot about Mahabalipuram, or rather I remembered it and tried to think about it but found that my thoughts went nowhere. What could you "do" with such an experience? After leaving Madras I travelled slowly northward by local trains, stopping here and there for a few days when the fancy took me, somehow managing not to get sick even though I thirstily and stupidly drank the water from the stand pipes in the railway stations. Eventually I reached New Delhi, where I walked until I was footsore among the great stone shapes erected by the Moguls and the British. With that I decided that I had had enough of India. I flew from Delhi to Iran, the land border between India and Pakistan having been closed because of growing tensions between the two countries.

Soon there would be war, and the violent birth of a new country called Bangladesh.

As I made my way through Iran and Turkey and entered Greece, I remembered Mahabalipuram less frequently. I was seeing new things every day, taking in as much as I could during the daylight hours, tramping around almost from dawn to dusk. In Greece especially the sheer beauty of the islands and the sea around them displaced much of what I had experienced in India. I ate a lot of good Greek food and gained back some of the weight I had lost. In the evenings, whenever I had no one to hang out with, I found myself wondering more and more about what I would do when I got back to Canada. I could not seem to find a sense of vocation in anything.

In the meantime, I had already met the woman I was to marry. Priscilla Evangelista, or Pressi to her friends and family, was a small, graceful, independent-minded Filipina living and working as an English teacher in Japan. For a year we taught at the same school in Kofu. Ours was to be in many ways a union of opposites, one that would survive twists of fate and challenges both to my identity and our marriage, the like of which we never could have foreseen at the beginning. Of course I was going to lose all or most of my eyesight: this much we knew. Looking back to that time in Kofu I find it odd, given how significant the occasion must have been for both of us, that I cannot remember revealing to Pressi the fact that I was going blind. But she can't remember it either. It has just blended into everything that followed.

What I do remember is the constancy of her acceptance even in those early days, an acceptance of my visual fate that was unconditional and fearless. When I first became aware of this in her it filled me with a grateful wonder. In the course of writing this book I asked her one day, all these decades later after I had experienced a long succession of unanticipated medical problems, if there hadn't been times when she worried about my continuing capacity to put bread on the table. She replied simply that she had always felt I would be able to manage, somehow.

2

The Functionary and His Mask

1 EYEING THE FOREIGN SERVICE AND ANGLING FOR TOKYO

When I got back to Edmonton in 1970 after my adventures abroad, I found myself starting – once again – from scratch. There was still no long-term plan, and now I felt the need for one. Right away I got a temporary job as a teacher of English to adult immigrants, in the summer program at Alberta College. Outside of class I tried to mull over my options, which was rather hard to do in the continuing absence of an inner call to any kind of profession. I liked this kind of teaching well enough, but wanted something more. I liked academic work, but after wasting time in behavioural psychology I had yet to zero in on an alternative field. Asian studies, perhaps? In any event I wanted to get back to Japan.

This was all very vague. I began to look at practical options that could give me financial security years down the line, when I finally lost my reading vision. I knew there were blind lawyers, and back in my freshman year I had entertained the thought of going into law. Now I looked at the idea again – not with any enthusiasm, but with an eye to basic financial needs. I learned that applicants to the Faculty of Law had to take something called the LSAT (Law School Admission Test); I could at least take the test, I thought, and then see. So that is what I did, leading to results that displayed how badly I was out of touch with myself.

I scored at the 93rd percentile on the LSAT. I stupidly took this as an objective indication that I would not only do well at law, but could live comfortably within the ethos and mindset of lawyering. On that

fanciful basis I applied to the program and was accepted. The upshot
was that right from the beginning of the course in September I found
myself in an environment that was not just unfamiliar, but downright
alien. Some aspects of legal studies were interesting in their own right,
but the more I got into them and the more I got to know my colleagues the less I felt I belonged in this line of business. Nothing
clicked for me. I really tried: I studied hard and was very active in
class and in debates. But by December I was sure I had made a huge
mistake, and quit. I have never regretted getting out, any more than
my colleagues regretted my leaving. The day I announced my decision
they clustered about me, slapping my back, pumping my hand, saying
how glad they were that I would no longer be present as a competitor.
Such was the ethos among the more aggressive strivers in the U of A
Faculty of Law.

Eventually I had to acknowledge how much my recent folly had to
do with my compulsion to build a safe little redoubt while I could
still read print, a place where I could eventually hunker down with
an on-site secretary-reader. What next, then? For the time being I
fetched up once again at the University of Alberta registrar's office,
this time as supervisor of the admissions section. This quick parachute
drop was arranged by the ever-flexible Doug Burns, the assistant
registrar who had hired me in 1967. It was at this juncture that I read
The Chrysanthemum and the Sword, a classic study of pre-war
Japanese society by the American anthropologist Ruth Benedict. I
loved the book.

I began to read voluminously in anthropology in the evenings and
on weekends. After a few months of this immersion I made another
stab at practical planning, supported this time by real interest. I
plumped for anthropology – a discipline that enables one to think
systematically about the otherness of an exotic foreign culture, while
intuitively feeling one's way into it right down at street level. I took
undergraduate courses the following year and master's program
courses the year after that. During the summers I worked with Doug
Burns to process the flood of applications to the fall session.

After a year in the master's program I got a bursary and was then
invited to do a "bypass," which meant gaining acceptance into the
PhD program without having to do a master's thesis. Soon after that
I was rewarded – to my surprise, gratification, and relief – with a
substantial Killam Doctoral Fellowship. All the way through this
process I enjoyed my studies, the company of my fellow-students, and

my work as a teaching assistant. The only problem looming on the horizon was the ever-tightening job market for young PhDs.

While all this was going on, Pressi was following her own trajectory of working and travel. She had stayed on another year at the school in Kofu to complete her three-year contract, after which she worked in New York State as a high school exchange teacher under the auspices of the Experiment in International Living. Then it was back to Japan to teach in Yokohama. We had kept in touch throughout, and Pressi was able to stop and visit with me on her way from New York to Yokohama. This reopened and rekindled everything. After she left I thought: This is absolutely crazy; we belong together. I proposed to her over a trans-Pacific telephone cable, fumblingly and croakingly, and she accepted. At the end of her term she joined me in Edmonton as a duly sponsored fiancée-cum-immigrant, and two weeks later we were married. Our world had turned.

Pressi got herself a stopgap job in a municipal government office, while I sweated over my doctoral thesis proposal. It was in the field of political anthropology, explicitly focused on Japan. I was fascinated by a seemingly impossible alliance between Marxist university students (the *Zengakuren*) and conservative, ultra-traditionalist farmers, the two demographics teaming up to violently oppose the construction of the new international airport at Narita. This campaign was destined to failure and was in the process of winding down, but it represented a commonality of radical elements that had captured the nation's attention. In 1974–75 my Killam Fellowship took us to Tokyo for a year of preliminary research and Japanese language study, an intense ramping up of the language tutoring I had enjoyed in Edmonton. We loved Japan and were delighted to be back there, despite some unexpected bronchial and back problems that slowed me down.

Yet I was still sorting out my options. To focus on the political culture of dynamic Japan, rather than the India that still haunted my imagination, that would be the more practical course. This did not mean, however, that I would end up as a university professor. As much as I enjoyed anthropology, I thought or hoped that a background in Japanese studies and more in-country experience would open up a broad range of career options. It was my interest in Japanese society and culture that had carried me into anthropology in the first place, but the dearth of entry-level positions in departments of anthropology was prompting me to look beyond academia. I was in my early thirties and increasingly preoccupied with the fact that, in Canadian anthropology departments, there were up to three hundred applicants for every available tenure-track position. Well, then, what about the foreign service? Under the prompting of economic necessity, practical ambition and growing curiosity, I wrote the foreign service examination in 1975.

I had read everything I could find on the Department of External Affairs (renamed some years later as Foreign Affairs and more recently as Global Affairs), and what I found left me intrigued but uncertain. "External" had in recent years lost some of the paramountcy and prestige it enjoyed during its heyday in the 1950s and 1960s, when US President John F. Kennedy characterized Canada's small but effective foreign service as the best in the world. But External was now a much bigger organization; there were growing pains and problems with morale, and the old ethos was giving way to something new. And yet the work itself seemed fascinating. I thought that if I could just get in I should be able to tune out the static, hunker down, and concentrate on my own work goals. This looked more and more like my best career alternative. I would miss the scholarly life, but I had the hope that my work as a diplomat could be usefully informed by my study of Asian political cultures.

The door to my new vocation opened on a blustery winter day early in 1976 when I went for a do-or-die interview, the anticipation of which had tied my stomach into knots. I had passed the examination and a preliminary interview, and this one would determine whether I was to become a foreign service officer. The session would be conducted by a panel of three diplomats who were travelling across the country to assess candidates. I wondered what they would be like and how we would get on together. I knew I lacked the smooth, glossy finish of the natural diplomatist; if I found myself in the company of three identical suits filled with three identically stuffed shirts, I would probably fidget or pull a long face.

What I could bring to the table – I assumed there would be a literal and very substantial table, for surely these mandarins would want to hold court behind a gleaming expanse of fine hardwood – would be my rather chequered job experience, an incomplete PhD, and my equally incomplete Japanese language training. As far as I was able to determine, External Affairs had never hired any candidate with my degree of visual impairment, and the department had no affirmative action programs designed for people like me. I had decided months earlier that I would have to be candid about my RP, but as I started out for my appointment I was still in a quandary over how best to do this. The venue for the interview was a downtown hotel with which I was totally unfamiliar.

I take an elevator up to the designated floor and step out, finding that the corridors are so dark that I can see practically nothing. I break out my collapsible white cane and go up to the door of the nearest suite, quietly feeling for the number. I find raised numerals that are easy to identify by touch, not a flat number plate. Had the hotel used tactilely indistinguishable number plates, the bane of all blind travellers, I would have gone back toward the elevator and borrowed the eyes of the first person I met. I had left myself time to do this.

When I find the right room I fold up my cane, slip it into the breast pocket of my suit jacket, and knock on the door. I am ushered into the room, and we all stand around as introductions are made. The bright light pouring through the windows dazzles me, so I drag out the introductions a little as my eyes adjust. Then we all sit down. I find that there is no table: the grilling will be conducted in slouch-inducing armchairs. I slouch and try to look relaxed.

In this interview I am taken through a series of imaginary situations involving problems at Canadian missions abroad. In each case I have to assume the role of the responsible embassy official and explain how I would manage the problem. The role-playing takes well over an hour, as I recall, after which we have a nice little chat. It turns out that these men are not mandarins and not the least bit stuffy, just regular blokes who know their business and are actually quite approachable. At a pause in the conversation, which seems to be winding down, I think: Okay – *now*.

I take a deep breath and tell them that I have a visual deficit, identifying it by name and mentioning that the condition is often progressive. I briefly describe its nature and the means I use to compensate for it, and then draw the folded white cane out of the inside breast pocket of my suit jacket and unfurl it with a flourish. There are murmurs of surprise. This, I explain, is for finding the right room in a dim hotel corridor and for walking around at night.

I pause to take in their reaction and receive any questions they may have, but they just keep gazing at me expectantly. So I go on, and find myself saying more emphatically than I had intended that my RP had never interfered with any job I had ever held. They could confirm this by contacting my references, should they wish to do so. I also say that the skills on which diplomacy places a premium are verbal and analytical, and it was these that I had been working for years to develop. I would retain them even if I were stone blind. Would the panel like to go back over any of my previous role-playing to reconsider or re-enact it in the light of what I had just said? They all reply that this would not be necessary, although one of them looks rather uncomfortable.

The meeting ends with smiles, more handshakes, and noncommittal good wishes. I leave, having no idea what to expect. It is not until I have gone down the hall, entered the elevator and begun the descent that I begin to tremble. As I exit into the lobby the hand holding the cane is actually shaking. Part of me feels that I pushed it too hard; another part is satisfied that I did the right thing. At least I played it the way I wanted to, by just being me. But what I meant by "me" was the new R P professional persona that I was in the process of fabricating. It felt brittle and didn't quite fit.

I was offered a position with External a few months later, and in August 1976 Pressi and I moved to Ottawa. I was the first legally blind candidate ever hired as a Canadian foreign service officer. During the next dozen years or so of postings abroad and assignments at headquarters I would lose most of my remaining functional vision, while still working and still constituting a minority of one. It was under these circumstances that I would become a striver, working against the grain of failing eyesight to validate myself in a long-drawn-out personal campaign of constant readaptation. As an unexpected consequence of this process, I was to learn that my professional persona was no substitute for real selfhood.

I began work as soon as we arrived in Ottawa, getting my first round-eyed look into the entrails of a large bureaucracy. As I moved around the department through a succession of short-term assignments, I found it hard to make generalizations regarding the work atmosphere and morale in the Pearson building – the sprawling headquarters of the Department of External Affairs and its foreign service. There were divisions where each officer was an isolated monad locked into his or her own little sphere of policy issues and procedural problems, in a climate entirely devoid of inter-monad camaraderie. Yet other divisions or whole bureaux possessed real group cohesion and high morale. Within or beneath the vast formal schemata of mind-numbing acronyms, headquarters was a little city made up of very different kinds of neighbourhoods, some of which you'd like to live in and others you wouldn't. But whatever the division and its ambience, everyone was intent on their tasks. As a rule the officers worked very hard everywhere, many putting in extravagantly long hours.

One unique feature of the place was the air of flux or impermanence imposed by rotationality, that is, by the movement of staff back and forth between assignments at headquarters and postings abroad. Sometimes people would take a second overseas posting in preference to coming back to the Pearson building, if they weren't too obsessed by the need to get promoted to the next rung in the hierarchy. There was a constant coming and going, especially in the summer. Under these circumstances, even the teams that had very good esprit de corps were relatively short-lived by the standards of more conventional workplaces. I wondered if over the long run this kind of turnover made people emotionally detached from their fellows.

As I got to know people in various parts of the department, I made it a point to tell them that I had RP even though I did not yet need to use my white cane inside the building. This revelation raised no eyebrows. Once you were in, it seemed, you were really in. By way of encouragement some of the older officers spoke admiringly of Robert Ford, the brilliant Russian language specialist, Sovietologist and long-term Canadian ambassador to Moscow, who had a serious degenerative condition that affected his legs. He refused to use a cane when dealing with the Soviets and began to rely on a wheelchair only when he retired. I found all of this both heartening and daunting: Ford was a legend and a genius and not incidentally a considerable poet, and I was just me – whatever that was. Nevertheless, I found to my delight that I was meeting officers with lively literary interests – men and women with strong backgrounds in the humanities or social sciences.

During that initial probationary year in Ottawa I kept plugging single-mindedly for Japan, as our first foreign posting. The personnel department knew that through my previous studies I had already completed the equivalent of the first half of the two-year full-time Japanese language training program offered at the US State Department Area Training Center in Yokohama. That was the program in which External's would-be Japan specialists were normally enrolled. However, personnel was famous for the kind of reverse logic that would gleefully or absent-mindedly dispatch somebody like me to the middle of Africa.

Our circumstances were changing very quickly, especially for my wife. We wanted children; Pressi, who was attending university in

Ottawa to upgrade her teaching qualifications, finally became pregnant. Our son Evan, who as things turned out would be our only child, was born in September 1977 – one month to the day after we landed at the new Narita International Airport outside of Tokyo. Narita had been fully operational for some time, although sporadic and ineffective protests by the radicals lingered on. We had got what we wanted: we were back in Japan, and now we were three. Despite my missing out on the opportunity to trace the devolution of the Zengakuren/farmer alliance, I felt pretty smug.

During that first year I was the cultural affairs officer, dashing around to promote Canadian musicians and artists who were eager to get a foothold in the lucrative Japanese market. We spent the following year in Yokohama, where I completed my Japanese studies at the US State Department training centre. Then in 1979 it was back to Tokyo again – four household moves in four years since leaving Edmonton. Now I would do a solid three-year stint in the embassy's political section, during which we had the rare satisfaction of living continuously under the same roof.

As soon as we settled into our new quarters, Pressi got herself a very good full-time job as an English language instructor to Japanese executives at Mobil Oil/Pegasus. This initiative irritated the head of the embassy wives' association, whose husband happened to be my boss, or rather my boss's boss. This lady laid down the law that Embassy wives should "work" (unpaid) only in support of their husbands, in the endless round of official entertaining. Pressi was not about to back down, though, and at the office I made it clear that she had my full support. In the end, my superiors just laughed the matter off. Meanwhile our household had been joined by one of our bright young nieces from the Philippines, Alma Evangelista, who having finished her degree wanted to spend some time in Japan. She stayed with us right to the end of our posting.

At work I concentrated mainly on Japanese party politics. Here I felt fully in my element, as a former and now resurrected political anthropologist. Political parties everywhere were just tribes, as far as I was concerned, and my political reporting was nothing but practical anthropology. I found the work as interesting as it was Byzantine, though toward the end I began to get a little tired of political operatives. Now it all feels as remote as a previous incarnation.

Morale at the embassy was buoyant, especially during the four years when Bruce Rankin was ambassador. With me as with others,

Bruce went out of his way to develop a genuine personal bond. He was old enough to be my father, and for the first time in my working life I found myself stimulated and encouraged by an experienced mentor. When I began to experience the significant degradation of my vision that will be described in the next section, Bruce gave me tremendous personal and strategic support. After his retirement in 1981 and our own move back to Ottawa a year later we remained in touch, and when he died of cancer it was like losing a member of the family. For me and for Pressi, Bruce Rankin stood for everything that was best about the foreign service.

During the five years of our posting, Pressi and I went through some interesting shifts of perception regarding Japan. Our previous experience in little Kofu had revolved around our students, a few good Japanese friends, and our keen interest in Japanese culture. My Japan-based graduate research also had a strong cultural focus. But in the metropolis we were seeing Japan writ large, hypermodern and impersonal. At a certain point the country began to go flat on us; the old Japan bubble somehow burst. This happened during a visit to the Philippines. After the warmth, informality, and openness of Pressi's people we found the metropolis and the society that ran it strangely alien. We had to find a new way to live there, and for Pressi this was based mainly on her relationship with her Japanese students. For my part the new optic was bound to be as much political and economic as it was cultural.

It was only then that I acknowledged to myself that there were aspects of Japanese society with which I had never been comfortable. I didn't care for the formalism and rank-sensitivity that shaped so many kinds of social interaction, or the powerful pressures to conform that were typically exerted on the individual by the group, or the way women were treated throughout Japanese society, or the intensely insular sense of national consciousness that could depict Japanese and non-Japanese almost as different species. Looking at how these tendencies were enacted all around me, I really lost perspective for a time. And yet Pressi and I continued to enjoy all the cultural riches and variety of entertainment that the city had to offer.

My negative attitude toward Japanese hierarchy and conformism didn't last. I found that the best way to get my work-related contacts into perspective was to really *talk* to them, talk to them about what they liked or wanted in their lives. Over sake in the entertainment districts at night they would certainly talk, sometimes vociferously, despite the limitations of my narrowly formal, unidiomatic Japanese. Although I did well in the Yokohama language program and ended up as valedictorian, I did not have a naturally good ear. I had to both labour at my Japanese and lubricate it. That's what gave me a mellower take on the metropolis – all those gallons of warmed sake consumed in overheated little bars.

Getting to the bars at night involved using my white cane, of course, and sooner or later this implement would itself become a conversation piece. Once we were deep in our cups and the proprieties began to fall away, my Japanese companions would often express amazement at my impairment and how I dealt with it. Visually impaired people in Japan tended not to put themselves forward, and I had yet to meet any Japanese with RP. I wish in retrospect that I had sought them out.

When I first started work at the embassy, my main worry concerning RP had to do not with myself but my as-yet-unborn son. Shortly after we were married in 1973 I had arranged for genetic counselling in the hope of determining whether my RP was inheritable. There had been no history of it in my family, and I urgently wanted to know if the anomaly that had come to me out of the blue could be passed on. After reviewing the report from my ophthalmologist and taking an exhaustive family history, with its trail of ambiguous blanks, the geneticist offered his opinion. Although a child born to us would be a carrier of the disease he would probably not develop it himself. There could not, however, be any iron-clad guarantee of this. That meant that when the hypothetical child became a living presence, I was determined to find out what was in store for him. Here was a case where I could not fall in with Pressi's reasonable tendency to let things well enough alone and deal with problems only as they arose.

So when Evan was only four months old we took him to a Tokyo hospital where he was subjected to an electroretinogram or ERG, the only diagnostic test that could show definitively whether RP was present in the eyes. The ERG technology of that earlier time required that subjects, including babies, be fitted with special contact lenses that were wired in to the machine. We waited in an adjacent room while Evan was tested, listening to his howls of protest. When it was all over the doctor came in to congratulate us: Evan did not have RP. Relief flooded into me and I turned to Pressi, beaming. She gazed at me reproachfully. "I *told* you," she said. And indeed she had. Just so, she had also told me right after the pregnancy was confirmed that she knew she was carrying a boy.

Why was I hell-bent on having the poor tyke tested so early on? No doubt I was propelled by my own early experience with RP denial, which once resolved left me a convert to the cause of early diagnosis and accommodation. I hurled myself at the ambiguity of Evan's diagnostic status and forced a verdict without having any clear idea of what I would do if it showed that he had the disease. I just felt it would be best to know the worst and thus be able to plan for it. I remember thinking that if he had RP I would have to groom myself as his confidence-builder and model, acting as point man in our forced sortie down the RP path. I thought that to do this – and here I was in the grip of my own brand of overcompensation – I would have to become a virtual poster boy for RP super-adaptation.

If anyone had asked me at the halfway point of our Tokyo posting what most concerned me about my own eroding visual capacity, I would have mentioned the increasing difficulty I was having reading Japanese script. Yet there was a more general concern percolating under the surface. As I riffle through my memories I find it rather odd, considering how hard and how variously I was working and playing then, that the image that predominates over all the others is so simple and prosaic, and yet so hemmed about with tension. It comes in a jaggedly uneven visual frame or outer visual boundary whose inevitable contraction represents a future threat. The image – or rather stream of images – is that of a very familiar Tokyo street as seen as I walk along it, empty-handed during the day and wielding my white cane at night. What makes these images significant is their nascent obstructiveness: signboards and display tables litter the sidewalk along a creatively irregular facade of shop fronts; overhead signs are placed so as to barely clear the heads of the Japanese, and so for me present obstacles at forehead level.

These potential impediments, their edges barely discernable just beyond my face and body, constitute the indistinct frame or outer boundary of vision. I had few problems with all this because I remained very alert whenever I was moving. Collisions were rare. Yet the challenge to navigation was real enough, and constant. Thus I ended up memorializing that happy time not with cultural images or the faces of the people I knew in Tokyo, but with this one composite image of what I was walking through, as I tried to stay within the oscillating frame and own those streets.

Sometimes when I felt the visual space around me to be constricting, I would think of the *kare-sansui* gardens in Kyoto, which I had first discovered and fallen in love with in 1969. They had induced in me an experience of great visual depth that somehow opened or relaxed my body-sense. But now on the rare occasions when my duties in Tokyo allowed me to visit Daisen-in, the feeling was one of nostalgia more than the old direct engagement and inner sense of expansion. It seemed that even as I had secured an interesting career, its all-absorbing character meant that I was losing touch with something else that was more subtle and elusive and important. I rarely thought about Zen, except in a cultural context, and I never thought about what had happened to me at Mahabalipuram.

2 DOWN FROM THE PLATEAU

By 1979 there was mounting evidence – especially the eyestrain I experienced when I was doing close work – that my central vision was beginning to degrade. Within a period of just a few months I lost all my remaining capacity to read the local newspapers. Peering at standard-size newsprint I could no longer distinguish the intricate kanji (Chinese-style characters) on which Japanese writing is largely based. This was ominous; even reading English was beginning to feel uncomfortable. If I was to have any future in this line of work, or in any other I could imagine myself doing, I was going to have to do some serious planning and regrouping.

The equal opportunity employment program at External Affairs had recently been extended to cover staff with physical disabilities, which made me eligible at least in theory for some kind of logistical equalizer or back-up. But first I needed more information about the altered sensory environment into which I was heading, and I knew I could get it only from the blind people who were already living and working there.

In the spring of 1980 I asked our headquarters staff in Ottawa to contact the Canadian National Institute for the Blind (CNIB) in Toronto and work with its staff to draw up an itinerary for me. This would overlap with our already scheduled period of home leave in Canada. The itinerary would include an ophthalmological assessment and a round of office visits with blind professionals in Ottawa, Toronto, and Washington, DC. My intention in making these visits was to learn how totally blind people in various fields did their jobs and ran their offices. This plan was strongly supported by Ambassador Rankin and eventually by headquarters.

When I reached Toronto I found that the CNIB had referred me to Dr John A. Parker, who was then a professor of ophthalmology at the University of Toronto. He was to have a remarkably long career, finally retiring in 2016. Dr Parker gave me a thorough examination, asked me to describe how my vision had changed over the years, and took a brief family history. He then gave me exactly what I had been hoping for: a prognosis of how my vision would degrade, stage by stage, over the coming years. He was able to do this because my case was apparently quite typical of one sort of early onset RP. My timeline as Dr Parker described it to me was necessarily couched in general terms, each of its transition points representing so many years from the present, plus or minus two or three. This chronology would prove to be very accurate.

What I particularly appreciated about Dr Parker's presentation was the way he described each transition point in terms not simply of loss but of the available technology that would ease my adjustment to the next stage. He even took the initiative, after we finished discussing the prognosis, of accompanying me to a nearby office at the university where a secretary who had RP was entering data on a computer system equipped with a large-print screen program. This young woman was obviously very much at home with her adaptive system.

The scheduled meetings with other blind people were more encouraging than I had initially hoped, with the exception of one jarring experience in Toronto that I will describe later. My new contacts showed me through direct, immediate examples the various sides of managing a career successfully without vision. I was introduced to new technologies and methods of organization, but just as importantly I met the confident men and women – lawyers, university professors, social workers, bureaucrats, and one engineer – who made use of them. They would become my future role models. One of these accomplished copers, Dr Jerry Neufeld of the University of Ottawa department of linguistics – for several years he also had a cross-appointment to the department of psychology – would become a long-term friend. Jerry grew up as a braille user, and the satisfying, hands-on physicality of that process was transferred eventually to the keyboard of a talking computer. The act of keyboarding was for Jerry intimately bound up with the creative process, and as a writer he was extraordinarily productive. He would give me invaluable help in my own later transition to digital media.

In Washington my most interesting meetings were with a blind economist and an employment equity officer, both working at the

State Department, and a blind lawyer at the Justice Department. During my visit to the State Department I learned to my surprise that the US foreign service was not open to candidates who had significant visual deficits. This restriction had great implications for the economist, who was permanently and frustratingly "grounded" in Washington. He explained that it was because of his blindness and not his previous training in economics that he was classified by the department as an economist rather than a foreign service officer; this ruled out any possibility of doing economic analysis and reporting from postings abroad. Apparently, the State Department had long taken the view that foreign service officers had to be physically capable of dealing with any emergency, including acts of terror. This stricture made State or at least its cadre of diplomats something of an exception among American government agencies, which otherwise went to considerable lengths to accommodate blind employees.

It was not for me to judge whether the special rules governing recruitment at the State Department were justified by special American circumstances. But it was odd to think that those Americans with whom I had the most in common, both in terms of our shared visual impairment and our similar interests, should be categorically barred from serving their country as diplomats. My comparative advantage as a Canadian made me all the more determined to keep working as efficiently as I could in Tokyo, and then back at headquarters. This meant that I was going to identify even more closely both with my job and my RP.

The decline of my reading vision continued after we completed our Japan posting and moved back to Ottawa in 1982. By 1984 I had lost the capacity to read normal-sized English print and was experiencing increased eyestrain whenever I performed any task that called for good, up-close visual acuity. Evidently I had finally reached the outer rim of the long plateau of comparative visual stability. From 1982 through 1984 I experimented with electronic devices such as the closed-circuit television reader, which allows the user to sharpen and magnify an image to whatever extent may be required. Unfortunately my intensive use of this device, with its hand-operated scanning platform, aggravated a pre-existing back and neck problem that was to eventually get much worse.

I finally took my print access problem to personnel. With the backing of my colleagues and the full support of the department's resourceful and persuasive Equal Opportunities Coordinator, Shirley Boles,

I made an unprecedented request. I asked that a full-time reader-secretary be assigned to work with me on a continuing basis, both during my headquarters assignments and on postings abroad. My assumption was that this request would meet with plenty of resistance from personnel, for it involved a novel redeployment of secretarial resources. Yet it was the only arrangement through which I could continue to do what the department expected of me. Much to my relief the request was promptly approved: the band of tension that had been tightening around my chest for months immediately began to let go.

My first reader-secretary was recruited from outside the department. I was surprised at the impressive number of candidates who responded to personnel's advertisement: after all, "reader-secretary" is an uncommon job category. Most of the candidates assumed, it seemed, that just reading out loud would be a cinch. As it turned out, there were very few who could read without stumbling or droning or getting lost, let alone type my dictation accurately and at speed. The hands-down winner was Karen Reid, a young married woman with two children in elementary school. The Reid family lived in one of Ottawa's more distant satellite towns. Karen was as cheerful and personable as she was efficient, and it was a pleasure to work with her. She did find the sheer sprawling size and impersonality of the Pearson Building a little intimidating – she characterized herself as a "small town girl" – and over the next couple of years she would find her long daily commute increasingly tiring. I was lucky to have Karen's support for as long as I did.

In Tokyo I had occasionally used Dictaphones, seeing their obvious advantages. The disintegration of my reading vision in Ottawa pushed me further in the same direction. Forced to abandon the quaint long-hand that was still favoured by my diplomatic colleagues – this was in the Old Stone Age, before personal computers displaced fountain pens and stenographers at External – I made permanent room for a Dictaphone right in the centre of my desk and began to "write" every-thing out loud. With Karen now available to quickly transcribe my reports and memoranda, my output significantly increased. This mode of production is very fast once it becomes habitual.

Both at the office and outside it I was now accessing the world of books and papers through a soundscape rather than a printscape. The only print I tried to read at work, and this with considerable difficulty, was the *New York Times Large Print Weekly*. At home all my leisure reading came to me in the form of cassette tapes from various libraries for the blind – Canadian, American, and British. I was of course aware as a lifelong bookworm that I had lost a precious resource, in two respects. First and most obviously I had lost the sheer volume and variety offered by all the libraries and bookstores I might ever care to visit. Besides that, I no longer experienced the particular and satisfying physicality that is involved in the act of reading. You can feel the heft or presence of a book, riffle through its pages, admire it if it is well-bound and the paper good, and above all curl up with it. You incorporate it right into your private physical space. Now the act of reading had been split down the middle in a new way: I was *here*, and the tape recorder – a functional but unprepossessing piece of machinery – was over *there*.

How did I feel about all this? I guess what mattered most was that I acknowledged the new way of dealing with the printed word as an absolute necessity. At first I felt a strong and even urgent need to accept my changed circumstances, and then actually felt the acceptance. The one thing that made this easier to do was the way I had absorbed my prognosis in 1965. At that time I had experienced the blunt delivery of the medical verdict as a relief, a dissolving of all ambiguity and denial and wishful thinking, and what I wanted again now was the relief of letting go. So I let go. I looked at my old life as a reader and said, in effect: *That's finished.* I found that the last lingering regrets dissipated in a natural way over the next couple of years.

This transitional period is hard to put into words because there is no received vocabulary for describing its hybrid nature. As experienced at the office it did not actually feel like a transition at all, a movement from relative sightedness toward blindness. There I was using one of the communication modes favoured by the totally blind – cassette tape – even as I could rest my eyes on the familiar contents of my office. It was the office of an adult illiterate who could not, need not, read the things he wrote. I was occupying a kind of mezzanine or halfway house between two more populous domains of experience, those of sighted readers and sightless listeners. This in-betweenness was not disturbing, but it was rather odd and unsatisfyingly indeterminate.

The one big problem with my new work system had to do not with dictated and transcribed output, but with the sheer volume of printed input. Even with the reader-secretary in place I no longer had the capacity to access and process large quantities of printed information. There had once been a time when I could speed read, but an oral reader cannot "speed speak." Nor could my reader read to me at all during those daily periods when she was transcribing my dictated memoranda or attending to other duties. Today a blind person doing my line of work would be far better equipped to manage the information inflow: he or she could tap into the department's digitized database and communications system, easily accessed through a personal computer equipped with synthetic speech. Sophisticated optical scanners would also enable the blind officer to "read" and store other printed material that was not already digitized. But in the mid-1980s the department's computer database had not yet been developed, and the available scanners of the day were not up to the task of reading poorly printed External Affairs telegrams with their broken letterforms.

Fortunately for me, I had landed an Ottawa assignment that allowed me to be highly focused and selective in my writing goals, and thus in the body of printed material that I needed to assimilate. I worked in the Policy Planning Bureau, where as an analyst dealing mainly with Asia-related issues I was granted an unusual degree of independence. This was an arrangement well suited to my declining visual capacities.

What troubled me was how those capacities were likely to affect my chances for further promotion. To illustrate the dilemma of expectations that can overtake ambitious people with failing eyesight who work in a corporate setting, I must say something here about my early prospects at External Affairs. Foreign service officers had to serve at the entry or FS-1 level for four years before they could be considered for promotion to FS-2. The average time spent in the FS-1 grade was running at about seven years. I was promoted to FS-2 in the minimum four years, and both Tokyo and the Policy Planning Bureau were considered to be excellent career steps. Thus I was on a trajectory that in the normal course of things would lead me – if I could keep up the pace in an intensely competitive environment – to an ambassador-level position.

But the next step upward would normally be a deputy director or acting director assignment, and this required a great deal of reading every day. You had to review all the paper being produced in your own division (the bigger and more active the division the better), keep abreast of developments elsewhere in the department, especially those that might have implications for your own shop, selectively monitor the daily flood of despatches from our missions abroad, and if possible thoroughly read useful publications such as the *Economist* and the *Far Eastern Economic Review* every week. I did not see how I could manage this. Even the upwardly bound officers at this level who possessed good eyesight typically carried work home with them every night, their briefcases bulging with hours of extra reading.

The other constraining or rather off-putting factor for me was the nature of the managerial work for which all this reading would normally be considered a necessary preparation. The more I saw of management at divisional level and above, the less it appealed to me. I simply had no interest in managing people, any more than I had in being managed. As for the substance of our work, what preoccupied the managers was not just a set of interesting foreign policy issues but the refraction of those issues through a complex and sometimes stultifying bureaucracy. For the upwardly mobile officer, a keen involvement in bureaucratic mechanics and territoriality was unavoidable as part and parcel of modern (and probably pre-modern) government. Dealing with these realities required a certain mindset that included a real interest in "process" – all those exasperating and time-consuming procedures required to get things done. I was definitely not process-minded. By temperament I seemed to belong exactly where I was, in a small and relatively autonomous "ginger group" whose role it was to question prevailing trends and come up with new ideas.

The policy planning shop had real group spirit and high morale, especially under the convivial leadership of Peter Hancock and his successor, Paul Heinbecker. The sensible course would have been to thank my lucky stars that I was able to work there, and just keep doing it until it was time for my next overseas assignment. But I was not attuned to the sensible course. By this time I had thoroughly internalized External's prevailing ethos of obsessive-compulsive careerism, absorbing it in an automatic and unreflective way. In one corner of my mind I was furious that the loss of reading vision stood in the way of an advancement that I both did and did not want. At the same time I was rather proud of the modest niche that I had with some effort carved out for myself. This split-mindedness pitted the restless striver, who could be as harshly self-critical as he was ambitious, against a more detached inner observer who suspected that the whole bureaucratic enterprise was at best a burlesque.

It was at about this time, when my new system at the office had been satisfactorily worked out, that I joined the board of the Ottawa RP Foundation. This was the forerunner organization of the present-day Foundation Fighting Blindness. I got involved with the RP

Foundation because I wanted to promote self-help groups for youngsters with RP – the kind of groups that could help them face and
better deal with the disease. But this kind of outreach proved to be
very difficult, for it kept bumping up against the sort of denial it was
intended to allay. Circulars and letters were not responded to; telephone calls were not returned. The RP youth scattered throughout
the community did not show much desire to get together, and given
my own early experience I could understand why. To meet as a group
for the express purpose of talking about that one problem they had
in common would force them to acknowledge how large it loomed
in all their lives.

The board itself was evidently rather uncomfortable with the goal
of helping people adjust to RP, for its dominating purpose and
explicit mandate was to "beat" the disease. All the considerable
talents and energies of the board were devoted exclusively to raising
funds for medical research. Although the fully sighted majority of
board members endorsed my idea of building a young persons'
contact network, they did so with some evident reluctance. They
seemed to have the reflex of trying to protect symptomatic RP youngsters from too much reality.

I began to wonder just who or what was being protected: Was it a
real whole person, with full native powers of adjustment, or a person
conceived of mainly as helpless victim? If the latter, did this imply
that sightedness is so essential to personhood or selfhood that its
eradication would permanently scar our identity? I felt that this could
not be true, yet I wanted to be able to prove it definitively. If there
were some means of logically demonstrating the separability of sightedness and selfhood – and I had no idea as yet how this could be done
– then sharing that demonstration with symptomatic young people
could help them to see their circumstances in a new way.

But it was not only inexperienced youngsters who needed this kind
of reassurance: even after making the practical adjustments described
above, I was beginning to feel that I stood in need of it myself. It was
true that I had accepted the loss of reading vision. And I continually
told myself, as an article of faith, that our core selfhood had to be
deeper than blindness. Yet as time passed my sense of who I was
seemed to be growing more ambiguous. Part of this was just the kind
of internal stretching and straining experienced by anyone who consistently works a lot of overtime, as I had done for years, and comes
to feel that some parts of himself are being left to atrophy. But there

was more to it than that. In working as hard as I did, I was not just compensating but overcompensating for the disadvantages imposed by RP. The ironic result seemed to be that RP was wrapping itself, stealthily but progressively, around my sense of self.

3 THREE FACES OF THE RP IDENTITY

With the benefit of hindsight I would now say that RP had become enmeshed with my sense of self in three distinct and even contradictory ways. First and foremost, in the sense that it was the prepared face that I presented to the world, was my professional persona. I invested a good deal of psychological capital in the relatively rare identity of a fully functional but partially sighted diplomat. At headquarters I always carried my white cane to the meetings I attended, even though I knew most of the layout of the Pearson building well enough to walk it in my sleep. I conducted a series of seminars on Canada-Japan and Canada-Asia relations with academics at Canadian universities, and travelled alone to various meetings and conferences abroad. These activities gave me the chance to show that a visually impaired officer was not impaired in the roles of representative or animator.

I especially liked the academic seminars as opportunities for puncturing the old stereotypes. I would make an entrance bearing a white cane, then settle in and deliver a long and detailed briefing without referring to notes. These performances were carefully prepared and designed to make an impression, but in retrospect I regret that they left me little room for improvisation or spontaneity. Whatever the particular topic may have been at each of these meetings, the unspoken subtext was always the same: my need for self-affirmation in the midst of eroding vision.

The seminars were one indication, one among many, that I was turning into a compulsive A-type personality. I was finding it difficult to relax, and this was starting to affect my relationship with Pressi and Evan. I was edgy and sometimes impatient. Evidently the persona or professional version of the RP self, who was an exacting taskmaster, was pushing down jangled roots into whatever the rest of me was. Yet because the persona was essentially a creature of the bureaucracy – a diplomat at headquarters is really just another kind of bureaucrat – I felt increasingly restless under the constraints of this narrow persona.

Thus it was that I began to write fiction in the evenings. I managed to get a short story and a novella published in national anthologies,[1] as the first steps toward what I hoped would be a set of interlinked stories set in Japan. When these efforts resulted in good newspaper reviews, it went completely to my head. The great, visually impaired Argentine writer Jorge Luis Borges had long been one of my culture heroes, and I began to have grandiose thoughts of becoming the Northern Borges. But when I tried to get started again I ran up against a formidable writer's block, one that I could neither break through nor understand, and my project of magnifying the blind persona through literature ground to a halt. It would be many years before I identified the source of that block.

Despite all my attempts to live mainly through my persona, I found with distressing regularity that the RP identity could manifest itself in a very different form. Underneath the persona and usually obscured by it was its virtual opposite, a partial-seer defined not by displays of ability but by feelings of disability. It would appear, for example, when I dropped some small and perversely mobile object on the floor and simply could not find it, or when unexpected sidewalk reconstruction or other kinds of barriers in unfamiliar locales made navigation particularly exhausting, or when the failing light made it impossible for me to recognize bus numbers during the evening commute back home. Such little problems do crop up in the daily lives of all visually impaired people, and they have to be dealt with not only outwardly but inwardly.

To inwardly react to physical obstacles or indecipherable bus number plates as exasperating affronts, as I sometimes did, was to take them "personally," in a temporary spasm of disabled self-identification. These little aberrations were something more than situational responses; they were expressions of the growing tension and self-doubt that was partly repressed by the professional persona.

As time went on, a cluster of annoyances of this sort began to crop up during my morning commute, or at least at the very tail end of it. I liked to get to work early; in these latitudes in winter, that meant the sky would still be quite dark when I reached the Pearson building. This made it hard for me to see; in my eyes the looming brown hulk of headquarters was not altogether "there." The bus dropped me off across from Pearson on the opposite side of the street, which meant that to reach the U-shaped entrance driveway leading up to the massive front doors I had to cross four lanes of traffic on Sussex Drive, a virtual expressway during rush hour. Despite the fact that there was no crosswalk at that point, the impatient commuters pouring out of the buses just swarmed across Sussex anyway. Some of the motorists in the oncoming cars seemed to regard these functionaries as potential trophies.

There was a crosswalk some way further down Sussex, but none of the commuters alighting on the north side of the street used it. In any event it was regulated by a traffic light that I had difficulty "reading." So I would barge out onto Sussex with everybody else, holding my cane, asking whoever happened to be next to me if I could take his or her arm. Sometimes I hesitated at the curb if the roar of oncoming traffic was particularly loud, in which case the runners would leave me behind and I'd have to wait a couple of minutes for the next incoming bus with its load of disembarking Pearsonites.

One morning as I stepped out in front of a parked bus I asked the man striding forward beside me if I could take his elbow. He laughed derisively, and in a very characteristic manner. I knew this man and could now dimly make out his features. "Jones," he said as he pulled me along, "how would you cope if I weren't here?" "I'd latch onto some other sucker," I snapped, but he had me there. As the blind educator and author John Hull once observed, there is for every blind person a sighted person just down his path on whom he is going to have to rely. I relied on this one only as far as the opposite curb, then broke off contact. Sometimes in these random allocations you end up with a real dud.

The next problem, once I had gone up the sidewalk skirting the U-shaped drive, was figuring out which of the many front doors was actually open. There was always only one, or at most one double-set. I could never visually identify it. There would be a great surge of people flowing past me, and the blurred and echoey aural cues they generated made it difficult to identify where the open portal might be. The Pearsonites were moving so rapidly and impatiently by this point that it was hard to be noticed even if I asked for help. If I had to characterize the feeling tone of the surge it would be one of irritability rather than eagerness to begin the day. Sometimes when I plunged into the herd and just followed its flow I would get to the top of the stairs only to find the door in front of me shut tight. Then, when I tried to move laterally to the next door, I'd find my way barred by a thick cord strung along a set of stubby metal poles. It was the sort of setup used for managing queues in theatres and banks, but here it made me think of cattle chutes.

Once I got into the building and walked over to Tower A, the final challenge was the elevators. The waiting area by the elevators was to my eyes extremely dim, and although each elevator had above it a panel of two lights that indicated either up or down, I could never make out whether it was the upper or lower light that was on. When an elevator arrived and the doors sprang open, everybody rushed forward and once again I would have to hesitate. I'd call, "Going up?" and wait, and sometimes have to repeat the question. By the time I got my answer, if I got one, it was often too late. These elevators were programmed to be impatient of laggards: after the briefest possible loading interval the doors would spring shut as unexpectedly and quickly as they had opened. Sometimes I would get caught between the doors as I tried to enter. I was never hurt because they would bounce back as soon as they touched me, but there would be a sharp clang and the experience was jarring.

That is how my working day began. Some mornings when the entrance ritual had been particularly exasperating I would indulge in the fancy, as I made the day's first pot of tea, that the whole thing was a plot. This cunning set of access problems – the misplaced crosswalk and kamikaze traffic on Sussex, the crooked lottery of closed and open front doors, the cannibal elevators – it all fitted together and could mean only one thing. Evidently I had become trapped in a kind of open-concept Skinner Box, but without the usual food pellets. It was a clever little experiment in Social Darwinism, dreamed up no doubt by the gnomes on the eighth floor in collusion with the municipal traffic department and the Otis elevator people. The objective of the experiment, and you had to admire the gnomes for their evolutionary long view, was to methodically reduce the number of expendable gimps or Untermenschen making it up to their offices during the morning rush. This was a nice example of what economists called structural adjustment.

One day when Karen was down with the flu I jokingly shared this intelligence with a temporary replacement secretary, who cried in a voice full of horror, "Oh no! Mr Jones, they wouldn't! Would they?" Startled, I stared at her. There was a single brief pulse of paranoia, and then I sort of blinked and came to. "It's all right," I assured her, smiling, "they'll never get away with it."

Of course it was easier to indulge in fantasy than to confront the uncomfortable truth, and the truth was that I identified personally with these morning glitches because they made me look bad in the eyes of others. This was an example of the kind of touchy reactivity that was part and parcel of the disabled version of the RP self. A practical solution to at least some of the glitches would be to get a guide dog, but I was not comfortable with dogs.

The disabled self also appeared out of nowhere when I found myself in circumstances that forced me, through the sudden and unwelcome juxtaposition of a bright visual memory and an immediate but ambiguous visual perception, to acknowledge how much eyesight I had actually lost. A particularly painful experience of this sort was my second visit to Wilton Park, a conference facility maintained by the British Foreign and Commonwealth Office in West Sussex, a couple of hours' drive from London. Wilton Park was a sixteenth-century manor house that had been rebuilt and added to over the centuries in a succession of architectural styles. Inside was a maze of rooms and passages that to the visually impaired visitor could be experienced either as intriguing or baffling.

On my first visit there in the mid-1980s to attend a conference on Japan, I had a wonderful time. I could not have managed without the cane, but with its help and the vision I still retained I could quite easily navigate, explore the building between sessions, and schmooze with the other delegates in the evenings. I had a rough but satisfyingly atmospheric visual impression of the facility's principal features.

But on my second visit a couple of years later I was shocked to find how things had visibly melted away. I now had to rely mainly on my cane to find doorways and trace passageways, and had to fall back on inexact memories of my earlier visit to maintain a sense of where I was within the floor plan. Visual boundaries had become very vague: the impressive vaulted ceiling in the great hall where we took our meals had completely disappeared. The food on the table could now be identified only by touch, and its dim outlines seemed to be a long way down from my face. It was only my solid contact with the chair that counteracted the feeling that I was floating in space, caught up in an enormous shadow-filled bubble.

For those few days at Wilton Park I experienced what I can describe only as loss of personal being. It was like a large hole within me, the palpable absence – if an absence can be palpable – of what had been a more-or-less functional partial seer two years earlier. On the flight back to Canada I had to do some hard work on myself to pull out of this funk.

After all, I told myself, I had done what I set out to do. I had made useful new contacts and was returning to Ottawa with a full set of substantive notes that I could apply to my current projects. This at least was something.

The diminished or negative version of the RP self re-emerged after Karen finally resigned. One morning she came into my office, sat down on her chair, and burst into tears. This is it, I thought. I got up, grabbed a box of Kleenex, and moved around the desk to sit down beside her. When she could finally speak, she said that she was tired out from all the commuting and had to find work at home. There was a secretarial job opening up at her childrens' school. When she hesitated, I told her that I was going to write the best darn recommendation either of us had ever seen. This provoked more tears, and for the first time I truly grasped the extent to which Karen had committed herself to helping me. Now, evidently, she was worried about how I would manage, and I hastened to assure her that all would be well.

But I had not anticipated what it would be like to spin my wheels when the support arrangements that kept me productively working abruptly collapsed. This was a frustrating period of several months' duration during which personnel could not seem to address the issue of replacing Karen. As a result my work was being impaired, and this drew me down by degrees into a simmering sense of grievance.

One morning when I was feeling particularly frustrated over this impasse, a colleague came into my office to read me a paragraph from a recent memorandum. It implied that my reader-secretary position was going to be permanently eliminated as an incidental consequence of a proposed general reorganization. I had not been consulted before this document was circulated, and it impelled me into immediate action.

In the end, after I intervened with the author of the memorandum, my all-important support system was reconfirmed. Some weeks later I was working once again with the necessary backup, and apart from that one bad patch the department consistently provided me with the resources I needed. Considering that these were still relatively early days when it came to equal opportunity policy development, External Affairs was quite forward-looking – thanks in large part to Shirley Boles.

But I can remember sitting at my desk after my colleague had warned me of what was coming, staring down at the memorandum I could not read, feeling a thick surge of impotent anger. What this anger expressed was an intense personal identification not only with my disability but with the vulnerabilities to which it gave rise. As I

sat there I thought about a radio program I had heard some weeks
earlier, a documentary on a recent convention of blind activists in the
United States. I had been shocked to hear one militant say with evident
bitterness that she wished the whole population could be struck blind.
"Then we would be top dogs," she explained. For the first time I felt
that I could understand such a state of mind.

After I was back to working at full tilt with a reader-secretary, one
in what turned out to be a long line of temporary helpers, I never
quite forgot the black taste of my earlier frustration. I was finally
coming to learn how, in the lives of visually impaired people less
fortunate than me, the sense of grievance and entitlement could distill
over time into a poisonous narcotic. If there was anything worse than
blindness and the unemployment that so often went with it, I thought,
it must be that soul-destroying bitterness.

The two versions of the RP identity that I have described here, the
confident persona and its frustrated alter ego, are conjoined through
the dynamics of retinitis pigmentosa. They are really two sides of a
single coin. To live with RP is to see in some situations and fail to see
in others. Because these experiences are the opposite of each other,
the forms of selfing that arise from them – i.e., the feelings of affirmative self-expansion or besieged self-contraction – are mutually contradictory. The one is positive, the other negative. It seemed to me
that the latter could not be completely done away with because there
were bound to be some situations that strongly invoked it. If the
faculty of vision was to be taken as an integral part of the public self
– and one certainly did tend to take it that way, even if there might
be a more authentic self that had yet to be revealed – then the best
one could do was to strive to keep the persona on top for as much
of the time as possible. When this failed, there was nothing to do but
grit one's teeth.

These two versions of identity did not exhaust the ways that RP
could penetrate the sense of self. At a level of the mind deeper than
that of the persona or the indignant griever that lay just beneath it,
there was an intense, anticipatory identification with the fate toward
which I was inexorably heading: that of total blindness. This buried
blind proto-self was almost always strongly repressed. But once uncov-
ered it had the quality of pure terror. I had discovered this terror, this
sense of utter self-annulment, back in 1980 during the fruitful round
of visits to blind professionals arranged by the department and the
CNIB. One of these encounters, which I came to value only in retrospect, showed me more than I had bargained for.

When I arrived for a meeting in Toronto with a man described on my itinerary simply as a social worker who had RP, I found myself facing someone whose visual deterioration was extremely advanced. That is, I was facing and looking at him in his swivel chair over on the other side of his desk: he was facing but not looking at me. He was not looking at anything, for his eyes had the unresponsive and in-turned cast of the totally blind. His haltered guide dog was snoozing off to one side. I still assumed at this time that the typical RP patient was left with light perception even after losing the capacity to recognize objects, but with a pang of anxiety I asked the social worker if he could see light. He replied flatly that he could not. After a few moments of silence, during which I went absolutely cold inside, he said that the last of the light had disappeared several years earlier. This man was about ten years older than me.

That evening in my hotel room I lay on the bed in a cold sweat and looked up at the ceiling, gripped by a shockingly primitive kind of fear as I anticipated that final darkness. This sense of inner annulment remained intense for what seemed like hours. Finally I made myself sit up, rubbed my eyes hard enough to make me see lights, and stared at the blank TV screen. I turned the TV on. I switched to the news channel, looking for the distraction of large-scale catastrophes. At this period I could still see the small screen fairly well, and for the rest of that evening and part of the night I drugged myself with images.

4 TRYING TO CATCH HOLD OF MYSELF

In the months following my encounter with the blind social worker in Toronto, I had tried to just forget about him and what he represented. But looking back on it a few years later I finally had to acknowledge that, somewhere along the line, I had slipped inwardly into a secret or at least implicit sort of bargaining. I evidently had an intense need to retain some little measure of visual consciousness, even if it was nothing but the bare light perception that would be of no use in distinguishing objects. It was upon this need and the assumption of its fulfillment that my confident professional identity was apparently constructed. My side of the bargain was to work very hard and do all I could to hold my position as the RP poster boy. It was all so ridiculous once you thought about it. With whom did I think I was bargaining? RP personified? God? I began to wonder what would become of my self-confidence and the performance that was linked to it if I went totally blind.

What baffled me was how I could have fallen back so far from the unconditional acceptance of blindness that had changed my life in 1965. I was sure that on that December night when I gazed at the Christmas lights and gave them up, I was prepared to relinquish not only visual form but light itself. Where in the intervening years did I make a wrong turn? I had done my exploratory travelling while I was in my twenties, to make the most of my lingering daylight vision: I had worked hard to develop the necessary adaptive skills, gone back to school, and found interesting work that allowed me to be completely open about my visual impairment. I had even let go of print. There seemed to be no fault, laxness, or avoidance in my adjustment to any of this. Was it just that the initial total acceptance of blindness was destined to be slowly compromised as I continued to claim and cling to the benefits of my all-important but deteriorating mobility vision? If that were so, then RP seemed like an especially pernicious way to go blind. It was as though its achingly long trajectory had been expressly designed to undercut even the most wholehearted early impulse to open up and accept the ultimate prognosis.

My questions about RP and its powerful but inconsistent entanglement with self-feeling were really queries about the fundamental structure of identity. Underneath the particularities of RP or of any other specific disease, the basic questions seemed to be the following: What is the self? Or if one prefers like the Buddhists to avoid using the term "self," what is our essence or fundamental nature? Is it subject to change, or is there some core that is immune to change? If the latter, then how is it that this core can apparently fail to know itself in a clear and consistent way? These were the puzzles to which I found myself returning in the evenings. I had already begun to read my way back into the Eastern philosophical tradition, and that was the context in which I placed or planted my uncertainties concerning identity and sensory experience. I concentrated at first on the unabridged spoken recordings of a few key works available from Recording for the Blind and the Library of Congress National Library Service for the Blind. These included Buddhist and Taoist texts and a collection of the major Upanishads.

I knew I had done myself a great disservice by allowing my early interest in Buddhism and other Indian philosophies to lie fallow. After my first stay in India in 1970, I had never quite got over the feeling that I had unfinished business there. It was not that I now wanted to throw everything up and join an ashram: I just had the sense that something in the Indian view of reality was going to help me find self-purchase, in the midst of deteriorating physical circumstances.

Those circumstances involved more than my declining vision. I had been having back trouble for years, and now in my forties it was getting much worse. The spinal problem was accompanied by widespread muscle pain and spasticity, and the doctors I consulted couldn't seem to do much about it. For the first time I had to face the possibility that medical circumstances having nothing to do with RP could some day curtail my work abroad. The channelling of so much self-feeling into my professional identity at External Affairs was looking more and more like a dubious long-term investment, psychologically speaking.

Meanwhile morale at headquarters was continuing to sag, to the extent that over the next few years the problem would be reported periodically in the press. The malaise was discouraging, sometimes depressing, and a damned shame. A succession of governments had failed, and would continue to fail, to adequately provision and renew what was still a very competent foreign service. Unfortunately, people with Japanese, Chinese, Russian, or Arabic language training were increasingly leaving the department to join the private sector.

As for me, I continued to be shielded from much of the prevailing funk because of the relatively autonomous nature of the work I was doing. At this time I was working with an exceptionally efficient and spirited reader-secretary, Gail Gow. But my old conflict remained unresolved; I was still periodically nagged by the feeling that I should be trying for further advancement. What continued to rankle was the knowledge that, apart from the problem of dealing with the increased paper flow, I knew I was capable of handling the work of a director or director-general.

The issue was settled one night when I did a simple thought-experiment, in which I imagined myself as a fully sighted manager dealing with all the bumpf and turf-nonsense I had so far been able to avoid. I saw instantly that I would hate it so much that I'd take the first opportunity to get out. Someone had to apply his hand to the gluey levers of process, the levers that keep the paper humping through the machinery even on those sad occasions when everyone knows that the end result will be the kind of bland, boilerplate Unspeak that doesn't achieve anything. But that person wasn't going to be me.

I couldn't and wouldn't do it, especially now that my sense of purpose was gravitating to my evening study program. And when I went abroad again I had no intention of forfeiting those evenings to the kind of numbing social round that was the unavoidable lot of the more senior officers. I remembered the clear conviction that had come to me on my very first day of primary school, when I began grade one as a late entrant. I had seen somehow that I was a singleton, neither better or worse than those around me, just different. And here I was again, seeing the same thing. It was about time I admitted that I belonged neither on the cocktail circuit nor in management, just as I had to acknowledge years earlier that I was not cut out for lawyering.

The next morning I met with my assignment officer in personnel, and went on record to the effect that I would neither seek nor accept further promotion. I would instead stick with the kind of work I was doing now, continuing to give it the same care and attention from 8:00 to 5:30, Monday to Friday, for as long as I worked at headquarters. As I walked back to my office I felt both new and raw, as though a layer of skin or a whole carapace had been torn away. All the better for finding out what really lay underneath.

By early 1987 I had been back at headquarters long enough that we were eligible for another overseas posting, and it so happened that an opening was coming up in New Delhi. I saw this as my last best chance to return to India under circumstances that would allow me to bring the different sides of my life, or even the different versions of myself, closer together. The Delhi assignment would include no supervisory responsibilities, and the job package looked interesting. As political counsellor I would once again have a fair degree of independence.

Delhi was the right choice, right for me and a welcome adventure for us as a family. That was important, for I had become very much aware that I had not been spending enough time with my wife and son. When my posting was confirmed Pressi plunged with anticipatory gusto into a great pile of books on India. Evan took to greeting me with a salaam and calling me "sahib" when I got home from work in the evenings. Finally it was time to pack everything up, and we gave ourselves over to the old familiar operations and rituals of decamping.

My new reader-secretary, Ann Johnson, was going through exactly the same process; she was being posted to India too, as my highly competent assistant for what we hoped would be a three-year assignment. I had hit the jackpot – Ann had already served at several missions abroad, and I was to find that she tackled everything with resourcefulness and zest. As a senior secretary she could have worked for one of the Gnomes on the eighth floor, but she wanted this particular adventure. Personnel arranged things so that we had several weeks working together in Ottawa prior to deployment, and this trial run cinched the deal for both of us.

I leave the final cleaning out of my office in the Pearson building to a quiet Sunday. The three tape recorders are already gone, included in our air shipment for quick retrieval. I pocket the last of my writing tools, the little microcassette pocket Dictaphone. As I pack up the remaining things from my desk I feel right with myself and full of anticipation. Something is being relinquished that I can't quite identify or don't yet want to acknowledge, but whatever it is it seems to be expendable. It isn't the professional persona, for this is still available. Lately I have been thinking of it as a kind of papier-mâché mask – a useful but removable face-saver intended only for diplomatic theatre. It will be something to stare out of as I deal with Indian officialdom. I take a last look around, pick up my half-empty briefcase, and leave the building with a light heart.

That evening after supper I wander out the side door down to the end of the driveway, then turn around and gaze back at our little house. I take it in, slice by slice, as the narrow beam of eyesight travels slowly across its breadth. I look in the same section-slicing way at our old birch tree, not the healthiest of specimens but one that somehow manages every year to fully leaf out. I look down the street, my gaze moving from one neighbour's house to another, seeing in turn each familiar flower bed and hedge. Then I just rest my eyes on the grass in front of me, waiting to feel something.

I know that I will not see these things again, at least not as recognizable objects. My central vision is deteriorating so rapidly that it should be pretty well shot by the time we return from India. But it seems as though I have accepted this, or at least come to trust that the total acceptance I had once known only waits to be rediscovered. I am more and more certain that the way to find it again lies in the reading and introspection that now dominate my evenings. As I walk back up the driveway, I feel more open to the future than I have been for a long time.

3

India, the Visual Conundrum, and Letting Go

1 THE NEW DELHI SENSORIUM

For whatever reasons – my age, perhaps, or the spiritual drought through which I had been living for years, or the worsening eyesight that made me want to experience as much as I could while I still had the chance – I was absolutely ready for India. From the night we arrived in New Delhi I found my senses opening up of their own accord. I was to feel none of the shrinking defensiveness toward hard Indian realities that I had experienced during my earlier visit in 1970. Pressi and Evan took an immediate liking to our new neighbourhood and our new house, a plain, sturdily built, unpretentious box that like the others on the street squatted squarely and securely inside its own walled compound. We quickly settled in.

I soon saw that the clear separations I preferred to maintain between home and the outside world, and between paid work and private study, were going to be blurred in interesting ways. Delhi lapped at our home in waves, bringing hawkers and would-be servants and cobra handlers to cry their wares and services at the front gate. If the *chowkidar* or gate guard was asleep and the gate unlocked, they would march up to the house to pound on our door and peer in through our windows. This could be irksome but it was also funny. Delhi entered our living space as competing streams of noise, sharp smells, intense radiant heat, and sand dust, the latter filtering in through the casements even when the windows were closed. Our small household staff and part-time grounds staff were Delhi in microcosm, a potent mix of Hindu and Muslim and Christian, intermediate caste and casteless untouchable, Indian and Nepalese, each newcomer replacing his or her predecessor at unpredictable intervals when things boiled over. The anthropologist in me found this a lot more interesting than frazzling, even when it left me frazzled.

My work at the Canadian High Commission was connected to my private study of India's spiritual traditions through the fascinatingly repulsive spectacle of politicized religion. A major part of my job was to report on Indian national politics and security concerns, including inter-communal strife. The issues involved in this strife – the politicization of religious movements and the impact of religious militancy on the secular state – were of the kind that had intrigued me since graduate school. I was now monitoring a major emergent phenomenon in North India, the funnelling of Hindu fundamentalist religious energies into militant mass movements bent on achieving political power.

Over the next several years this phenomenon would come to be known as *Hindutva*, a term that can be translated as "Hinduness" or, more ominously, as "Hinduization." The latter connotes the deliberate marginalization and pressuring of India's non-Hindu minority groups, particularly Muslims and low-caste or casteless Christians. Although the sectarian activists made up only a fraction of the country's Hindus, they directly challenged the tolerant pluralism that was so admirable a feature of Indian democracy.[1]

The High Commission was a good vantage point from which I could track these developments, through the simple expedient of talking to people who understood them. This involved reaching out to community leaders, politicians, and journalists. The post was a positive work environment; we had an able crew that was glad to be in India, half a world away from headquarters. I was able to hit the ground running, so to speak, because of Ann Johnson. She was a naturally good oral reader and a skilled transcriber, and we started pumping out reports in our first week.

The senior officer who countersigned my despatches was a nice guy and a very competent diplomat, even if his cultural assumptions and sense of propriety were occasionally a little old-fashioned. When he learned that I was interested in Indian spirituality he warned me gravely not to let news of this leak out to Ottawa, or headquarters would stop reading my political reports. I just laughed and said that they wouldn't, and they didn't. Given the tensions of the time, my reports on communalism and separatism would have been read and absorbed even if I had dictated them in the full lotus position stripped

naked as a *sadhu*, and studded my text with Sanskrit footnotes. This
was, after all, only two years after Sikh terrorists had blown Air India
Flight 182 out of the sky over the Atlantic, killing all 329 people on
board. Most of these victims were Canadian citizens of Indian origin.
The small minority of Sikhs who were committed to violent separatism constituted a threat that neither India nor Canada could ignore.

But it was Hindutva that would continue to connect itself most
closely with the personal interests that had brought me to India.
Although this movement was imposing real distortions onto Indian
social and political life, it was clear to me that the aggressive actions
of the Hindu bully boys were as unconnected to the Vedanta I was
studying as the violent Crusades were to the teachings of Jesus. As I
watched events unfold I felt that every Westerner who was attracted
to Indian spirituality should have the chance to see what I was seeing:
the sharp distinction between genuine spiritual teaching, on the one
hand, and the bellicose communalism that distorts and misuses it, on
the other. On the broad plane of power politics, no country is "spiritual." Whatever was of real value in the Indian religious classics could
be determined only by freely inquiring individuals, not by political
cadres or militant gangs.

Most of my evenings were reserved for those classics. Sitting in the
fusty but comfortable study at the front of our house I accessed these
texts in my usual way, through the bridging medium of audio tapes.
My sensory recall of that room is another one of those composite
memories that sum up the experience of being in a particular place
over a considerable span of time. Here the memory is only incidentally
visual; it is far more auditory and olfactory, tactile and kinesthetic.

In the first place, the fact that the study faced the street made it a
cube of pulsing sound. The English output from my tape recorder
had to negotiate space with the Hindi that seemed naturally to belong
in the room. It emanated from the itinerant hawkers and passers-by,
from the soldiers just across the street on permanent guard duty in
front of the house of a Cabinet minister, from the garrulous autorik-
shaw drivers at the taxi stand, and from the blaring public address
system of the girls' private school just beyond. Periodically a dense,
omni-tonal white noise would come surging into the room as wild
parakeets – hundreds of them at once – alighted on the big tree in
front of our house to hold one of their conferences. There was also
the rackety sound of vehicles, anachronistic chuggings and grindings
from an earlier era when gas engines had fewer cylinders and no

mufflers. Somehow none of this interfered with my weekend and evening studies, and this amazed me at first. I could tune into the ambient sounds when they were interesting but had no problem tuning out again.

As I sat at my desk I could always smell Delhi, that heady mixture of hot dust, petrol, and diesel fumes, whiffs of flowering or rank or rotting vegetation, fresh dung and dried dung burned as fuel, hints of spices and of sweat. I was aware at regular intervals of my throbbing back muscles against the back of the chair, sometimes aware not just of hearing the text but of my whole body receiving the sound of it, and appreciatively aware during sandstorm season of the silky powdery film slowly materializing on the surface of my desk. I could feel my sweat as a kind of second skin when the air conditioner was off, and then the welcome cooling of all my surfaces when the system was switched back on. Only as incidental to all the above did I register my surroundings as a visual space, a volume of pleasant amber or butterscotch light containing blurry visual objects.

Of course in this particular setting the eyes had little to do. But the reason I remember and occasionally still dream of this scene, of me just sitting and studying and noting the sensory background, is because it epitomized a fundamental change. In all kinds of circumstances now I was finding my attention redeployed away from vision toward the other senses. Whenever I was moving I was still obliged to attend to the thorny combination of visual cues and visual limitations, but that was just a practical necessity. In a deeper sense I was actually losing interest in eyesight. This was in inverse proportion to my wanting to take in the world in other ways.

The claim that I was beginning to emotionally separate myself from vision may seem absurd to people with advanced RP or other forms of major vision loss, who like me have experienced a desperate attachment to deteriorating eyesight. But I was tired of such clinging. I had become aware of the clinging as a psychological phenomenon in its own right, a subtle tension distinct from the visual experience it was irrationally aimed at preserving. This tension was and always had been the strain in my strained sensing, or a very large part of it. Tuning into the strain and regarding it objectively was like finally noticing, with a sense of my own foolishness, that my fingertips or the palms of my hands had long been covered with glue. I wanted it off. I was fed up with the strained, exhausting attention that goes along with deteriorating vision: I was just beginning to discover that it was

possible to let go of the strain, to inwardly dismiss it, and find that
that strain can dissolve without the image itself dissolving.

No degree of straining or clinging could make my eyesight any
more useful than it was, or preserve it for any longer than the disease
process would allow. This growing conviction that visual attachment
was a superfluity I could ill afford was directly connected to my
private study program. That is why my memories of living in India
– of interviewing local contacts and making Indian friends, of exploring the temples and mosques, of poking through the bazaars and
touring with my family, of picking my way down our back lane and
trying to avoid the piglets – all revolve around or refer back to that
scene in the study. It was in that room, fortified by the material I was
taking in, that I took a long-overdue look at my presumptions concerning the nature of the self in relation to visual experience.

When we moved from Ottawa to New Delhi in the summer of
1987, I included in our shipment a number of Western texts that
would provide a kind of counterpoint to the Indian classics. This
Western material, which I sourced from Recording for the Blind and
the US Library of Congress (National Library Service for the Blind),
all had to do in one way or another with the idea of the self. The
recorded texts were drawn mainly from the fields of philosophy,
developmental psychology, cultural criticism, poetry, and theology. I
was rereading authors whom I had known to be deeply interested in
the dynamics of ego development, or with false social constructions
of the self, or with other barriers to self-actualization. It does not
matter after all these years who they were or what they had to say;
what seems important in retrospect was my intention in reading them.
I simply wanted to open up the question of the self as broadly as
possible. During my last year in Ottawa the entanglement of vision
with identity had led me to frame a few basic questions concerning
the self, as spelled out in chapter 2, section 4. In Delhi I was now
referring those questions directly to the texts, or rather to the different
perspectives that they represented, just to see what would happen.

If in this project I had any one Western guide who turned out to
be more influential than all the others it was John Keats, a great poet
rather than a philosopher or social scientist. Keats famously encapsulated his own attitude toward life and art in a concept he called
"negative capability." He described the flowering or opening-up of
this inner faculty in the following terms: "When a man is capable
of being in uncertainties, Mysteries, doubts, without any irritable

reaching after fact & reason ... [rather than] being incapable of remaining content with half-knowledge." In other words, in our search for truth and beauty, negative capability engages our capacity for deep intuition, as distinct from falling back on familiar notions and conventional reasoning. This attitude requires an acceptance of mystery, and a willingness to remain suspended in a state of doubt or half-knowledge – rather than grasping at premature conclusions through impatience. Negative capability is thus a state of openness toward the real, toward the truth that remains partially veiled.

I felt sure somehow that the Keatsian orientation of alert and non-judgmental openness – of negative capability – could be very fruitful in addressing the riddle of our fundamental nature. For the first time in my life I was allowing the question of the self, whose referent is the very experience of being, to fully stretch out and demonstrate its reach. The effect of this deliberate irresolution was not the radical destabilizing doubt that some of my Western authors had described, but a new receptiveness to experience. I not only took in my new environment in a less filtered or more immediate way, but was newly attentive toward the senses that allowed me to do this. It was in this context that I began to feel the sensory shift described above, the heightened attraction of the non-visual senses. They had become a source of interest in themselves, as though up to now I had not really known them.

Such was the background of intention and new experience against which I addressed myself to Buddhist and Vedantic teaching, after a few months of concentrating on my Western sources. The Buddhist texts that I had on tape included Edward Conze's overviews of the history of Buddhism, his more specialized monographs on ancient Indian Buddhism, most of Daisetsu Suzuki's major works in English, and oddments such as The Tibetan Book of the Dead.

But I think I already knew from my earlier experience in India that in the end my path would take me into Vedanta. Among my sources on Vedanta and popular Hinduism were books by or about two prominent figures in whom I was particularly interested at this time: Ramakrishna and Vivekananda. Ramakrishna was a late nineteenth-century Bengali sage whose personal experiences crossed and re-crossed the porous boundary between Vedanta and Hindu devotionalism, or Bhakti. He was revered both for his embodiment of love and his open-hearted ecumenism, which encompassed a profound respect for the teachings and implicit world view of Jesus.

In the following year I would see a vivid example of Ramakrishna's continuing influence in the form of a slum-dwellers' cooperative organized by the Ramakrishna Association in Calcutta. The kind of community development work done by the association is the Vedantic counterpart of what some Christians, particularly liberal Christians, call the social gospel. I was to find the slum-dwellers' cooperative quite remarkable for its innovativeness, vigour, and tenacity. These determined people gave me a whole new perspective on the poor of Calcutta, from whom I had fled in 1970.

Ramakrishna's protégé Vivekananda was an austere intellectual, which seemed to make him an unlikely student of his emotionally labile teacher. In the early years of the twentieth century Vivekananda did more than any other Indian preceptor to introduce Westerners to Vedanta. I had on tape the full set of his books on the various schools of Indian yoga, among other works. I also had texts on Indian art by a number of authors, and Coomaraswamy's intriguing study on the linkages between Greek and Indian mythology.

But the most important of my resources were my taped copies of the major Upanishads and the Bhagavad-Gita, key sources for early Vedantic thought. I read and reread them over and over again. During these months I attended evening classes on the Bhagavad-Gita given by a swami at a local college, sitting in the cramped and steaming basement lecture hall as the one and only foreigner. On the weekends I studied Patanjali Yoga, an eight-fold spiritual path that included yogic posture and breath control and was quite different, as I discovered, from Vedanta. My gentle and sincere teacher of Patanjali Yoga was Mr Das, who reminded me of a warm and loving Italian Catholic priest we had known in Japan, Father Cerizza Virginio.

My tape-recorded texts added up to fewer than thirty volumes at this time, but taken together their broad scope allowed me to see Buddhism and Vedanta in terms of their similarities more than their differences. The two traditions evolved out of the same substrate of Indian religious thought. They are primarily concerned with bringing to light our fundamental nature, referred to in Vedanta as "self" and designated by the Buddhists as "Buddha-Mind" or "the Mind of Clear Light or Suchness." Both Buddhism and Vedanta teach that our real identity is neither the body nor the senses, nor the conventional mind of thoughts and sense-perceptions. Both insist that we are profoundly and tragically ignorant of our real nature, and that the result of this ignorance is the compulsion to cleave desperately to the transitory and the unreal.

I had no difficulty relating this to my own life, especially to my long-standing entanglement with failing vision. When I thought of the little ways in which the particulars of my own experience answered to those of the texts I was studying, it seemed to me that what Buddhism and Vedanta were all about was not exclusively the attainment of enlightenment, if that rare state is to be understood as an inexpressible and thus perhaps incommunicable transcendence. Surely, one would hope, it was also about seeing life clearly and living it unobstructedly right here and now.

In the course of my reading during the warm Delhi winter of 1987–88 I was particularly struck by passages in two Upanishads, and by the mental images they invoked. In the Katha Upanishad the importance of discriminating self from non-self is illustrated by the famous chariot analogy. The body is represented by the chariot, the senses by the horses pulling it, and the world of sense objects by the road down which the horses and chariot are rushing. The charioteer stands for the intuitive or discriminating faculty of mind that grasps the real significance and proper place of the senses, while the reins and bridle are the practical aspects of the mind that guide the senses in the right way. In the absence of discrimination and guidance the senses claim predominance over mind and body. They become runaway horses, a condition that in the analogy stands variously for uncontrolled sensuality and avarice, ignorant materialism, and hopeless confusion concerning our real nature and path.

The most startling thing about all this to the Westerner who encounters the Katha for the first time is the place of the self, Atman, in the analogy. The Atman is neither the chariot nor the charioteer, neither reins nor bridle nor horses. In the imagery that the Upanishad deploys with so much care, the self is the rider positioned behind the charioteer. His form or presence is not visually described, because the Upanishad makes it clear that he is not physical, not perceivable by the senses. Not even the higher mind can grasp or know the self through thinking. That is why Atman is hidden *behind* the charioteer, whose thoughts and attention are normally directed forward.

And yet the higher mind or charioteer is capable not only of the practical exercise of its faculties that the horse-mastering analogy depicts, but of a very special kind of intuition as well. The mind that is firmly established in discrimination and in harmony with the senses can eventually open or surrender itself to the real self, the Atman, through a mediating insight that is far deeper than thought. In the Upanishads the practice that invites this insight is referred to as *yoga*, sometimes translated as "meditation" or "introversion." It is a kind of looking within or looking back into oneself. Self-realization through introversion is the real purpose of the charioteer's life-journey.

As I sat in my study reflecting on all this, the one aspect of the chariot image that impressed itself upon me most strongly was the distance between the Atman and the horses. I was thinking, in this regard, of my collapsing central vision. According to the Upanishad all the components of the chariot equipage are non-self, but of these it was the sense faculties – those horses out in front – that were farthest removed from our real identity as Atman. The intended implication was obvious. To be helplessly attached to damaged senses rather than maintaining one's centre of gravity in the discriminating mind was not only a source of pain, but evidently a kind of false selfing, a confusion regarding one's basic identity. It mixed up visual perception with self-being. The effect of this conflation was to make the words "I" and "seer" virtually synonymous.

Within days of reading the Katha I discovered another text that put my personal circumstances into even bolder relief. A late Upanishad known as the Maitri declares that there is a perfect oneness (non-separation) of the Atman, the self, and Brahman, the absolute reality. The deep inner confirmation of this teaching – i.e., Brahman-realization – is presented in a highly concentrated and singular way. It involves macrocosmic/microcosmic parallels, an ancient esoteric physiology that includes a mysterious "heart" and energy channels, and a yoga that draws upon these subtle entities to achieve a vividly described breakthrough experience. According to the text, the energy induced by this yoga is called "lightning" or "light," for "in the very moment of going forth it lights up the whole body" (Maitri, chapter 7, verse 11). This phrase pulled me up short: I hit the pause button on the tape recorder. It reminded me of something similar and significant, something I had heard in a completely different context long ago. It lurked silently, frustratingly, just beyond the edge of retrievable memory.

When I pressed the play button to resume the reading, this is what I heard: "The person who is in the eye, who abides in the right eye, he is the god Indra and his wife abides in the left eye. The union of these two takes place within the hollow of the heart ... That is the channel that serves both of them by being divided into two, though but one." I stopped the machine again and for some minutes sat there, thinking. Then I began to laugh, a rather wild sort of laugh that ratcheted upward into a war whoop. Two things had just happened. First, this symbolic account of uniting the identities of the two eyes, coupled with the reference a sentence or two earlier to the "light" within the whole body, had triggered the memory that up to that point had been out of reach. The parallel quotation was from the Gospels; later I confirmed it to be from Matthew 6: 22–23. There Jesus says, "When thine eye be single" (or in some translations "whole") "thy whole body will be full of light." Whether this close textual similarity was only a bicultural coincidence or some kind of arcane cross-cultural connection, for some reason it just delighted me. A Himalayan rishi was shaking hands, so it seemed, with the Galilean prophet.

But second, and far more meaningful in terms of my own circumstances, was the special significance conveyed by the figure of the two eyes in both texts. I grasped that significance, or at least felt that I had done so, and reacted accordingly. The resulting whoop had been so loud that our chowkidar, who happened to be just outside, tapped urgently on the study window to make sure I was all right. And by Jesus and Indra I *was* all right. I had just heard a two-thousand-year-old philosopher put me wise to the fact that the two eyes, in their natural roles as our most powerful and far-ranging sense-faculty, stood symbolically for the dualism that can be resolved only through a realization of Brahman within the heart. That is to say, there is a kind of spiritual impediment that is associated especially with sightedness. This put a whole new light (so to speak) on the prospect of going blind. Why should I *not* laugh? The irony – the backhanded, unsolicited, unavoidable nature of this learning opportunity – was enough to break you up.

Of course I was acutely aware – how could I not be? – that to lose one's eyesight was to lose a precious life-tool, an unparalleled, marvellous adaptive device. But the teaching context in which those two eyes make their appearance has to do not with practical coping but with what the Maitri calls non-duality, oneness, which for the Upanishad was the ultimate goal of spiritual aspiration. The unification of the two eyes described above is certainly not a reference to neural-visual processing – listening to the tape I knew it could hardly be that, in a pre-neurological culture. It is a disclosure through metaphor of an apprehended non-duality that obtains at a deeper level than sensing. This was, apparently, a direct intuition of undividedness both within and without. Thus the Maitri verse quoted above goes on to say, "The seer sees the All and becomes the All everywhere."

The designation of the realized sage as a "seer" who has discovered a new way of "seeing" is not an incidental or gratuitous metaphor. Eyesight is unique among the senses in presenting reality panoramically as an array of individual material objects, one of which (the closest, the one right "here") is taken to be one's natural self. The panoramic view as cognized breaks down into an endless succession of material/conceptual dualities: this thing as distinct from that, this category of things as compared with some other, the "I" right here as totally distinct from the "you" over there, and – by fateful extension – your category of human being as utterly "other" than my own. In the symbolism of the Maitri, then, it is natural that the two eyes should stand for the dualism that typifies not just raw empirical experience but empirical thinking.

I did not yet have all this thought out on the day I had my unexpected little eureka experience with the Maitri, but the passage that extolled an inner transformation or unification of vision struck me as being based on a profound insight. I had felt for some time that the faculty of vision was closely bound up with acquisitive materialism, a narrow literalism, and the downplaying or even denial of any reality that could not be plainly seen. And I was by no means exempt: for me as with others, functional vision was the quintessential empiricist and duality-reinforcer. The reinforcer whispers, "Just look at that beautiful thing over there – wouldn't you love to have it, instead of the shabby one you already own?" This is the conventional representation of separateness and acquisitiveness, the virtual opposite of the Maitri vision of an apprehended underlying unity.

The reader may feel that I was understandably just seeing what I wanted to see in the Maitri, and that my account had to do mostly with my own imagination and the force of my circumstances. Certainly I was totally unschooled in the art of parsing this kind of foreign, historically remote, and sometimes strange material. But, as I came to understand over the succeeding years, the Upanishads are open to interpretation, and within that tradition there is nothing amiss in deploying intuitive imagination to address immediate spiritual goals and needs. Beyond that, though, I was convinced when I read the Maitri that it was really onto something, that I was too, and that they were the same thing. For me it all had to do with the distinction between outer ophthalmic vision and inner "seeing" or self-realization.

But I must own that at this time I was not only drawn to the quite unimaginable goal of Advaitic realization, but in equal measure wary of it. I remembered the powerful but virtually uninterpretable impression that overtook me when I gazed out from the temple at Mahabalipuram, and how I had withdrawn or drifted away from that state of irresolution. In some sense that I could not get my mind around, it seemed that I had failed. So the two big interconnected questions in 1988 were how far I wanted to go into Vedanta, and whether I had what it takes for such a journey.

I knew there would be no free lunch: the cancelling-out of visible dualities through vision loss would not in itself uncover an underlying wholeness. For that you needed yoga. Despite Mr Das's earnest attempts to teach me correct posture and breath control, and not-withstanding my readings in Vivekananda, I had little real grasp of the broader yoga tradition. The yogic path, whatever it entailed, would probably be very hard. But I did have the thought that, given sufficient time, an involvement with some kind of yogic practice might have the effect of shifting problems such as vision loss away from the centre of one's attention, to a place where they could be cooled down and better managed.

It seemed that something like that was already happening, spontaneously, without my having found a "practice." Just to read the Upanishads was a compelling and refreshing experience, despite all the textual puzzles. The interest of the texts seemed to be one of a piece with the vividness of India itself, of Delhi just outside the window. I had the feeling when reading the Upanishads that the world might be experienced in quite a new way, both through the senses and in thought. But I remained mindful of my Keats and his counsel of negative capability; what I needed to do now was to keep the process of enquiry open without signing on to anything. This could allow things to unfold slowly and naturally while inner resistance gradually softened – or so one might hope.

The Upanishadic Atman, in particular, was too big a concept to make for quick assimilation. All I could do was to just let it germinate. If anyone had asked me at this time what the Vedantic self actually was, or in what sense it was inseparable from Brahman, or what non-duality was really like, I would have said quite honestly that I did not know in the least. As to my own experience of self, despite my inner uncertainties I was about to receive a welcome glimpse into what belonged to self and what properly lay outside it.

2 DISENTANGLEMENT FROM IMAGES

The precondition for this glimpse was my continuing absorption in the Indian texts, nothing more. I just kept studying. Whenever I came upon an Upanishadic reference to the self as a principle separate from body and senses I would just sit with it for some moments and then put it into safe storage, so to speak, tucking it away below the surface of the mind, where I could retrieve it from time to time and stare at it. It was on one such occasion in the spring of 1988, sitting quietly in my study with the tape recorder turned off, that I realized all in a moment with a distinct inner click that I had always been a reality different from physical form, body-feelings, and external sensing. This reality, the "I" that I truly was, was the simple and indubitable presence that lay at the dead centre of all my physical and sensory experience. I felt this with total conviction. Discovering the actuality of that presence was evidently the change, or the first part of the change, that I had come to India to experience.

This was not what people usually call a peak experience. It was something else, a small but clear pulse of direct intuition. It called forth the kind of satisfaction one feels at seeing through a long-standing error – seeing through it clearly enough to banish it, at least for the time being. I think that inner click was the distillation of every other moment in my life when I had found myself quite naturally regarding the sensate body as a kind of object, as distinct from the observing subject. What was particularly significant about that object, right at the moment, is that it included the two little gelatinous spheres called the eyes. I felt myself as the immaterial centre in relation to which the whole sensate body, eyes and all, was manifestly off-centre. It was so clear and obvious, the difference between being right "here" and the body and sensory apparatus being "there."

And then, when I roused myself from my abstraction and glanced up, I was startled to find that the act of seeing had somehow aligned itself completely with what I had just been thinking and feeling. The familiar images of the objects in my study had not changed – in themselves they were as constricted and blurry as before. But I seemed to have moved back from these images in some subtle but significant way. I saw what was there without any sense of being entangled or implicated in it. There was a feeling of relief, as uncomplicated and satisfying as a taste of menthol, as though a welcome cooling element had been introduced into the normally tense experience of trying to see. Like the mental click of a few moments earlier, this was not a transcendental experience; it was more like the release of a long-standing pressure or the removal of a habitual load. It was a freeing-up into what felt normal and right.

Over the next few days, as I walked around the house or yard or the grounds of the High Commission, I continued to see in this functionally unchanged but existentially transformed way. I savoured the relief of it. I thought of it as "seeing" my own seeing, that is, of being aware of seeing as something external to myself. To step back from damaged eyesight in this way had the taste of freedom, and this I found far more important than the quality of the images themselves. I was no longer a visually permeated self confronting a world of dissolving objects, but a non-visual self aware of the visual function as an impersonal flux of light and colour containing vague shapes, both nameable and unnameable. It was a mind-show in which my sense of self-involvement was mercifully reduced and relaxed. In emotional terms, as regards to the tension of the previous state and the relief of the present one, there was a great difference.

I could now register vision as the entirely objective and wholly impersonal phenomenon it so obviously was. In reality it had never been anything else. But this confirmation of the impersonality of the visual process did not imply that I myself was experiencing some kind of depersonalization or an ebbing-away of identity. What I experienced was a decoupling of self-feeling from vision that would allow the self, in the months and years to come, to be the autonomous observer of vision loss rather than its subject or victim. Further vision loss would not happen *to* the self but be witnessed *by* it.

This was the separation between our fundamental nature and the business of sensing that my Buddhist and especially my Upanishadic texts, notably the Katha and Maitri, so vividly invoked. Quite unexpectedly I had experienced seeing, or the faculty of vision, in a way that philosophers from many schools, both Eastern and Western, would characterize as "detached." The day I discovered this serene

detachment from vision and absorbed its significance was the day, to
return to my earlier figure of speech, when I began to wash the glue
from my hands.

All of this was felt intuitively rather than thought through. After
all, what had especially captured my attention was not a logical argument for such an inner detachment but a fertile metaphor, that of the
Katha chariot. I saw myself as having moved back from the precarious
business of clinging bareback to one of the horses into a far more
secure position – if not that of the hidden Atman, then at least that
of the discriminating charioteer. It would be a decade later during my
systematic study of Advaita Vedanta that I would see this incident in
its overall context. But it was the immediate experience of letting go
of that tight, long-standing identification with the faculty of vision
that changed once and for all my relationship with R P.

I thought it would be hard to explain what had happened to me to
anyone unfamiliar with the Katha Upanishad and the view of identity
that it presents, but I found that the simplest possible account struck
a responsive chord. To those closest to me – Pressi and Evan, a few
friends and colleagues – I just said that I had managed recently to step
back from or let go of my visual problems. This they had no difficulty
in taking in; they could see for themselves that I was more relaxed.

If I had not distanced myself from the experience of seeing in the
manner described above or in some other way, I would have remained
tied to my degraded eyesight in the three mutually contradictory ways
depicted in the previous chapter. Both the professional blind persona
and its frustrated alter ego would have retained their potential as
alternative or contending identities. The third alternative, a helpless
anticipatory identification with total blindness, would have continued
to lie in wait for me. These three versions of mistaken identity were
all based on the presumption – a totally invalid presumption, as I
now understood – that vision was not only integral to the self but an
especially important aspect of it.

My disidentification from vision did not mean that I was now
identifying even more strongly with the other senses, by way of substitution or compensation. That was not necessary. Evidently, the
healthy alternative to clinging to vision was to stand back from *all*
the senses and enjoy them from that slight but courteous distance
that allows them to function clearly. What actually happened, it seems,
was that the new experience of stable detachment from vision helped
to ease a subtle but long-standing tension that had stood between me

as observer and the entire sensory world. I found that it was possible, through newly relaxed attention, to be at a slight, comfortable remove not just from vision but the other senses as well. The change was refreshing – it was the senses themselves that seemed to be refreshed. This was a further blooming of the non-visual senses that had some- how begun as soon as we arrived in New Delhi.

The timing and particular nature of my new discovery owed itself to the concentration I was bringing to the Upanishads, reinforced by the compelling necessity that I was facing. My vision was continuing to go rapidly downhill, and I knew that I had to accept what was coming at the deepest possible level. This was the imperative that transformed the experience in my study from its initial phase – that of feeling absolutely sure that I was some principle or reality that lay deeper than body or senses – to the succeeding phase, where my attention was drawn to the unexpected change in my visual orienta- tion. If the potential for an opening-up into the Vedantic sense of self was present in any of this, it was in the initial phase, but evidently I was not yet ready to stay with that and go more deeply into it. I had a powerful need for what happened next, the more limited but crucial freeing experience of detachment from vision. I revelled in the unfet- tered openness of this kind of seeing, despite the continuing blurriness and ambiguity of the objects on show.

Could this experience be taught to others? That was the question I kept returning to over the next couple of months. It seemed to me that in circumstances where the degree of vision loss was not as yet so great, and the pressure of finding a new way of relating to vision not so urgent or stress-inducing, the person living with RP might be able to move toward visual detachment in a more gradual if irregular way. The precondition would be some teaching that emphasized the virtues of detachment, if not Vedanta or Buddhism then perhaps Greek or Roman Stoicism. Under its promptings a youngster caught up in this situation could begin to experience vision objectively, falling back into the old attachment out of habit, then re-experience the objective view again, and so on until the counter-habit of detachment from vision became more secure. But this separation from visual clinging would remain vulnerable to cancellation so long as the relationship between seeing and self remained ambiguous.

Vedanta, as I was beginning to absorb it through reading its early source material, considerably lessened that ambiguity. I was to even- tually learn that the later Advaita Vedanta of Shankara eliminated

the ambiguity altogether, logically and categorically, revealing self
and sensing to be entirely separate. Yet in New Delhi the Katha
Upanishad proved to be a sufficient resource for me to "reset" myself
into the new perspective as often as required. The old conditioned
identification with vision would temporarily re-emerge from time to
time as my eyesight further declined, notably during difficult patches.
These were the times when I was especially worried about something,
or experiencing insistent physical pain, or struggling with some particularly confusing visual array. Such circumstances could sometimes
rekindle the old mental tension that had yoked me to images. But
visual attachment was no longer an autonomous mechanism. It was
more like an electric fan that was slowly winding down after the
disconnection of its power cord.

   During the remainder of that first year in Delhi, as I was getting
used to detached or unselfed seeing, I began to discover that even
when the visual changes were unhelpful or dysfunctional in a practical
sense they could still be viewed with genuine curiosity. They could
even be received with a certain wry appreciation for their oddness.
This sometimes happened when I took time out, in the sense of literally stopping in my tracks, to take in the visual flux unresistingly as
pure spectacle. The weaving together of my disintegrating central
vision with the freshened input from my other senses would remain
intriguing even when it was confusing. As for the business of getting
about, white cane work was to become more difficult but never
unmanageable – at least not as a consequence only of vision loss.
Many years later when I lost the capacity for long solitary walks, this
change was due to other physical factors.

   The new sensory mix sometimes struck me as poignant, in a non-
threatening and quite impersonal way. One could see how fleeting and
contingent our sense-impressions really are. To accept this fact of life
had a distinctive emotional taste, one that I remembered from those
first few weeks after receiving my prognosis in the winter of 1966. I
was apparently returning to the inner condition from which I had
welcomed those Christmas lights back in frozen, snowy Edmonton,
as something to enjoy fully and then ungrudgingly relinquish.

3 A SET OF MOGUL PICTURES

My changing disposition toward vision and visual degradation in
1987–88 is preserved as a set of memories, all of them of things seen

in Northern India. These mind's-eye pictures have dimmed somewhat but stubbornly refuse to dissolve, even after all these years. Over the next few pages I will present a selected few, as though this were a slide show. Taken together they will seem like a travelogue, and on one level that is in fact what they are. After all, everyone likes to show pictures of places he has visited, especially when they are out of the ordinary. My slides qualify on that score, because even as I beheld these scenes they were only partially "there." As such they may serve as curiosities for the normally sighted reader.

But what I want to convey through these images is something other than or more than a washed-out version of ophthalmic experience. As received by the average viewer, such a presentation might seem clinical or even a little spooky. Yet at this juncture I was learning by degrees to accept what I saw, and so to become engaged with an increasingly disordered and occasionally incoherent sensorium. It was a sometimes difficult transition, as you will see. But it is amazing what you can make out of coloured bits and pieces that can seem at first not to add up to any whole.

One of these scenes finds me in Old Delhi in the courtyard of the Jami Masjid or Friday Mosque, one of the largest mosques in India, built in the mid-seventeenth century by the Mogul emperor Shah Jahan. I have just come out of one of the reception rooms in the cloisters, where I was granted an hour-long interview by the grave and courteous Imam. I look up above the cloisters and glance along the top of the high wall: there they are, the black flags of martyrdom, mounted as though on battlements. I turn my eyes away. Now I can stop talking and thinking about politics and inter-communal strife; I will just stand here at the back of this vast open-air prayer space and take in the marble rising up before me.

The great mosque is flanked by two four-sectioned minarets. I run my eye up each of them in turn, perceiving with some difficulty the white marble piping that runs around the sandstone column at regular intervals. Then I gaze straight ahead at the facade of the mosque. Before I first visited the Jami Masjid the previous fall I had primed myself with my favourite guidebook, Alistair Shearer's *The Traveler's Key to Northern India*.[2] Shearer describes how the symmetrical plan of the mosque leads the eye naturally from the minarets along the series of arched openings in the facade, five on each side, to the iwan or principal arch right in the centre. This is the main entrance to the mosque. He also explains how the positioning of the magnificent central dome well back from the facade draws the mind's eye magnetically right through the iwan into the vaulted darkness within.

Is this what I experience? No, and I am not sure it is what the person with normal, full-field eyesight experiences. His wide gaze is not so much led to the iwan as gathered effortlessly into it. As for me, my circumscribed vision is neither led nor gathered but must search, feature by feature, for what it seeks: the beautifully shaped iwan perceived at last as a welcoming darkness. I mentally enter through it not because my attention is pulled by the recessed dome – I cannot even see it now – but because I know what lies within. The interior of the mosque is an empty prayer-space whose object of contemplation is the mihrab, the concave niche in the back wall of the mosque that shows the direction of Mecca. The mihrab is said to be joined to Mecca by the qibla, an invisible axis whose substance may be thought of metaphorically as the concentrated devotion of the worshippers.

I withdraw my attention from the mihrab and again scan the face of the mosque. It is all like a dream. I have to train my tunnel vision on each feature in turn and concentrate in order to draw its shape and colour out of thin air, or rather out of the marvellous clear light, and then watch it dissolve back into the light as my eyes tire. Only the dark unwavering mouth of the iwan, as my gaze returns to it, seems substantial enough to retain its shape. I would like to walk up to the iwan and enter through it, to feel what it is like to be swallowed by that cool darkness. But I would not care to break the sightlines of the faithful who are already scattered around the precincts on their prayer mats. So I stay where I am, content to watch this mirage of a mosque whose components keep going in and out of existence.

I wonder as I stand there if anyone could set eyes on the Jami Masjid and fail to be moved, if only a little, by its noble beauty. Islam is not my particular spiritual path, but this place makes me want to learn more about it. I do not know it yet, but eventually I will discover in the writings of the great thirteenth-century Islamic sage Muhyiddin Ibn 'Arabi (Ibn Arabi) a teaching that, at its deepest level, is identical to Indian Advaita Vedanta. Ibn Arabi urged us to recognize and unconditionally accept the transient character of all experience, and the ephemeral nature of the sensory world itself. Real inner freedom, he warned, can be won only when we open our hearts to change and stop clinging to sensory phenomena. He encapsulated this counsel in a simple mantra that would serve as my guide during the final stages of vision loss: love the forms and let them go.

On another day I am browsing in the big arcade situated just inside the Lahore Gate, the main entranceway to Delhi's massive Red Fort. When the fort was constructed by Shah Jahan as another one of his great works, this area housed his courtiers and attendants. Now it contains a lively bazaar of little shops or stalls selling traditional wares and antiques. I am standing at a table laden with old brass, looking down the arcade toward the inner gate that opens into the fort's interior. I am trying to decide whether the vague shape I see through the gate is part of the intricately carved Drum House, but I can't make it out.

Here in the relative dimness of the arcade I can see even less. I have been pottering among the stalls for a good quarter of an hour, which once would have been more than enough time for my eyes to adjust after the midday glare on the street outside. But everything is vague. These days I can no longer draw a line between the problems of dark adaptation and those of central visual acuity. Objects lighted well enough that they ought to be clearly identifiable are as often as not blurry, or even half-dissolved. At the moment the object in question seems to be a brass incense burner, judging from its smell and touch-shape and the heft of it in the palm of my hand. Visually it is ambiguous, not quite an object at all.

All around me is a steady pandemonium of voices that blend into a kind of acoustic curry, sharp exclamations momentarily spiking up and then dissolving back into the pungent babble. It is rather comforting – the sound of human continuity, of appetite and commerce, of different ethnicities and classes somehow managing to rub along together. What I see is the visual equivalent of this: a swirl of unidentifiable semi-forms, some of them moving and thus presumably human, all claiming their own spaces but fitting in with one another. I stand there taking it in, feeling relaxed.

I am still holding the little brass artifact; I raise it up to my face, not to my eyes but my nose, and smell its tangy old brassiness. I have an absurd impulse to cram as much of it as I can into my mouth, in order to know it orally as a baby would. This may seem strange, but during my sensory realignment I found for a time that I wanted to get down to a level of non-visual experience that was primitive or primal. What would it be like to totally set aside memory and preference and really taste this thing, just as it is, or run my hands all over that big thing over there? After squeezing and rubbing the brass a little more I put it back onto the table.

I begin to wonder how I would manage if I were one of these trad-
ers and blind as I am now, or blinder. Well, I am sure I would know
the identity and quality of each of my brasses by touch and memory:
my fingertips quite easily discovered the two rough impurities on the
one I was holding. And I would have a sharp-eyed boy to watch my
table and check the denominations of incoming bills. As for the out-
going, I would dispense them by the same means I use now when I
go shopping, drawing them out of a compartmentalized pouch organized in advance. But if something in a customer's voice set off my
internal Cheat Detector – I assume every experienced trader has one
of these as standard mental equipment – I would ask him straight out
to give me bank notes only of the right denominations, reminding
him that we come together in the all-knowing sight of Allah. If he
still tries to pull a fast one, the boy would nudge me and I would yell
bloody murder. Then my fellow-traders from the neighbouring stalls
would rush over and swarm the wretch. No problem.

Even as I indulged in this little fantasy I asked myself reflectively
why I was doing it. After all, I was not an Indian and would never
wind up as a small trader. Apparently I was becoming interested, for
the first time, in how blind people manage in circumstances that dif-
fered sharply from my own. I had begun to feel a connection with
poor and working-class blind people that hadn't been there before.
It was at this time that I drew rather heavily on some of my Indian
connections to get our gardener's six-year-old son admitted to a school
for the blind, a course of action that otherwise would have been out
of the family's reach. It was the obvious thing to do, and the little guy
was already a real coper.

Another memory from this series is that of the Qutb Minar complex, a twelfth-century Muslim site in Delhi that incongruously contains a much older and stubbornly resistant Hindu artifact. The
complex includes the Qutb Minar, an imposing minaret standing
five stories high; the Quwwat-ul-Islam-Masjid, or Might of Islam
Mosque, the oldest mosque in India; and the tomb of Iltutmish, the
conqueror of Hindu Delhi who built these structures. But what especially fascinates me here is the fourth-century iron pillar that stands
in the courtyard of the mosque. The inscription confirms that at its
original site, location unknown, it was erected to the Hindu deity
Vishnu (God in his Aspect of Preserver). Tradition has it that it was
brought to this site in the tenth century, before the Muslim invasions.

Just why the later Islamic iconoclasts allowed it to continue to stand here is something of a mystery.

As I walk past the Qutb Minar toward the mosque I can feel the heat of the sun radiating off the minaret's red sandstone. I pause and look up. At this close range my eyes cannot even begin to take in the size of this massive thing. Nor can they distinguish the warm red of the sandstone, the visual analog of that radiant heat, nor make out the decorative fluting on the lower stories. All I see is a shimmering, almost pulsing brownish cylinder that reaches up and up. When I get to the courtyard I turn back for one last look at the minaret, seeing it as a thick and featureless "I" or exclamation mark looming high above me.

Once inside the courtyard I ignore the partially fallen arched screen that forms the facade of the mosque, and walk slowly toward the iron pillar. People are chattering in Hindi and some other language I cannot place. The voices abruptly cease as two little groups on either side of the pillar become aware of the tall thin foreigner who is approaching them carrying a long white stick. I wonder who I am about to meet. When I reach the pillar I place my hand on the warm wrought iron, which I know from my guidebook is completely free of rust. My appreciative if undiscerning gaze runs up and down the well-crafted, sun-dazzled column: this is an exclamation mark cut more to my size. I begin slowly to circumambulate the pillar, the fingertips of my left hand trailing over the Gupta inscription.

"Hello!"

I stop and turn toward the speaker. She is a young girl in pigtails, in her early or mid-teens judging from her voice. Her features, as I slowly take them in, seem to belong to Central or even North Asia. Perhaps she is an ethnic Tibetan down on a school visit from Leh. Three other girls whom I suppose to be her schoolmates crowd in behind her, giggling and conferring in the unfamiliar language I heard a few moments earlier. The lead girl gazes at me rapturously; evidently I am quite a sight. I gaze upon her with reciprocal delight. She is manifestly if blurrily charming, and so innocently unselfconscious. I become aware of her faint but pleasant buttery smell. Soon we are all practising our English, and I learn that their native language is indeed Tibetan. These are the first Tibetans I have ever met. Over the coming year my path will take an unexpected turn that will lead me to another Tibetan, a revered, austere Buddhist monk.

When the girls have gone I once again rest my hand on the pillar. I rub it slowly back and forth, feeling the smooth but slightly irregular metal texture, then breathe in the good iron smell absorbed by my palm. I would like to be able to taste the pillar, just as I wished to taste that little brass object in the Lahore Gate arcade.

There is a discreet, throat-clearing cough a few feet to my left; someone else has moved up to join me. I make him out to be a neatly turned out old man. He begins to address me in excellent English and it soon becomes apparent that he is very learned. He tells me all about the Gupta empire, answering my questions with authoritative precision. When we have exhausted this subject he asks me, begging my pardon, how I came to lose my eyesight. I explain. "Bad luck," he says, "but today your luck will be good. You have exceedingly long arms." I laugh, for I know what is coming next.

This was not my first visit to the Qutb Minar complex. When I was backpacking through India in 1970 I came to this very spot and jokingly performed the little ritual that is described in all the guidebooks. According to the tradition, the aspirant to good fortune will get whatever he wishes for if he stands with his back to the pillar, stretches his arms around behind and succeeds in linking up his fingers. Apart from the tallest Rajputs and Sikhs there are few Indians who can do this, but it turned out that I could. Now this dapper little man is urging me to try it again, explaining the tradition and praising the restorative powers of the Hindu pillar. I know he is wishing that my vision be made whole, and how could I disappoint him?

I turn around and lean back against the pillar as he cries, "Wish! Wish!" My hands meet on the other side, and I am treated to delighted Hindi exclamations and ragged applause from a scattering of onlookers. When I let my arms drop the old man seizes my right hand, pumping it up and down with joy. I thank him and silently reiterate my wish, the same wish I made in 1970 and then allowed to slip out of my mind, and out of my life. It has nothing to do with eyesight.

Over the next couple of months I take some summer leave, a few days at a time, so that Pressi and Evan and I can visit destinations that lie within motoring distance of Delhi. One of these little tours takes us to Agra, whose main attractions are the Taj Mahal and another impressive Mogul fort. Then we drive on to the abandoned imperial city of Fatehpur Sikri. I had read about this deserted citadel years before and particularly wanted to see it.

Fatehpur Sikri is located on an isolated redoubt, a rough bluff that overlooks the flat plains of Uttar Pradesh. In its day it was home to one of the grandest courts in Asia, that of Akbar the Great, housed in some of the world's most beautiful and sophisticated architecture. Moving the court from Agra to this forlorn place was the inspiration or folly of Akbar himself, who initiated work on the building site in 1569. The court took up residence in the 1570s and construction continued until 1584, when the city was abruptly abandoned. The reason for this withdrawal is unclear but may have involved an insufficiency of water.

We assumed we were going to a tourist site where there would be other sightseers and probably some locals from nearby villages. But when we arrive we find total emptiness. No people, no animals, no birds, not even the sound of wind to break the stillness. There is just one little man by the side of the road who offers to be our guide. As we tramp up into the citadel he tells us that he has had no work, meaning no visitors, for weeks. I have to take care not to stumble as we move up and down the crumbling steps and broken pavements; preoccupied with my cane work, I see little at first. I feel or hear the buildings as sources of echo, our scuffling feet resounding hollowly off the sandstone walls. The place feels frozen and oddly emptied out, emptied not only of people but of material reality. It is rather unsettling. I would never have thought that monumental buildings could convey such a sense of nullity.

Our guide leads us by a zigzag route from one notable site to another, pausing at last before the Panch Mahal, or five-story pleasure palace. All this time I have been waiting for my eyes to "adjust," although there is nothing wrong with the light, so that I might see some coherent images. But all I see is a bewildering succession of fragments that do not connect, and broken planes that do not cohere into anything at all. I feel a growing dismay. I am beginning to realize that the construction of these buildings was not guided by any grid or rational plan; apparently, they were all raised more or less haphazardly. There are no broad thoroughfares or proper streets, no regularity of spacing that would allow me to identify specific images as a component of this or the outer boundary of that. I hear Evan nimbly scrambling up what must be an outer stairway of the Panch Mahal, but when I look toward the stairs – those sketchy parallel lines must surely be stairs – they seem to lead up or dissolve into nowhere. It is into this nowhere that Evan has already disappeared.

My restless visual memory began of its own accord to dredge up some of the strange, sketchy images that were first invoked when I read a short story by Jorge Luis Borges, "The Immortal."[3] The story depicted an abandoned city that was utterly alien, in the sense that it was never intended for humans either in its conception or its grotesque execution. It was a geometrist's nightmare, a place where all normal spatial relationships were telescoped or collapsed into one another. That impossible place, I think, is where I am right now. This is fantasy, of course, but still I feel a constriction in my chest.

Then I manage to collect myself and inwardly recede from what I am seeing – I think I actually shifted backward a few inches, in a brief little surge of physical literalism – and then I remember. I reaffirm that vision is an entirely impersonal function, and that I am separate from what I see. The brokenness of these images belongs to the images themselves, and not to my own nature. No matter how bizarre they may be, they cannot touch me or diminish me, only inconvenience me. The visual mind that enfolds those images is not an aspect of the self, but stands subtly apart from it. The self or inner knower simply beholds what is on show.

Nevertheless these particular images apparently have something to say, and I now try to be more open to them. This changes things – not the images themselves, but what they now seemed to signify. It is as though my quirky and unpredictable eyesight has entered into the heart of that strange insubstantiality or negation that I have been feeling since I got here. Seen through these eyes Fatehpur Sikri illustrates the inescapable law of transience, which eventually breaks down all material things. The disarticulated planes that I see when I stare at the Panch Mahal can be taken as an unasked-for glimpse of the future, a true anticipatory vision conjured up by the stark reductionism of RP. It is a visual fast-forward to the far distant day when everything here will inevitably lie in shards and fragments. I think of the famous inscription that appears over the main arch of the citadel's triumphal gate: yes, they are exactly the right words. I turn to our guide and ask him to lead us to the Victory Gate.

We follow another winding course and then mount the long flight of steps to the massive gate that was erected to proclaim Akbar's imperishable glory. We pass through the main arch, the gate towering forty metres above us. Once inside the courtyard we can look back and see the prescient message up above the arch. I do not need to see it. It is a verse from the Koran attributed to Jesus, whom Islam honours as a great mystic and ascetic. Our guide translates it aloud, probably relying on his memory of the Koran rather than on the old defunct script that only a few antiquarians can read. "Said Jesus, on whom be peace, the world is but a bridge. Pass over but build no house upon it. He who hopes for an hour hopes for eternity for the world is but an hour. Spend it in devotion, for the rest is unseen."

After this we leave Fatehpur Sikri, descending slowly through the silence to the road where our car is parked. Our driver is clearly glad to be leaving. As we set out on the long drive back to Delhi I think about the inscription on the Victory Gate, and this puts me in mind of what I had seen at the Taj Mahal in Agra two days earlier. I first saw the Taj in 1970, drinking it in for three days and two miraculously bright moonlit nights. At nighttime the great tomb was no doubt far fainter and ghostlier to me than to the other gazers in the garden, though I had loved my image nonetheless for that. But all these years later when I stood before the Taj beside Pressi and Evan, who were encountering it for the first time, I was presented with an utterly different kind of image. I heard Pressi's intake of breath and her long, soft "Ohhh!" I heard Evan say "Neat!" But I just stared in fascination, unable to speak.

To set the context I should explain that when I visited the Taj in 1970 I had consciously worked to build up a kind of constructed image of the whole building, as seen from well back. I often did this during my travels when I came upon something that was monumental in size and extraordinary in its effect. In the case of the Taj this process required several little forays up close to grasp the complex octagonal structure of the base, and the other details that tended to blur as I moved further back. Eventually I arrived at an image of the overall form that was part immediate percept and part imaginative construct, the two merged seamlessly together.

What I saw when I took in the Taj with Pressi and Evan almost two decades later was a dazzling example of the effects of time on the perception and memory of the person living with RP. The dazzle was probably to some degree literal, for the afternoon sun bore down on my compromised eyes in a way that drained away detail even as it bestowed luminescence. But the resulting image was like nothing I could have anticipated. It was lucent and ethereal, so apparently insubstantial as to seem almost transparent. None of the structural detail was left; everything had fused into a single shimmering light-shape that was completely new and yet entirely recognizable. It was more like the platonic Idea of the Taj than its actual embodiment. Of course I knew that its origin was optical rather than metaphysical, an effect of the sun on my retinas. But it was so achingly beautiful that I could not dismiss it as a mere symptom of damage. It was really a kind of gift. I think I finally mumbled a thank you – at any rate I said one inwardly. I didn't try to identify to whom, or at what, it was directed.

4 REGARDING FACELESSNESS

The experiences recounted above were among the first fruits of my relinquishing the life-long emotive habit of clinging to eyesight. This habit was on its way out, and now and then its very absence would pop up as a singular fact. I would be slightly startled to notice that the old habit had dissolved, that it just wasn't "there" at all. From this time onward the new stance of non-judgmental detachment from an increasingly scrambled visual array would help me to cope with the necessary practical adjustments, as first this task and then that could no longer be done in the old, visually dependant way.

Of course, these readjustments were at times exasperating and exhausting, for they involved hard work. I always tried to deal with the frustration and resulting muscular tension on their own track, so to speak. This was the track of rethinking and relearning how to do things, of repeatedly starting over again, of continuing to slog ahead one step at a time even when I felt like quitting for the day. There was also the track of blowing off steam, of cussing and blaspheming when I felt like it, and having an extra slug of gin to fortify my tonic water when I got home and folded up my cane. But in the larger domain of just being and living, the enquiry into which I had immersed myself had already granted me a great boon. It had banished once and for all my fear of blindness. From the summer of 1988 onward I never again experienced anxiety at the thought of a lightless future.

If for a moment I may get ahead of myself by a couple of decades, I can report that every time I thought the last of my light perception had finally vanished – this was to happen repeatedly after 2004 – I had the satisfaction of accepting this apparent terminus without feeling the least pang of existential fear or self-diminishment. Nor was there any anxiety about what might be called the mechanics of practical compensation, for by then I had long-established daily routines that required no eyesight, and thus no light.

In Delhi in 1988 I was on a more even keel than I had been for years. I was quite simply happy – happy in my work and family life, happy in my studies and cultural explorations and travels, consistently happy despite the leaking away of my remaining vision and the steady amplification of my back pain. I took this simple happiness as a sign that I was on a path of growing self-purchase, a path that was based on something more than mere speculation or wishful thinking. The key finding as I understood it was that the self – the real self, in itself and as itself – was not a seer, and did not require seeing for its own self-sufficiency.

If my revisionist view of the self in 1988 had been based on a falling away from reason, and if my disidentification from eyesight was a mere illusion, it would have been very difficult for me to respond to the next stage of visual disintegration in the way I actually did. I was just entering that phase of central vision loss when faces – the faces of my colleagues and friends, of my wife and son, and of the visual "me" staring back out of the mirror – were blurring into featureless ovals that conveyed no identity.

Because I saw Pressi and Evan every day and my colleagues at the High Commission every weekday, the gradual disappearance of their faces from my world was almost imperceptible at first. The visual memory that marks a startling change is not of them but of an Indian soldier, or *jawan*, many of whom I would see during my long walk down embassy row before work every morning. Theirs were faces I would normally only glance at.

It was my habit to take this exercise no matter how high the temperature. I liked walking, and in early morning before the embassies opened the long access road was virtually empty of traffic. As I plodded along, swinging my cane, I could expect to see the jawans posted at each embassy gate grinning at me gleefully. Their work must have been boring, and the spectacle of the mad blind *ferengi*, or foreigner, was perhaps the only break in the dullness of their morning routine. Who but a mad ferengi would be out here walking in this heat when he could be sitting in his air-conditioned office? Who but a mad blind man would be toiling along with a stick when he could be driven? Whenever I greeted one of the jawans in my meagre Hindi he would snap to attention, but nothing could break that grin. Or so I thought.

On this particular morning I was walking past the French embassy when I happened to glance over at the jawan sentry and saw him remove his broad-brimmed hat, probably in order to mop his brow. With that gesture his face was now unobscured. It froze me in my tracks: I just stood there and gaped. For one dizzy moment – perhaps I really was going mad, after all – I thought his face had been melted by the sun. Toward the bottom the faint crescent of the white teeth was disappearing as the man lost his smile, no doubt in reaction to my intense stare; above it the rest of the face seemed to have been scraped entirely away. No eyes, no nose, no ears or hair. Then I thought: *Of course.* What an ass I am. It's only the R P, the next stage of it. I couldn't think of anything to do or say so I just walked on.

Apparently the intensely bright sun did have something to do with that dramatic effacement, not by rendering flesh into melted butter but simply through its temporary damping of my inadequate central visual acuity. As I walked along and thought about this I realized that the factors involved were actually very similar to those that had given rise to that gossamer vision of the Taj Mahal, except that this time I would have preferred not to have seen what was on show. I began to scour my mind for recent memory-images of what Pressi and Evan looked like at home. By the time I got back to the gates of the High Commission I knew that I had been deliberately ignoring or downplaying the increasing blurriness of their features. As I passed through the checkpoint – more jawans, more snappy salutes and big grins – I drew in a long, shaky breath and slowly let it out. This is what I always found myself doing whenever my visual world halted in its serene rotation, lurched backwards, and developed a new set of fractures.

What happened after that? I have had to stop to puzzle this out, for my next definite memory of effacement is from several months later, and once again it features someone other than Pressi or Evan. It is an image of my reader-secretary, Ann Johnson. This is another of those generic or template memories that depict not a specific occasion but something I saw every day, in this case Ann walking toward me down the hall of the Chancery. I know it is Ann because of the characteristic sound of her tread. As she comes nearer I begin to make out her form, which is an Ann-form, and then her dress, which is somehow an Ann-type dress. When she is quite close to me I can blurrily see that her dark hair is where I would expect it to be, done up Ann-ishly about her head rather than hanging loose over her shoulders. I smile at what was once a fresh-complexioned face, reduced now to a pallid disc containing no discernible features, and try to direct my gaze to where the eyes used to be. By now I am used to this. It is not upsetting, just weird.

Between the unexpected apparition of the faceless jawan and the workaday presence of faceless Ann many months later there lay a critical period of inner realignment, one that I cannot reconstruct from memory. But of one thing I am sure: this realignment or letting-go was worked out at home in the company of my family. It seems that as we carried on with our normal domestic routines I had simply got used to the fact that the faces of my wife and son were less and less available to me, finally disappearing for good at some vague point that was indistinguishable from the blurry continuum. It was inevitable that this process should sometimes leave me feeling sad and regretful. I doubt that even a sage could lose the capacity to see the best-loved faces in his or her life without feeling pangs of regret. But these reactions were always temporary. They did not involve the kind of grief that typically arises from the permanent loss of loved ones or treasured things, as distinct from images.

I felt – and I do mean *felt* rather than figured out or wilfully hoped, for it was far more a matter of knowing through the heart than of reasoning or believing – that Pressi and Evan were no less present and accessible to me than before. Just as I was essentially not the seer, they were essentially not the seen. The main thing for all of us was to adapt to my not being able to make eye contact when we were talking. It was important that the same sense of inner contact should still be there despite the absence of gaze meeting gaze, especially during those ordinary little exchanges whose real point apart from the details of the moment was the affirmation of our interconnected lives.

We did adjust. In time I would feel when we were together how we all breathed the same air and occupied the same space, or at least adjacent spaces. This sense of an enfolding, pervading space was more comforting to me even than touch or voice. It was nothing mystical, just an awareness of the same essential co-presence that sighted people affirm when they look into each other's eyes. It came to me as much through the pores of my skin as through the mind.

As for the face in the mirror, I found its slow dissolve intriguing rather than frightening. Eventually, as the reflection became feature-less, I was able to just note the change without resistance, knowing that this was not a great and momentous relinquishment but a passing away of no particular importance. I saw the vague presence in the mirror as not-I. What I meant by this was not just that my real face was still intact, on this side of the glass, but that my real being was not facial or even physical.

Later I was to consult published accounts of vision loss that describe how blinded persons sometimes feel the need to touch their bodies and especially their faces to confirm that their identity is still whole. I experienced none of this. My body with its distinctive mug was still familiarly there, in the sense that I could confirm its contours through touch, but what was primary to identity was neither the body nor the face. It was the inner, mysterious knower that knew these things to be other than itself.

Everything I have laid out in this chapter was somehow one big thing with no parts or edges, a sort of flow or movement that I find even harder to label than to describe. So I just think of it as my inner realignment. By the end of our first year in Delhi I understood that it was for this that I had to come back to India – for the sensory aspect of the realignment, first of all, and beyond that for the corresponding, still preliminary opening-up of a less restricted experience of being. Given my circumstances and the implicit needs that had been pressing on me back in Ottawa, I made the right move.

India became my teacher, indirectly and unsystematically at first but tellingly just the same, through the symbolic language of the Upanishads and a spirit of place that consistently engaged all my senses. India – my India, not the political or economic entity but the old tradition of enquiry that still offers the means to a greater self-purchase – helped me to keep going blind. It taught me how to do this without lapsing into panic, depression, or bitterness. Yet I was only getting started, against the grain of an obscure inner resistance, on the Vedanta that would require me to go much more deeply into myself.

4

Vedanta, the Ego, and the Flesh

1 RE-ENTER SHIVA

During our second year in New Delhi I was wrapped up even more intensely in my work at the High Commission. The daily intensity was leavened somewhat by the little visitor who occasionally fetched up in Ann's office, connected to my own. When I was dictating to Ann I could sometimes hear through the open door the experimental cooings and sputterings of little Sarasa, or Sarah, Ann's newly adopted baby daughter. Ann had wanted children for years, and in New Delhi she finally took the necessary steps. The orphanage that she had approached was very receptive to the prospect of a foreign adoption, and it was my honour and pleasure to write the letter of recommendation, and sign the necessary papers, that would eventually generate the visa for Sarah to enter Canada with her mother. But for the time being Sarah was the High Commission's prize daughter, everyone's pet.

Outside of working hours I continued to explore my sensory-cultural environment, and whether at home or moving about the city or at the office I was able to further consolidate my new way of experiencing eyesight. But this year was to mark a turning-point that would soon end my foreign service career and constrain many aspects of my active life. From 1989 onward I would have to deal increasingly with medical problems other than blindness. In this chapter I will describe what led up to this life-change, and how at this time I tried through my own forms of experimentation to remain engaged with the Indian spiritual tradition.

One day when Pressi and I were browsing through a bazaar we had not visited before, we came upon a display of well-crafted

Natarajas. The heavy metal statues were almost two feet high and
their details were particularly fine, as Pressi could see and as I found
by running my fingertips over them. This was the same Dancing Shiva
that I had first met up with on a far more formidable scale in that
bedroom in Madras during my previous visit to India. Once again I
was struck by the grace and poise of the dancing figure. Yielding to
nostalgia, I bought one of the statues and we took it home.

The Nataraja was not for show. He belonged in my study, not in
the living room where we entertained. After I had found a place for
the statue on the low bookcase near my desk, I traced once again the
high-arching line of the left leg, the tip of my forefinger moving
deliberately as though I were reading braille. I felt a pang of envy for
the figure's suppleness and physical strength. This was just a momen-
tary concession to a literal, physical iconography that portrays the
deity as a four-armed but otherwise anthropomorphic god. What the
Shiva really represented, as far as I was concerned, was not physical
at all. I had read enough Vedanta by now to superimpose onto the
Nataraja a non-theistic, non-corporeal interpretation, and this depersonalization of the Shiva-figure had the effect of making it not
less interesting, but more. This was not the way a Hindu devotee
would conceive of the Shiva, however.

What interested me now was that each hand of the four-armed figure
had a particular significance, either cosmological or eschatological.
In his upper right hand Shiva holds up the hourglass-shaped drum of
creation that pulsed the universe into existence; in his upper left hand
he brandishes the bowl of fire symbolizing the final conflagration that
is destined to destroy everything. The circle of flames within which
the great figure dances represents the same fate. This set of symbols
may be taken as depicting the ancient vision of an oscillating universe,
with space and matter exploding initially out of a Big Bang and then
expanding enormously, only to slow down and contract and finally fall
back into itself in what some Western physicists call the Big Crunch.
This process was believed to be cyclical, repeating itself over and
over again as the macrocosmic analog to the microcosmic cycle of
individual birth, death, and presumed rebirth. I knew that this arcane
cosmology had fascinated Robert Oppenheimer, the physicist and
student of Sanskrit who is remembered today mainly as the "father"
of the atomic bomb.

Shiva's third and fourth hands, which hold no objects, are con-
formed into specific gestures (*mudras*) the significance of which is

aimed directly at whoever is viewing the statue. The lower right hand lies open in an attitude of benevolence and bountiful giving, while at the same time indicating the leg that is raised in ecstatic dance. What this open hand offers is the sanctuary – and, ultimately, the eschatological salvation – that can be found at the feet of Lord Shiva. Interpreted more abstractly and inwardly, Shiva's hand can be taken to offer the path to liberation set out by the various Hindu scriptures, including the Vedantic. The corresponding mudra, known as Holding Steady or Fear Not, formed by the lower right hand, is presented to confirm that these paths may be followed without succumbing to fear.

Why fear? The answer is conveyed by the tiger skin that Shiva is wearing, and more graphically by the little figure or homunculus on which his right foot floats, or rests, or – more ominously – on which it bears down. The tiger may be interpreted as the slayer of the ego, that defensive sense of "I" that fears its own demise. The homunculus is sometimes identified as the worshipper who is seeking sanctuary at Shiva's feet, or as a demon, or sometimes as ignorance. But for all practical purposes this beleaguered creature is the human ego. Thus the homunculus need not be taken either as an imaginary monster or some kind of conceptual abstraction; it can stand instead for the ego-sense, the bottom-line sense of individuality of the you or me who stands gazing at the symbolic tableau.

Eventually I came to feel that while the Nataraja tableau makes for vivid iconography, it is ambiguous when it comes to the complex business of valuing or devaluing or even identifying the nature of the human ego. The ego as we know it certainly has its ugly side. As a supposed separative self its default position when under pressure proves all too often to be pure selfishness. The raw ego-sense that squats at the core of the personality can lock the mind and will into the kind of defensiveness, aggression, self-seeking, vanity, and pride typically conveyed by the term "egotism." On top of that, or rather beneath it, is a generally muted fear that under adverse circumstances can ramp up into anxiety, or even terror. This is the ego's fear of its own marginalization, of its undoing, and finally of its inevitable and permanent demise. In this reduced and stressed-out condition the ego becomes our distorted personal homunculus, ground down under the heel of whatever wrathful deity we have been conditioned to believe in.

In the setting where I first implicitly encountered the problem of the wilful ego and a judgmental God – the local church that I left in disgust when I was sixteen – the problem was addressed by a

Bible-thumping minister, who saw our teen group as a potential nest of vipers. We were apparently sinners, sinners in mind and soul if not yet in body, inheritors of an original sin that was somehow sexual in nature. Our basic self (he did not use the word "ego" because it was not available in the Bible) was just plain bad, bad enough for hellfire. In retrospect, it seems ironic that our packaged introduction into hell and damnation should have been served up in the United Church of Canada, which over the succeeding decades would evolve into one of the most liberal of the mainstream Canadian denominations. In adulthood I did not identify as Christian. But as the reader will see later, I did develop a fascination with the profound (yet at times seemingly contradictory) teachings of Jesus.

In New Delhi in 1988 I was looking into a teaching, Vedanta, according to which our fundamental nature or true selfhood was spiritual, not physical or salaciously mental. Nor were we essentially the ego, which Vedanta identifies as a kind of false self. In Vedantic teaching there were references to personal ego-based faults or impurities, designated as *kleshas* – I had come upon the same term in Buddhism – but these could be rectified eventually through understanding and appropriate forms of practice. This struck me as an insightful and humane perspective, though it clearly called for discipline. I was on the other side of the world now, both geographically and philosophically, trying to get my bearings. So far, at least, I liked this new spiritual terrain.

The most important discoveries I had made in Delhi had nothing to do with sin and much to do with sussing out the ordinary ego. First, I had found that the conventional sense of self or ego identifies intensely with the faculty of vision, and second, that this identification can be given up or dissolved even during the challenging process of vision loss. I had experienced this as a great liberation. But now I found myself wondering if I had it in me to disidentify from the physical pain that was becoming increasingly obtrusive, and sometimes disabling. The source of this pain was not a vengeful deity or "bad karma," but straightforward physical factors that could be traced back to early injuries.

My circumstances seemed to lead to an interesting question: If I managed to disidentify from this aching body and indeed from the whole psycho-physical complex, what then would I discover my self to be? Could it be the deep self referred to in the Upanishads as the Atman? That was just too "big," surely. To me the answer seemed to be a discovery of oneself as simple consciousness – an individual consciousness. This would be the consciousness that observes the mind-stream, the body, and the external world. Yet I found it surprisingly hard to wrap my imagination around the notion of an individual consciousness-self, which kept coming up in my mind's eye as a vague mist confined in a bell jar.

Perhaps the consciousness-self is after all a universal reality which in some mysterious way is common to us all. I couldn't seem to get my mind around this idea, either, even though the Upanishads suggested this shared selfhood and sometimes confirmed it explicitly. There was only one Atman, which was characterized as non-dual or transpersonal. It seemed clear from the texts that this was not to be taken as anything remotely resembling the "hive mind" of an insect colony, in which individuals function rather like organs of a single entity. The Atman clearly had to do with a shared consciousness, not with a delegation of functions within a community. But how could the immediacy and intimacy of conscious "inner space" be transpersonal? This was a question I would seriously address only years later, after I had worked through some gut-wrenchingly "personal" problems back in Ottawa. The focus for some time to come was going to be on individuality – mine.

In the meantime I had become intrigued, in a mildly appalled sort of way, by the fact that in most of the serious philosophical, spiritual, and scientific disciplines I had looked into, the individual as conventionally conceived is given short shrift. To take a broad objective view, the lone human being is completely expendable, of no account whatever in the general scheme of things. And yet we prefer to position ourselves at the centre of our universe as privileged existents. To the extent that we do so, we are fantasizing. We are setting ourselves up to be demoralizingly swatted down, well before we are actually finished off.

Earthquakes do happen, wars rage, and civilizations decay. On the more intimate or immediate scale of events, a young person is unexpectedly killed or contracts cancer or begins showing the symptoms of RP. The inflexible, literalist religion I had rejected in high school tried to rationalize these blows of fate, all of them based on the laws of nature devised by a presumably "good" God, by promising a final settling of accounts that would make everything right in the end. But, to go on the available evidence, the very nature of things – and by extension its presumed source or ground – is no respecter of persons.

Yet at the deeper reaches of all the major spiritual traditions there is a very different view. Plato and his Greek predecessors had expounded the concept of Necessity, which identifies suffering as an inevitable consequence of physical creation. The twentieth-century Christian thinker and contemplative, Simone Weil, illustrated Necessity with the dead-simple example of gravity. Divine law having ordained that bodies fall downward instead of floating upward, it follows that humans who lose their footing at the lip of a precipice have their heads smashed open. The early Greek Stoics whom Simone Weil loved, such as Chrysippus and Cleanthes, celebrated creation and natural law and Necessity in its totality. Cleanthes' beautiful and moving *Hymn to Zeus* extends its unconditional praise even to those aspects of nature that normally frighten or appall us. This poem strongly appealed to me; its overall tone of unconditional acceptance seemed right.

In the Book of Job, which is arguably both the most profound and the most outrageously ego-threatening document in the Jewish Bible, an unflinching and awe-inducing vision of reality is revealed to Job by the voice in the whirlwind. Job understands what he is shown, and his grievances are transformed into profound acceptance. Acceptance is the real point of the story, an acceptance so unqualified that it reaches down far beneath the claims of the ego. Acceptance is in fact the *only* significant theme presented in the Book of Job, notwithstanding the subsequent and entirely phoney Hollywood ending that highlights an absolute welter of divine gifts. Many modern scholars take that ending – the "payoff" for Job's "submission" – to be a much later and gratuitous interpolation.[1]

Jesus similarly urges his disciples in Matthew 5:45 and Luke 13:1–4 to accept the fact that natural law does not discriminate between good people and bad. In the former passage (the Sermon on the Mount) God is shown to make his sun rise on the evil and the good and send rain to the just and the unjust alike; in the passage from Luke, Jesus states flatly that certain men who were killed by a falling wall or tower were as likely to have been good people as sinners.

What these teachings have in common is a veiled or implicit critique of the ego's unreflective enmeshment in judgmental dualism. So long as we insist on things going this way instead of that, on winning instead of losing, on attaining to these goods and not to those ills, on remaining perfectly healthy without losing any of our faculties, we are just sitting ducks. To ward off anxiety we choose to repress the knowledge – Job's knowledge – that life as it actually comes at us is an admixture of the desired and the undesired, the glorious and the terrifying. But in presenting their sere and daunting vision of reality, both Jesus and his ancient predecessors in the Jewish wisdom tradition were telling us that, however difficult it may be to achieve, there really is a radically different, fearless, open way of living – of just *being*.

The most widely known Vedantic presentation of this extreme truth, the truth that the exalted is co-mingled with the terrible, appears in the theophanic or God-revealing eleventh chapter of the Bhagavad-Gita. It is a beautiful but harrowing vision – harrowing only if resisted – of a great, flaming, creative/destructive cosmos that is not only the work of "God" but, metaphorically speaking, his very substance. This is the Indian counterpart to the Book of Job. Studying it as I did in New Delhi and repeatedly going back to the eleventh chapter, I found in it a truth and gravitas that made my problems of failing vision and growing pain seem smaller and more natural, less "special." It was in this general frame of mind that I had turned to the Katha Upanishad and appropriated its chariot analogy, as described in the previous chapter.

The parallel between Indian Vedanta and the most rigorous versions of Judaism and Christianity was emphasized by the Vedanta teacher Rama Tirtha, during his lecture tour of the United States in 1902–1903. The most important feature that the Eastern and Western teachings have in common, he said, is a single shared spiritual law. In Vedanta and Buddhism this law is called Dharma; in the three Abrahamic religions it is identified as the terrible or "jealous" aspect of God. What the law requires of us is a large-hearted acceptance of things as they actually are. This is not the pseudo-acceptance that is born of defeat and the giving up of hope, but the affirmative acceptance that rises of its own accord when the bare, defensive ego-sense is nudged away from our inner centre. To go through this inner displacement, one thinks, may be the hardest thing in the world.

These traditions hold that it is precisely because we make a little god of the ego that the real God or ultimate reality, referred to by the Jewish Scriptures as a starkly anthropomorphic "He," is said to be "jealous" of it. However you try to conceptualize the greater reality, as God or Dharma or physical law or something that is ineffable and thus not really conceptualizable at all, the very nature of things pushes us sometimes quite mercilessly to get beyond the constrictive ego-sense. It is not so much this brutal pushing as the ego's automatic and frantic resistance to it that forms the real core of our suffering.

Rama Tirtha identifies the two great symbols of this suffering, and of its possible transcendence, as the Cross of Jesus and the Trishula of Shiva.[2] The Trishula is a trident, the weapon wielded by Shiva in some of his many representations. Its points, like the nails that go with the Cross, are driven not just into the flesh but into the ego that identifies with the flesh. The dilemma of the ordinary, non-Christ-like human being who is impaled by medical circumstances is only secondarily the impalement itself; his primary dilemma is a lifelong physicalized egohood that makes detachment from the suffering body or degraded senses very difficult.

Vedanta claims that the surest way to acceptance of our own circumstances, whether ordinary or extreme, is through introspectively seeking out our hidden self-sufficiency. Thus from a Vedantic point of view one of the most noteworthy depictions of Shiva in Indian art is the Maha-Yogi, Shiva as the prototype meditator and teacher. He sits before the viewer in stillness, immersed in meditative absorption. He may or may not be depicted with a serpent, and he may or may not be covered with the ashes of ego-renunciation. What counts is not so much the symbolic accessories or the specific meditative posture as the self-knowledge that the latter represents. If the Shiva so depicted is interpreted as representing high Vedantic attainment, his experience of selfhood would be so wide-open, integrative, and life-affirming that it would reject no aspect of fate, no matter how daunting.

It is the inner openness of the Maha-Yogi, one might say, that serves as the "space" out of which the spontaneous energy of the Nataraja erupts into dance. But I found myself wondering if a Vedantin and a Shivite, taken together, would approve of this figure of speech. At this time I was just becoming aware that I was conflating two traditions, the higher Vedanta and the theistic path of Shiva (Shaiva Marga), each of which has its own distinctive set of features. I was fascinated by Vedanta to the limited extent that I understood it. On the other hand – or was it the same hand? – I had never forgotten my nightly encounters with that towering Nataraja in 1970.

It didn't matter to me then if Vedantic philosophy and Shiva iconography were mixed together; as far as I was concerned the Nataraja, dancing within his circle of cosmic fire, was the Atman depicted anthropomorphically. The dance was joyous, and this was reason enough for the ancients to have placed it at the heart of their Bang and Crunch cosmology. It would be a few years later, when I finally got down to serious study, that I realized the importance of grasping the real differences among these various traditions. They present distinct and in some cases incompatible ways of conceptualizing God – or Ungod.

2 THE COILS OF THE EGO

What makes the religio-philosophical view of life described in the previous section so striking, especially to those of us who grew up immersed in the escapist popular culture of the West, is the honesty with which it addresses the human condition, and its rejection of easy answers. Whether you view the more demanding of the Indian spiritual paths as philosophy or religion or as symbolically encoded depth psychology, they are definitely for adults. It is tough stuff – tough in the sense of tough love. When Vedanta adopts a religious mode of expression it does not so far as I could see fall back on prayers to be let off the hook, or promises of posthumous rewards. It concentrates instead on the challenge of inner transformation, the uncovering of our essential nature, asserting on the basis of millennia of experience that such an uncovering really is possible. It is this discovery that is identified by Vedanta as the key to realistic, affirmative, open-hearted living. It all sounded quite wonderful, on tape.

But what about the stubborn ego? This was the question I kept returning to in 1988. The macrocosmic scale of Vedantic symbolism was a little overwhelming, and of course the "I" who saw it as disproportionate was the ego itself. My doubts about the possibility of Vedantic realization were based in part on a concern that I might lack the intuitive capacity for separating myself – my real self, assuming that the latter actually exists – from the stickiness of the ego. Given the fact that the ego usually just crouches there deep inside, defending its little turf while emitting alarm signals, one has to seriously wonder how it is possible to learn to meditate like Maha-Yogi, and so slip free from the ego's coils. Anyway, who was I to take on such a thing? My energy was being sucked into amplified reporting on current political developments and national security concerns.

Yet my thoughts kept returning to the ego's sheer obduracy. It seemed to me that the bare, defensive ego-sense or individuality, whatever it might prove to be in itself, was implicated in every fundamental division of experience I could think of – I versus you, I as subject confronting a world of objects, I resisting whatever fate I might wish to avoid, I as the arbiter of the good and the bad. The problem of the ego was implicit throughout the Upanishads and vividly represented in the Bhagavad-Gita in the person of Arjuna, the conflicted and frightened warrior.

Nevertheless I had learned for a certainty that whatever else my true self would turn out to be, it was not, and need not be, an ophthalmic "seer." Considered in retrospect, the fear of blindness that I had known at different times in my life seemed now to be entirely the work of the homuncular ego, in its self-appointed role of endangered seer. The bare ego-sense clung to the body and senses not just out of habit but in order to feel more real, more substantial. It feared to be otherwise. But I had found that in some contexts the fear turned out to be hollow or even a kind of bluff; in the switch to a de-egoized visual detachment the homunculus was simply ignored. One might go further and say that in that particular kind of situation the homunculus simply vanishes.

I kept wondering what it would be like to relinquish all the ego-based modes of identification – not just the sensory but the physical, mental, and emotional. Then presumably there would be nothing left from which to fashion an identity that would be truly unique and individual. It was hard to imagine such a pass, and it left me feeling divided. On the one hand my reservations seemed to spring from the ego itself, and they were quite revealing. They showed that when the ego was feeling threatened and stripped down, it was very much aware of its own inherent poverty or insubstantiality. In this sense it was weak and vulnerable and thus no match for the real self, whatever that might be. On the other hand, I was periodically gripped by doubt in the face of Vedantic teaching – a doubt about my fitness for such a project, given the painful memories of early sexual interference that sometimes pushed up to the surface of my mind. That is when I felt like a real homunculus, malformed and cut down to size.

As I sat in my study the day I brought the Nataraja home from the bazaar, gazing speculatively at the Shiva-figure, I thought of what it had been like in Madras to have his far larger representation looming at the foot of my bed. This scene had always been enacted in the evening, which meant that to my eyes the illumination was consistently dim and atmospheric. The effect was a kind of frozen moment, with Shiva always in the very act of manifesting out of nothingness. Taking him in involved a premonitory, egodystonic fear, not an urgent recoil but the kind of alert, wary defensiveness that attends the sense of intriguing but darkly shadowed possibilities. I was very much aware throughout that I was playing with imagination, as though scripting a myth. But there was something else that ran entirely on its own track: the fear of having to let go in some very large way that my mind could not compass. Recalling this in New Delhi I found it strange that some of that old fear could sometimes unexpectedly recur, for most of my subsequent experience suggested that the fear was completely unjustified.

For example, the line that connects the great Madras Shiva to the downsized version I acquired in New Delhi runs straight through an incident that occurred in Ottawa a couple of months before we moved to India. As part of my reading program on identity or selfhood I was then studying one of the basic works of the twentieth-century German philosopher Martin Heidegger, *An Introduction to Metaphysics*. This book was recommended to me by a friend and foreign service colleague, Rob McRae. Rob has a PhD in philosophy and the kind of mind that neatly accommodates the logical, the metaphysical, and the bureaucratically doable. He was about to be posted to Czechoslovakia. At the end of our India assignment Pressi and Evan and I would spend a most enjoyable week with the McRaes in Prague, notwithstanding the constant spinal pain that would eventually ground me. In Prague I would get a taste of how Rob monitored the tumultuous but largely non-violent protests of the Velvet Revolution.[3]

Despite the modest or deliberately ironic title of the Heidegger book that Rob had urged upon me, that tome was by no means a light and easy "introduction" to metaphysics. It sought to recapture the direct and unobstructed vision of reality experienced by early Greek philosophers, a direct vision that was lost in the later attempts to erect competing philosophical systems. Heidegger's text was as dense as anything I had ever read, yet it gave the sense of something inexpressibly simple and powerful that lay behind the language and drove it on. Once I got into the book I found it hard to put aside, despite the warm weather and long, light-filled Canadian summer evenings that normally would have drawn me outside into our backyard. For a couple of weeks all my evenings were spent at my desk, holed up with my tape recorder.

At one point toward the end of this process I found that I just had to stop, for I couldn't think anymore. As I sat there, I closed my eyes for a few moments and took in my mind as a pleasingly empty space. Then I opened my eyes again and turned off the power button without glancing at it – the recorder was within easy reach just to my left

– and my gaze fell automatically on the object in my direct line of vision. This was the attractively asymmetrical, roughly finished Japanese tea bowl that habitually rested in front of me near the outside edge of the desk. It was one of those ordinary things whose presence you register without really taking it in. But now I was staring at it, filled with incredulity.

The bowl was absolutely radiant, blazing with what seemed to be an inner rather than a reflective light. This light was not an emanation such as a halo or corona; it was integral to the cup itself, as though the cup were made entirely of light. It seemed far more real than the everyday visual object whose shape it had assumed. What glowed or burned before me in the shape of a tea bowl was an intense naked presence the like of which I had never seen before, an affirmation of pure raw being. The thing seemed almost alive.

To view such an object was to be filled by it completely. There was none of the ordinary sense of an observer *here* looking at a bowl *there*: there was just the bowl. I was present simply as the open conscious space that contained the bowl. For a brief but measureless interval, that one object was the world in itself and the whole of experience, uniquely and fiercely beautiful. The attendant emotional tone was that of sheer wonder.

And then – *Stop. I'm not ready for this.* The ego-sense swarmed out of nowhere back into its accustomed position at my end of what was once again a two-ended visual tunnel instead of an open visual space. The experience was over, decisively short-circuited by the killjoy who had thrown some breaker switch. The killjoy consisted simply and starkly of the threatened sense of ego-based individuality, the tight little inner observer that, however tenuous it might sometimes seem to be, did not want to disappear again. With the return of this defensive, separative "I"-feeling there arose a sense of disappointment and even mortification. A chance combination of circumstances or rare good luck had crystallized this opportunity for me to experience something new and significant, just at the time when I was soon to lose the capacity for seeing an object of this size clearly and all at once. And I had blown my chance through fear. Or so I felt.

Later with a little reflection I amended my judgment. I did not totally squander the opportunity but had actually experienced the altered state for a few critical moments, giving myself over to it without resistance. And what had happened to me was by no means unique: many people have written about this sort of thing or described it to friends. For those with normal field vision it often occurs in a restful or striking natural setting, as a feeling of deep immersion into the landscape. In my case the experience was not the result of luck or chance but the intense focus on Heidegger's text. This had drawn me into a kind of meditative absorption.

I learned something of significance from this incident. That little contraction of fear or pusillanimity (the word means literally small-mindedness) was not in itself a characteristic of egolessness. How could it be when it was the ego's reappearance that generated the fear? During the moments of actual absorption when the ego was not present there was no fear at all. The reaction set in only when the mind started up again, and remembered that it was supposed to be affirming the presence of a tight little personal "I." The mind had spooked itself like a small child alone in his dark, safe bedroom, a child who remembers a scare story about the Boogeyman.

There was nothing "mystical" about this experience, if by that word we mean either the mental projection of something that really isn't there, or the attainment of a realm separate from the everyday world. What I experienced was just a glimpse of the way things look when the ego withdraws, which is in fact the way they always are in themselves. The world is not flat and dead but vibrant. And to see this vibrancy was evidently to share in it. When the sharing is especially clear and unimpeded, with the distinction between subject and object temporarily eliminated, it is really a kind of grace.

During ordinary states of absorption or receptivity we simply overlook the significant absence of the individual ego-I that we normally take ourselves to be. For some of us – for me at least, ambushed as I was by my tea bowl – it is necessary to be pulled into an uncommon kind of sensory experience in order to realize that the usual sense of individual self-existence can simply disappear. Apparently it was the most natural thing in the world for it to be spontaneously, painlessly blown away. Was there a means of deliberately getting back into that state?

Turning this question over in my New Delhi study, I leaned forward in my swivel chair and reached out to the Shiva statue, touching the squashed homunculus. The ego inside me wasn't quite this easy to put in its place. Whenever I tried to sideline or override the arrogant thing it just popped up somewhere else, usually in a different shape. I wondered, as I squinted at the dimly visible humanoid figure, if my heightened apperception of the Japanese tea bowl was linked to my more recent discovery of detachment from vision. In a sense, the transformed tea bowl furnished a precedent for what was to come: the two experiences were categorically similar, in that each in its own way involved the suspension of the sense of ego that normally permeates the act of seeing. And each of those incidents occurred as an unlooked-for response to concentrated metaphysical study. I knew that what drew me back to the incident in Ottawa was a desire to enter more knowingly into its ground or source, an experience of total fearless absorption. If I could do that, and as a result find greater self-purchase and resilience, it might help me deal with my mounting spinal and sciatic pain. For that the internal homunculus was useless.

However, over the next few months in New Delhi there would be no further bouts of metaphysical study, speculation, or experimenting. The mentalist was about to be enmeshed by what he came to think of later as the Revenge of the Flesh.

3 FACTOR X: THE CENTRIPETAL PULL OF THE BODY

By the end of 1988 the long, slow increase in bodily pain had at last reached a level that compelled me to ask myself whether my current mode of life was sustainable. It took a positive effort of will now to keep my attention directed outward toward the activity of the moment, instead of having it sucked inward to lodge in the aching or stabbing sensations that dominated the inner landscape of bodily feeling. My work output was as yet unimpaired, but sitting had become so difficult that I had to lie down at intervals on a yoga mat spread out on the floor of my office, where I listened to Ann read to me and dictated my telegrams to headquarters. The High Commission's resident Canadian doctor knew all about my back problem and the efforts I had made to accommodate it. He could do little but suggest that I might finally be approaching a watershed.

The main medical subject of this book is RP and its entanglement with self, but the eye disease and its management never occur in a vacuum. In every RP life there is sure to be some other issue rumbling away, some Factor X that intersects with the problem of vision loss and makes it more difficult and complex. It might be family or marital strife, conflicts at work, financial woes, substance abuse – any of the problems that can complicate or distort a life. My Factor X was pain in the spine, long nerves, and muscles. When I began to write this personal narrative I decided to make only the minimal necessary references to the pain problem up until 1989, because this would reflect the way I was actually trying to live my life. My way of dealing with Factor X was to ignore it as much as possible and carry on. But the pain and inflexibility were always there as a drag or limiting force. It was in Delhi that I finally began to feel the full cumulative effects of decades of overcompensation, of pushing too long and too hard.

The back problem began when I was fourteen. Its onset may have been due to a diving accident, but degenerative disc disease does not necessarily require a trigger incident to get started. At any rate it was after my spectacular bellyflop that the pain began in the lower back and the sciatic nerve running down the left leg. A three-week family road trip had been scheduled to begin a couple of days later, and the long hours of cramped sitting exacerbated the pain. No doctor was consulted, either en route or when we returned home.

That fall I began high school, and for the next three years the back problem was part of the general funk or muddle through which I was slogging, deeply uncomfortable in my own skin. Just as I then thought of my visual limitations as a kind of personal ineptitude, I regarded the situational back pains as signs of weakness. Sports had become doubly fraught: in track and field events I would strain my eyes and nerves to avoid collisions, only to wind up limping off the field with resurgent sciatic pain. This made me feel like a wimp. At home the problem was dismissed as growing pains, and once again no doctor was consulted.

When at seventeen I learned I had RP and plunged into reactive denial, I buried the back problem with the visual. Between bad patches of nerve pain I forgot or turned my mind away from it. At university I tried to do what my friends did – swim the strokes that are hardest on the lumbar spine, go canoeing, carry my own canoe – thus adding to the mounting strain on the affected disc. I didn't push myself into these activities so much as sleepwalk through them. But eventually the increasing symptoms became difficult to ignore. Instead of taking pride in my unusual height I came to see it as a ridiculous joke; I was apparently a failed vertebrate.

All of that changed completely in December 1965. When my denial was shattered and I finally "owned" my RP – that is the way I would have expressed it then – I was ready to own the rest of me too. I made an appointment with an orthopaedic specialist who ordered the usual tests, and it was only when he went over the results with me that I learned that I had a herniated disc. By this time things had progressed too far for any sort of preventive measures to make much difference. The disc soon ruptured to the point of incapacitating me, and surgery was performed to remove the extruded material. The results were successful enough that for several years I was relatively free of pain. I adopted a regimen of back exercises and avoided heavy lifting, and accepted the back condition as something I could manage by applying the right skills. When I set off for my Japan adventure in 1968 I wore an ultra-light backpack with very little in it.

In 1972 I experienced a flare-up of the old symptoms, and tests revealed that more disc material had been extruded from the lumbar spine. A second back operation followed, and this time the results were not quite so positive. After this I would have moderate chronic pain that slowly over the years became immoderate. In 1980 during our Japan posting I went through a bad period that had me bedridden and crawling to the bathroom. This went on for a week or so. But lots of people had sprung backs; it was a straightforward enough problem, and I still figured I could keep slogging along with mine.

It was during the five years in Ottawa after the Tokyo posting that I began to experience pain not only in the lower but the middle and upper spine, the hips and sacroiliac joints, and the muscles of the back, shoulders, and neck, together with increasingly frequent and severe muscle-tension headaches. I didn't understand it, and neither did the doctors I consulted: it would be many more years before I got even a provisional diagnosis. I tried chiropractors and standard physiotherapy, but nothing changed. I thought that at least part of the problem must be the long hours I was working in relative immobility at my desk, so I began to go swimming in the evenings and on weekends. But although I enjoyed swimming it didn't help much with the chronic pain and growing stiffness, and eventually even the swimming became difficult. This in brief was the background to the deteriorating situation that I faced in New Delhi in 1988–89.

In January 1989 I decided to give myself a little break – an extended weekend – both from my work and my Vedantic texts. This would allow me to attend a four-day seminar on Tibetan Buddhism to be conducted by Kyabgon Drikung Chetsang Rinpoche, an eminent lama of the Kagyu school. I was interested in the Tibetan Kagyus because they had preserved the Yogacharin teachings, one of the ancient Indian schools of Buddhism I had been reading about. When I arrived at the Ashoka Mission I found that I was the only attendee who had not taken Buddhist vows of one sort or another – and the only one to sit

on a chair. The others sat cross-legged on the floor or arranged themselves on benches. My back hurt like hell, but I was determined that
that should not interfere with my absorption of what the Rinpoche
had to say. This turned out to be a beautiful explication of classical
Buddhism in all its intricacy and logical consistency. More specifically
it was a presentation of the *mahamudra*, a path to liberation favoured
by the Kagyu school.

As I sat there day after day for four days, listening intently, a part
of my mind was entangled with the pain and exasperated with the
entanglement. I was also very aware of the irony of my situation.
Here I was, nailed to the body and listening to a teacher whose lead-
off subject just happened to be suffering or *duhkha*. Vedanta highlights the same concept and labels it with the same Sanskrit word.
The Rinpoche told us that the only effective way to deal with duhkha,
either as physical or psychological pain, was to see how the false sense
of self became attached to body and mind. I had known for months
that this was what I had to do with aversive body-sensations, just as
I had done with vision. And at the Ashoka Mission I had the perfect
opportunity to do it, to witness the sense of "I" that was all snarled
up with the hot grid radiating from my spine. But deep down I was
furious. I just wanted the burning to stop.

Yet the enmeshment with pain existed in only one part of my mind,
the introsensory. With the greater part I was listening to the Rinpoche's
discourse as he laid out the elements of the Kagyu path, attending to
it closely, admiring and thinking about it in the rest intervals, and
making detailed notes on a pocket Dictaphone during the lunch
periods. All of this happened at centre stage; the pain itself and my
negative reaction to it were pushed into the wings. I could split the
mind in this way just as all of us can when we really have to.

At the end of the fourth day, as dusk was falling, I was straining to
focus on the closing ceremony through a pulsing tangle of whole-body
pain so dense and thick that it seemed to spread out halfway across
the room. I watched the dim forms of the Tibetan monks, these patient,
generous, impoverished refugees who were doing their best to help
us, as they elevated their offerings of flowers and fruit against the
background noise of grating traffic and a nearby dogfight. For some
reason I found this little ceremony deeply affecting, and was unexpectedly moved to tears. I felt immensely glad that I had come.

I pretty well collapsed when I got back home, and for a week or so
I could not walk more than a few steps. Attending the Buddhist

seminar had not in itself caused any further damage to the spine, but once I got back on my feet it was obvious to me and to Pressi that I could not go on like this. It was also obvious to my colleagues: arrangements were made to have me medically evacuated to Ottawa. By February I was installed in an Ottawa hotel room and enrolled in an intensive two-month program at the Ottawa Rehabilitation Centre, a component of the General Hospital complex. Pressi was worried sick, but she had to stay behind to care for and encourage Evan. For the next two months we relied on weekly telephone chats to reassure one another that everything was just fine.

However, the results of the program were not encouraging. I was diagnosed with chronic and refractory spinal pain caused by degenerative disc disease and the resulting long-term mechanical changes to the spinal column. Superimposed on this was myofascial or soft-tissue pain syndrome, a clinically recognized condition of indeterminate origin. Once again my back did not respond to physiotherapy, and the occupational therapists were unable to come up with alternative seating that I could tolerate. My only recourse was to medicate the pain as necessary and "pace" my activities. Given the nature of my work, which involved close monitoring and reporting on political trends and crises, this was hard to do.

I went back to India to work as much as I could, but found it very difficult to put in a full day. Finally I accepted the inevitable. I began to wind up my affairs, and by late summer we were moved back to Ottawa. In the fall I got started on the intricate business of qualifying as an official hypergimp under the government employees disability plan, and although the application process took time the result was never in doubt. In January 1990 I was declared disabled and put out to pasture. And that was that: the functionary had disappeared, not just from Delhi and Ottawa but from my life.

I hoped that after that my physical condition might settle down a little, but it slowly degraded and got more complex. It would take another fifteen years for further changes to be attributed to a rare genetic disorder known as NARP, which I will describe in subsequent chapters. What I was heading into without knowing it was a kind of figure-ground reversal in my sensory and physical life. Years before it was the manifest symptoms of RP that had constituted the figure or foreground reality of daily functioning, while pain simmered in the background except during acute episodes. But starting in that second year in New Delhi it was this new complex of symptoms, this elaboration of Factor X, that would tend to push into the foreground of awareness. Even during its bizarre final stages RP was to be a less significant issue in my life, replaced eventually by the relative stability and predictability of total functional blindness.

It was with very mixed feelings that I was shunted onto the disabled list. I felt sorry, to put it mildly, that there would be no more postings abroad. The department had given me some great opportunities – not just to go here and there and do this and that, but to do it all with some very smart and interesting people. But the professional role of foreign service wonk had long ceased to have any bearing on my sense of identity. The old diplomatic mask or persona had been left on the shelf inside my office at the High Commission in Delhi: there it would slowly gather dust and leer down invisibly on my successors. As for the kind of work I would have been doing back at headquarters, I had to admit that I wouldn't miss it. I was physically drained, and there was relief in the thought that I could at last begin structuring my days around the ups and downs of my physical condition.

Of course I was frustrated, sometimes intensely, by my physical limitations and sometimes immobilized by them. Pressi and I were also concerned about the reduction in my income and her uncertain job prospects. She would once again face the classic dilemma of the repatriated foreign service spouse – that of having to start over from scratch yet again. At least I would have the opportunity to concentrate whatever energies I could muster on my avocational interests. Fortunately mine was not the kind of pain problem that completely overwhelms the patient and compels large and continuous doses of narcotic painkillers. I had latitude between the episodes of bad pain and exhaustion to experience a relatively clear mind, and so pursue my private studies and my interest in writing. I even had hopes that the focus on study or writing could at times be a way of de-emphasizing the pain.

The broadest question that arose out of my changing circumstances was not their practical implications – the adaptive strategies could be worked out one step at a time – but the overall meaning that would attach to this kind of life. What did I make of this new state of affairs, or what did it make of me? This was not an abstract but a "personal" question bearing on identity. One of the ways in which the question could be expressed was the one that had goaded me during the Tibetan Buddhist seminar: When pain cannot be eliminated, are we bound to identify with it? Is our "I" or essential nature inseparable from the afflicted body, no matter what the Buddhist and Vedantic philosophers may say to the contrary? If so, had I managed somehow to disidentify from the eyes and faculty of vision only because getting free of them was "easier" than disidentifying from pain?

For many people, especially those whose pain is truly overwhelming, the problem of aversive sensation is the greatest challenge that the body imposes on the life of the mind and the life of the spirit. Even in my own less extreme circumstances, it was only slowly and by degrees that I learned how to accommodate the strong centripetal pull of my body, while dealing with the peculiarities of late-stage R P. As to where I might now invest my available energy, the mature Advaita Vedanta that developed out of the Upanishads was the goal toward which I was implicitly heading during my time in New Delhi, the Buddhist seminar notwithstanding. But once I was back in Ottawa I sometimes approached that goal sideways or crabwise with my attention fixed on something else.

The reason for this indirection or faltering is simple enough. It is hard to absorb and live a philosophy such as Advaita amid the scatter and unexpected lurches of ordinary life. Distractions, competing priorities and inner uncertainties can clutter or seemingly obliterate the path. I can illustrate this in spades by picking up my narrative again after our move back to Ottawa, and describe some of the twists and turns that I never could have anticipated.

5

Into the Pre-visual Centre

1 SKIRTING THE EDGE

Making the transition to life back in Ottawa, which would be our home from now on, proved to be easiest for the youngest of us. Evan slipped effortlessly into the local student scene without a backward glance toward India. The adults, meanwhile, had to retrench. The provisions of the disability allowance make it very difficult for its recipients to experiment with part-time or occasional work, even if they could rally the physical capacity to make the attempt. So while I stayed home Pressi began the hard slogging and networking required to establish herself locally as a teacher of English as a second language.

My first priority in the winter of 1989–90 was to learn braille, which I found I quite enjoyed once I got into it. Priority number two was to get myself up to speed on the new voice-output computer that would greatly enhance my capacity to store data and write independently, once I had something worth writing. As I worked away at the word processing, screen-voicing, and other programs, I had to exercise patience to accommodate my continual back and sacroiliac pain. I found that this kind of pain imposed non-negotiable limits on how long I could work at the computer, even when I got down on my back with the keyboard propped up against my thighs.

When I had grown sufficiently familiar with this new system to think of really doing something with it, I found myself taken anew by the old urge to write fiction. The would-be Northern Borges was back. It was amazing: there he was, big as life, offering or demanding to be my new official persona. It would take time before I was able to see that under his writerly veneer he was the same old ego who had been there all along. He hated the idea of my getting any more deeply involved in ego-bashing philosophical studies. He quickly set up camp in a region of my mind that was soon given over completely to authorial ambition. There was in all of this the simple desire for self-expression through writing, but this healthy impulse was bundled inside an ambition for critical acclaim and financial success.

Yet in an entirely separate space within my skull, so habituated had I become at External Affairs to the dissociation of doing Official Persona work during the day and private study in the evenings, I was continuing until late every night to read just the sort of thing that challenged all forms of conventional identity, authorial or otherwise. Some of this material was being recorded by the generous local volunteers whom I had recently recruited and equipped with specially adapted CNIB tape recorders. I was very aware of the split between the daytime and evening regions of my mind, and found this schism uncomfortable because it marked an apparent conflict or uncertainty regarding my fundamental goals. Did I want to penetrate deeply into Indian spirituality, or become a literary lion? For the time being I played at not letting the one part of my mind know what the other was up to.

In my attempts to create fiction I struggled for over a year to develop one story idea after another – I noticed with some discomfort that they were becoming more and more autobiographical – but it was no good. I kept getting stuck: the writer's block was still there, still apparently unresolvable. I just couldn't believe that I had totally lost the chops that enabled me a few years earlier to write fluently and get published. There was something going on that I didn't understand, and finally it began to give me the creeps. In the end I did not delete my drafts but moved them to an obscure sub-subdirectory on my hard drive, where I could just forget about them. This was the digital equivalent of burying a body in the backyard.

For a few weeks I keenly felt the absence of the project that had given definition to my days. But my reading interests were branching out of their own accord into new areas, and these represented whole libraries of material that even a full-time study program could scarcely begin to tap. If I needed a new label for myself, and of course I told myself that I didn't, it would be that of the self-starting private student or autodidact. What better avocation for the retiree? Yet whenever I ran into former colleagues who asked what I was up to, and told them, I seemed to draw a blank. They invariably asked what all this philosophical head-banging was good for, and how I could even do it without "taking courses" or otherwise getting officially certified.

My new reading interests at this time were opened up and stimulated by poet and essayist Dennis Lee, whose investigations into Western philosophy outstripped anything I had attempted in that field. I was fascinated by his books, specifically those in audio format that were available from the CNIB. I have recently gone back to one of those works, *Body Music* an intense and intimate exploration of poetics.[1] In 1989 or 1990 I impulsively wrote a letter to Dennis Lee through his publisher, outlining in a fumbling sort of way what I had been up to. He responded with enthusiasm, and a canny sense of what I might be ready to look into next. So it was that Dennis became my host or maître d' for the rich, vivifying feast served up by the Western spiritual tradition known as the negative way or *via negativa*. As I was to learn over the following years, the insights opened up by this tradition proved in many cases to be strikingly similar to the disclosures of Advaita Vedanta and Buddhism.[2]

Dennis led off by urging me to read two basic books: Michael Sells's *Mystical Languages of Unsaying*[3] and Raymond Blakney's *Meister Eckhart, A Modern Translation*.[4] The Sells book was like nothing I had ever read. It was a selective but highly authoritative account of how the most gifted and iconoclastic thinkers within the Christian, Islamic, and Jewish traditions implicitly deconstruct our conventional notions regarding "God." They accomplish this potentially dangerous and revelatory work by drawing upon the logic and ingenious cosmology of Neoplatonism. The result, as arrived at by brilliant intuitives such as the Irish theologian John Scotus Eriugena (c. 800–c. 877), the German Neoplatonist Meister Eckhart (c. 1260–c. 1328), the anonymous author of the fourteenth-century work of Christian mysticism, *The Cloud of Unknowing*, and the Spanish Islamic sage Ibn Araby (1165–1240), was the evocation of an absolute and all-encompassing reality that was both immanent and transcendent. This should have been more than enough for me to absorb and ponder over. But during this same period – and here once again I was effectively partitioning my brain into two separate work stations – I was studying Nagarjuna (c. 150–c. 250), the Buddhist philosopher who most effectively negates and cancels out all conventional realities. I took all this in, floating above the whole show without putting my money on any one tradition or champion.

I had to admit to myself that I found Nagarjuna and the masters of the Western negative way more interesting than much of the

Vedanta I had read up until then. Yet my most important experiences in India – with Mahabalipuram Temple and the Shiva-figure, with the Gita and Upanishads, and with visual detachment – seemed to point me toward the higher or Advaita Vedanta. I still had the feeling that Advaita was the richest seam of usable ore I had yet come upon. If I had made it a point of finding out what the Upanishads had led to in subsequent Vedantic thought, I would have discovered a natural entryway into Advaitic insight. Why was I now turning from the potential I had glimpsed in the Upanishads to alternative traditions? The new material was marvellous in its own way, but I began to wonder about my priorities. Something was holding me back from the higher Vedanta as I then muddily sensed or conceived of it, an obscure uneasiness concerning its demands on the interior life. By contrast, my purely intellectual engagement with Eckhart and Nagarjuna was unthreatening and enjoyable.

Over the months an odd sort of pattern emerged. The uneasiness I sometimes experienced when I toggled back and forth between Vedanta and my new resources proved to have something in common with the guardedness that would steal over me in New Delhi when I sat still and allowed the mind to go blank, as the first step toward searching inwardly for what I thought of as the bare individual consciousness. And curiously enough, the negative reaction provoked by my recent attempts to write autobiographical fiction had the same sort of inner taste, though more concentrated and "personal." I dealt with these sources of negativity – or rather didn't – by suppressing or "forgetting" them. There was something down inside me that I did not want to "see."

Fortunately this internal resistance did not interfere with the refreshing experience of detachment from vision. I still practised it, if objective seeing can be called a practice. This was a pretty good indication that insight into one kind of false selfing, the kind that is based on an indiscriminate identification with eyesight, could be liberating even for people who were wary of plunging into Advaita. An insight could also spread out beyond its original boundaries. Visual detachment had first been triggered by the conviction that the real self was not the physical apparatus with its senses; since then I had come to feel that the self also stood back from the entire psychophysical complex.

Because that complex includes our most cherished mental representations of identity, the implications seemed huge once you got a glimmer of them. If the real self stood separate from all our notions regarding selfhood because unlike them it was not in itself a mental construct, then it could not be accurately represented by any concept within the mind. In other words, the real self was literally unthinkable and inconceivable. It would have to be known in some completely different, non-conceptual, intuitive way.

Every so often during that period I would impulsively say something that seemed to be aimed at this different kind of knowing, startling both myself and whomever I happened to be talking to. One day a young man I will call Eddie recounted to me in some distress a dream he had had the night before. It was about his girlfriend and himself. His relationship with this young woman had apparently become tangled up in contradictory feelings that both drew the couple together and pushed them apart.

What struck me as I listened to Eddie was the way the dream was depicted. As sometimes happens during dreams, the dreamer was viewing himself the way we normally view another person, from a little distance, as though the dreamer were floating outside his own dream-body. The principal image of the dream was that of Eddie and his girlfriend standing and embracing each other, locked together fiercely in a way that was both clinging and combative. The two figures were saturated with all the charged thoughts and feelings that my young friend had been wrestling with for days.

When Eddie finally fell silent I said the first thing that came into my mind. "If you were observed to be the man who was standing there all tangled up with his partner, and saturated with his own feelings, then who or what was doing the observing?" This produced a kind of startle response. "That," he said in a voice that had risen abruptly in pitch, "puts a whole new slant on things." Then we just sort of stared at each other. Or rather I could feel him staring at me. I said, "Isn't this actually the way it is all the time even outside of dreams? The only difference is that when we're awake the observing of what we conventionally take to be ourselves comes from somewhere deep inside." After that neither of us knew what to say. I wish I could have found the right words, for I think Eddie went away with the feeling that he was harbouring some kind of incubus.

It was also at about this time that Pressi and I were inveigled into attending a cocktail party, one of those wretched stand-up affairs where people just mill about and don't get properly fed. Going to such a function didn't make much sense because of the strain it

imposed on my back, and after this one I never went to another. The
room was uncomfortably crowded. Pressi soon disappeared into the
flow, and after a few minutes I was joined by an acquaintance whom
I am going to call Radhika. Our talk quickly turned to her current
spiritual involvement. She was a member of a New Age Hinduish sort
of group with its own guru, a man whose teachings were based on
an unfortunately literalist interpretation of one of those old Indian
myths that has its counterpart in many other cultures. The myth had
to do with an original divine light or fire, which had lost some of its
substance when part of the light was divided up and encased in multiple, scattered embodiments.

"I now know what I am," said Radhika in a voice brimming with
confidence. "I am a tiny speck of divine light."

I should have kept my mouth shut. No doubt my back was already
sore from the standing, and perhaps I was grumpy. At any rate I said,
"Have you ever seen it?"

"Seen what?"

"The speck of light." She hesitated, and I went on. "The only way
to actually know that you are such a thing without taking somebody
else's word for it is to observe it yourself. But even if you did, who
would be the 'you' who did the observing? And who would be the
speck of light?"

She just stood there. Oh no, I thought, you've done it again. You
oaf. You're not fit to be in company. Then some friend of hers popped
up and claimed her, and we got separated in the surge. I never saw
Radhika again, but I heard a few months later that she had quit the
group and was getting married to a regular sort of worldly guy.

When I looked back later at these incidents and a couple of others
like them, what intrigued me was the spontaneous and unguarded
nature of the responses I provoked. Nobody tried to get around the
questions. Nobody said, "Go on, it was just a dream and dreams
don't make any sense anyway," or "Part of me observes myself and
the other part gets observed, so what's the big deal?" Apparently the
abruptness and seeming naïveté of the questions made this kind of
sophistry impossible.

The effect of questions like these is to undercut our fixed notions
that we are some kind of object, physical or mental or a combination
of the two, turning that perspective inside out. This applies whether
we are observing someone else or ourselves. The observer discovers
that he or she is occupying a position separate from body and feelings

and thoughts – separate, in other words, from everything we take to be the objective self. This would include Eddy's tense body and tangled emotions, and the imagined object that was Radhika's speck of light. With the exception of that non-existent speck, it is possible to pull back from all these physical or mental elements and simply observe them. This "works" because the invisible observer-position is real – although it is normally only implicit or hidden. In the exchanges that I described above the switch of perspective is definite enough and rapid enough that the observer has a rare moment of disorientation or wonder, during which the usual sense of identity and placement evaporate. I would learn years later that this kind of experience is identified by Advaita Vedanta as subject/object discrimination, a means for analytically and experientially identifying the true observer-self.

The encounters I have described here were not a mere game in which I as interrogator enjoyed an advantage. In asking the questions in the way I did, just blurting them out without premeditation, I found myself occupying the same peculiar locus as my companion. What I was trying to discover was not a new and better idea about the nature of self, nor an ego of any sort I had ever heard of, but something far more existential and immediate: the inner experiential place where the "I" – perhaps the *real* "I" – observes the mind, body, and world. I called it my centre. It was the conviction that this centre must be real that had led me to my first experience of detachment from vision in New Delhi. Now I was trying to find that centre in a new way, one that had nothing to do with vision. I was compulsively asking other people to find their centre so that I might find my own, like a dog who has forgotten where his bone is buried and expects his litter-mates to point it out to him. It was all backwards: I was subcontracting a job of excavation that I could only do alone.

2 JUST BY WALKING

Fortunately for me there was one prosaic daily activity, that of white cane walking, in which some intimation of the subtle centre could naturally arise. In fact it had to arise: it was hard for me to enjoy a long walk if it didn't. To make this clear I have to begin with the experience of the sighted walker, as our standard of comparison. His or her movements are to a great extent unmindful or automatic. When a person with normal or at least adequate eyesight goes for a walk, it is vision that is chiefly responsible for the sense of spatial context

in which she gets from here to there. Her other perceptions and sensations – sounds, odours, the feelings of the moving body – are fitted
into or referred to the stable visual manifold.

All this happens effortlessly in a way that both facilitates mobility
and reinforces naive visual materialism. In the sighted walker's unreflective mind it is the visual image, say that of a big eighteen-wheel
truck, which not only has primacy over but actually seems to propa-
gate the sound of the air horn and the smell of diesel. It is always the
visual percept that "has" other sensory attributes as its apparent
auxiliaries. There could never be a sound or odour that "had" a visual
image, in the sense of entraining it as a subordinate phenomenon. In
other words, the visual materialist automatically takes the image to
be the physical thing-in-itself, the "thing" that actually generates the
associated sounds, odours, and touch sensations.

By the early 1990s my vision was no longer the paramount sense
faculty. My light perception still gave me a sense of visual space, but
because of my by now extreme tunnel or pinhole vision that space
was only straight-ahead space. I could perceive nothing but the way
before me and that only very vaguely, often failing to see obstacles
right in my path. The dissonance between vision and touch – the cane
locating over and over again those little obstacles that the eyes could
not see – made the visual array seem increasingly unreal.

This sense of unreality was reinforced by the excessively fractional-
ized view that presented itself whenever I looked off to either side as
I continued to walk forward. Each of these glances opened up another
narrow and entirely novel slice of space, its contents determined by
the extent to which I turned my head or shifted my eyes. These discrete
slices of vision were totally unconnected with one another; there was
no subliminal sense of a broad field or background within which they
could cohere. There was in fact no real visual environment – just
isolated visual events.

On top of that, the position of a visual object would often be indeterminate when its shape and identity were ambiguous. It could seem
to be far off at one moment and startlingly near at the next. This abrupt
and entirely illusory spatial transposition of things was a further element that sometimes rendered dreamlike the ordinary experience of
going for a walk. The upshot of all this was that my residual sightedness was becoming increasingly unreliable even as a secondary component of practical navigation. The very sense of visual presence – both
my own presence and that of the world – was becoming tenuous.

As a result, the space that I experientially occupied when I went for my long daily walks was mainly non-visual. It was to a large extent proprioceptive, opened up and marked off by my swinging arms and legs and by the oscillating axis connecting my right hand to the swinging cane-tip. This was a felt space that travelled with me, so to speak, remaining constant no matter how far I got from home. It varied only as a consequence of my tactile discoveries – those unseen obstacles that when touched with the cane, and skirted as I veered to the left or right, effectively reshaped my walking-space. Overlying this proprioceptive space was the larger space opened up by sound, especially the sounds of approaching cars and traffic farther off, of near and distant birds, and the flat or echoing cane taps directly before me. The third spatial element – and this was the problematical one – was the interconnected planes and lines of muscular or nerve pain. This pain had the potential, if it became too obtrusive, of blurring the envelope of proprioceptive space and roughening or even impairing my gait.

These circumstances raise two basic questions, or at least they did for me. The first had to do with simply understanding the great sensory change I was continuing to experience, which when you stopped to think about it was quite mysterious. Here I was with vision that had been reduced to a narrow array of images that were sometimes uninterpretable. Yet for most people it is normal field vision that acts as the frame for all the other external senses, as in the example of the eighteen-wheeler above. The inputs from those senses are regularly referred to visual evidence to give them material substance, to invoke the physical "thing" that is being perceived. Thus one might think that the shredding away and disappearance of vision would be experienced as a gaping vacuum, a background nothingness against which episodic sounds and vagrant touch sensations and passing odours would come into being, fail to cohere, and eventually melt away. I knew that something like this could be experienced at first by the person who is suddenly and totally blinded.

But my moment-to-moment experience, as fragmentary as it sometimes was, still had an underlay or foundation of coherence. Something was somehow managing to tie together my disparate sense-impressions into a whole. Because of my fragmented vision, that whole could at times be very inadequate and exasperating, but it was always a single field of experience that belonged somehow together. Even in conditions of total darkness this something, which I was reluctant to prematurely identify by name, was serving as the receptive ground of my immediate sensing. It was deeper and more constant than the sense-data themselves.

This receptive ground was not a neurological structure. I am aware that the brain has a remarkable capacity to "rewire" its intricate synaptic networks in response to serious loss in one sensory modality, so that the other modalities may be integrated and coordinated in new ways. But what I am referring to here is an actual inner presence, "inner" in the sense that it belongs to the broad category of conscious-ness, as distinct from brain. Given the right kind of attention, it can be directly experienced, intuited, or "felt."

But at the time I am documenting here, this was a very subtle and sometimes elusive presence. Yet whenever I dissolved absent-mindedly into it, the presence turned out to be nothing other than the light of awareness – awareness of the inflow of sensory phenomena. I found that when the awareness was clear, that is, not gummed up by me, the coordination of the external senses went well, and walking was reasonably efficient. When, on the other hand, this awareness was occluded because I was distracted by something, there would be trouble. And yet one had the feeling that this awareness was still "down there" or "in there." The metaphor I employed for this uniquely subtle reality or agency was that of the ground bass, as deployed in certain types of Western and Indian classical music. The bass note is always there, always sounding, although one might not be consistently cognizant of it.

My second basic question was not phenomenological or analytical but entirely practical. It had to do with my future as a pedestrian. How was I to continue walking like this, with inadequate vision and with increasingly compromised muscles, and avoid the inner tension that would make white cane walking an exhausting ordeal rather than a good workout? I was concerned about this, for in recent years the combination of vision loss and steadily amplifying pain had been paring back the opportunities for simple physical pleasure. As a way of getting my circumstances into perspective, I compared myself first to the sort of RP patient who had my degree of vision loss and used a cane, but was still tied desperately to half-dissolved images, and then to the RP patient who was trying to compensate by ignoring images and pouring everything he had into intense cane-work.

Because of his clinging to unreliable and transient visual phenomena, the person struggling with RP who could not let go of images was not grounded in anything real. And because of the resulting distraction he was only half-aware of what his cane arm was doing. His attention was jerked about from moment to moment by competing inputs of image, sound, touch, and body-movements, with nothing constant to inwardly anchor them. This turned not only practical mobility but self-feeling into a very jagged experience, even in the absence of physical pain. Yet the only real difference between this person and me was that he had not yet discovered visual detachment.

A different sort of problem faced the other person with RP, the one whose response to white cane training was to intensely identify with what his cane arm and legs were doing. He was grounded in the wrong thing. Over-identification with body movements creates tension, just the kind of muscle tension that I now had to avoid. The great problem for this man as for the other described above was a want of detachment – detachment not from images, in his case, but from the stress of being a tense physical "doer."

As for me, my circumstances were such that I was being drawn by one welcome factor, that of visual detachment, and pushed hard by another that was not welcome at all, my nerve and muscle pain, to find a way of walking that was both alert to all sensations and relaxed. I had already developed the habit of processing visual information from what I had come to think of as an unperturbed interior position. I knew that this "inner" place or space was not in itself visual but pre-visual. It was my pre-visual conscious centre. It seemed to me that some of the stress of white cane walking with compromised muscles could be diluted if I could enlist or confirm this same interior space as the single centre from which I not only saw detachedly, but might walk detachedly. To knowingly and relaxedly be that centre would mean letting go of the habit of imposing myself onto the pain sensations, in an effort to dominate them, and the alternative habit of trying to pretend that they did not exist. Evidently I *as consciousness* had to form the counter-habit of just observing sensations from within, without becoming entangled in them. This seemed like a tall order.

As I made the first steps toward reorienting myself in this way the bare ego-sense tried as usual to interfere, just as it had done prior to the letting-go into visual detachment back in Delhi. Now, despite my best intentions, it was doing its damnedest to wrap itself around aversive body-sensations, clinging to them stupidly as the aggrieved sufferer, clinging so tightly that there was no space between them and the sense of "I." Or the ego would sometimes do the opposite, fleeing from the pain into the mind where it would compulsively count my steps or repeat a word over and over again in order to distract itself. In either case it was trying to affirm its illusory sense of being the real centre of things.

The ego had plenty of opportunity to play these games, for in the first half of the nineties I was experiencing a set of problems that had not yet been properly diagnosed. White cane walking exacerbated this condition by provoking muscle knots, spasticity, and pain in the right arm, shoulder, and neck, and extreme tightness in other muscles running up from or around the scapula and clavicle. I equipped myself with the lightest possible aluminum cane and learned how to take some of the edge off the muscle pain through stretching, pressure-point release, and the application of heat and cold, as the problems stubbornly persisted.

What I learned during those first years back in Ottawa, just by walking, was that despite these physical problems it was sometimes possible to be at an inner remove from the aching body when it was in motion. Of course there were days when muscle knots or spasticity compelled me to head back home and down tools, but there were other times when I could centre myself in relation to body-feelings in exactly the same way as I did with respect to visual images. I was also discovering that the same kind of detachment was possible in relation to the ordinary, vagrant thoughts and memories that typically arose during the course of a long walk. They could be allowed to just come and go. It seemed that every form of experience, from external sensing to internal feelings to mental operations, had exactly the same inner "centre." This was the place where the sense of core identity or I-ness should base itself all the time, I thought, for it had the paradoxical quality of being perfectly open to everything yet at the same time slightly but tellingly separate from every form of suffering.

It was this deep, nonphysical centre that served as my experiential manifold. It took in the presence of my moment-to-moment percep-tions and tied them together as their common ground. So far as I could see, the most fitting words for this inner reality were conscious-ness and its synonyms – awareness and sentience. I was coming to think of this presence – and more and more it really did have the feel of an actual presence – as consciousness pure and simple, conscious-ness as distinct from all perceived phenomena, the inner light of awareness. Consciousness illuminated every type of experience, physi-cal or mental, while somehow retaining its own autonomy. That is why it felt so satisfying to be centred in it. I had seen in Delhi that consciousness was not the ego and could not be found as an object; nevertheless, it could evidently be "felt" as spacious clarity or clear inner space. This kind of self-presence could at times be deeply affirming in its own right.

The experience of centredness described above, that special feeling of being the locus or rather the very actuality of autonomous consciousness, was the "thing" I had been trying to identify in my exchanges with Eddie and Radhika. The alert subtle centre was the reality that stood back from the whole psycho-physical complex. It was this consciousness-centre that had observed the swirl of body-based emotions and mental agitation in Eddie's dream; it was this that would have observed Radhika's speck of light if there had been any such thing. In this kind of experience as in every other, consciousness itself was the ultimate registrar of whatever came up. In all this it remained in itself apparently changeless.

I am writing about this retrospectively, of course, and I have to remind myself that at this time I tried to intuit these things rather than thoroughly thinking them out. Sometimes the feeling or intuition of consciousness as a living presence quite deserted me. That is because it can be very hard to knowingly and consistently occupy the bare I of consciousness. During my walks I would lose this centre over and over again and have to recede back into it. Sometimes, when the muscle or nerve pain was especially distracting, I couldn't "find" the consciousness or awareness-centre at all. It seemed to be nothing more than a notion, an imagined inner place which, curiously enough, I sometimes managed to stumble into by accident.

There was another form of distraction that cropped up during those walks, and I found it even more galling than my frequent identification with pain. It really rubbed my nose in my inability to remain centred. It went like this: sometimes as I paced along with some problem or other nibbling at my mind, I would get inwardly entangled in a bout of compulsive chain-thinking. These chains emerged mechanically from the unresolved problem. To be wrapped up in chains of pointless and obsessive thoughts not only amounted to bad strategy for the visually impaired pedestrian, but was a kind of bondage as well. It was somehow demeaning. I had never felt this so strongly before.

But on an especially good day – when the pain level was not too high and my thoughts were not driven by some new idea or burdened

by any particular problem – I could for a brief, welcome interval fully
occupy the centre, walk in a relaxed way that disengaged me from
the pain, and believe implicitly that this mode of being was absolutely
natural. It was in fact so natural that by rights it ought to be there all
the time. I wanted to fix it in place, patent it, bottle it, swallow it
down again and keep it safe within me once and for all.

Yet whenever in pursuit of this constancy I tried to reconcile the
conventional ideas of self and consciousness, I could get thoroughly
hung up. I tended to automatically objectify that which I had found
to be uniquely subjective: the inner light. This reversal of categories
(from subject to object) was apparently an artifact of thinking, perhaps
an unavoidable one. But then again when my mind was quiet and
not busy thinking, there was nothing that could be more obviously
present than the simple light of consciousness. That was when it felt
like the self. And even if it hadn't felt like anything at all, the bare
fact of its being right at the heart of all my sensing and knowing
meant that it was categorically – almost geometrically – my centre
or essence. Everything else – body-feelings, body-form, and the mind-
stream – were its dependent satellites or adjuncts. They were just fine
where they were, off-centre.

All this may give the impression that I was making some headway
in my project of clarifying the self, if not in detaching myself from
pain. The truth was more equivocal. Circumstances had made it possible for me to recede, at least irregularly or occasionally, into the
position of the interior observer who is mindful of the psycho-physical
complex and the shifting terrain. But I had not as yet taken to heart
the necessity of discipline, of finding a way to consistently return to
the detached perspective every time I lost it in a spurt of mental
abstraction or uncomfortable body-identification.

And there was a more serious problem: at this time I absolutely
could not have turned my attention inward to recede deeply into my
own consciousness – not even for the important practical purpose of
making myself more centred. Any attempt to probe through serious,
concentrated, introspective meditation would have been blocked by
my lifelong fear of what might be revealed. It was this fear, as I later
confirmed without any doubt, that was responsible for my finessed
and ambiguous attitude toward Advaita, and my failure to write
frankly autobiographical fiction.

As it turned out, however, none of this emotional back-pedalling
could prevent me from reading my way into two illuminating books

on the Advaitic version of Vedanta. These books, both by Arthur Osborne, introduced a broad international readership to the life and teachings of Ramana Maharshi, widely acclaimed as the most influential Advaitic master of the mid-twentieth century.[6] Once I got into Osborne's collection of Ramana's original works and the complementary biography of his life, reading the two of them back and forth, I found myself as it were in mid-air. It was as though I had launched myself off an ordinary-looking diving board only to find that the pool was edgeless and apparently bottomless. Here there was no catechism and no resort to logical analysis. Here there was an experience of boundlessness as Ramana knew it, a way of being that dissolved the boundary between inner and outer. One could fall into this or seem to do so, only to be pulled back by ego-based defensiveness. At least that's the way it was for me: I was both shaken and gratified.

The effect of discovering Ramana Maharshi – even as I was forced to reconfirm my inner defences – was to kindle within me a rather desperate desire for inner wholeness. The consequence of this development was the biggest personal crisis of my life, one that threatened me in a far deeper way than the original revelation of my RP. This crisis took the form not of a breakdown but a break-in, the smashing of the internal blockage or barrier against myself that had been erected during my childhood. Because of the nature of the problem that had compelled its construction, I knew that removing the barrier would badly mangle a particular self-construct to which I had long clung, and turn my life upside down. This could even have the effect of separating me from Pressi and Evan.

3 FACTOR Y: THE RETURN OF THE REPRESSED

When a person who faces the prospect of blindness gets into the habit of referring to some other life-problem connected with it as Factor X, my own example being spinal-muscular pain, and then later finally acknowledges the existence of a completely different problem that has always been just as tightly entangled with the threat to selfhood, the second problem deserves to have its own label. Thus: Factor Y. In my case I tried to hide Factor Y – my repressed homosexuality – not only from others but also from myself, to the extent that such self-deceit is even possible. Younger readers, and especially young gays who came of age after the Stonewall riot of 1969 launched the gay liberation movement, may find such

massive denial incomprehensible. The fact that I gave my homosexuality absolutely no expression in behaviour or speech, and as
little as possible in thought, owed something to the prevailing
homophobia of an earlier time; I was born in 1943. But the internal
repression owed much more to specific childhood experiences.

From the age of eight I was subjected to methodical sexual invasiveness and abuse, which I could neither avoid nor reveal to anyone
outside the tight circle of exploitation and emotional blackmail. What
made the abuse especially difficult to bear was the way in which it
violated primary relationships and poisoned family life. The effect
was such that by the age of thirteen I had indelibly connected what
had been done to me with the gay feelings that were pressing for
release. To acknowledge myself as gay – or rather as an "invert" or
"homo," in the language of the day – would have been to capitulate
to the abuse in some irremediable way, and surrender to its effects.
And I could not bear the thought that I had been not only used but
"turned" by my abusers.

Neither the particulars of the abuse nor the identities of its perpetrators are relevant to this study. But my resulting struggle with homosexuality is relevant in two ways. First, it illustrates how RP denial
in youth and early manhood can be complicated and reinforced by a
quite different kind of repression, one that stains the sense of visual
inadequacy with the deeper tint of a supposed unmanliness or unwor-
thiness. And second, the issue of sexual identity bears directly on one
of the principal themes of this book – the refractory or veiled nature
of the real self. All physical and psychological attributes, including
visual capacity and sexual orientation, no less than racial markers
and religious conviction, raise exactly the same question with regard
to self. Are they intrinsic or extrinsic to self? How much gravity is to
be assigned to each attribute in the context of a whole life? Can we
decide that ourselves, or is their relative importance fixed by nature?

I could if I chose go back over this and the previous chapters and
write a complete, full-length, between-the-lines second text made up
exclusively of the censored portions of my thoughts and feelings over
all those years. It would not just fill in the gaps of my narrative but
knock it awry, for the two texts would be based on contradictory
versions of identity. The inner split was so marked that it was like
being two persons. The public person, really an ego-ideal, was heterosexual; the other was left unnamed and did not bear scrutiny. He

or it was the personification of all the pathology that had been directed onto me during my childhood and early adolescence.

This dark version of the "I" got mixed up with my early R P denial through an implicit or half-conscious association of ideas. I saw gayness, like blindness, as a stunting or deformation of the whole self or whole man that I deeply needed to be. The spinal problem was part of the same perceived self-diminishment. I have already mentioned how in high school I would limp off the field after a track meet, exhausted by the visual strain of avoiding collisions, feeling the sciatic pain in my leg as wimpishness. What I did not mention was my further discomfort in the locker and shower rooms, where I shrank from my own nakedness and met no one's eyes.

All during high school I was painfully shy and withdrawn, socially inhibited by my own internalized homophobia. It was only after starting university that things opened up into a more or less normal student life with its close friendships and partying. But the combination of night blindness and gnawing doubts about my masculinity made dating an awkward business. Between my caneless blunderings and sexual self-doubt I often felt when I was with a girl that I was quite cut off from her. Looking back on those scenes from where I am now, I am free to call the tight invisible box in which I so often found myself by its proper name: the closet.

The repression of the knowledge of impending blindness is remarkably similar in its dynamics to the repression of gayness. Both conditions involve wilful denial, a desperate need to "pass" as normal, and an inner region of self-alienation. It is not just the conflicted gay but the unacknowledged R P sufferer who is "in the closet." It was in large part the pressure of being doubly closeted that finally pushed me, on that cold winter day in 1965, into accepting the visual fate that the doctor had so bluntly confirmed for me. Something had to give, somewhere.

My life would have followed a completely different course if at the same time I could have accepted my gayness. That would have been very difficult but not impossible, for I had initially gone to the doctor for counselling. I told him something about the early sexual abuse, referred to my uncertainties over my sexual orientation, and described the growing feeling of inner pressure. It took the doctor no time at all to assure me – categorically and with confident authority and without asking any questions – that I was not a homosexual. He said that although my early experiences might have been of the sort that could in many cases skew a boy's sexuality, in my own case the seemingly gay feelings were just "a temporary confusion." I remember his words exactly.

Apparently I did not conform to whatever stereotype served as this man's understanding of "inversion." I had told him about my crushes on a series of girls, and he took this fact alone to be proof positive that I was "normal." His assessment of me turned out to be dead wrong, but I was enormously relieved. I needed to believe him.

So it was that I set about remaking my life on the basis not of full but half-knowledge of the problems I was to face. With my growing confidence as an RP coper, and official certification as a heterosexual, I found that the old reserve that inhibited my contacts with girls had evaporated. When getting to know someone I would tell her about the RP as a simple matter of fact. I discovered that the girls I really liked appreciated this candour and understood immediately that the cane was a tool for living, not a sign of weakness or marginality. For the first time I was getting intimately involved with girls, with the usual unpredictable consequences. I was absolutely charmed by feminine beauty and I relished the energy of entanglement even when the entanglement went totally haywire. But inside this real need for involvement was a completely unreal sexual identity. Now after all these years I can only marvel at the plasticity not only of human behaviour but of what lies behind or within it, the private inner experience that can be shaped as much by chance, accident, and wishful thinking, as by genuine knowledge and desire.

My initial headlong rush into dating was dampened when I went to work for the family counselling agency in 1966. No doubt I was drawn willy-nilly to that line of work because a part of me was still trying to reopen the old sexual issue that had been buried rather than resolved. Unfortunately, my experience with the agency's director – the inveterate manipulator described in chapter 1 – could have the effect only of reinforcing my inner split. The man was absolutely obsessed with homosexuality. This was the issue that stood, or rather lurked unnamed, between us.

One of the director's key devices for discombobulating the men on his staff was to imply, subtly or not so subtly, that some of them were not entirely straight. He had a way of darkly insinuating the term "latency" into a conversation, as a deliberate if coded reference to this issue. On one memorable occasion he scrawled the word onto a blackboard during an evening "development" or "rap" session attended exclusively by the agency's male counsellors, then turned around and glared at us, waiting for someone to say something. I couldn't believe it. This man fancied and to some extent presented himself as a Freudian. But if he had ever actually studied the handsomely bound set of Sigmund Freud's complete works on show in his office, he had forgotten that Freud's usage of the word "latency" was a reference not to buried homosexuality, but to the natural stage of childhood development that precedes puberty. Some of the others sitting in that room must have realized this too. Yet none of us said a word.

With me at least (I can't speak for the others) the director could be more insinuatingly personal, even when resorting to indirection and anecdote. One day I accompanied him as he paid some kind of agency-related business call, and while we were walking back to the office he casually observed that a former client of his had recently committed suicide. "Lovely man," he added, "a homosexual." I glanced at him and saw that he was smiling. I had the distinct impression that he was making this up, just vaporizing, supposedly for my benefit.

On another occasion he described a grotesque tableau that he had unexpectedly come upon late one night in Montreal, when he was taking a short cut through an alley. Five or six policeman were standing around a man who was lying motionless on the ground. One of them was giving the man a kick, rounding off what had evidently been a group assault. Another policeman began to urinate on the prostrate figure. "Homosexual," the director explained, that in itself supposedly being a sufficient explanation. He claimed that he plunged into the scene and rescued the victim.

I didn't believe that for a moment, nor indeed any of the story, for once again his account had the quality of a tall tale fabricated for a specific purpose. But the question of veracity was really immaterial. Taken together with the earlier reference to his dead client, the message was clear: if you give in to being queer you will be brutalized by the enforcers of public decency and sexual orthodoxy, and eventually die by your own hand. At the time this lesson was conveyed to me, in 1966, homosexual acts between consenting adults were still punishable in Canada by imprisonment.

There was another, even creepier, side to the director's manipulations and invasiveness. I described in chapter 1 how he would sometimes come in very close and stare into my eyes, softly laying his hands on me. They were mesmerizing eyes, which as I recall could sometimes take on an almost violet tint, and he certainly knew how to use them. Once when he was up close and had me well and truly locked on, he told me in an intense half-whisper that I must above all else develop the right kind of male friendships. By way of clarification he added "I won't go up your ass." I must have just gawked at him. After that I found myself wondering what had gone on below decks during his years in the navy.

The director contrived and for the most part succeeded in projecting an image of tough, swashbuckling hypermasculinity. But there were odd indications, openly displayed, of something else. There was the inappropriate touching, inappropriate in the sense that it did not respect personal boundaries, a liberty that the director took with members of both sexes. And there was the kissing. The director not only kissed his grown and half-grown sons – nothing wrong with that, in itself – but made it a point to tell us repeatedly that he did so.

It was clear that he liked young and youngish men, staffing his agency mainly with them. I was struck by how often he would offer the observation that this or that young man was "good-looking." As for the style that the director favoured when he set out to look good in his own right, I was surprised when I first saw him in his tuxedo. Its simple blackness was enhanced by and elaborately frilly, lacy shirt front and cuffs, an unusual male fashion statement in the conservative Alberta of the mid-1960s. I asked a couple of staff members what they thought of it. After some hesitation, they both responded in effect that they guessed he could get away with it.

During my time at the agency, the impact of the director's complex persona and invasive ministrations were such as to muddle and obscure the issue of my buried homosexuality. To the extent that the director was inwardly clear about what he was doing, this may have been the result that he intended: to muddle and freeze things, so that the impulse that got buried and frozen would stay that way. But could such a crude imposition really work, or help? When I was alone with the director I felt, but could not acknowledge in so many words, that I was being drawn into the ambit of a truly unwholesome force. Some of his former associates would eventually refer to his portable force field as his egomania, or sociopathy, or raw chauvinism. Some would see him retrospectively as a repressed homosexual. In any event, under his gaze I had become morbidly self-conscious in my relations with both men and women. When I resigned from the agency it was with a feeling of gnawing irresolution. Whoever and whatever the director was, his effect on me had been stunting and self-falsifying.

However, I was young and an accomplished denier. Things brightened considerably when I replaced the charged atmosphere of the agency with an ordinary administrative setting at the university. Back at the agency under the inner pressure cooked up by the director, I had hurled myself compulsively into finding a new girlfriend. The resulting nascent romance didn't work out, to put it mildly. On that occasion, the energy of entanglement had led me into a truly awful if temporary mess. By contrast, against the background of relaxed and friendly office life at my new university job, I had a pleasant, no-strings affair with a strong, self-sufficient woman who was older and wiser than I was. It continued until I left for Japan.

Over the succeeding years I lived the kind of life that was tailor-made to confirm my normalcy: more crushes and dating and emotional involvement, and the relationship with Pressi that deepened into love and permanent union. But underneath all this, the gay feelings that the doctor back in Edmonton had assured me would be "temporary" remained unextinguished. I tried not to think about those feelings, which resulted only in a stress-inducing doublethink. This inner tension amplified the muscle tightness that went along with extreme and ever-narrowing tunnel vision. I was quite aware of how my body was tightening up over time, as unseen obstacles seemed to be closing in on it; I could also feel all too well how vagrant currents of gay thought or feeling were translated immediately into additional bodily tension. Even when I reacted by making myself go blank inside, the extra tension remained.

The strategy of gay repression was reinforced even more by the birth of Evan in 1977. I wanted above all else to build a stable, normal family life, one that could offer him the sane and secure home that I had never had. That meant that our home could contain no undercurrent of sexual unsureness or ambiguity. The problem was that even by reminding myself why such an undercurrent should not be tolerated I was actually bringing it back into being, inside myself. Then I would have to cancel it out again. The classic description of this contorted inner process, set into a broad and sinister political context, is to be found in George Orwell's novel *Nineteen Eighty-Four*:

To forget whatever it was necessary to forget, then to draw it
back into memory again at the moment when it was needed, then

to promptly forget it again. And above all, to apply the same process to the process itself – that was the ultimate subtlety. Consciously to induce unconsciousness, and then once again to become unconscious of the act of hypnosis that you had just performed. Even to understand the world of doublethink involved the use of doublethink.[7]

I persisted in a policy of more or less continuous internal suppression for another seventeen years after the birth of my son. Although I managed through compartmentalization to enjoy many aspects of my life and work, the five-year period in Ottawa between our Tokyo and New Delhi postings was marked by a growing emotional edginess and physical tension. These symptoms evaporated in Delhi as I began to discover the clarity and benefits of Vedanta. The result was not only a permanent disentanglement from vision, but two years of buoyant, conflict-free lightheartedness.

Once we were back in Ottawa again this happiness began slowly to dissipate into the default state that I called "normal." The falling-back was the inevitable result of the old, unresolved repression. On a particularly dreary night of frozen rain in March 1994, I finally acknowledged to myself that I could no longer avoid grappling with the question of my sexual orientation. What led me to this conclusion was not the recurrence of internal dissonance, which I might have continued to rationalize and endure until I cracked, but the realization that I was debarring myself from the very self-knowledge I craved. Coming to terms with my sexuality seemed to be a precondition for realizing the deeper self of Advaita Vedanta.

It all came down to shame. I had always been ashamed of the thing itself, the homosexuality that would not stay buried; now I was ashamed of the way my self-falsification had lately sabotaged my study program and made introspective meditation impossible. There was also the shame that had been inculcated into me by the director, who in the dimmer reaches of my mind was perhaps a stand-in for my two original abusers. But most of all I was ashamed – ashamed and exasperated to the sticking point – at having allowed this issue to fester my whole life long. So I set about making arrangements to go into therapy. The counsellor I engaged for the purpose was a man whom I knew in a parallel, non-professional context.

For the next several months my life was dominated by the sessions with the counsellor and the long bouts of private, intense introspection through which I prepared for them. I was determined not to fail this time. I began layer by layer to dredge up and examine every aspect of my buried homosexuality. I was sure that no health care professional could do this digging for me; I had to do it myself. And there was so much of it: what came to light was a sunken continent of repressed longing, the forms of denial and rationalization to which it had given rise, the self-referential homophobia that I sometimes projected compulsively onto others, and the stubborn self-blame that went back to my earliest childhood.

Even the three versions of the RP false self that I had left behind me turned out to have been tied to sexual identity. The official persona of the visually impaired but competent diplomat had been implicitly heterosexual, and thus a real man. But both the frustrated alter ego who was half-blind rather than half-sighted, and the helpless deeper identity who harboured so much fear of total blindness, had been implicitly queer. In this primitive and reactive level of the mind the unconscious associations lined up like this: visual dependency = unmanliness = effeminacy = faggot. Thinking of these imagined linkages during the bad patches when I felt visually exhausted was like trying to walk forward while chained to a set of heavy iron balls, one behind the other.

As the process of inner scrutiny grew more intense I began to have a series of vivid and sometimes horrifying dreams. These encompassed both the early trauma and my present condition. They seemed to be charged with urgent meaning, but were encoded in a symbolic language of visual tableaux that I found at first hard to penetrate. The dream images that were on show were far more sharp-edged and vivid than the things I routinely saw during the waking state. I focused all my energy on trying to understand them, convinced that understanding must somehow be attainable. This was, after all, my own mind.

On the mornings after strong dreams I would go to my study and just sit still. I stared inwardly at the remembered dream-images until some spool of associations began to unwind, leading me eventually – when I got lucky – to the hard significance I needed to see. This always had to do with my feelings for men, which under normal circumstances were half-suppressed and defensively rationalized. The important thing was to open up to the image and wait in negative capability until the associations began to appear. I did not try to apply, cookie-cutter fashion, any of the ideas about dreams that I had picked up from reading Freud and Jung.

I found that when it came to my sexual dilemma the dream mind was deeper and far more knowing than the waking "I," for the dreamer presented in his own visual language the very insights that the waking "I" lacked. Thank God I hadn't waited any longer to do this work – I was as yet still sighted in my dreams. Later I was to learn from my further study of Advaita that the visual symbolism of meaningful dreams is the work of *buddhi*, an intuitive faculty that most of us possess.

The basic role of the counsellor was to be a sympathetic ear and provide support while I was thrashing through all this. Beyond that he had to confirm or challenge the conclusions I was drawing from my dreamwork and introspection, but as a matter of course he almost always confirmed them. I think it was clear to both of us – at any event it was crystal clear to me – that for all practical purposes I had become both analysand and analyst. The one area of exception was my periodic retreat back into implicit denial. Only the counsellor was in a position to catch these lapses and alert me to what was happening.

As we approached the end of the process the counsellor began to reflect back to me the conclusion that I myself was increasingly putting into words: I had never been straight or even bisexual. I was gay. But then I got stalled in a penultimate stage in which I was re-experiencing some very old, corrosive feelings that were rooted in specific memories of abuse. I seemed unable to get past them or to break their association with my now apparent gayness. And yet I knew that most contemporary clinicians had dropped the old notion that homosexuality was the result of early abuse or family dysfunction. While that kind of history could entrench a lifelong habit of guardedness or implicit mistrust of authority figures, as it had with me, sexual orientation seemed to stand on its own. It was not entrained by any other class of experience.

It was hard now to avoid the conclusion that my early history was not the cause of my half-buried gayness, but on the contrary the reason for its repression. I had been conditioned to fear and loathe something that may have been encoded in my very protoplasm. And indeed, the first indicators of a complex genetic basis for homosexuality were just then coming to light. As to the psychology of gays, I myself had seen evidence in the persons of gay teachers and artists and diplomats I had known that a homosexual could be as well-balanced and strong in character as anyone else. But I did not want to be one. The old, shame-based internalized homophobia continued to eat through me.

When the resolution of this impasse finally occurred, its form and timing took me completely by surprise.

4 A BURST OF OPENNESS

I head down my usual route on a hot steamy day in August, trying to release some of the pent-up strain by going for a very long walk. I am weighed down by a sense of leaden oppression and feel so tired I can no longer think; I just walk and walk. My vision sees the sky as darkly overcast despite the heat. It seems as I pace along that the dim light through which I move is indistinguishable from my own inner murk. Although I am usually very attentive to the sounds around me, and had formed the habit of processing them into my forward movement as a matter of course, my footfalls and cane-taps are as distant and muffled as the noise of traffic several blocks away. I am quite turned within, and everything in there is silent and static. The sense of self is buried somewhere within the inner awareness that attends to white cane walking, but even this seems clouded and dull.

After perhaps half an hour of this numb plodding, it just happens. Out of the blue I find myself confronted with a very simple but momentous thought: *Just say yes.* And I do so, instantly, not pausing to consider the vast implications. It is at that moment that I finally and fully acknowledge my gayness. I accept it not resignedly and grudgingly as an unavoidable fate but positively and unconditionally, as something to be totally affirmed. I just open right up, from the inside out.

That single moment changes everything. The long-accustomed and burdensome feeling of heaviness is gone from my shoulders, upper back, and the back of my neck. My body is buoyant and tingling, borne along by a joyous inner airiness that is wide open and receptive to everything. The audible world flows in. The sounds of birds and kids and dogs must have been there all along, but now they are unimpeded and ringing clear. They sound marvellous and new, as though I had never heard such things before. "I am gay" has given way to an affirmation of being so simple and unqualified that it could be expressed only as "I Am." It seems strange that I should be walking exactly as before, the legs and cane having worked automatically during the inner transition.

Over the following days and weeks the most dramatic external manifestation of this inner breakthrough was a conspicuous lowering in the level of my chronic physical tension. I started to loosen up all over, and felt as though I had been detoxified. The easing of muscle tension was so marked that my excellent massage therapist, Arlene Cybulskie, finally asked me what big thing had changed in my life. So I told her. She responded with personal congratulations and a kind of professional satisfaction. "The way you were always bunged up here, here, and here," she said as she kneaded my back with her clever hands, "finally makes sense. You were carrying around all that stress."

Now, I know that when an intensely affirmative experience of selfhood is triggered by an equally intense struggle to accept one's homosexuality, any attempt to explain or even describe what happens inevitably gets tangled up with sexual politics, or more deeply with the vague notions about selfhood on which sexual politics are based. Some readers of this book who belong to the heterosexual majority may be dismayed by the turn of events described above, because they would seem to lead inevitably to the breakup or at least the deep disruption of a family. Some gay readers on the other hand may see such a breakup as the regrettable but unavoidable cost of "coming out."

Both types of readers take it for granted that sexual orientation is a fundamental aspect of the self, so much so that the sexual behaviour that is driven by it seems to have the irresistible force and legitimacy of self-validation. But my own story was to follow a different line. At the moment when the self so dramatically declared its presence it accepted my gayness without qualification: nevertheless, I found that it did not compel any fundamental change in my circumstances. It did not have an "agenda."

I "came out" to my wife and later to my son, and was overwhelmed by their understanding and support. I came out to my oldest friends, to former foreign service colleagues, and to people I knew in the local blind community. I made new gay acquaintances, some of whom would become long-term friends. Bookworm that I am and would always remain, I launched myself into a crash reading program on gay studies supported by volunteer readers. In this venture and in my outreach to the Ottawa gay community I was encouraged and aided by David Rimmer, proprietor of the gay bookstore After Stonewall. I began to march with my white cane in Gay Pride parades.

But at no point did I seriously consider breaking up the home I had made with Pressi and Evan. Nor did I initiate a substitute or parallel gay sex life. Thus it was that I became a minority within a minority within a minority: a blind "out" gay man who chooses to live a quiet family life with wife and son, a life centred on philosophical and religious study.

Yet it was right here within this unbroken domestic scene that an obvious question loomed: What about Pressi? In all this was she not getting a raw deal? This was a misgiving I had to face, and work through. Because of marrying me she has not experienced the kind of rich, long-term bonding with the sort of man – a heterosexual man – to whom she would normally cleave. This struck me at first, unavoidably, as irremediably sad. Yet Pressi had been in no hurry to get married; she had declined the proposals of previous beaux, and incredibly enough she somehow conceived for me an abiding love. It was that unconditional love, and nothing else in my previous experience, that unfroze my heart and taught me for the first time how to love in return.

Yet the cumulative tension generated by my unresolved and unvoiced inner conflict had worn me down, and that tension came between us. When I finally broke free of my denial and came out to her, I tried my best to explain everything. I told her that I had never stopped loving her even during the hard and scrappy times, including our current economic squeeze. The effect was immediate: now, as she moved about the house during her daily routine, she would sing – just sing unaffectedly in her fine lyric soprano, with a particular lilt I hadn't heard in years. Not for the first time in my complexly simple relationship with Pressi, I felt a sense of gratified and bemused wonder.

As for my new outreach program, the gay men I was getting to know received me variously as a real comrade, a friendly visitor, or a peculiar case. I knew that some of them felt that my life lacked authenticity because it did not include sex with men. On the rare occasions when someone expressed this opinion in so many words, I replied simply that I am what I am. That meant that I was not moved to abandon my wife and best friend of thirty-three years, or to engage in a double life based on deceit. What I did not say, because I knew that I would not get anywhere, was that my questioner was mixing up sexual experience with the self as such. His was the language of unintentional and perfectly sincere conflation, a usage so common that we rarely question it. Whenever words such as authenticity or falsehood are applied to a person's lifestyle, they implicitly refer not just to how he behaves but to what he has made of himself inwardly. The latter is taken to add up to an identity, which may be either real or deluded.

What I saw in the conflation of gay sex with selfhood was a parallel to the false selfing that typifies a certain class of blind persons, those who tend toward strong politicized leadership within agencies for the blind and the blind community generally. This parallel is not based on sex as such or blindness as such, but on something deeper and less obvious that the two groups share in common – an unconscious mechanism of intense, assertive, politicized identification with their own bodily sensorial experience.

This common feature comes into focus when contemporary gays are compared with the blind American activists of two generations ago. The latter reacted to blatant and pervasive structural discrimination against the blind by creating a powerful lobby, the National Federation of the Blind (NFB). The highly effective NFB equal rights program was coordinated by militant cadres who identified completely with their condition. That is, they identified not only with the actual phenomenal experience of blindness but with the hard-won mobility and braille-based communication skills that supported their work. From my conversations with blind American professionals who came of age in the late 1960s, I gather that the blind self-construct of the NFB militants was absolutely central to their sense of who they were. This construct was more deeply rooted and elaborated – and far more politicized – than the blind official persona that I cultivated at External Affairs.

Now consider the situation of gay people. Like the blind they are conspicuously distinguished from the majority because of one key attribute. But while the attribute of visual impairment results in the kind of discrimination that is based mainly on the stereotypes of helplessness and unemployability, a gay sexual orientation can provoke the far more visceral reactions of hatred, fear, and contempt. It is hardly surprising that a minority who have faced millennia of persecution and ridicule because of this one innate difference should reactively or defiantly affirm that attribute as the very core of their identity. Thus for many but by no means all gays it is sexuality – sexual experience as such and sexual orientation as an identifier – that becomes the informing principle for elaborating and validating a life.

This attitude or mindset is sometimes called gay essentialism. Over the years gay essentialism has been promulgated as ideology or enacted as political defiance by groups such as the Mattachine Society, the Radical Faeries, ACT UP, and Queer Nation. But more often it appears as the product of personal reinvention or spontaneous acculturation on the part of gays who are struggling to accept themselves and help one another. Gay essentialism is a belief in, and an elaborate argument for, a specifically and uniquely gay culture, ethos, and psychology. What this amounts to is a theory of a gay self, which has been embraced by a great many political radicals and moderates alike. Over a period of five decades it was in large part these men and women who fought for full human and civil rights for all gays and lesbians. Their success – together with the remarkable evolution in social attitudes that followed upon that success – helped even me, in the depths of my repression, to finally come out. I owe those activists an enormous debt.

At the same time, however, the idea of a specifically gay self should be judged on its merits. That this kind of self is really an artifice vulnerable to destabilization is demonstrated by those lives in which two or even three attributes compete with one another to dominate the identity. This sort of thing just seems to happen, for life is complex and people are not really unidimensional. The classic, wrenching example from gay life is the conflict between sexuality and membership in a homophobic religious community. A more contemporary American example is that of the ambitious young Republican party official who is constantly pulled between his real need for solidarity with his fellow gays, and his equally strong commitment to conservative political and social ideology. These two sources of identity are in some respects poles apart, and the result for the person so divided can be an intense experience of cognitive and emotional dissonance.

Once again, there is a parallel with the experience of blind and partially blind people, especially those who try to break out of their predetermined roles and penetrate some elite group in the larger society. In the case of the visually impaired but highly competitive runner Marla Runyan, whom I mention in section 3 of the introduction, the result was conflict between her intense desire to join the ranks of the superbly able Olympians and her deeply conditioned self-construct as one of the disabled. In my own experience at image-conscious External Affairs, the conflict was between wanting to look smooth, presentable, and self-reliant as a diplomat, and having to insist in some settings that procedures be altered to accommodate my needs as a blind person. I experienced this tension as a petty but irksome zero-sum game played between two competing self-constructs.

The perspective offered above can be extended to those cases in which other sources of identity – race, ethnicity, disabilities other than blindness – must vie for prominence within the complexity of a life as lived. What all such examples show us is that there is no obvious way of solving the riddle of identity so long as we take ourselves to be a sum of disparate bits and pieces. And even when a person stubbornly claims one and only one attribute as his essence and raison d'être – the uncompromisingly militant gay, the blind equal-access lobbyist who is filled with a sense of grievance and entitlement, the fire-breathing evangelist – we get the feeling that he could do with some rebalancing. But although recalibrating the relative importance we assign to our various attributes may improve the quality of our lives, such adjustments have nothing to do with our real identity. Even when bits and pieces rub along together without much friction they are still bits and pieces.

It is possible to have a very different experience of self, and discovering this was the most important single thing about what happened to me in the summer of 1994. While the experience involved acceptance of gayness, the emergent self that made acceptance possible was not based on identification with that or any other attribute. The presence that witnessed and accepted the uncovering of my gayness and the continuing erosion of my vision was not in itself either sighted or blind, straight or gay. The one vital fact about its nature that makes it available as food for thought by any reader of this book is that it did not belong only to "me." That unexpected pulse of self-affirmation was not bound to any personal name or ID number, and it had no mark or feature that would restrict its identity to gays or blind people or any other group.

Such a self was neither a material object nor a mental construct concerning identity. It was neither an ego nor a personality. In earlier instantiations it had presented itself as the unique reality that since 1988 I had been thinking of as my "centre" – that presence that appears and reappears throughout the pages of this and the previous two chapters. It was a kind of subtle inner space, but had no specific physical location. One could call it the centre because at times of alert, intense, but self-contained sense experience it seemed to lie implicit at the very heart or inner core of that experience. It was our in-gathered essence, directing its attention straight outward even as it remained mostly veiled.

But on the occasion described in these pages it burst forth in its true guise as the light of consciousness. It was unobstructed, immediately present, space-like. It was this and nothing else that said, "I Am." No matter what extrosensory and introsensory phenomena the light took in as I walked along, it maintained its consistent identity as "I." This, I thought and felt through and through, was the Ur-I that underlies all our experience and imagined identities. I knew and felt this absolutely, and didn't need any book or teacher to confirm it for me.

The extraordinary thing about the light of consciousness is that it is utterly, ignorably ordinary. It is present all the time as the consciousness that illumines the body-mind and the great world but is taken entirely for granted, gazed through as though it did not exist. Yet when the presence of that light becomes clearly apparent we instantly have the conviction that it has always been "there" as our primary experience of being. That too is remarkable – that this discovery should actually feel like a rediscovery, as though we had been fully conscious of consciousness all along.

It is so incredibly simple. What I am vainly trying to describe here is just awareness indivisibly aware of itself, that and nothing more. Yet in its simplicity, which is to say its complete absence of inner distinctions or divisions, consciousness has the quality of complete self-possession and self-sufficiency. Once you experience this even if only briefly, you never quite lose the feeling that nothing else is needed to complete you. Because the light of consciousness has no material substance there is nothing within it that could be lost or damaged; because it is complete in itself there is nothing outside it that it needs for its identity. And its very immateriality makes it wide open and accessible to whatever requires attention. There are no obstructions within its clear spaciousness that would resist the attributes that have been assigned to us, by fate or karma or the laws of science, or if you prefer, by God.

Whether the attribute in question is the skin colour of a despised minority or the blindness that would otherwise stunt a life, or the innate sexual orientation that some people love to hate, it is taken in and bathed in the light of acceptance. It turns out that the attributes we cannot change find their proper place not as pseudo-identities but as the objects of unconditional acceptance. At the level of the generative light of consciousness we are all the same, and all potentially capable of "seeing" ourselves without inner division or alienation.

That is what I eventually concluded from my own experience, and from the conviction that my consciousness was in no way unique.

It is a peculiar feature of my biography, then, that I should have been led to the general perspective spelled out above by struggling with the very specific, personal problem of sexual orientation. But the greater issue for the reader of this book may be the very idea that our core identity could be anything so seemingly reductionist, so elusively unobjectifiable, so unsatisfyingly non-individual, as the naked light of consciousness. How could anyone live in that way, and who would he then *be*? Perhaps this author simply had an odd experience from which he might be expected to recover. Or perhaps his blind view of the world was just too disconnected from reality to take our individual identities seriously.

Here I can only say, as I did toward the end of the introduction, please just wait and see. In what is to come you will find that over the succeeding years my consciousness-based view of selfhood only deepened. But more to the point – when it comes to alternative world views, and the kinds of self-constructs that are fitted into them – we are going to see as we move through the following chapters that the conventional materialist understanding of reality is not as solidly based as we suppose. It is a shambles, and in fact an illusion. Nor is normal sense-perception, left to itself, a sufficient judge of what is real and what is not.

In 1994 my own view of reality already owed a good deal to Advaita Vedanta. I doubt that I could have come to terms with my sexual quandary without Advaita, as I then understood or half-understood it. It was basic Advaitic principles that somehow short-circuited my defences: caught between the alternatives of a conflicted identification with gayness and a complete rejection of it, I was presented apparently out of the blue with a third alternative. The man in my kind of dilemma who does not know about this alternative – that of welcoming gayness from the depths of a self that does not identify with anything – may never fully resolve his conflict, no matter what kind of life he lives or what he chooses to call himself. I am thankful every day of my life for having found that third way.

And that, crammed into as few pages as it takes to show what was really at issue, is the story of how I came to terms with my oldest and deepest identity conflict. The brief definitive experience of altered perspective that came upon me during that long walk did not render me fully and continuously wide open, in the manner of a realized sage, and over the following months the light of consciousness usually affirmed itself in a quieter and less dramatic way. But my breakthrough experience convinced me beyond all doubt that what is called "spiritual" is already present in ordinary life. Spirit is the light at our core that not only illuminates life but actually experiences life. If we are prepared to be open to the light and really attend to it, and recede unresistingly into it, it will confirm our essential commonality. It is out of that commonality that I can say, factually but non-identificatively, "I am gay."

I will never find the right words to adequately thank Pressi for her support, encouragement, and patience during this period of transition. She has an inner quality that I can best characterize as discretion, a capacity to wait and not interfere that granted me the space I needed to find my way. When I came out to her she understood completely the necessity of being out with others, and actively shared in that openness. She never had any doubts about the final outcome – the reconstitution of our life together around the same old sinewy and resilient bond of love. Together we are still family, however much we may differ as bundles of this and that.

One last point regarding Factor Y: once I had come out I found that the puzzle of my writer's block had been effortlessly resolved. The failed novella that I had squirrelled away on my hard drive was absolutely permeated with Factor Y – it was really an attempt to come to terms with my buried homosexuality without revealing to myself what I was doing. When I recently reread it I was both amused and appalled by its convolutions, which were the inevitable product of my once again chasing my tail with the inner eye squeezed firmly shut. Even when I discovered in the fall of 1994 that the block was gone I felt no desire to rewrite the thing. My writing interests had somehow changed, and I was no longer impelled to wear the costumes and masks of fiction. This is when I first had the thought that one day I might try to write something on blindness, or Advaita Vedanta, or both at once.

5 LOOKING FOR MY OTHERS

You cannot go through the kind of interior change described above without discovering a parallel shift in your disposition toward other people. When you stop to think about it this makes complete sense; it is almost like a syllogism. If (A) the clearest, most affirmative and joyous experience of identity shows you to be not some definite thing but pellucid, receptive consciousness, a condition that leads you to wish that consciousness might somehow open up even wider, and if (B) this experience makes it obvious that deep down it must be like this for all of us, inherently clear and potentially expansive, then (C) you find yourself as a matter of course becoming less reserved and more open to your "others," and responding to their openness whenever you sense it. In my case this was felt as the easing of an old inner rigidity or restraint that had often excluded me from a sense of connectedness or fellow-feeling.

From late 1994 through 1995 I found that my ordinary daily relations with people, from old friends and neighbours to casual social contacts and taxi drivers, were taking on a new tone. I simply liked being in company more than before, even when I didn't have much to say. What I especially liked or found intriguing, as odd as this may sound, was just the sense of the other's presence. No words or images were required. And this interest was present whether I was "out" to the person or not. All this can be summed up by saying that for the first time in my life I no longer felt like an outsider, a monad who was barred somehow from full social intercourse.

I was now beginning to rely more heavily on volunteers, and not just for oral reading. Keyboarding was getting more difficult as my arm, shoulder, and upper back muscles became more refractory, and my fingers gradually stiffened up with joint problems. One of the means I hit upon to get myself some personal assistance – apart from the standard option of approaching the CNIB – was to post a notice downtown in a lively and welcoming gay bookstore, After Stonewall. I was looking for volunteers to help me explore gay literature, to survey the work of Western writers influenced by Vedanta and Buddhism, and to deal with some of the typing. All of that amounted to a pretty big order for any one volunteer, but over the years I did surprisingly well in finding people interested in helping me with this or that part of the package. Some of these colleagues – for that is how I thought of them – became long-term friends for me and Pressi.

In 1994–95 I conceived a desire to make direct contact with a qualified Advaitic mentor. This was another natural consequence of letting down my guard; perhaps now I could lay myself open to the intuitive gaze of a real teacher. For several years I had known people who in one way or another were pursuing an interest in Advaita Vedanta, and I had benefited from my many discussions with them.

But none of them was a *jnani* – a fully self-realized or enlightened sage. The Indian Advaitic texts stated categorically that none but a jnani could serve as a mentor. I knew that even in India realized sages were exceedingly rare, compared with the legions of self-styled gurus whose principal concern was to drum up business for themselves. In North America the search would be even harder.

Here it must be added, however, that the very texts that debar all but the true jnani from the position of guru go on to say that the assumed necessity of an external guru is to some extent based on a misconception. The real guru – the Atman, or "commonal" or universal self, our actual source of spiritual insight – is within us. The role of the jnani, for the aspirant who is lucky enough to know one, was to help him or her turn inward toward the Atman. In this there was something of a parallel to certain kinds of experiences that crop up in Western therapy or counselling. This parallel had struck me during my recent struggle with Factor Y; a more open experience of self had come from within, not from anything the counsellor said or did.

Little Ottawa was becoming big enough that it was beginning to figure on the international guru circuit. One day I went to an advertised public talk by an Asian spiritual teacher who was making quite a name for himself. This was my first exposure to organized public guruism. The speaker's presentation, which was really a piece of performance art, left me cold. Its subject might be described as Vedanta Lite, or Don't Worry Be Happy. This man went on to build a formidable international organization and secure a place as a frequent media spokesman for Eastern spirituality. But for me he was just a negative model, a kind of New Age entrepreneur.

Soon after that I began to participate in an Ottawa group organized around an itinerant Advaitic preceptor of sorts who travelled regularly from city to city. This man took great care to identify himself not as an enlightened guru or any other kind of guru, but simply as a "friend." Yet over the months I found increasingly that the periodic meetings or get-togethers were taking on the form and tone of a *darshan*. In the Vedantic and broader Indian tradition a darshan is a kind of audience in which a supposedly enlightened or at least highly advanced teacher offers counsel and support. The regulars who attended these meetings were very nice people, and I enjoyed being with them. In the evenings when the meeting room was dimly lighted they would take the initiative to help me to a seat, usually the privileged place right next to the amiable preceptor.

But in the end I concluded that this man did not have what I was looking for. After I stopped going to the meetings I felt that I had had the experience of being "grouped," which is the New Age or guru-circuit equivalent of being "churched." It is a communal experience of blending into a warm, welcoming, and uncritical circle in which everything flows easily and some kind of ultimate fulfillment seems to be guaranteed. This can be very misleading.

One of my most memorable experiences at this time was with Joan Ruvinsky, an accomplished Montreal-based yoga teacher whom I first met in Ottawa. To most of her students Joan teaches the physical-meditative art of Patanjali Yoga, reinforced by a study of the Yoga-Sutras on which the practice is based. I had tried to learn and practice the *asanas* (postures) of Patanjali Yoga in New Delhi but had been constrained by my back and joint problems.

What interested me about Joan's work was that she was also one of the very few people in North America who teach Kashmiri internal yoga. Internal yoga is a feature of Kashmiri Shaivism, which at one time in India was among the strongest regional expressions of Advaita Vedanta. This kind of teaching focuses on the *prana-maya kosha* or energy-body. In Vedanta, the five koshas or "sheaths" are the succes-sive layers of the body-mind as we actually experience them (see chapter 7, section 1). The prana-maya kosha comprises the subtle energies, accessible to direct experience under certain conditions, that underlie our ordinary experiences of internal phenomena such as breathing, position or posture, movement, and physical pleasure or pain. Joan had assured me that I would be able to do this kind of bodywork despite my physical limitations.

So one day I took the bus to Montreal and spent the afternoon with Joan, learning how to experience the energy-body. One way is to remember and enter into the experience of engaging a group of muscles – those that lift the hand, for example – without actually causing an external movement. Such an experience is hard to describe because it is neither physical nor mere imagination. In recent years a modified version of this kind of internal focusing has been incorporated into athletic training and rehabilitation.

But the most remarkable opening during my hours with Joan occurred a little later in the day. She had set me to do very slow body movements with complete attentiveness. At one point, sitting on the floor in a loose and unforced cross-legged posture with my upper body rotated far to the left, I was swivelling my head slowly toward the right. This is an uncommon combination of movements, which as a result is free of the sense of routinization. All at once in the middle of this exercise the conventional sense of embodiment simply disappeared. There was just space and within that space a more subtle kind of energy, or *prana*.

It was a beautiful moment, one that despite the uniqueness of its features somehow had a familiar taste. That space was exactly the same space that I had melted into at the moment when I accepted my homosexuality. Then it had been filled or charged with an energy I could describe only as joy. It was the same space I sometimes felt while reading some arresting passage in a Upanishad, or some other Advaitic text, an inner space that seemed to have no discernable outer boundary. Thanks to Joan Ruvinsky I had found another way into it. This was a way that she clearly knew well, and for her it was very much a path of the heart.

A very different path – that of the head and nothing but the head – was exemplified for me by a fellow student of Advaita whom I knew over a period of years. It took me some time to realize how singular his view of the Advaitic tradition really was. One day I tried to give this co-seeker a full account of the breakthrough into visual detachment that I experienced in New Delhi – this would have been sometime during the first few months after we returned from India. As I began to lay out the Katha chariot analogy my friend interrupted me with the impatient observation that he found the Upanishads "unreadable," as compared with logic-based philosophical writing. He then launched into a disquisition on some contentious point in Western philosophy. I just held my peace and listened. I never again broached with him the subject of Upanishadic symbolism. Nor did I ever mention my unphilosophical and no doubt unreasonable evenings with the four-armed god in Madras decades earlier, or my experience at Mahabalipuram, or the unexpected disclosures that will be described in the next chapter.

For this man, who had studied philosophy and other disciplines at two of the world's great universities, Advaita was deep thinking, rational inquiry – that and nothing else. It was in part because of this attitude that he had recommended to me the equally well-educated Advaitic preceptor described earlier, the one who held periodic group darshans in Ottawa. My friend seemed to assume that the non-intellectual qualities of mind that the classic Advaitic sources attributed to the sincere student – dispassion, resoluteness, forbearance, the capacity to stand back from experience and simply witness it, meditative concentration, love and compassion – would all somehow arise naturally as a result of correct analysis. I found this view one-sided and naive, despite the fact that I myself was beginning to discover the liberating power of Advaitic reasoning.

The hyper-rationalist and I eventually went our separate ways, and I have not seen my former friend and would-be mentor for many years. I am not identifying him by name here because he does not occupy this page in a way that would allow him to present his side of what became a long and contentious argument. As a debating partner this man did me the real if unintended service of taking so inflexible a position that it challenged me to find my own balance between reasoned inquiry and the other essential elements of the spiritual path. Because this kind of dogmatism is essentially an ideology, it fortifies the ego that identifies with it.

But the other extreme can be even worse. When it comes to the loose scattering of groups and networks that might be called Western Vedanta, the sort of extremism that has misled the greatest number of people is not the one espoused by my former friend, but its exact opposite. This is the view that the exercise of reason has absolutely no place in opening up the life of the spirit. That is simply a wrong idea, and when it is propagated by a guru its numbing effects can disable not only the intellect but common sense as well. This lays people open to unhappy consequences.

A notable example of this was the late guru/entrepreneur known as Bhagwan Shree Rajneesh, or Osho. His financial empire, the trappings of which included a conspicuously displayed fleet of Rolls-Royces, was based in part on his followers' wilful suspension of their own faculty of judgment. A sign at the entrance to the Bhagwan's preaching tent in his Poona ashram read "Shoes and minds must be left at the gate."[8] I never had occasion to meet any of the Bhagwan's disciples, but I did get to know a number of seekers of a similar cast who believed implicitly that the intellect was the enemy of the spirit. I found this shocking and saddening; it seemed to me that the anti-rationalist's hatred of the mind was as misguided as the anorexic's hatred of the body.

The trick was to know how to use the mind, judo-like, to expose its own unexamined errors regarding the constitution of self. That wasn't easy, but eventually I found that it was doable. I confirmed this by taking in the Advaitic literature and experimenting with its teachings. But first I was moved to go more deeply into my experience of vision loss – into the "inner space" that it opened up. As I illustrate in the next chapter, this space proved to have radical implications for the fundamental nature of things.

6

Vision, Science, and the World-Illusion

1 THREE UNCONVENTIONAL PERSPECTIVES ON SEEING

Ever since my posting to New Delhi, I had harboured a notion or hunch regarding the special role of vision in constructing our conventional understanding of world and self. Was the sense-world "real" in the way we assume? In the mid-1990s my engagement with this question was reinforced by three highly original writers: Douglas Harding (1909–2007), Jacques Lusseyran (1924–1971), and John Hull (1935–2015). These men – two then living and one dead, one sighted and two blind – had each in his own way grasped the limiting or even misleading nature of ordinary visual experience.

The British writer and teacher Douglas Harding, who was fully sighted in more ways than one, taught a remarkably direct and immediate method of seeing into our real nature. He first introduced Western readers to this new way of inner seeing, actually a very, very old way rediscovered at intervals across the millennia, in his little classic *On Having No Head*.[1] It was published in its original form in 1961. An expanded version brought out in the early 1970s was very widely read and much discussed among seekers of various persuasions.

Over the following decades Douglas conducted thousands of workshops around the world, introducing participants to his growing repertoire of ingenious in-seeing "experiments." These show through various stratagems how to access or invoke the basic experience introduced in *On Having No Head*. Because this "in-seeing" is really a kind of inner attentiveness, an opening-up into one's own consciousness, it can be accessed as much by the blind as by the sighted.

In the many books and articles Douglas continued to produce he carefully laid out the experiments step by step for the reader to try. He set them into a context that was both immediate and universal, showing how the in-seeing can securely ground the practical business of daily life, and documenting how it is depicted explicitly or implicitly in the literature of many of the great religions. Above all, his writings demonstrate by example how this in-seeing can become deeper and deeper over time. The Harding experiments offer one way of tapping into that mode of experience that in this book I refer to as "inner seeing." Inner seeing as I employ the term refers to direct, experiential knowledge of our deep inner constitution – of our normally obscured selfhood.

I read *On Having No Head* in the early 1990s and was intrigued by its principal claim: that the most important common feature of the world's great religions was neither their basic moral injunctions nor their ideas about the divine, but a single core insight into our true nature. When I tried out the first and most basic of the in-seeing experiments presented in the book, one expressly designed to invoke that core insight, somehow it hadn't worked for me. I was left with nothing more than the idea of what I sometimes called one's "centre."

In 1994 I read Douglas Harding's *Head Off Stress*, which was both a revelation and a delight. By this time I was ready for the Harding method, largely because of breaking through the inner defensiveness that had been all wrapped up with Factor Y. I now found myself open to the book's carefully laid out suite of experiments. They were brilliantly conceived, simple to do, direct in their effect, and far-reaching in their implications. What they evoked in a unique way was the same wide-open, space-like awareness that I had experienced through other means over the past year. The uniqueness of the Harding approach lay in its utter simplicity, the way it immediately reversed the arrow of attention so that it was no longer vectored outward toward external objects but straight inward into consciousness itself.

It would be quite fruitless for me to just comment on the *Head Off Stress* experiments and describe them in a general way, and equally fruitless for you to just read my words. The person who is new to this resource has to actually perform the experiments himself or herself in order to get their point. You can do this by going to the lively web site coordinated by Richard Lang: (http://headless.org/contact/richard-lang.htm). Its email address is headexchange@gn.acp.org. It was on this website that some of my in-turning experiments for the blind were posted in the mid-1990s.

After I finished reading *Head Off Stress* I wrote to Douglas Harding, and when I received his warm and encouraging reply I began to make plans to attend a workshop he was scheduled to give in Barre, Massachusetts, a couple of months later. As I expected, getting to Barre wasn't exactly easy. I had to make arrangements with airline representatives for the bulkhead seating that could accommodate my long legs and ease some of the pressure on my lumbar spine, which meant convincing them to waive the usual rule that debarred blind people from occupying that particular space. I had to take a special, lightweight plastic chair, back braces, and a rolled-up yoga mat as luggage, and enlist the help of Travelers Aid in Boston to guide me to the rental car and carry my gear.

Once I was set up in Barre I found that sitting through the workshops was physically challenging but deeply satisfying. Doing the experiments in a group setting felt perfectly natural, as an experience both of deep introversion and spontaneous sharing. To the extent that I and my fellow participants could tell from comparing notes after each experiment, we had all experienced the same voluminous open space where we would normally find ourselves all bunged up. This way of getting together and sharing views was not based on cultishness or the need to be led, but on a simple and transmissible means of looking within that required no validation by any authority. Naturally enough I associated the result – that experience of space that was both inner and outer – with Advaita Vedanta.

But I would eventually discover that Douglas himself was no Advaitin. He was a resolutely non-affiliated practical guide with an independent mind. What he revealed to people was the one kind of immediate experience that could instantly if temporarily cancel out our conventional sense of identity and plainly reveal the boundless no-thing within. Douglas refrained from identifying this inner reality with any specific religious tradition and made it plain that he would not act as anyone's guru. But he and his wife and co-teacher Catherine proved to be great friends.

From our first meeting in Barre to his death in 2007 at the age of ninety-seven, Douglas cordially and consistently refused to comment on my successive attempts to interpret what the experiments told us about the real nature of the perceived world, and its relationship to consciousness. The important thing, he insisted and reiterated through our many exchanges of letters, was to just see what the experiments point to and then ground oneself in that clear, spacious reality. He certainly did so himself. As the years passed, it was apparent from Douglas's published writings and private correspondence that his experience of all-encompassing consciousness was becoming more and more profound. At the same time, as a kind of parallel, his own religious sensibilities were becoming more explicitly – but always non-dogmatically – Christian. He made no attempt to impose this sensibility onto others.

At lunchtime on the first day of the Barre workshop I had some difficulty finding my way from the retreat centre to the building in which the food was served. It was typical of Douglas's thoughtfulness that, noticing this, he materialized unobtrusively by my side to show the way. As we walked along together and I plied my cane, I experimentally put myself back into the reversed perspective that made the workshop so vivid. The effect was remarkable. It was exactly the kind of awareness-centred, physically relaxed openness that I had been struggling to secure in my attempts to go on long walks with the white cane, against the grain of nerve and muscle pain.

Of course I was experiencing that openness now in the perfect security of walking with a guide, but I felt sure that it had great potential for helping me smooth out my solo navigation. I told Douglas how it felt to walk like this, which naturally enough came as no surprise to him. He said that that was the way of it for everyone who got the point of the experiments. I should just allow the perspective to settle in and become habitual, he went on, and in the meantime not lose my way while I was caught up in the buoyancy of the experience.

It was at Barre that Douglas first shared with me his conviction that it was people like me – blind or nearly blind people – who are in the best position to turn inward and fully experience our fundamental nature. I was surprised at how definite his views were on this subject. Then I thought of the Maitri Upanishad. I told Douglas how this text associated the faculty of vision with the illusion of dualism, but he replied firmly that that was not what he was talking about.

Indeed, as I was to learn over the years from our re-enactment of the ancient debate between dualism and non-dualism, Douglas and I would have to agree to disagree about certain basic philosophical issues. I would find, as many others would find, that the experience of wide-openness invoked by the experiments was correspondingly wide open to interpretation. With repeated immersion and habituation and some thought, for example, that intriguing experiential space

– which is somehow both inner and outer – would seem to be consistent with the single, non-dual foundational consciousness adum-
brated by Advaita Vedanta. But there are many other possible glosses.

Some years ago during the course of my long correspondence with
Douglas, he eventually identified himself – and these were his exact
words – as "a dyed-in-the-wool dualist." He took this position in large
part for the most humane and understandable of reasons: the incom-
patibility, as he saw it, of a non-dualist understanding of reality and
his own person-to-person relationship with his beloved wife, Catherine.
But back in Barre he was already urging me to grasp something having
to do with eyesight that he took to be far more consequential than the
question of whether the reality that lies beneath all appearances is
essentially divisible or whole. "You'll see what I mean," he predicted.

As my object-vision completely fell apart over the succeeding years,
I was to realize the perfectly obvious sense in which Douglas had
been seized, to an extent matched by few other sighted people, by an
insight into what might be called the generally unremarked "down"
side of external vision. This had to do with the gobsmacking, anaesthetizing, hypnotic power of images, the last distorted versions of
which slowly dissolved from my life. Television had long ceased to
be part of my experience, and I had become intrigued at how sighted
people could spend hours and hours every day and evening staring
at a cathode ray tube, or a plasma screen, or a computer monitor, or
the ridiculously small visual display of a mobile device, not out of
necessity but through choice or habit. I began to think of this passive
staring as a kind of stupefied bondage, one that blind people are
spared whether they like it or not.

But the drawing power of images was not confined to these electronic gizmos; the whole visible world exerted the same pull. For the
sighted, it was so easy and natural and useful for consciousness to be
directed outward to images, never learning how to reverse itself and
penetrate its own depths. I'm sure it was this easily formed and hard-
to-extinguish habit of visual out-turning that Douglas had in mind
when he insisted that the blind were more likely than the sighted to
discover the potential of inner seeing.

He was onto something there, but even for the totally blind the
experience of inner seeing doesn't just happen. When there are no
longer any visual phantasms served up by television, and when even
the natural world of visual objects has completely melted away, it is
true that the blind person will in one way or another turn inward.

But this may be for either good or ill. All too often the blinded person who can no longer participate in the external world in the same old way falls back on the solace of body-feelings, through alcohol or overeating or a cocooning form of sexual preoccupation, or into a mind that is now given over to brooding fantasy or chain-thinking (i.e., entrapment in a long, winding chain of fruitless thoughts). The trouble with this is not that it amounts to an involution but that the involution does not go deep enough. It stops at the embodied and mental forms of ego. The blind man or woman may need some instruction from an in-seer to learn that one can go much further in, right down into the consciousness-self we all share.

Yet I did know of one remarkable blind man who seems to have discovered the consciousness-self completely on his own, and then consistently lived out of it. Jacques Lusseyran, a hero of the French Resistance and survivor of the Buchenwald death camp, was born sighted but lost his vision completely at the age of eight. In his autobiography, *And There Was Light*,[2] Lusseyran describes how he began to look within himself soon after he was blinded and discovered a "light" emanating from a deep place he knew nothing about. This place was both within him and beyond him – "beyond" in the sense that he as an embodied individual was not the source of the light but its recipient. The light illuminated everything, and he came to see the whole world as existing within and because of it. He equated it with life itself, and attributed to it the strength and inner sustenance that helped him survive the horrors of Buchenwald.

What was this light? In some ways Lusseyran's description of it is strikingly similar to Saint Augustine's account of the Light of God that he found at the very centre of his own soul, a Light that for reasons of doctrine, piety, and religious dread he had to regard as utterly other than himself. But Lusseyran's light was the discovery of an eight-year-old whose view of reality was not yet shaped or limited by religious indoctrination. Quite on his own, he came to recognize the light as a universal principle. He identifies it as the real source of all his apperception through the non-visual sense faculties.

Expressed in those terms, it would seem to correspond to our own implicit, taken-for-granted light of consciousness, the irreducible inner observer of our sense-impressions in all their modes. But in Lusseyran's case that light was charged with an unusual degree of continuous attention. It was this faculty of strong, sustained attention that seems to have been responsible for Lusseyran's skill in blind navigation, which was formidable enough to distinguish him as one of the very few who live up to the stereotype of having some kind of super-ophthalmic "sixth sense." Significantly, he did not claim this skill or the power of attention that supported it as his personal attributes. He insisted that both were entirely the work of the light itself.

Lusseyran warned his sighted readers about the addictive material-ism that can steal by degrees over those who habitually allow their undiscriminating gaze to go wandering wherever it will. In a booklet entitled *Against the Pollution of the I*, he describes how the gaze fastens itself to one image after another, inducing covetousness and numbing discriminative judgment, losing interest in each visual dis-play and moving on to the next.[3] This may sound like the scolding of a Catholic moral philosopher with an especially ascetic cast of mind, and Lusseyran was indeed both a Roman Catholic and a pro-fessor of philosophy. But the more I read him the more I felt that he was trying to draw our attention to a danger or self-limitation inherent in ordinary sensory life. It consists in construing our self, through a half-conscious presumption of symmetry, as a kind of inner object that proves in the end to be just as contingent and lacking in abiding value or meaning as the myriad outer objects we see every day.

Well, Lusseyran was long gone, and just as I had sought out blind professionals fifteen years earlier to learn about their practical orga-nizational skills, I now wanted to talk to a blind person who might share some of my interests – including perhaps an interest in Vedanta or Buddhism. I began by doing some networking in the hope of mak-ing contact with blind or visually impaired people who had found the phenomenology of vision loss interesting as a subject in itself. But I didn't have much luck and soon ran out of network. It was at this point that I read John Hull's *Touching the Rock*,[4] which proved to be the most penetrating account of vision loss I had ever come upon. I found out that Dr Hull was scheduled to visit Ottawa in a matter of weeks, which was certainly a fine stroke of serendipity, and I was able to make arrangements for him to give a public talk at the local CNIB. Hull's frank but supportive presentation on the existential challenge of vision loss made a strong impression on his listeners, as I was able to confirm by contacting those audience members I knew in the days that followed.

John Hull lost the vision in one eye in his teens and became totally blind in his late forties. Born and raised in Australia, Dr Hull lived in Britain for many years. He taught at the School of Education,

University of Birmingham, retiring in 2009. His critically acclaimed books on the process of vision loss and total blindness are compelling phenomenological studies that stand in a class by themselves. His method, apparently so simple but rarely achieved in such depth, was to open himself completely to the experience of blindness and especially to touch and sound. The result was the vivid evocation of a world that lies parallel to that of sightedness. *Touching the Rock* is not just about going blind but about *paying attention* to going blind, paying attention so intently and fearlessly that the process is revealed to be something stranger, more engrossing, and more ambiguous than we could have predicted.

What particularly struck me about *Touching the Rock* was that although its author's path to knowledge and acceptance seemed superficially to be the opposite of the one urged by Douglas Harding – that is, a turning of the attention outward toward sense-experience rather than inward toward the conscious source of that experience – both strategies lead in the end to the same questions. What is the self? And what is real? It seems to have been John Hull's experience of blindness, above all else, that prompted his immersion into phenomenological inquiry. At one point in the book, where he contrasts the fitful, episodic, discontinuous nature of sounds and touch-sensations with the smooth continuity or reliable "thereness" of visible objects, Hull writes, "The sighted person lives in the world; the blind person lives in consciousness."

When I discussed this passage with Hull in a follow-up telephone conversation a few days after his public lecture, he was prepared to go further than he had done in print. He said that what sighted people think of as the visible world, the world they live in, is the forms of their own visual consciousness. What Hull meant can best be appreciated, I believe, by first considering the nature of sounds and touch-sensations and the way people react to them, and then comparing this with visual experience. Because specific sounds can be so fleeting, often manifesting only for brief moments before they disappear, it is clear to people that they are sense-impressions rather than the actual objects that give rise to these impressions. And although touch can confirm in a very definite way that a thing is right there concretely in front of us, we know that the touch-sensation is not itself the object being touched. The touch-sensation lasts only until we draw the hand away, after which we either see or assume that the object itself is still "there."

This kind of distinction between hearing and touch on the one hand and their respective objects on the other ought to apply in exactly the same way, one might think, to seeing and the objects of seeing. A visual percept or image arises within the mind, and as a mental phenomenon it should be considered as utterly distinct from the visible object in the external world. But, as I suggested in the second section of chapter 5, what actually happens in everyday perception is that we take our images to be the visible objects themselves. What makes a visual image appear to be a thing-in-itself "out there," according to Hull, is mainly the steadiness of its manifestation within the mind.

A simple comparison will illustrate this. Your ordinary experience tells you that your tactile impression of your favourite chair is not the chair itself, and that your acoustic impression of the radio is not the radio itself. In these cases it is perfectly clear that your touch and sound sensations are not in themselves material objects. But when you take in the visual representations of chair and radio, you are sure that what you are experiencing is the actual objects as they are in themselves rather than images in the mind. The steady gaze seems powerfully to confer a completely independent physical existence upon your own visual percepts, and quite unlike sound and touch the gaze can do this effortlessly and continuously across a broad, three-dimensional panorama.

What this means is that our common experience of external visible objects is nothing more or less than an imaginary externalization of our visual consciousness. Hull summed up this state of affairs with the observation that the world of the sighted is more deceptive than the world of the blind because its objects seem to have an absolute reality that is really an effect of visual consciousness. Thus it is the experience of the blind and not that of the sighted that is closer to the way things really are, at least in the negative sense that the blind are not tied to images that masquerade as objects.

I was pleased and rather relieved to have had those exchanges with John Hull, for they showed that there was someone else who was following a track that was at least in one respect parallel to my own. I had finally met a blind person who could, up to a point, enter intuitively into my experience of vision loss, and echo its implications back to me. For my part, I had been aware for some time of the peculiar fact that sighted people take images to be the actual source or ground of the smells and sounds that accompany them. My example of this in the previous chapter centred on the image of a big diesel truck. I continued to marvel not just at how normal sightedness came bundled with a habit of mentally externalizing the images, but how the sighted did not seem to notice the bundling.

But what I was especially preoccupied with now was a series of odd incidents that I myself had been having, which involved a certain kind of visual anomaly or illusion. They had begun years before my personal crisis of 1994 and continued intermittently afterward. There was something about them that nagged at me, and I found myself almost waiting or wishing to see the next instalment.

2 INSIDE THE MALL: REALITY OR APPEARANCE?

These experiences occurred in various visual settings. The one I describe below – the definitive one, as it turned out – happened in the Rideau Centre, a large shopping mall in downtown Ottawa. The Rideau Centre is complex enough in its layout that even sighted people are apt to get lost there at first. The architect apparently had an aversion to right angles; the corridors of shops comprising the main part of the mall meander in a curvilinear and seemingly arbitrary way. To the blind person it was an absolute labyrinth. Wandering around in it made me feel like a token in a bizarre board game, the rules of which were revealed only to the sighted. I thought I had sussed out a couple of reliable routes through the snakes and ladders by fixing in my memory a series of faint but useful visual cues, at the places where corridors branched or re-branched. But one day in January 1995 I got horribly lost. I couldn't identify anything: the visual display had muddled itself into a complete mess in which there were no identifiable objects at all, and no directional indicators.

Finally I backed up against a wall, holding my cane with both hands, and just stood still with my eyes closed. I took some long, deep breaths and tried to let go of the tension in my shoulders. I wasn't worried about getting stuck – I could always ask someone to help me out – but I wanted to see first whether I could make something out of this jumble. Opening my eyes again I let the gaze pan very slowly across the plane of visual incoherence. And I do mean "plane." There was absolutely no sense of three-dimensionality, just a perfectly flat display of vague colour-shapes that seemed so uniformly close to me that they may as well have been painted onto my eyeballs. Not only were there no things there but no "there" there, no depth of space in which things could inhere. All I could do was keep panning, waiting for some tiny sliver of recognition.

But when recognition came it was not as a sliver, an isolated piece
of this or that: all at once the flatness exploded outward into space,
a space that was instantly filled with more or less recognizable objects
in a coherent array. I felt like whooping for joy, as I had done in my
New Delhi study the day I broke through the surface of the Maitri
Upanishad. For the first time, I had observed the visual phenomenon
closely enough to be sure of what had really happened. The spectacle
that I was now taking in was not the physical structure we call a
shopping mall, but my visual consciousness in the very act of recon-
stituting itself. It was mind rather than matter that was on show.

I had been treated to a demonstration of how the mind creates
within itself a virtual world – the misleadingly solid-looking visual
world described and interpreted by John Hull. Such a world is a
marvellous display made up entirely of sensory-mental projections.
The two-dimensional mess that I was stuck with for perhaps twenty
long minutes was an image within my mind; there was nothing
remotely like it "out there" in the shopping mall. But I had now seen
that very image, in all its flatness and incoherence, suddenly blossom
into three-dimensional coherence. The full 3-D image was the same
mode of reality as the flat image from which it had sprung, the mode
of visual consciousness. The open secret that RP makes so obvious
when it produces the kinds of effects described here is that the
"objects" perceived by all kinds of seers exist within and not outside
of consciousness. This is true whether their visual capacities identify
them as good, bad, or indifferent seers. It turns out that the sensory
mind is not merely passive like a photographic plate but active, as a
creative force.

Right then and there in the mall I knew that sooner or later I would
have to write about this. The unprepared RP patient cannot help but
find such an experience unnerving, even eerie. The spacious visual
world suddenly collapses into a flat smear, then just as suddenly reas-
sembles itself. The first half of this experience casts the patient into
a baffling nowhere. There is the strange sense of one's body being
marooned in a real spatial environment, but at the same time trapped
within something else that is claustrophobically intimate. The "something else" is the collapsed visual mind, which is not identified as such.
This is an instance of real ontological confusion – that is, of finding
oneself unable to recognize the mode of reality that one is occupying.
Such an experience is grist for the mill of ontology, that branch of
philosophy that seeks to reveal and distinguish among the various
modes of being.

The more I thought about it, the more I wanted to draw out the veiled implications of this kind of sensory-mental projection – not just for RP patients, but for people with normal vision as well. These implications had to do not with ophthalmology or neurology, but with the critical link between perception and the world that we believe exists independent of perception. In what follows I will document and try to account for the most amazing feature of our sensory-material life, with its conventional, unexamined world view: the extent to which that view is permeated with illusion. Over the centuries the Eastern and Western negative way traditions, including Advaita, have claimed that our commonplace ideas regarding the nature of things are utterly wrong. Nevertheless, the story of a literal, physical creation set forth in the scriptures of the three Abrahamic religions has had the effect of implicitly validating our materialistic notions of what the world is.

It was only with the advent of empirical philosophy and modern science, as sketched very briefly below, that the traditional world view was effectively refuted. To confront this truth for the first time can be rather jarring, and a little disorienting. But the new picture of the world presented by contemporary science is by no means malign, or inhuman, or some kind of cosmic joke. On the contrary, the world-illusion that we take to be reality is actually a benign and adaptive product of human sensory evolution. Moreover, I hope to show in this and the following section that the new model of reality is consistent with a deeper understanding of self, and a more profound experience of being. It is on that basis that I will try to demonstrate how an authentic view of self and world can liberate the person facing vision loss from irrational and unnecessary fear.

Fortunately, at this point in my long-term study program it so happened that I was supplementing my focus on Indian philosophy with the basic works of the British empirical philosophers, notably George Berkeley. I was also beginning to explore the strange world view of modern physics, which had direct implications for interpreting what happened in the shopping mall. Later I would zero in on two other disciplines, evolutionary biology and developmental psychology, which helped to clarify what befell me that day. In all this I was caught up in a remarkable adventure having to do with appearance and reality, bondage and release. All I can do here is to summarize what came to light as I worked my way through unfamiliar terrain. I must leave it to the reader to adjudicate what follows, and to extract from it – I hope – something of personal value.

George Berkeley (1685–1753) demonstrated in his brilliant analysis of vision that what we take to be external visible objects are really visual percepts within the mind. As we walk toward such an object, and here Berkeley is reminding us of something we have known all our lives, the "object" seems to grow bigger and bigger as we approach it. Then as we walk around it taking it in from all sides, we find that its shape is continually changing. That is just what I saw in the Rideau Centre that day after my visual mind re-assembled itself. I slowly circumambulated a small display table, watching it morph as I recalled Berkeley's basic argument.

His fundamental point is very simple. Ordinary physical things do not grow or shrink or radically change their shape just because we are looking at them from this or that position. What varies is the mental image of the thing within the sensory mind. Berkeley wanted us to grasp that, whatever we may believe the presumed external object of perception to be in itself, a mental image is entirely different. Mental phenomena are of the nature of mind and do not exist outside of mind.

I gathered from my overview of Berkeley's major works[5] that his findings could be interpreted in at least two ways. The radical interpretation – the one embraced by Berkeley himself – is that there is no material world "out there" at all, existing in its own right. There are only the sensory-mental projections that we experience, which in themselves are immaterial. The other interpretation, the one I follow, is that there is indeed a "world" existing apart from our perceptions of it. That world, however, does not in any way correspond to our sensory-mental experience. It is a hidden world, unimaginably strange.

As I began to explore particle physics and quantum theory, what I found defied not only our ordinary experience and constructs but the outer bounds of ordinary imagination. It turns out that physical objects are comprised almost entirely of empty space, haunted at rare intervals by minuscule subatomic particles that in themselves take up virtually no space at all. Indeed, the particles known as electrons and quarks are regarded by some scientists as point-particles, which have absolutely no spatial extension. The total aggregate of all classes of particles is so small, so ephemeral, so almost not there, that the physical world must be taken to be an emptiness, or nearly so. This state of affairs amounts to an outright negation or refutation of our conventional idea of "substance" or "matter."[6] The new, dematerialized model of the world was the result not of speculation but empirical investigation, made possible by the spectacular technological advances of the twentieth century. The new technology has allowed us to probe the constitution of the world right down to the level of the individual atom.

There is another aspect of physics, specifically of quantum mechanics, that totally negates the continuity that we would naturally ascribe to a real physical world. Physicists have determined that subatomic particles are manifest, that is, existent, *only when they are being observed by a human or a measuring instrument*. Between observations they are non-existent, mere potentials that have not been actualized. And that is utterly baffling – to everyone.[7] Richard Feynman (1918–1988), the late acknowledged dean of quantum physicists, used to observe famously and frequently that *nobody* understands quantum mechanics.

Yet the fundamental facts of modern physics – the virtual emptiness of the "physical" world, and the spooky here-again-gone-again manifestation of its basic components – have been affirmed repeatedly for the better part of a century. Erwin Schrödinger (1887–1961), the co-founder of quantum mechanics and a Nobel laureate, was prompted to ground this strange new world view in Indian philosophy. In his book *My View of the World*,[8] Schrödinger drew upon Vedanta and Berkeley in his search for coherence. Later, other physicists such as Robert Oppenheimer, David Bohm, and Arthur Zajonc would be fascinated by the ontology and metaphysics of Vedanta and Buddhism.

Berkeley's philosophy and the findings of modern physics are vectored, it would seem, toward utterly different versions of "reality." But taken together they provide us with a picture of where we really stand, or float. On the one hand, Berkeley's phenomenological acumen – and here I refer only to his analysis of sensory experience, not to his deeper religious philosophy – demonstrates straightforwardly that the "world" we experience is an intricate skein of sensory mind-forms. Such a "world" can be categorized non-judgmentally as an illusion, in the simple sense of not being the physical array we take it to be.

On the other hand, contemporary physics has demonstrated unequivocally that the underlying, actual world of subatomic spook-bits – suddenly appearing, just as suddenly disappearing – is equally lacking in conventional physical reality. Moreover, we cannot get any direct sensory access to the rarified world of the physicist. This means that we have only the directly accessible but wholly immaterial sense-show in which to make our lives. When I first took this in I experienced a little *frisson* of vindication, for in the three or four years leading up to the Rideau Centre incident I had been seized by the fact that people really do take stable, continuous visual images to be physical things-in-themselves (see section 1 above).

I soon found that contemporary evolutionary biologists such as Richard Dawkins, steeped as they are in the findings of the new physics, routinely refer to the common objects of sensory experience (including our own bodies) as beneficent, adaptive illusions. Dawkins's deployment of the term "illusion" is in no way intended to downplay the importance, beauty, and breathtaking complexity of the world-show. To me, the most intriguing thing about his account of perception, as presented for example in a lecture at McGill University several years ago,[9] is his explanation of how the world-show actually arises.

According to the standard model arrived at by evolutionary biology and neurology, our sensory system has evolved in such a way as to create intimate correspondences among our seeing, hearing, touching, smelling, and tasting. The consequence is that when they are experienced, these multi-modal clusters of sensation are projected as seemingly free-standing physical objects existing on their own. Such sensory phenomena comprise what scientists refer to as the sensorium. As Dawkins emphasizes, the sensorium is wonderfully adaptive: it is made up of the very phenomena that allow us to get about, secure food, and stay alive. It is nothing more or less than a boon bestowed by nature, as interpreted for us by Darwin and Dawkins.

The point to be emphasized in all this is that the adaptive process outlined by evolutionary biology strongly conditions us, from moment to moment, to take the sensorium to be a real physical world. Even after we have grasped that a world and a sensorium are utterly different propositions, we repeatedly "forget" this distinction under the pressures and routines of everyday life. As we deal with the sensorium, which seems reciprocally to be dealing with us, or actively bearing down upon us, we automatically take it as pure, hard physicality. This presumption is normal in the sense that it is deeply inculcated into us. But as we shall see, such a presumption can under some circumstances be painfully and ironically maladaptive.

If it is hard to credit that the "physical" world is a sense-show, it can be even more challenging in a personal way to realize that the new science implicitly questions the presumption of an individual physical self. The human body as actually experienced (including internal body-feelings) is part and parcel of the sensorium. As such it is not a thing-in-itself. And even if we could reach down experientially into the subatomic realm, a physical sense of identity or selfhood could not possibly be based on weird particles that "exist" only discontinuously. How could we possibly take ourselves to be exotica that are unperceivable, virtually uncognizable, and for the most part inexistent? I can toss off this rhetorical question now, but I confess that it took some head-banging before that stubborn head finally came to terms with the "personal" implications of the new physics.

All things considered, we would seem to have no choice but to plump for the sensorium and make the most of it. When we do this we find that we are free, perhaps for the first time, to radically reconsider our identity. Although we will find for the most part that we continue to act and feel and think according to the terms of our old, materialistic conditioning, we are free at any moment to turn back to the evidence that reveals our manifest body to be an immaterial aspect of the sensorium. Reviewing the evidence has the effect of opening us up, extracting us from what we had unthinkingly taken ourselves to be. That means among other things that we do *not* have to believe that we are in essence a skin-bag filled with aging flesh, bone, gristle and body fluids, endowing the whole with an imagined, materialistic self-existence. And indeed, sometimes without having to think about it people really do recoil from this blood-and-guts identification, preferring to "have" a body rather than to "be" one. The entity or agent that would most likely "have" our body would be our old friend the ego – whatever the ego eventually proves itself to be. As I observed in chapter 4, section 2, the ego is oddly opaque and illusive, or sometimes marginalized and downright inert. Here one might recall these words from W.B. Yeats: "fastened to a dying animal/it knows not what it is."[10]

The considerations outlined so far in this book – the riddle of identity, including our highly questionable physical identity, the illusive or refractory nature of the ego, and the daunting capacity of science to highlight these uncertainties – apply to each of us, whether we are visually whole or visually impaired. Now: because this book explores selfhood in the context of vision loss I will turn back to the person with RP, having in mind especially the one who has undergone experiences similar to my own. We will address the problem of his or her further visual deterioration, and see what happens when the passage into total blindness is informed by the revolutionary modern world view presented above.

It was almost a decade after the Rideau Centre incident that I came upon the resource that casts a unique and clarifying light on "personal" challenges such as total vision loss: the insightful, liberating account of childhood development and ego-formation articulated by Swiss psychologist Jean Piaget (1896–1980). I found that Piaget's developmental psychology further clarified the overall perspective represented by George Berkeley, evolutionary biology, and a whole raft of physicists, in the sense that Piaget sheds new light on our conventional empirical identity. For example, I could now get a more immediate sense of how Richard Dawkins's adaptive illusion "works," as a pseudo-subject confronting a world of pseudo-objects.

Piaget's depiction of how the infantile sense of ego first arises, and is then consolidated, is justly celebrated.[11] He describes the first uncertain, tenuous, and temporary manifestation of the ego-sense as a function of external perception, the sensory perception of conventional objects. Later on the nascent ego-sense becomes consolidated at the point when the infant forms the definite impression that external realities exist continually in their own right. This breakthrough is referred to by developmental psychologists as "object permanence," the conviction that things exist "out there" even when we are not perceiving them.

The sense of independent reality that has been conferred upon the object of perception now exerts a powerful reciprocal effect on the ego-sense. The upshot is that the ego takes itself to be a real, self-existent, continuous entity – this despite the fact that it dissolves every night into dreamless sleep, as pointed out by Advaita Vedanta. A close reading of Piaget confirms that the ego is not an entity at all, certainly not in the sense that we take a physical body to be an entity. It is instead a mental program, a set of assumptions and routine reactions geared to practical empirical life. But well beyond that, the ego bestows upon itself an intense, defensive conviction of its own reality.

The question, then, is how the ego's conviction of its own self-existence can be maintained when the necessary ties to a complementary object-world begin to unravel. Late-stage RP experience is a good (that is, an intense) case in point. People who have RP develop in the usual way, caught up in a duality within which the sense of a solidly real perceived world is balanced against the sense of a firmly established perceiver. What makes this process so significant and fateful for us, and for other people with untreatable progressive vision loss, is the special role of eyesight. Although the non-visual senses can provide the ego with a sufficient impression of permanent objects in its external world, they cannot do this with anything like the efficiency, vividness, and panoramic inclusiveness of vision. In this regard, the ego might be said metaphorically to feed with a particular avidity on images.

The corollary of this is all too obvious, and all too wrenchingly lived out by many people with RP. As the retina slowly disintegrates, it is natural that there should be concern, then worry, and finally fear. This fear envelops the ego, which in the formative years appropriated the role of self. At this critical juncture the ego finds itself boxed into the stressful position of the self as *seer*. When any ego that strains to function as the putative seer loses its capacity to see, it finds itself facing the prospect of its own total annulment or demise. Yet the ultimate source of that fear is nothing more or less than the ego's unthinking, automatic, deeply conditioned habit of identifying intensely with the faculty of vision. The consequence of this habit is an increasingly frantic clutching after whatever measure of eyesight still remains. At this point it is as though the visually identified ego needs images in the same absolute and desperate way that the body needs oxygen.

This is what it means to see clingingly instead of detachedly, caught up as we are in the unfounded conviction that our sightedness is an indispensable part of our selfhood. For someone with RP to live out of the continuing conviction that sightedness and selfhood are inextricably entangled is to be subjected to a very bad trip indeed. As the patient anticipates the obliteration of the visual world, this "trip" takes on a unique quality of entrapment, becoming in effect a waking nightmare. Fortunately this entire process can be unmasked, clarified, and cancelled out, as an unfortunate set of wrong ontological assumptions.

The process of unmasking or clarifying is by its very nature a kind of release, a liberation. One becomes liberated from a false view of reality. The sense of fear attending final-stage vision loss is based all along on the conviction that a real self in the form of a visually obsessed ego is "losing" a real world made up of conventional physical objects. The truth is that these two interlocked elements – this kind of "self" and that kind of "world" – are illusory. What makes it so difficult to break free of this dilemma is the implicit assumption that the supposed subject and its apparent object are fatefully entwined, standing or falling together. This mindset goes right back, of course, to the infantile conviction of object permanence documented by Piaget. If it were put into words, the mindset would go like this: I (the ego) remain whole for so long as the world (the realm

of materiality) remains both real and accessible. This way of looking
at things, based entirely on illusion, "works" consistently only for
those with workable vision. It is the standard adaptive strategy innocently embraced by the sighted, a strategy that is goal-oriented, automatic, and unreflective.

The saving grace for a person facing imminent blindness is that he
or she has the inherent capacity to "see" (i.e., inwardly grasp) what
is really going on. To exercise that capacity is to realize that the standard model is ontologically haywire. The resources introduced in this
section allow the person with late-stage R P to identify the conventional
view of self and world as a kind of fiction. We can of course acknowledge that this fictional view is adaptive, for the sighted, or more
generally the ego-bound, but we who have R P can well do without
it. For the blind or even sighted person to finally see through the fiction, and let go of false identifications, is to wake up. Awakening
opens the way for the true self, the subtle, commonal self, to slowly
make its presence felt.

For me, piecing together this coherent metaphysical perspective
and applying it to my own circumstances was a unique and abiding
pleasure. Nevertheless, this logical but seemingly radical decoding of
the vision loss crisis is not for everyone. Fortunately there is a much
simpler, common-sense approach that does not require people with
R P to familiarize themselves with the rather specialized materials
offered here. Given the degraded condition of late-stage R P percepts,
it can be gently and persuasively pointed out to the patient, by a doctor or a friend, that the forms to which he or she is clinging are not
actual objects. They are images that bear little resemblance to what
they supposedly represent. Why cling to them as though they were
actual, functional realities? Here the R P patient is left free to continue
to believe in a conventional physical world, even as he or she is
encouraged to just let go of the visual garble that is impeding rather
than helping. The person with R P (or any other blinding disease) can
be told – and this is the unalloyed truth – that no self, no *real* self,
could "lose" its own reality just because ophthalmic images are fading
away. It is the eyes and not the self that go blind, a fact of life that
will be confirmed deep inside when the last remnants of vision have
faded away. I know this to be true, and many others do as well.

John Hull, whom I introduced in the first section of this chapter,
realized after an intense period of fear and suffering that the real self
definitely does not go blind. In this regard our journeys were

remarkably similar, despite the fact that my intuitive sense of a foundational reality was oriented toward the Upanishads, while his was firmly grounded in the Old and New Testaments. In an email message to me dated July 19, 2009, Dr Hull confirmed that he began his descent into blindness encumbered by an intense identification with vision, "which was why I thought at first that I was experiencing the loss of self when it was actually only the tearing away of vision from the self." In what he described as a descent into consciousness, he concluded that the real self lies much deeper than the visually obsessed empirical self or ego.

After receiving this email I contacted Irene Ward, an old friend in Ottawa whose RP is very similar to my own, and shared with her Dr Hull's conclusions. "That's exactly right," Irene responded, "and I wish I had known it thirty years ago when I was struggling with the final stage. It would have made things a lot easier." Dr Hull and Irene and I, and many other people with impaired vision, learned that it is possible to see images knowingly.

To see knowingly is to see in a direct, disentangled way that images are simply images, manifest only within the mind. By all means make use of them for as long as they remain useful, but please, please do not depend on them or defer to them as though they were little material gods. Eventually you will see that you do not need images at all in order to be inwardly whole. In fact, the practice of detached and non-judgmental seeing seems in itself to invite a kind of quiet and subtle inner wholeness or sufficiency, even when the eyes have declined to the point where there is no longer anything much to see. Letting go of poor images without rejecting or demeaning them is a form of acceptance, and over time this begins to have the quality of self-acceptance.

In this short but concentrated section we have explored a great range of actual or possible experiences – metaphysical, psychological, gut-wrenchingly emotional, not to mention the full panoply of sensory experience projected as a "world," and the depiction of a subatomic sub-world that even the physicist acknowledges to be downright weird. I know there must be some readers who are at present feeling a little up in the air, even though the perspective we have opened up would seem to be potentially freeing for the person who is entangled with failing vision. Eventually some fully sighted reader will ask the inevitable question: "What about *us*?" With everything seemingly turned upside-down or inside-out, this clear-eyed skeptic wants to

know how he can now feel that he is permanently grounded in something real and sustaining. What would that something be?

Here I must fall back on my own experience. I find that there is
an inner ground, a deep and buoyant ground that appears to spread
out far beyond the limitations of the individual sensory mind. This
kind of perspective is documented in the annals of many spiritual
traditions, and in the growing literature on transpersonal psychology.
Such a discovery not only acknowledges but celebrates the sensorium
just as it is, that marvellous artifice. A great many people have had
preliminary, temporary glimpses into this ground or substratum,
including me. In that regard I have as yet rendered only half my
account of what actually happened in the shopping mall. In section
3 below I will try to describe the great singularity that came to light .
– a clarifying reality that already abides within us all, but is rarely
attended to. For most of us its full implications are hard to interpret
at first. The most important thing about this experience is that it is
available in equal measure to the fully sighted, the visually impaired,
and the stone-blind.

3 THE GREAT LIGHT OF CONSCIOUSNESS

The full story of the Rideau Centre incident is that when the two-
dimensional mess into which the shopping centre had suddenly collapsed propelled itself with equal abruptness back into three-dimensional
coherence, I knew not one but two things as certainties, the one being
the flip side of the other. First, as already reported, I knew instantly
that the array of projected forms was physically unreal. Second, however, at that same moment it was crystal clear to me that everything
I was seeing owed its presence – its very existence – to the light of
consciousness. The display items in the mall and the structure of the
mall itself were "there," all right, but I was sure that consciousness
contained the whole and somehow *was* the whole. And with that I
felt that I had come home in an entirely new way.

Consciousness had claimed everything as subsidiary to itself. In so
doing it was strongly affirming not only its own lucent presence, but
its entailment and grounding of everything that appeared within it.
During that long hot walk the previous August, when I was still in
the grip of my internalized homophobia, the light of consciousness
had disclosed itself unexpectedly but healingly as the real I. What it
did not then reveal was that the sidewalk and grassy verge, the trees

and birds and all else, were manifest only through – and as – the reality of that light. By contrast, the entire display in the shopping mall was a completely unbroken field that shone as undivided consciousness. It seemed, especially at first, that there were no real divisions or separate things. Everything was uniformly luminous, with a span and depth of subtle luminosity that I had never seen before.

The direct and unmediated "seeing" that reveals the individual objects of the waking state to be virtual, ephemeral things, manifesting within the context of a whole consciousness, is a watershed experience – and not as rare as one might suppose. Such an experience in no way demeans or devalues the waking state and its sensorium, as we shall see below and in the next chapter. I found that the self-disclosure of the sentient light, which for me at this juncture was both the source and the "substance" of every single thing in the mall, was far more significant than the accompanying cancellation of the display's conventional physicality. Such a disclosure is life-affirming in a singular way: it erases the distinction between the depths of consciousness and the breadth of the sensory world. In its great reach, all-inclusiveness, and sheer beauty, it leaves no room for alienation.

The sense of self or "I" in such an experience is not the ego: it is the selfhood that is inherent in the light of consciousness itself. Here there was a subtle but vivid presence, seemingly edgeless, which in a confusing but agreeable way was both "I" and much more than "I." Its very immediacy meant that it must be the consciousness that I had always taken to be my own; on the other hand, the more I stayed with it, in it and as it, the more it seemed to reach far beyond the boundaries of personhood. I must admit that this presence invoked a certain sense of awe. The most obvious word to designate such a presence is consciousness, so I employ that word here, but the singular quality and boundless depth of that light suggests two other terms: spirit, and ground.

I had evidently crossed an internal/external boundary into something new, new at any rate for me. By whatever words it might later be labelled and further described, this reality was commodious, complete in itself, and freeing: that was apparent right from the beginning. Its cardinal feeling-tone was that of generous all-inclusiveness, of consciousness containing the objects of common experience as actually/factually as a raisin pudding contains its raisins. Now and then there arose a corrective counter-feeling, to the effect that because these objects were demonstrably illusory they

lacked the conventional physical "thinghood" that would allow them
to be "contained" at all. I saw this contradiction as a problem of
language that one day I would sort out, and soon fell into the habit
of thinking of the sensorium as being contained, embedded, or even
"enfolded" within consciousness.

There was a certain satisfaction in conceiving my immediate sensory
experience in these terms: that of being able to receive the objects of
perception as a real and direct gift of consciousness. The giver was a
consciousness that was not merely personal, a fact that I kept coming
back to with a sense of wonder that could only stop and stare, so to
speak. I had entered into a mode of experience that not only fore-
shadowed, but offered a bridge into, the world of the Upanishads. As
I had begun to learn during my posting in New Delhi, the Upanishadic
world was open to variant interpretations. My own experience and
working assumptions at this point were different in some respects
from what might have accrued from following a specifically Advaitic
path, but that did not matter for the time being. Because this book is
for the most part a personal record I will take the rest of this section
to highlight those aspects and implications of my new condition that
soon led me into intensive Advaitic study, and proved over the long
run to have lasting value.

The most important change is that I had finally begun to taste
consciousness as it really is: an actual dominant presence. During the
event in the mall there was no evidence of anything lying outside of
consciousness and in fact no "outside" at all; although the visual field
itself was limited, the great consciousness that seemed to contain it
gave the sense of being unbounded. I found myself half-remembering
lines from a poem by the seventeenth-century poet Thomas Traherne,
the authorship of which I confirmed with my friend and volunteer
reader Sonia Tilson:

The sense itself was I.
I felt no dross nor matter in my soul,
No brims nor borders, such as in a bowl
We see. My essence was capacity,
That felt all things[12]

The "I" that presented itself to Traherne in this poem was, I feel,
the same capacious and indivisible light that illumined the Rideau
Centre. As clear, featureless awareness the light is always the same

"everywhere." Its intense self-affirmation in the mall strongly suggested that consciousness and existence (or perhaps consciousness and being) were two names for the same "thing." I was aware that at this stage I must be in what might be called the shallows of this sort of experience. Nevertheless I came away from the mall convinced that it was only through such an experience, preliminary as it no doubt was, that the life-enhancing actuality of the consciousness-self could be entered into.

It was this experience that confirmed for me, once and for all, that the consciousness-self was not distinctively individual. That is, the incident did not involve a strictly personal, exclusionary experience of self. There was, for example, none of the old familiar feeling of "I am I and none other." Nor did the mind serve up any personal pronouns – no "me" or "mine" – that would attribute the self-luminous consciousness to one person only. Just as in the preparatory incident of the previous August, when the light of consciousness had propelled me into accepting my gayness even as it revealed itself as a reality that was deeper than sexual orientation, it disclosed itself in the Rideau Centre as the "I" that had nothing to do either with sightedness or with visual impairment. At the same time, it grounded and affirmed that impairment. This as in the previous incident was a measure of its fullness and generosity, its unconditional acceptance.

What happened to me that day was entirely positive, an experience not of material loss but of intelligibility and gain. That was quite remarkable, as I thought after the fact, for the context had been that of total visual collapse. Collapse might well have occurred again at any moment, as I walked on. But I felt secure and confident. Within or as this consciousness I was safe – safe not necessarily in the "physical" sense, but in the felt presence of self-sufficiency. One had the impression that the sufficiency was foundational and unconditional, that it was always available wherever one happened to be. In that regard, what I used to call the "centre" had spread out in all directions.

I would not be surprised if the reader judged this incident to be an oddball happening that lies beyond the ambit of his or her own experience, both actual and potential. As such it would be seen as peculiar to the author. But I believe that what I fell into that day was something that could make anyone's life better: a more affirmative and secure sense of foundational selfhood. The experience described above is so simple, so grounded in the present moment and uncluttered by theory, so clearly expressive of the consciousness available to us all, that it

would seem to be the exact opposite of a one-off or singleton or quirk.
That pre-ophthalmic light is there, all right, its verification requiring
only that we somehow open up to it. We then find that it contains
everything within our ken.

The incident in the mall convinced me that this kind of opening
must have occurred to many, many people. Once you know what to
look for you can find signs of it not only in explicitly spiritual literature
but in the memoirs, poetry, and private correspondence of intuitives
such as Thomas Traherne, William Blake, Walt Whitman and Alfred,
Lord Tennyson. They *knew*. As I will describe in chapter 7 it is certainly
possible, given sufficient time and patience, for any interested seeker
to prepare for and eventually invite a glimpse into the consciousness-
based nature of things. We will see that this can come about through
an Advaitic practice known as mindfulness or witnessing.

In the meantime, I will try to sum up what we have seen so far in
simple, plain, non-poetical terms: the objects of common experience
do not exist in themselves but are somehow inseparable from consciousness; as such, they constitute a sensorium rather than a physical
world; we are, however, massively conditioned to keep regarding that
sensorium as a physical world despite all the countervailing evidence
from modern physics; and, for many people, this situation continues
unresolved until some unexpected event vividly exposes the plain
facts of sensory existence. As turned over and digested in the mind,
the opening becomes a direct, experiential complement to the critique
of materialism set out in section 2 above.

It is right here that a reader with a conservative world view, whose
skepticism is tempered with a generous measure of curiosity, asks a
pointed question: What's all this stuff good for? Quite a lot, actually.
Here's a partial list of the implications.

1 It turns out that what we call common sense is good at practical
   adaptation, but poor at ontological revelation.
2 With regard to the specific kind of ophthalmic/personal threat
   addressed by this book, it also turns out that you as the consciousness you truly are will never go blind, for consciousness
   is deeper than sightedness or blindness and is unaffected by
   the latter.
3 More broadly, the light of consciousness is wide open to the
   sensorium and registers the whole lot unresistingly; what this
   means is that, to the extent that you can align your sense of self

with consciousness as such, you can learn to un-self the experience of sensory degradation in any of its modalities. In the same
way, you can mindfully insert a buffer of detachment between
the consciousness-self and the somatic experiences of aging. At
my stage of life and with my particular infirmities, I find this
buffer invaluable.

4 As for the ego, the experience of RP vision loss illustrates a
   more general theme bearing on our compulsive, ego-driven identification with the elements of the sensory body-mind. When the
   person going blind begins to sense the presence of the consciousness-self, or even when she begins to seriously question the
   validity of a self based on nothing but egoized identifications,
   there can be a liberating kind of inner "reset." She may discover
   – and this is further to point 2 above – that she can at last begin
   to give up the old (and by now careworn) habit of surrendering
   her sense of self to the benighted visual ego, that is, to the ego in
   its particular mode or identity as "the seer." She may finally realize that the seemingly doomed "seer" is just a mental construct,
   an imaginary ophthalmic entity that doesn't in the least know
   what's what. An imaginary entity doesn't know *anything*.

In consequence, the sense of self will deepen, or perhaps for a time
simply shift into the other sensory modalities. These too can now be
viewed more objectively, less clingingly. There will be a corresponding
sloughing-off of accumulated, somaticized stress. I can tell you first-
hand that this decompression can be felt as a great boon.

The paradigm outlined here – compulsive identification with something that lacks the kind of reality ascribed to it by so-called common
sense, followed by clarification and the relief of letting go – can be
applied to many challenging experiences, both extro- and intro-sen-
sory, experiences to which the ego would normally react with fear or
righteous indignation. I will provide examples from my own experience in the following chapter. But here I must at least mention in
passing one benefit of "seeing" things as they really are that I would
not have anticipated in advance. When it finally really sinks in that
the actual status of the objects of common experience is that of sense-
forms having absolutely no existence apart from consciousness, there
can be a diminishment of the old ego-based urge to buy and possess
things as a form of supposed self-enhancement. The practical result,
I found, was that after 1995 I could live more comfortably on the

reduced pension that necessarily follows from enforced early retirement on medical grounds.

But there are deeper benefits. When it finally sinks in that the sense-
forms comprising our own bodies have no reality outside of consciousness, there can be a fundamental shift in what philosophers refer to
as the experience of being. The full implications of this shift may not
at first be apparent. Advaita affirms that our true being is commonal,
transpersonal, supra-individual, as represented by the concept of the
Atman – the universal self. According to this teaching the Atman
concept can in due course open up for the seeker into a direct intuition,
that of an apprehended universality of the basic selfhood that we
share with all our "others." The reference here is very specific; this
transpersonal selfhood is the clear and transparent "light" that illumines all minds, not some shared feature contained within those
minds. From the experience in the mall and its reconfirmation over
the following years, I came to feel sure that that "light" in its very
formlessness and featurelessness was one and the same for all of us.

Such a commonal light, if it were acknowledged and attended to,
could be the basis for a much broader fellow-feeling and sympathy.
The idea or presentiment of such a commonality may lie behind the
remarkable Jewish injunction to love one's neighbour *as oneself*
(Leviticus 19:18), taken up and reiterated by Jesus in Matthew 22:38,
etc. What do these injunctions actually mean? According to many
Jewish and New Testament scholars who are linguistically equipped
to parse the original Hebrew or Greek, we are not told in these passages that we should love our neighbour to the same extent that we
love our self, or that we should take our neighbour to be our self
metaphorically; we are instead to love him literally *as our self*. Such
an interpretation is of course not only onerous – "Wait, I'm supposed
to love *him*?" – but revolutionary, seemingly impossible.

In Matthew 25:34–40 Jesus goes on to present one of his challenging, variously interpretable parables. The setting is seemingly posthumous and celestial, with the righteous (in effect the disciples to
whom Jesus is telling the parable) gathered all together in his presence.
He recounts how they fed and clothed and nursed him and visited
him when he was in prison. They express puzzlement, pointing out
that he had never been in such straits, so they could not possibly have
performed any of those acts for him. Jesus responds with this:
"Inasmuch as ye have done it unto one of the least of these my breth-
ren, ye have done it unto me."

What Jesus seems to be invoking in this exchange, with its implicit emphasis on a helping or giving that somehow reaches beyond the identity of any individual recipient, is an apprehended oneness or co-identity that involves them all. Yet evidently it was only Jesus who was able to feel this commonality fully and directly. Given this fact, his purpose was to implicitly query the conventional notion of individuality (which as we would express it is based on the ego), while indirectly suggesting a shared transpersonal ground. An Advaitin would identify this ground as the light of consciousness; given the separate existence of individual body-minds, that light would seem to be the only common feature that is wholly shared by the group. We can speculate that for Jesus, at least, that light had the ineffable quality of spirit.

We may have heard or read reports of what would seem to be a conscious ground that is shared among individuals, or perhaps we have experienced a little taste of this kind of thing ourselves. Such an experience generally involves love, spontaneous love as distinct perhaps from the mandated love of those old Levitican injunctions, and typically it seems to include the knowledge that the oneness or commonality is not at the level of the different individual bodies or personalities. When I was struggling with my internalized homophobia in 1994, I came across an account of such a union that meant a great deal to me. It was in Paul Monette's *Borrowed Time*,[13] in which the Pulitzer Prize–winning author describes his partner's desperate battle against AIDS: "Six weeks before Roger died he looked over at me astonished one day in the hospital, eyes dim with the gathering blindness. 'But we're the same person,' he said, in a sort of bewildered delight. 'When did that happen?'"

This is what can sometimes occur when the terrible process of terminal illness somehow manages to burn away rather than reinforce one's exclusive identification with the individual body-mind. What Roger Horowitz glimpsed was a oneness of person, as he expressed it, that underlay the particulars of their relationship and was clearly based – just read the book for yourself and you'll see – on love. As I was to learn from my reading of Advaita Vedanta a few years later, Advaita identifies love as the heart's intimation of non-duality. Indeed, when I first read *Borrowed Time* I was sure even then that the kind of love those two men experienced must in its essence always be very much the same, whether the sometimes rocky path that leads to it is gay, straight, familial, or avocational – along the lines, for example, of a dedicated religious community. All these paths lead to the same door, which in some circumstances opens exactly wide enough for two.

In this chapter I have tried through various means to deconstruct the conventional world view and to present in its stead a consciousness-based ontology. Despite our obsession with conventional objects we actually live as and through consciousness, both in ordinary daily life and our deeper experience. Given the kinds of misunderstandings and problems outlined in this book, we might wish to get to know consciousness a little better. This means reversing the arrow of our attention and going down deeper into consciousness itself. I am not talking about mysticism but a form of direct knowledge, which most of us in our busy lives never get around to seeking or even recognizing as a possibility.

Every life has its turning points, and what happened in the Rideau Centre that day was one of mine. In an absolutely direct, simple, non-conceptual way it changed everything. In drawing upon my old audio cassette diaries I have allowed the sometimes earnest or urgent or even proselytizing tone of the original to stand, for nothing I have seen subsequently of life as we live it, and of visual false selfing as we suffer it, would lead me to alter my analysis or dilute my prescription. What I especially liked about the Rideau Centre experience was the way it opened up the big questions about the nature of things, only to swing back inevitably to the nitty-gritty of RP phenomenality and the jittery ego that is entangled with it. This was a way of grounding philosophy and science in the particulars of daily life as some of us have come to live it. I also liked the fact that the potential egodystonia that lurks within our contingent and fragile sightedness should have been exposed and parsed as a result of a visit to a large glitzy shopping mall, a venue that is expressly designed to feed the ego's fantasies by attracting its hungry gaze. The irony would have tickled Jacques Lusseyran.

My commentary here has been informed by my study of Advaita in the years following the adventure in the mall. But my description of that experience is based squarely on the account that I dictated onto audio cassette later that same day. This was a first leap or fall into an ontology and metaphysics that would eventually, years later, sort itself out. As the next two chapters will illustrate, there would be new medical and practical difficulties that sometimes occluded my consciousness-based perspective. Nor had I yet got down to the deepest level of unresolved, somaticized childhood trauma, which would continue for seven more years to constrict my life in ways that I scarcely understood. But over the long run the new perspective could not be denied.

The Advaitic classics that I would absorb over the coming years did not focus as intently as I have done here on the ontological status of visual forms, because those works were not intended specifically for seekers who were undergoing a vision-related identity crisis. But the classics do in the end affirm the truth that all the objects of common experience would be utterly nonexistent without consciousness, and that to go down knowingly into consciousness and relinquish one's maladaptive attachments is the way to a better, clearer life. If you have RP you may well have to deal at some point with the same kind of curious phenomena that I experienced in the Rideau Centre. Please believe me that it is far better to understand such an experience in the terms outlined in this chapter than to react to it helplessly – angrily, egocentrically. Leave the visual experience of egohood to those who can innocently enjoy it – the fully sighted who see clearly but do not know *what* they see. For those of us who have RP it is better to live in the truth. The truth may stretch our commonplace minds, but it really can be freeing.

7

Learning to Live an Ancient Teaching

1 TAKING IT IN AND LETTING IT WORK

In the second half of the 1990s I began the long and deliberate process of liberating my sense of selfhood from the constrictions and contradictions of our conventional, illusory identity. I did this by focusing all the energy I could muster into absorbing the classics of the Advaitic school of Vedantic philosophy. I knew from my previous reading that Advaita Vedanta is widely considered to be the most challenging and logically consistent of the orthodox Indian philosophical systems. Its most famous proponent, the eighth- and ninth-century monk Shankara (Shankaracharya), is generally regarded as India's greatest philosopher.

The key Advaitic texts were finally becoming available to me in an accessible format, and I immersed myself in their core teachings and methodology. What made this study program possible was the generous and skilful support of Dana Mullen, Sonia Tilson, and the late John Rogers, the three volunteer readers who recorded a formidable amount of Advaitic and related material onto cassette tape exclusively for my use. Their practical help and friendship has been an inestimable gift. All three were retired university teachers, and it was in part because they were interested in learning more about Indian philosophy and spirituality that they volunteered for this work.

Our journey into Advaita was for all of us a new and uniquely challenging form of learning. Advaitic core teaching can at first seem novel and exotic and remote, as though one were looking in on it from a considerable distance, while at other times it may feel exacting and highly technical. With familiarity and application, all of that eventually changes. Because of the sharpness and directness with which the Advaitic texts trench into the question of our real identity, reading them can become an intense and very "personal" experience. That is because the truth-claims and direct revelations of Advaita can be threatening to the embedded ego, as I was to experience. But over the long run I would find that the clarity and beauty of Advaitic thought invite a kind of inner affirmation, or direct recognition. At a certain point I began to apply these teachings – as though this had been planned all along – to my changing sensory-medical circumstances.

I will try here to present a thumbnail sketch of Advaita Vedanta – an exercise that may only show why such a summary is impossible. With a subject such as this, words can only fail. That is because the Spirit, or Ground of Being, or Brahman, or whatever we want to call it, is ineffable – a word that refers to that which is beyond all words. Language is invariably about division, the "this" as distinct from the "that," while the label "Brahman" refers to that which has no divisions at all, no opposite, no "others," and no qualifiers. Yet the student of Advaita is somehow compelled to speak or scribble about the indescribable, as I am doing here.

Advaita is a vast and many-sided philosophy, but it does present at least one feature or finding that readers of this book can immediately seize upon. More than a millennium ago classical Advaita anticipated (and phenomenologically demonstrated) the kind of scientifically informed world view presented in chapter 6, the key finding of which is that the "physical" objects we perceive are illusory. To be sure, Advaitic ontology begins gently and reassuringly by acknowledging the conventional, empirical realities. These consist of individual subjects and the multitude of objects they perceive. This is but a provisional position, however, one that Advaita proceeds to take totally apart. Through careful analysis Advaita shows that the objects of common experience are but sensory projections, while a close examination of the ego-based subject reveals it to be nothing but a mental construct that "exists" only during the waking state. The ego is neither an entity nor a viable self.

But quite apart from these pseudo-selves and the illusory sense-show, Advaita posits a reality that is absolute and unqualified: Brahman. It is against the reality of Brahman that illusory subjects and their objects of perception manifest, and into which they all inevitably dissolve. In the ancient Advaitic teaching the student is introduced, perhaps from his earliest years, to the Upanishadic teaching on Brahman, the ultimate reality from which we are in no way separated. Expressed most simply and starkly, Brahman is the actuality and universality of consciousness and being. These two elements, consciousness and being, are the metaphysical realities that in their essence prove to be not only inseparable, but non-different from each other. That is, Brahman may be thought of as a being that is so complete, unlimited, and unqualified that it includes the capacity to consciously know itself. Correspondingly or reciprocally, Brahman is a consciousness that is so intensely present to itself that, metaphorically speaking, it has the density and immediacy of pure being.

This primal condition of Brahmanic non-duality, as consciousness/being, is expressed concisely by the word "Advaita." Advaita means indivisible or undifferentiated. It is the ultimate goal of Advaitic study and immersion to realize through direct experience the wholeness of Brahman, the Brahman that is already right here, right now. The Upanishads present this unitary reality in various ways, most famously through myth, metaphor, and rhapsodic invocation. But the most telling passages in the Upanishads are those which, out of the blue, equate the commonal self in which we all share – the Atman introduced in chapter 4 – with the absolute reality of Brahman.

These challenging Upanishadic passages are known as the Mahavakyas, a word that may be translated as the Great Affirmations or Great Equations.[1] It is the purpose of the Mahavakyas to reveal how an individual self is an illusion, and how the Atman-consciousness that we all share is indistinguishable from the consciousness of Brahman. The way to penetrate the Mahavakyas is to grasp how the attributes regularly assigned to a conventional self, and to a conventional creator or personal god, turn out to be parallel examples of inconsistency or self-contradiction. What remains after these two sets of accretions are stripped away is an intuitive sense of the single ineffable reality that is our true nature. This "stripping" and the realization to which it leads is an exemplary demonstration of the transcultural, Eastern/Western negative way introduced in chapter 5, section 1.

It is tempting to draw parallels between Brahman and other iterations of the absolute that have evolved out of the negative way: the Tao, the indefinable Suchness of Buddhism, the plenum void of Neoplatonic Christian mystics, and the godhead proposed by those Jewish, Christian, and Islamic theologians who sense that there must be a unique and absolute reality that lies beyond any conventional definition of "God."

The problem is that this unique reality, unveiled through a process of sheer negation, tempts the student or devotee to say something positive about it. Such a positive characterization would only have the effect of once again veiling Brahman: it is better to remain silent. If something must be said within the context of the Advaitic tradition, it can be legitimately couched in terms of complete non-duality. One simply observes that the full realization of Brahman by the seeker cancels out the dualities of I and thou, the human and the divine, consciousness and matter, subject and object. Such a realization is a very rare achievement, one that is said to be charged with joy and an indescribable depth of being.

This kind of spirituality is not for everyone. Even after I committed myself to a serious program of Advaitic study, I found myself half-resisting the idea that enlightenment could ever be for me. Yet I soon discovered that I could not pull out of Advaita, now that I had entered into its early stages. I was caught up in a classic attraction/avoidance conflict; I was very aware of this, and found the situation intriguing. Now, the reader may view with either interest or healthy skepticism the twin claims that Brahman is real, and that a supra-egocentric enlightenment or Brahman-realization is actually possible. That does not matter for our investigations throughout the remainder of this book. I am not an adept in Advaitic spiritual practice, but an auto-biographer who wants to get on with his story. That story will reflect aspects of Advaita to the extent that its teaching continued to get under my skin. Eventually I became not a disciple – I never had a live teacher – but a kind of trial-and-error journeyman. In the rest of this section I will begin to lay out some very practical and life-enhancing resources offered by Advaita, those that found application to my sensory and physical problems.

The new study project and its applications were the natural culmi-nation not only of my earlier reading in Vedanta but my more recent experience with the quirky phenomena of late-stage RP. These startling manifestations were of a character that positively invited a thorough reconsideration of our most basic assumptions – assumptions having to do with our worldly identity, and the nature of the sensory world itself. The axis around which my thoughts turned, as I continued to interrogate the implicit truth-claims of the senses, was the Rideau Centre incident described in the previous chapter.

What mattered most about that watershed experience was not so much the refutation of physical identities that are conventionally assigned to sense-forms, but the lucent presence of a consciousness that was both the ground of those forms and the essence of my self-hood. Moreover, the manifest consciousness-self seemed to be an expression of a completely affirmative, almost palpable sense of being. This sense of being was non-exclusive, as I emphasized in chapter 6; it was apparently transpersonal. I could experience this but not yet adequately conceptualize it.

In 1995–96 I was beginning to take in the stream of audio recordings issuing from my enthusiastic volunteer readers, even as my physical/sensory life was becoming more complicated. In the wake of the Rideau Centre incident the new consciousness-based perspective did not fade away, and this was the most important fact of life bearing on my reception of the tape-recorded Advaitic material. It was the clear light of consciousness that brought the material alive, and it was against this positive background that I would experience the continuing deterioration of my eyesight. Over the succeeding months and years I found that the perspective opened up by Advaitic teaching was not only habitable from day to day, but buoying.

Here by way of illustrating the natural, unforced, and almost ordinary nature of the consciousness-based perspective is a short passage from a diary that I kept during the first year of my reading program, 1995–96. With a few slight modifications, this is one of the several diary excerpts describing white cane mobility that were eventually published in the literary journal *Ars Medica*.

Today I went for a walk all the way down to the river for the first time this season. No problems. Very pleasant. Only a little dizzy and shaky. There was just one moment on the far side of the eastern parkway when I got completely turned around, at the point where I had to find the beginning of a gravel slope that leads down the hill to the bike path. I stood there gripping my cane, not sure of what was before me. Was I facing toward the slope or the river or the trees? I listened very carefully, and while I waited for sound cues I slowly turned my head and looked around a full 180 degrees, seeing a dimensionless incoherent wash of blurry shades of grey with no edges anywhere. And I thought, how eerie this is, this visible something that is really nothing, this unrevealing light that seems to cling to my face. It could be either the great empty space of the river valley or a dense copse of trees just a few feet off. This is what my sensorium has become, still predominantly visual but often formless.

Soon I got my auditory cues and turned to face what I now knew was the beginning of a downhill slope. It was only then that I began to feel, with my face, the sense of great volume extending far beyond me. Was this imagination? Will I one day be able to sense the voluminousness as soon as I enter such a scene, direct and untranslated and without the need for confirming audio cues, as some long-experienced blind people can do? Whether I do or not the remarkable fact remains that this luminous, ephemeral river valley is spread out entirely and only within my consciousness. That is the real marvel.[2]

What is described above was for me a new world view, one through which unexpected problems could be addressed by using new life-tools and techniques drawn mainly from Advaita. I will try to illustrate a single key theme – that of a livable and fertile "middle ground." This "ground" may be conceived of as lying between two distinct alternatives. These are (1) the conventional view of the world and self, based on unreflective materialism, and (2) the profound serenity of full Advaitic enlightenment or self-realization.

The middle ground that lies between this set of polarities is simply the living-out of the new understanding introduced in chapter 6. This understanding recognizes the first polarity as a product of the adaptive evolutionary process, a pragmatic mindset that remains livable for so long as circumstances do not unravel in any of the many ways that can shred our self-confidence, or even our sense of self. By contrast with this conventional and vulnerable mindset, the non-materialistic middle ground is open to the light of consciousness in a way that eventually brings it forward as the ultimate adaptive resource. The feeling-tone that characterizes the middle ground is that of curiosity, venture, and flexibility, and by degrees it involves a relinquishment of egocentrism. This is not the enlightenment of the second polarity above, or anything remotely like it. It is instead a program of inner opening and self-examination that proves to be far more adaptive than the first polarity. I have found that occupying this middle ground definitely beats taking oneself to be a virtual sitting duck – a material thing among things – when material circumstances change for the worse.

I hope to show as we proceed that it is in large part the practical utility of basic Advaitic teaching that makes a habitable middle ground possible. It may seem surprising that a philosophy that occupies itself with the biggest of the big metaphysical questions should be able to help us with specific life-problems, yet this is the case. It is especially under the weight of problems that pose a real existential threat that Advaita reveals itself to be something more than a set of remote and inert dogmas. Advaita is a way to inner clarification and decompression based on ideas that are meant to be tested out, and here we will look at some of the clear and accessible means by which they can be tested.

Our examination of visually entangled false selfing will illustrate how the general process of Advaitic self-clarification works. Advaita is a means to knowledge that remains one and the same whether the object of refutation is the ego-based self in all its forms or just one of those forms, the visual. In either case Advaita aims at direct insight through the exposure and negation of our conventional beliefs. This is the seeing of a truth so clearly that it effects an internal change. To see simply and directly that a particular self-construct is false and maladaptive is to begin letting it go, and to begin letting go of the fear, resistance, anger, and unhappiness that may be wrapped around it. One falls back from this complex into a more secure anterior position where the sense of self deepens of its own accord – subtly, perhaps, but sometimes dramatically.

Many people have experienced a slow, gradual, but cumulative opening into the hidden light of core consciousness, which is our true selfhood. Because that selfhood is real it can by degrees impress itself on the empirical mind. Consider for example a seemingly ordinary old woman in a retirement home, as I imagine her. Over the years she has found herself attending to her inner openings and subsiding more deeply into them, because they seem to be significant. When she takes in the sight of her gnarled, wrinkled, liver-spotted hands, considers the unreliable state of her failing memory and the great changes that time has wrought on many of her most basic convictions, and just gazes across the room, she experiences something that if put into words would go, "But *I* have not changed." Now and then she does frame the experience in language just in order to stand back from it and consider its remarkable fidelity to itself, shifting it into the third person. She thinks, "It never changes," and "It is always here."

If a person such as this should go blind, she may well find some of the adjustments difficult because of her age. But that inner self-affirmation would remain unchanged, for it arises out of the clear inner light that has no degradable features. This dignified, untutored old lady has never heard of Advaita Vedanta. But if she were given the opportunity to look into it, she would immediately recognize as familiar and valid its teaching on the importance of disidentifying from both the body and the stream of mind-forms. That is something she has gradually worked out for herself, for she knows that she is something deeper, clearer, and simpler than these. She cannot name it, this presence that illumines her from within. She just says, "It is right *here*," indicating her heart rather than her head.

What I find truly remarkable is that sometimes we can spontaneously let go of some kind of suffering without realizing as yet that we are also letting go of the identification with body and senses to which the suffering had clung. That is exactly what happened to me five decades ago when I first said yes to blindness while sitting in that doctor's office in Edmonton. This was long before my introduction to Advaita, or any other school of Vedanta. When I took in the doctor's prognosis without the spasm of resistance that might be expected at such a moment, I let go of the fear and denial that was attached to the besieged sighted self, without quite grasping that I was also beginning to relinquish the notion of sighted selfhood as such. It would not have occurred to me at that point to describe what was happening as the repudiation of a false self in favour of the true, but something of this sort was registered inwardly.

As I sat there opposite the silent and watchful doctor, the mind represented this inner change in the only way it could. It conjured up the vivid image of a sheer chalk cliff face. That dead-white but otherwise featureless expanse was of course blindness itself, entirely filling up and nullifying the visual field of the mind's eye. But the cliff was climbable – that was the vital point. In this symbolic rendering, the self was coming to terms with blindness by metaphorically scaling it and leaving the old, vision-entangled mode of egohood behind. And yet this real self was not in itself blind. The climber knows the difference between himself and the object he is climbing. Implicitly, then, the real self would have to be a principle distinct from both the presence and absence of vision. It must stand apart not only from vision but also from the other bodily senses and probably the body itself. This is what I half-knew or guessed, but could not yet put into words.

Advaitic teaching helps us make this kind of implicit discovery far more explicit and certain, by opening the way to insight into what we are and what we are not. Without this insight the person with RP is apt to slip back into visual false selfing under the increasing pressure of degrading eyesight, as I did during the years 1980 through 1987. All that may be required to lift the patient out of this regression is the simple presentation of an equally simple idea – the idea that there can be a secure experience of self in which the senses can be observed without identifying with them. It was this idea, mediated through the Upanishads, that resulted in the breakthrough experience in my New Delhi study (chapter 3, section 2).

What these snippets from my biography illustrate is a particular mode of experience that Advaita values and seeks to further develop. I have referred to it directly or indirectly at various points throughout this narrative. It consists of taking oneself to be a locus or centre of consciousness from which all aspects of body, senses, and mind can be acknowledged and accepted for what they are, even as they are recognized as not-I. In Advaita this centre of consciousness is referred to as the witness (*sakshin*). The witness is not a person or any other kind of entity; it is quite simply one's bare sense of "I" in the formless form of clear consciousness. Its lucent presence will normally be obscured by the egoized mind.

It is in and as the witness that we can come to see in a vivid and direct way the distinction between subject and object, the real and the unreal, inner freedom and circumstantial bondage. In section 3 of chapter 6 I made an observation about the very real possibility of self-acceptance in the midst of failing vision, as follows: "the practice of detached seeing seems in itself to invite a kind of quiet and subtle inner wholeness or sufficiency, even when the eyes have declined to the point where there is no longer anything much to see." This was in fact a description of the witness mode of consciousness.

One of the principal methods that Advaita has developed for invoking the witness is a special kind of attention to what might be called our total, ego-driven constitution. This is a method for examining the various aspects of our conventional identity with such impartiality that we seem to be seeing them for the very first time. The initial step in this process is analytical: the body-mind is disaggregated into five orders of gross and subtle matter referred to metaphorically as "sheaths" (koshas). These are the successive layers of our ordinary identity experienced physically, sensorially, mentally, and emotionally. Each sheath or kosha has its own phenomenality, appearing as a certain class of phenomena.

Starting with the outer gross body and moving inward, the five koshas are scrutinized in turn to determine whether any of them, singly or collectively, or specific components of one or more of them, actually measure up to a reasonable understanding of what the self could be. The most important criterion for making this determination is the distinction between subject and object. The actual practice of subject-object discrimination is frequently rendered by Advaita as discrimination between the seeing and the seen. This all-important and startlingly immediate form of ontological reasoning crops up in an implicit way in other spiritual and philosophical traditions, but so far as I know it is only Advaita that makes its nature and implications crystal clear. Subject-object discrimination is the real key to understanding why neither the objective body nor the objectively present flow of mind-forms can be the observing subject – i.e., the witness.

The second step in kosha work, one that follows naturally from grasping the analytical distinction between subject and object, is to actually contemplate the sheaths as not-I. If the first step helps us to think outside the box of conventional identity, the second allows us to feel ourselves as an inner reality independent of the five categories of our immediate inner experience. That is, when we knowingly view the koshas simply as objects of knowledge we spontaneously take up the position of the provisional subject or witness, feeling the change without having to think about it. It is from this new and deeper position that the various aspects of the personality can be seen to belong to the mental koshas, not to the consciousness-self that witnesses those koshas. Yet this is *not* an exercise in alienation or rejection. To witness the complex personality from the depths of the consciousness-self is to see it, perhaps, with a non-judgmental sympathy that may not have been available before.

There is nothing "theoretical" about kosha work. It is a direct and unmediated knowing of oneself in a new way. For a time this will be felt simply as the confirmation that one is detached, as the witness, from all five koshas. The observant and autonomous witness seems to be right "here" at dead centre, while the kosha components are just "there," slightly and interestingly off centre. By degrees this may give way, as I intimated earlier, to the feeling that the witnessing consciousness actually contains the koshas within itself, or alternatively that it somehow "grounds" the koshas. This is part and parcel of the fluid and flexible experience that characterizes the "middle ground" referred to above.

It is worth knowing in advance that the switch into the role of the witness will at first be temporary. For those who are new to kosha

work, the experience of being the witness tends to give way to conventional embodied egohood when it is necessary to turn from the
practice to the demands of ordinary life. But we can go back to the
exercise, or rather to some specific application of it, as often as it
occurs to us to do so. The most obvious application is to inwardly
"see" as not-I some component of the body-mind that is giving us
trouble right at that moment, without rejecting or disowning it. This
is actually a remembrance, an immediate inner "click" that takes us
back to what we realized about self and not-self through the praxis
of kosha work. Sometimes we feel the click, sometimes we don't. In
this regard kosha work is not a panacea for the wrenchings of egoism,
but it is an invaluable step toward detached self-containment. It
provides a foundation of active self-knowledge upon which other
practices can later be developed, practices that are far more a matter
of inner "seeing" than any kind of "doing."

As for my own introduction to this resource, I discovered kosha
work in the late 1990s through reading the Advaitic classics, most
notably the Commentaries of Shankara. I entered into kosha work
in minute detail, sheath by sheath and component by component,
repeating the procedure many times over. In doing this contemplation
or reorientation I was entirely untutored; I just focused my attention
on particular aspects of the body-mind, and allowed myself to experience the perfectly obvious fact that I contained them without being
them. I could view all the koshas as not-I without feeling in the least
alienated from them, allowing them to replace one another in awareness as I took in each phenomenon in turn. This experience felt more
and more natural and wholesome the more I did the exercise.

Even in those early days I came to think of kosha work as practical
ontology. While its ultimate goal was a rare kind of knowledge, its
cumulative effect even for a neophyte practitioner like me was to
steadily dissipate the suffering generated by false identifications.
Experiencing the koshas by the light of subject-object discrimination
is a way for people with eroding eyesight to do deliberately what I
had done spontaneously in New Delhi: disidentify from failing vision.

It struck me after learning the value of kosha work that we moderns
are really in a unique position when it comes to challenging the presumption of an intrinsically sighted self, a presumption that can make
the experience of going blind so awful. We have seen that it is possible
to draw upon some of the interlinked findings of modern science,
especially those of developmental psychology, to reveal as hollow the

conviction that the image-obsessed ego is an inherently real entity. When we couple this science with the Advaitic kosha work that shows both through reason and direct inner "seeing" that the observing consciousness-self is entirely separate from all five sheaths, and thus from the restless ego-sense, the combined effect of the modern Western and ancient Indian disciplines is powerful. It is like having not just one observer but two who take in the same truth from two different angles, and then have the satisfaction of sharing their mutually confirming notes.

2 SPIRITUAL PRACTICE AS STRESS MANAGEMENT

The coping strategies that I have learned to apply to my changing physical and sensory circumstances can be thought of either as stress management techniques or spiritual practice – they are actually both. Within the Advaitic canon there are traditional practices or exercises that calm the mind and open it to metaphysical insight and practical coping. Such practices invite a welcome loosening of our habitual attachments, so that in our regular daily round the mind can remain open and rest in simple, alert, motiveless awareness. This is a flexible and relatively de-egoized mind, one that can be turned toward a succession of goals as external conditions change.

Before I got into the kosha work outlined in section 1 above I had wrestled for many years with the problem of how to develop a practice, for unlike most students of Advaita I was not a personal disciple (*chela*) of a specific guru. Learning about the applications described in this and the following section – and, more importantly, developing the habit of actually using them – did not happen all at once. This required time, immersion in those texts that had something to say about practice, and real soul-searching on my part. The latter had to do with my ongoing unease regarding the adequacy of my own latent capacities, and the question of how "deeply" I wanted to go.

Advaita sees not just kosha work but many other applications of its teaching as a dyad of two closely linked practices or experiences called *viveka* (discrimination, discernment, ontological insight), and *vairagya* (renunciation, detachment, disidentification). Viveka and vairagya are not in the least esoteric. As experienced they are quite straightforward, but it is helpful to see as clearly as possible how the two concepts or practices fit together. Viveka means seeing the difference between the self and the not-self, or the real and the unreal. This means seeing that the phenomena we desire or value lack the absolute reality and identity that we normally assign to them. As experienced while the attention is focused specifically on some aspect of the koshas, viveka arises as a little or sometimes great eureka-moment in which one says in effect, "I am not that." To keep Sanskrit usage to a minimum I will render the term viveka as "discrimination" wherever the context allows.

The second concept, vairagya, refers to an inner realignment that to some extent arises naturally and spontaneously out of the viveka or intuitive discrimination referred to above. Vairagya means letting go of those objects of desire that you now realize lack the kind of absolute reality you normally attach to them. But most critically it means disidentifying from those bodily and sensory and mental forms that up to now you have taken to be your actual self. The chief example of vairagya presented in this book is the letting go of one's tense and anxious attachment to declining vision. This disentanglement does not involve effort, and in fact is not a "doing" at all. It is more like a shift of viewpoint, a seeing of some phenomenon from a new and more secure position that is farther back from the old. As we proceed through what follows, I will in most cases render the idea of vairagya as "detachment" or "disidentification."

The conjoined practices of discrimination and detachment fit together in the following simple way: if discrimination is realizing the truth about what you really are and what you are not, detachment or disidentification is falling back and being at ease with that truth. The most straightforward way for me to illustrate these two concepts and the connection between them is to cite specific instances from my own experience. To do that here, I first have to describe some of the physical and sensory changes that I have experienced since the mid-1990s.

The physical-sensory body is really the best place to begin when considering how spiritual practice ought to be applied. Considered as a material object of attention, the body is closer to us than anything else. Considered as a source of trouble, as a consequence of illness or pain or the degrading of its faculties, the body can impinge upon the mind more powerfully than almost anything else we can imagine. What I have had to learn over the past twenty years, sometimes against the pull of an indignant resistance, is how to accept physical and sensory decline as an opportunity for spiritual practice rather than an impediment to it. Remaining open to the final stages of RP was only one aspect of this process.

By the mid-1990s I was experiencing worsening muscle pain both in existing and new areas, increasingly frequent muscle spasms in response to white cane use or other normal activities, deep body and joint pain, sudden episodes of fatigue when I would have difficulty in concentrating, and hard-to-control headaches of a new kind, caused by instability in the upper cervical spine. In 1996 a rheumatologist whom I consulted about these problems catalogued my various trigger points and announced straightaway that I had fibromyalgia. According to him this diagnosis would account for the foregoing cluster of symptoms, excluding only the mechanically generated headaches. It was fibromyalgia, he insisted, that the doctors at the Ottawa Rehabilitation Centre had provisionally labelled as myofascial pain syndrome back in 1989.

I didn't know what to think. When I researched fibromyalgia on the Internet it seemed somehow rather "iffy." I found that some of its victims were preoccupied with their condition to the point of obsession, staying online for long rap sessions during which they reinforced one another's frustrations. I wanted no part of that. So I followed my own exercise program, avoided the chat rooms, and directed my attention elsewhere.

The amplification of pain continued into the late 1990s, and because I was finding it more and more difficult to sit in most chairs I increasingly confined myself to home. We no longer went to concerts, and had friends over rather than going out to visit them. The problem of maintaining a comfortable body position was further aggravated in 2004 by an unexpected flare-up of lower back and sciatic pain. Tests revealed that in addition to the already ruptured lower lumbar disc, which was now extruding more material, two others were bulging and putting pressure on adjacent nerves. These too could rupture. Since then I have been constrained from bending forward or lifting anything weighing more than a couple of pounds.

During this period I was also experiencing an odd heaviness and unresponsiveness in the legs, some degrading of fine motor coordination in the fingers, a growing tendency to drop things, occasional unaccountable lapses when I could not pronounce words correctly, and a gradual worsening of a balance problem that had been present in a small way for many years. This set of symptoms fell into place in 2006 when I was diagnosed with a rare condition known as NARP (neuropathy/ataxia/retinitis pigmentosa), which is caused by one or more point-mutations in the mitochondrial DNA.

The clinical picture of NARP includes not only the RP that I had come to know so well, but a gradually worsening ataxia or muscle coordination problem, progressive nerve damage in the legs, feet, arms and hands, and according to some reports a tendency for muscles to fatigue or "crash" when they are subjected to extra demands. The ataxia and lower-limb nerve damage have significantly affected my gait, which gradually became unsteady and irregular, and more recently downright shaky. I have also begun to have problems with swallowing and choking, and the earlier sporadic difficulties with speech production have become more frequent. One way or another these various symptoms can be attributed to NARP, although other factors could be involved.

NARP is congenital, which means that I have had it all my life. It has been the hidden context or foundation for my visual problems, an untreatable disease so arcane that most doctors and even most ophthalmologists have never heard of it. Considerably fewer than 1 per cent of RP cases can be attributed to NARP. The presence of the disease may be indicated through a muscle biopsy, but a more secure diagnosis can in some cases be had through genetic testing. As to the long-term implications for me, I hope simply not to end up in a wheelchair or fall prey to the dementia that afflicts some NARP patients. But sometimes I find myself thinking about the logistics of living on wheels without vision. I also have to remind myself now and then that it is the complex mind-stream that succumbs to dementia, and not the simple but foundational light of consciousness that illumines that stream. This is by way of self-reassurance.

A new factor in recent years has been a recurrent dizziness. This too may be attributable at least in part to the NARP. But according to an ENT specialist whom I consulted, the emergent dizziness could also be linked to a bout of viral meningitis I had when I was in Tokyo in 1980. The virus would have disappeared after the original attack, but it might have damaged the inner ear balance mechanisms in a way that could be stirred up by my more recent, ataxia-based unsteadiness. Whatever the provenance of this dizziness, even when I am sitting quietly it can range from light-headedness to something like real vertigo, accompanied by an exacerbation of the nystagmus (involuntary movement of the eyes) that is always present. During these episodes I experience an inner swirling sensation, which obtains whether my eyes are open or closed. I am glad that I have learned to view phenomena from a detached centre of observation, for this allows me to experience the dizziness and swirling sensations without being totally sucked into them.

But the main problem areas to which I have applied this practice of detachment have been the final stages of RP and the management of escalating chronic pain. As I was getting involved in kosha work it so happened that I was being pulled into the stage of RP experience that I came to think of as visual chaos. This was a ramping-up both in complexity and frequency of the kind of visual illusions that I had first experienced in a smaller way in India, when we visited the deserted city of Fatehpur Sikri. Visual chaos is a shattering not only of coherent form but of visual space itself. Figure and background are scrambled into eccentric shards and planes of ambiguous orientation, the latter appearing to lean outward at one moment and inward in the next. It is impossible to know whether the indefinable forms you are seeing are smallish things right in front of you, or medium-sized things a few yards off, or large things a block away, or non-things that have no tactile counterpart.

There is an unstable two-stage version of visual chaos that begins with the sort of flat, two-dimensional scramble that typified the Rideau Centre incident, followed by a sudden opening-out into three dimensions. For a brief moment I seem to be experiencing something recognizable, but the merest shift of the eyes plunges me back into a two-dimensional "space" in which nothing makes sense. Sometimes this space is filled with incoherent debris that looks for all the world like fragments from an explosion. They hang in mid-air as though frozen in time by ultra-short-exposure photography. This sort of phenomenon is experienced by some but by no means all late-stage RP patients.

I found that in practical terms visual chaos was something worse than the mere absence of functional vision. It is the dysfunctional presence of the utterly bizarre, a display so dissimilar to normal visual forms that most people with RP who experience it have great difficulty describing what they see. The illusions can be very disorienting, stopping you dead in your tracks when they unexpectedly appear. When this happens even on familiar ground, all you can do is check out the acoustic and tactile cues and resolutely walk straight ahead into the distorted pseudo-object that is not tangibly there.

I understood that what was happening to me was at least in part a cancelling-out of the mind's capacity to project and maintain normal, three-dimensional visual space. Evidently my raw visual percepts were so degraded that they could no longer trigger those all-important, context-creating visual memories. Of course I had to deal somehow with the resulting mess, and I did this through a practice that reinforces visual detachment. During the period when the visual illusions were at their most lurid – this went on for over a year – I concentrated my kosha work on the visual function as such, so that it was the mental experience of seeing rather than the projected visual forms themselves that became the object of my attention.

In sessions of quiet introspection at home, I would look slowly across the living room and attend not to the fragmented or fantastic visual garble but to something that was more subtle, capacious, and somehow more inward: the actual presence of the visual mode of experience. This was vision as such, vision as a kind of field or volume, vision as distinct from its specific objects or sense-forms. It is what Advaita refers to simply as the visual mind (*jnanendriya*). To attend to this as a vague, subtle object of awareness in its own right is to make deeper the all-important inner distance between subject and object. That is, when you are aware of the visual field or mind-space as an object of attention you have interposed an extra degree of detachment and disentanglement between yourself as witness and whatever specific visual forms happen to be present. Now the witness consists of a deeper and more stable pre-ophthalmic consciousness, and this inner recession of the observer reduces the unsettling effect of the visual garble.

I would then try to carry the same kind of detachment into the streets by walking the most navigable portions of my daily route. During these expeditions I made it my top priority to keep myself recentred deep within myself, well back from the visual mind. In that way I could experience the visual mess within the mind's eye objectively instead of being spooked or swamped by it. This had the effect of forestalling the re-emergence of the visual ego that identifies so clingingly with the mind's eye itself.

I was learning that when you are caught up in late-stage RP, it is nothing short of a saving grace to realize with each step you take that you are *not* the degraded visual mind, that amorphous pseudo-subject, but the witness that observes that pseudo-subject. On particularly good days the experience of being the witness would gradually expand from the subtle limitation entailed in being some kind of fixed inner observer, into the far greater openness of a deeper consciousness. This was the consciousness that grounded all the modes of extro- and intro-sensing. To walk knowingly within that consciousness was an experience of buoyancy, clarity, and unforced alertness. These openings into globality were temporary, contracting after a time back into the sense of being a particular witness. But while they lasted they were a real boon.

That is how I was able to maintain a fair measure of the visual detachment I had first discovered in India, allowing the mechanism of chaotic visual projection to just toggle through all its weirdest settings. Of course visual chaos could impose real difficulties when it came to the practical business of getting from point A to point B, and I had to find a new way of "riding" the other senses without getting all tensed up. The early months of navigating through visual chaos were pretty choppy; as I will show below, the demands of walking through a new and incoherent set of sense-impressions with tight and refractory muscles could be exhausting.

Nevertheless I found the visual phenomenality of what was going on fascinating. I owe it to the freeing effect of vision-related kosha work that I was able to get through an intense and demanding period not only with a fair degree of equanimity, but also with unreduced curiosity and even a certain sense of privilege. The special effects were really something to see, and I was one of the relatively few who could see them. But the occasional experiences of a whole and undivided consciousness were far more important to me.

All this made me feel that, in some respects at least, I was beginning to learn how to face daily sensory life with the right kind of detachment, without surrendering my sense of the whole. But there were some problems that I had real difficulty in managing, or even figuring out properly. One of these had to do with the changing nature of mobility demands. Sometimes during my walks, when my course became uncertain and I had to strain for auditory or tactile cues, the sense of centredness or calm detachment in relation to body and senses would completely deflate into tense muscle-identity. These were the "bad" days. Once I perceived I was going astray it took only a moment for my sense of presence to bind itself tightly to the whole body. That meant that the experience of walking in vast, wide-open consciousness was cancelled out. I could feel a tightness even in my facial muscles as I listened hard and probed with the cane. It wasn't the visual chaos as such that was the matter; it was the intensity with which I was periodically latching onto sound and touch.

I understood from kosha work that I was separate from the faculties of hearing, touching, and introsensing (i.e., the sensing of inner body-feelings), just as I was from seeing. When I found myself tightening up and straining for aural cues I could "reset" myself anterior to all these senses by pausing for a moment and relaxing into that remembrance. The problem was that walking presented me with a constant stream of shifting sensations and navigation tasks, and in trying to respond to these I couldn't very well keep stopping to recentre myself. That way I'd never get anywhere.

The problem gradually got worse. By the late 1990s I could walk loosely and freely within the amplitude of the consciousness-self only when the navigation demands were routine. When they became challenging everything turned inside-out and I became nothing but the tense body, or so it seemed. I felt that in trying to keep moving in the face of these circumstances I was lacking in some basic competency or understanding that I couldn't even identify.

There was a second problem bearing on my relationship with the body, one that was present whether I was out walking or doing things at home. This had to do with the sense of self in the presence of pain. Here I must first say a word about how an ontology that is based on consciousness understands the phenomenon of pain. We can tease out the conventional presumptions regarding the manifest reality of pain by referring such an experience to the parallel one of touch, i.e., the touching of external objects. As we saw in chapter 6, section 2, evolutionary biologists such as Richard Dawkins understand how the combined effects of touch and vision generate a powerful and entirely illusory sense of a physical entity existing independently in itself, outside of consciousness.

A comparable illusion is produced by the introsensation we call pain, occurring in close combination with the extroperceptions of touch or vision – that is, feeling the pain deep within while touching or looking at the body surface. It is right here, when we are asked to apply to the introsensed body the same radical scientific findings that in chapter 6 clarified the immaterial, space-like nature of the external world, that we may finally draw the line and protest. It is one thing to acknowledge that external objects are really sets of sense-forms that do not exist outside of consciousness, an acknowledgment based (however unenthusiastically) on the evidence of particle and quantum physics. But it is quite another thing to admit that the internal, intimately introsensed body is also illusory. I really hurt, the subject protests: how can I not be "real"?

Our inner microcosm of strong body-feelings, which we are conditioned to take as proof positive of our being a real, solid, physical entity, seems to stand in natural apposition to all those entities "out there." We unthinkingly take ourselves to be the material subject against which the array of entities "out there" stand in the complementary position of absolutely real, solid objects. Solid out there, we believe, and painfully solid in here. What really lies behind this conventional experience, in which vagrant body-feelings are taken to be a continuous material lump, is the ego's intense need to become something definite and concrete – something absolutely real in itself. Practically speaking, the ego-based compulsion to identify with introsensations is another aspect of a general evolutionary adaptive strategy, one geared toward organic self-protection. That is, we are able to retreat from those external entities that can do us harm.

But consider the dilemma of the person – you perhaps – who is living with chronic pain. Your body-pain is inescapably actual, a fully present manifestation, and it is so obtrusive and demanding a form of sensing that it seems to compel the most literal kind of objectification. You are drawn into taking that pain to be an unnegotiable aspect of a material body that is existentially engorged by suffering. And this is where the evolutionary adaptive strategy seizes up and confounds itself. Because you so unconditionally identify with your malign introsensations, it is as though you were constituted or constructed of pain. What could be more outrageous and imprisoning than that? Thus the conventional assumptions associated with physical selfing tighten into another one of those bad dreams, in a way that parallels the key conviction that vision loss attacks our selfhood.

That much I understood. But the phenomenon of pain proved to be more complex and stubborn than I supposed when I first got into kosha analysis. On the one hand, I had been able to confirm that kosha work as applied to inner body-feelings could indeed bring a real sense of release, an inner "seeing" of body-pain as not-I. The pain would still be there within consciousness, but at the moment of clear seeing or insight it was as though the observing "I" was buffered by a little zone of cool space that gave it some separation from the suffering. Pain received from this little distance could disclose itself to be less malign than pain that was close-up and invasive. This way of seeing pain was a concrete example of how the discriminating of self from not-self could result in a welcome degree of detachment.

On the other hand, there were bad times when the pain besieged that little zone of separation and penetrated right through it. This did not totally cancel out the intuitive distinction between self and not-self, for the pain was still located ever so slightly on the side of the not-self, but it did dull the buffering effect. These were the times when staying detached was hard, as the ontological facts became blurred and the enveloping consciousness seemed to contract. Often when this happened I would fall into the old habit of inwardly turning away from the pain, trying to ignore or even deny it. I would take up some task that I could physically manage or stubbornly press ahead with my reading and note-taking. The upshot of this periodic oscillation between acceptance and rejection was a growing feeling that there was some mystery about pain management that I didn't grasp. Sometimes I just blamed myself for not being able to let go into a deeper detachment.

A third and very different kind of problem in dealing with the body was being fuelled by my increasing distractedness or absent-mindedness, which sometimes made me lose track of what the body was up to. I had a tendency to half-consciously pick things up while I was bombing around the house and just as abstractedly put them down again God knows where, my thoughts a million miles away. A day or so later the objects would be classified as officially missing. This kind of absent-mindedness was very sloppy drill for a blind person, and it had physical consequences. I would bump into door jambs or room dividers with the very head that was mentally out to lunch.

This made me feel stupid, but it was asurefire way of recalling me to the present moment. Only then would I realize where my mind had been, immersed perhaps in the argument of some text I had been reading, or caught up in a loop of useless chain-thinking, cycling away automatically like a hamster on an exercise wheel. Surely there must be some durable state of mind that could forestall this kind of thing. But what was it and how could it be secured?

My problems with navigation, pain management and absent-mind-edness did not undermine my conviction that discrimination and detachment were absolutely invaluable practices. I had tasted their fruits in a variety of contexts, over and over again. I continued to blame myself rather than the practices for my apparent failure to consistently realize their potential. As for my broader Advaitic study program, it continued apace without road blocks or time off. I was totally immersed in the teachings of Shankara, and I understood more and more why he was judged to be Advaita's most effective proponent of discriminative detachment. By now I was making a slow, methodical second pass through A.J. Alston's monumental, six-volume *Shankara Sourcebook*,[3] and finding it ever more absorbing. It was just that this philosophy seemed to be all too separate from my sometimes exhausting daily grind.

But I finally twigged to the fact that my three problem areas had something in common, something that was really very obvious. I called it "noise." What I meant by this was the internal static made up of competing sensory inputs, or physical pain, or random trains of thought, all of which had the identical effect of distracting me, sometimes dangerously. Maybe there was another dimension of practice I knew nothing about – one having to do with living with the static, one that could both complement and make more room for discrimination and detachment. But what might that be, and how could I access it?

3 THE SUBTLE ARTS OF EQUIMINDEDNESS

At the end of the nineties – I can make this sound more portentous by calling it the end of the millennium, which it also was – I was introduced to the specific type of spiritual resource that I'd been missing. This happened through Bill Gayner, one of my volunteer reader-typists in Ottawa, who had moved to Toronto to work as a psychotherapist at Mount Sinai Hospital. He had once lived in a Buddhist residential community. Bill began to tell me about the practice of mindfulness, a meditative art derived from the Buddhist tradition.

Mindfulness is an ancient and venerable mental discipline that invokes and brings forward one of our most important natural faculties, the faculty of fully attending to whatever comes into the mind. This deliberate attention is a basis for really coming to know ourselves, and fully taking in our sensory world. If the ordinary mind tends toward distractedness and scatter – and indeed it does – mindfulness by comparison is consistently purposeful. It is the relaxed but alert practice of lightly placing the attention upon whatever is to be observed, of maintaining that attention, of lightly leading it back to the present moment whenever it slips away. This is quite different from what we usually think of as mental concentration, which is very much a "doing" and involves a degree of intensity or effort. Mindfulness is a non-doing. It is a simple but fully conscious and undistracted being-there, an unruffled "inner seeing" that has real staying power.

Once I grasped in a general sort of way what mindfulness practice entailed, there were two things I knew for certain. First, I saw that this was the resource I had been lacking in my efforts to deal with the three practical problems described in the previous section. Second, and this was quite a discovery, I realized that the mindfulness practice that Bill had come to by following a more or less Buddhist path was for all practical purposes very much like the resource that the Advaitic texts referred to as "witnessing." To take up this resource is to observe events or phenomena in the detached mode of consciousness known as "the witness." When I introduced the concept of the witness earlier in this chapter I described it more in terms of an experience of inner autonomy than as a deliberate technique, but it lends itself to the latter usage as well. As a cultivated practice, mindfulness or witnessing is very old, belonging as it does to the deep common bedrock of the diverse Indian spiritual tradition. It includes the directing of sustained attention not only to the various aspects of one's own body-mind, as in Advaitic kosha work, but to any phenomenon in the external environment. Whatever its application, it fosters the development of equimindedness or equanimity – that is, the maintenance of a serene, non-judgmental inner balance.

The actual practice of mindfulness or witnessing must have played a key role in developing the Indian ontological tradition I had been reading about for years. In both Advaita Vedanta and Buddhism, mindfulness/witnessing was the most direct and self-reliant way of cultivating insight into the deep nature of things. Thus the word *vipassana*, the technical term for mindfulness in the ancient Pali that served as one of the principal languages for early Buddhist teaching, is often translated into English as Insight Meditation. Whether the teaching context was early Theravadin Buddhism, the later Mahayana Buddhism or Advaita Vedanta, one of the principal goals of mindful attention was to see through direct experience that the various physical and mental components of our supposed individual self are by their very nature non-self, and utterly impermanent. This was a large part of what I had come to think of as "inner seeing." In the Buddhist negative way, the principle to which the practice of mindfulness is ultimately referred is called the Emptiness of Emptiness, the final negating of all negations.

Graduated-step programs for developing competence in mindfulness were laid out in great detail in the voluminous Buddhist literature; in Advaitic texts, however, references to the parallel practice of witnessing were generally brief or even cursory. They usually took the form of an injunction to simply be the witness. In Advaita, which was never as highly organized or codified as Buddhism, the teaching of witnessing was not "textbooked" in a standard and comprehensive way but left to the discretion of individual teachers.

Buddhist mindfulness training began to filter into North America in a significant way in the late 1960s and 1970s, when young American meditators who had studied and practised with Theravadin teachers in Southeast Asia and Sri Lanka returned home eager to share what they had learned. Over the next few years the benefits of mindfulness practice would be affirmed and applied by medical professionals, most notably in a very effective program known as Mindfulness Based Stress Reduction (MBSR). This was exactly what its name denoted: a practical program for managing stress through the cultivation of a balanced and flexible mind. MBSR was developed in the late 1970s by Dr Jon Kabat-Zinn and his colleagues at the University of Massachusetts Medical Center, as a core program of their stress reduction clinic. This work was informed and supported by the emergent discipline of behavioural medicine, which has clinically confirmed the health benefits of meditation.

MBSR is based squarely on the technique of Theravadin vipassana, and in that regard it is in no way a dumbed-down or New Age tourist version of mindfulness training. It is the real thing. As taught, however, it has until recently made very little reference to its Buddhist origins. Its purpose has been the secular and pragmatic one of skilfully dealing with stress from a calm and detached centre, and to this end it can be taken up by anyone who simply wants to make life more manageable and fulfilling. The components of MBSR include sitting meditation, a form of directed attention known as a body scan, and simple hatha yoga performed mindfully.[4]

This original version of MBSR eventually became the most successful and widely disseminated stress management program in North America. It is taught today at hundreds of clinics and community centres in the United States and Canada. When the program is practised at home, it can include the cultivation of mindful attention whenever the body is in motion or performing routine tasks. This ambulatory form of mindfulness, which keeps you fully alert to what you are doing and where you are going, is absolutely invaluable if you happen to be blind or visually impaired.

Whatever the variations in content, mindfulness practice is extremely simple because it really has only two elements – the act of observing and the phenomenon being observed at any given moment. Yet it is far from easy. Integrating it into daily life requires application and patience, as Bill attested from his own experience. I confirmed this for myself by going through an unsatisfactory series of fits and starts. It was only when I really committed myself to the basic practice and then gave it time to open up that I learned to apply MBSR to my special problem areas of outdoor navigation, pain management, and growing absent-mindedness.

It was a challenge to maintain the attention in any context, but for me the problem of outdoor navigation had a special twist that made it particularly frustrating. This was the seemingly unavoidable subversion of the experience of walking relaxedly in the light and space of the consciousness-self, which subsumed the objects of common experience. To walk confidently in such a context was one aspect of a new mode of being that had arisen as the most wholesome development in my life: the clearly felt presence of consciousness, awareness aware of itself, as my deepest and most expansive feeling of being. Before the advent of visual chaos I could usually walk comfortably enough in that great conscious space, although muscle spasms or tricky navigational problems might make the experience short-lived.

But now I was struggling with divided attention. Although I was not spooked by the phenomena of visual chaos, I could not help but be distracted by them. My attention was being pulled back and forth between the useless visual illusions and those all-important tactile and acoustic cues, even as I was trying to remain centred in aware openness. Whenever the terrain became difficult, the non-visual cues began to clamour for attention. To resist this clamour was impractical and only generated tension; to accede to the clamour in a rush of concern was another kind of tension. Either way I lost that buoyant sense of centred, self-affirming consciousness.

It was a real conundrum. How was it possible for awareness to confirm simultaneously and with equal clarity both its own lucid presence and the presence of sketchy but essential sense-data? How could it do this while disregarding the inessential but obtrusive visual mess through which my cane and body-form seemed to be ploughing? Perhaps I was asking for the impossible. A fully sighted pedestrian

who had been introduced to space-like awareness through a spontaneous experience or the Harding experiments could easily walk in
safety through that space and experience its buoyancy, but perhaps
this was beyond the capabilities of the late-stage RP patient with
chronic neuromuscular problems. Should I just reconcile myself to
the loss?

When I got the MBSR training tapes and began to use them, I had
to admit to myself that despite my familiarity with the Advaita
Vedantic concept of witnessing as applied to kosha work, I was entering into the general practice of witnessing as an absolute duffer. Among
the North American Vedantins I had met, witnessing was lauded as
a virtue but not taught as a transmissible skill. I decided to blank out
my idea of what the witness was and follow the MBSR tape. I started
by sitting still and just listening to the tape, trying as directed to shift
my attention lightly from the breath to body-feelings to areas of actual
physical pain to ambient sounds to ideas within the mind, back and
forth, simply observing them in a state of neutrality. Whenever I lost
this detachment – and of course I lost it over and over again – I reset
myself back into it. I knew it would take considerable time and practice
to become both steady and flexible in my attentiveness, but the method
was clear and easy to grasp.

Eventually I ventured into mindful walking outdoors. From my
preliminary practice of following the tape and trying to walk mindfully inside the house, I had concluded that whenever I was in motion
it was an absolute necessity that my full attention be directed to tactile
and acoustic cues – even if that meant losing the feel of the deep centre
of consciousness and its great spacious expanse. For the blind walker
there really is no alternative. When I began to practice outdoors, toiling down the familiar sidewalk that was closest to our condo, I found
that any attempt to maintain through sheer willpower the sense of
immersion within consciousness had a perverse effect. It seemed to
objectify that consciousness, turning it into an ersatz "thing" that
bore no resemblance to consciousness itself. I think I had had a whiff
of this problem all along, but hadn't wanted to own up to it.

Now I found as I walked that there were two radically different
ways for the person who is trying to remain detached from visual
chaos to direct his attention outward. He can do this unmindfully,
which means half-consciously clutching at percepts and identifying
urgently with the body, or he can walk with the attention resting
lightly and flexibly on the percepts and sensations that are really

useful. The difference between these two approaches was amazing. Of course I was just a beginner, but I could see that it really was possible to allow body-feelings and useful external cues to manifest without becoming entangled with them.

To realize this possibility, you have to acknowledge the presence of garbled and meaningless visual images without actually attending to them, vectoring the attention in an unforced way to sounds and touch-sensations as they arise. It is a matter of simply tuning in, without compelling anything or being compelled. You keep witnessing that portion of the mind-body flow that makes some kind of sense, the portion that is non-visual, inwardly moving back from its acoustic and tactile components whenever you feel yourself beginning to anxiously adhere to them. Once you get the hang of this, you find that the sensate body is quite capable of correcting its course in an appropriate or even automatic way. It requires only practice. In my own case I practised mindful walking at first only on familiar ground, gradually extending the range and duration of my walks.

The sensory muddle that I had looked upon as an obstacle turned out to be my teacher, for it pressed me into learning how to walk with real but unforced attention. I couldn't really manage without being mindful, unless screwing myself up into a big tight wad just to walk down to the mini-mall qualifies as "managing." To get there in a reasonable state of relaxation required me to keep remembering what it felt like to be in the unique state of just being the witness, and to return to that remembrance over and over again whenever it slipped away. I did not have to break my stride in order to do this. This was living right in the present moment step by step, instead of worrying about the next step and the one after that and about what would happen when I got down to the corner. That I could actually walk in this way, amidst visual chaos and with my imperfect body, was a real testament to the remarkable potential of witnessing.

I don't want to give the impression that any of this was easy. There were plenty of times, especially during that first year, when the going got rough and my attentiveness slackened, and even when it didn't I could still occasionally get lost. Yet I could return at any moment to the unguarded but somehow secure place where I could observe the muddle without being the muddle. I knew the feeling of that place – it was the feeling of the space-like awareness I'd been so jealous to preserve. Incredibly enough – and this was a real bonus – it was coming back.

It began to arise of its own accord whenever I had walked for some time in alert but unperturbed observing. And why shouldn't this spaciousness arise? Awareness is our fundamental nature. I was right here walking and awareness was my essence, encompassing the moving body and the whole larger show. It had been Douglas Harding who first introduced me to the light and spaciousness of awareness, which I eventually claimed as my primary experience of selfhood: now mindfulness or witnessing was demonstrating how I could preserve and walk through that awareness-space despite my sensory and physical handicaps.

The Advaita I was now studying placed all this into a far greater context, that of a consciousness that was indivisible and thus transpersonal. At this stage the three resources in which I had seen so much potential – the Harding experiments, the panoramic Advaita study program with its teachings on kosha work and witnessing, and the MBSR program of mindfulness training – were effectively aligned with one another. The contemplative and active modes of awareness were like two sides of a single coin, and the long period of "contraction" was coming to an end.

Over the next few years the intense manifestations of visual chaos gave way first to scrappy remnants and then to faint scribbly sketches of nothing in particular, and then melted into something entirely new. For want of a shorter and snappier name I called it the post-chaos ocean of empty light. This light was different from anything experienced previously, and like the chaos that preceded its emergence it is by no means experienced by all RP patients. Gone were the last vestiges of visual interference, of non-things manifesting out of the murk. And the murk itself had evened out into a uniform light that had no definable tonality, being neither colourless nor merely grey. Sometimes it shone with a pearly iridescence. This empty light was a definite presence, in the sense that it had volume. While visual chaos had often seemed two-dimensional, a flat plane pressing up against the face, the world now opened up again only to reveal its emptiness.

This restored sense of three-dimensional volume was mysterious, for it did not depend on any direct perception of relative object-placement within the environment. Nor did it depend on remembering being in the same place before. It was entirely visual, pure visible space with no contents. It asserted itself in all environments, familiar or novel, as an experience of vast extension. This extension was endless in every direction, including straight down. The world had become a submerged Atlantic of filtered light. It was quite spectacular and beautiful in its own way, and there were times when the edgeless consciousness-self as I then conceived of it seemed to re-identify or objectify itself as the great pearly light all around me.

Now, boundless empty light could in theory represent the opposite kind of mobility barrier to the one served up by visual chaos. If chaos seemed to be an almost palpable jumble into which one might crash, bottomless light is the nothingness into which one might fall. I walked through this light by attending to the firm tread of my shoes upon the pavement, and by remaining mindful of all the other non-visual cues that seemed to come out of the light itself. After the excesses of visual chaos I didn't mind the fact that the light contained no forms.

Even when this abstract iridescent space finally gave way to simple unseeing, it would be mindful awareness that helped me to keep walking with a reasonable degree of efficiency and enjoyment. Compromised muscles in my cane arm and shoulder might compel me at times to cut my walk short, but as I did I was navigating out of the unresisting conscious centre. That meant that I was walking in acceptance even when I had to turn around and go back home. When NARP and other factors finally made those long rambling walks impracticable I would think of this change as a trade-off. I missed the walks, but what I had lost was more than offset by the gift of steadier awareness. Awareness could be lightly sustained – sometimes – even in the presence of pain.

Pain was of course a big item in its own right on my MBSR agenda, the second of the adaptation problems that had been with me for years. Because in one form or another pain is a permanent presence in my life, I have the permanent vocation of working with it. There is a lot that could be said about living with pain, for as a subject of medical and psychological inquiry pain management has spawned a large and growing literature. But as I am writing here about mindfulness practice and its applications I will limit myself to one topic: how the experience of pain can be subtly altered by witnessing it.

If we interrogate ourselves we may find that we are already half-aware of this capacity to transform our experience of bodily discomfort by closely attending to it. A mindfulness teacher can appeal to this capacity by doing the interrogating for us: "Have you ever noticed that your awareness of pain is not in pain even when you are? I'm sure you have. It is a very common experience, especially in childhood, but one we usually don't examine or talk about because it is so fleeting and the pain so much more compelling in the moment it comes upon us."[5]

Witnessing pain is something you learn about by developing a regular practice of sitting meditation, in which you get used to placing the attention on a variety of phenomena, including feelings of bodily discomfort. It took me a long time to settle into such a practice, for reasons I will discuss later. But even my early experiences of sitting with pain were enough to show me that the more you do this the more capable you become of doing it again. Yet in a certain basic sense each time is like the first time: you are always the same witness, even if the pain changes. As that witness you just keep observing the pain without fighting it; when you find yourself reacting to the pain you watch the reaction, observing it non-judgmentally as something that is just there. When the reaction begins to recede or soften – which it often does under patient observation – you go back to attending to the pain itself. This cycle is repeated for as long as the meditator chooses to keep the session going.

It can be a very intense experience, as it was for me one day in 2000 when the spinal and sacroiliac pain was particularly bad, and I was doing my best to just stay with it. By the time I got to the end of the forty-five minute session I'd set for myself I had confirmed that one could remain apart from the pain to a surprising degree, even while consciously and steadily taking it in. Feeling vindicated despite my exhaustion and nausea, I took the heavy dose of codeine that I'd avoided up until then. I had the thought, which turned out to be totally wrong, that I had seen through this problem once and for all. I wouldn't have to open myself to pain in this way again. That of course was the somatic ego speaking; it didn't like the unresisting consciousness that took in pain, but it loved codeine.

In trying to convince myself that I didn't need to develop a practice of sitting receptively with pain I had fallen into the error of putting mindfulness on the same footing as kosha work. The great lesson to be learned from the koshas is that they are the observed while you, the real you, are the observer. Once you have got that point you have got it for keeps. I had examined the koshas many times over, not because the first survey was insufficient but because it delighted me to revisit the remarkable truth. On the other hand I did not want to make it a habit of sitting mindfully with the raw spinal pain of the energy-sheath. Surely this was unnecessary; I already "knew" that the pain was not-I.

The problem with this position is that there is a great difference between mentally grasping a basic truth regarding the nature of our bodily phenomena, as important as that may be, and actually living it. Kosha work, which as explained above is an exercise in discrimination and detachment, makes possible a particular kind of insight into our true nature that allows us to disidentify from whatever elements of the sensory body-mind are under observation. This can be done, I emphasize once again, without rejecting or demeaning those elements.

What mindfulness adds to this process is a cultivated capacity to observe the body-mind with sustained attention, and to maintain that inner gaze even in the presence of an emotional or physical pain that would normally make us recoil. Over time the pain is received into a deeper level of insight and acceptance. Kosha work says, "Use your head and see that you are not the pain nor the body that houses it, and recede inward." Mindfulness says, "Open your heart and see what pain is when you allow the fear and indignation and negative judgments associated with it to be seen clearly. See how these reactions slowly dissolve within the mind when you give them sufficient time. Then see yourself as the wide-open awareness that can accommodate the pain itself." To the extent that you can do that you have a truth that you can really inhabit, and that is something much more than knowing the truth in principle.

I know this must sound austere, but it is something you can work up to in stages. In committing myself that day to a 45-minute session of mindful attention to very bad pain, I was diving into the deep end without really knowing much about swimming. It would have been perfectly all right to medicate that particular pain earlier in the day. As I confirmed when I began to learn more about mindfulness practice, no legitimate teacher is going to ask you to play the masochist or martyr in dealing with a pain problem. Sometimes, it is true, the teacher may encourage you to focus on bad pain during a meditation session in order to learn how to strip it of fear and hatred, the fear and hatred that make it seem worse than it actually is. I do this when the pain is front and centre and presents me with the choice of either maintaining my equilibrium by facing it, or putting myself into a state of agitation by strongly reacting to it. Some pain is so overwhelming that it blots out the possibility of such a choice, but mine usually allows me to incorporate it into my practice.

Observing pain directly without shrinking from it is only one element of the mindfulness practice that helps us deal with aversive sensations. The broader approach to pain management through mind-fulness is to open up a fuller life in which the pain will in general be less prominent because it is less attended to. This is the strategy of the MBSR program as a whole, with its emphasis on learning how to flexibly redeploy the attention during meditation. This skill is then applied to the wonderfully relaxing resource of the body scan, and to the satisfying practice of simple mindful yoga. These activities have the effect of "backgrounding" the pain. But the most immediate resource for withdrawing the attention from pain is to absorb oneself in following the breath, and this is what I do during routine household tasks. I also fall back on the breath during long waits in the poorly designed chairs that seem to be standard issue in doctors' waiting rooms, and during interminable rides in uncomfortable cars. I can still feel surprise when I am reminded all over again how effective this simple stratagem really is.

But even for the student of mindfulness who sticks with his practice, living with chronic or disabling pain is tough. It is a vocation that is imposed without prior consultation or consent, like being born into a caste of hapless and indentured rock-breakers. This arbitrariness used to make me think there was something about pain that I didn't yet understand, some secret meaning or significance that lay just beyond my grasp. Once revealed it would smooth my way to living with pain more intelligently, as a kind of specially informed pain savant.

This was just intellectualism, my usual mode of retreat from unpleasant circumstances. The truth turned out to be simpler and starker. What pain asks of us, as an uninvited teacher, is that we just look straight into it without resistance. There is no way we can do this so long as we continue to view pain egocentrically. In the ego-based experience of pain we identify intensely with the body and take the pain as an affront, seeing the body-part that contains it as a traitor or the victim of alien attack. The pain itself is felt to be either malign or utterly meaningless. In the latter case it faces us as blankly as a stone sphinx, but this sphinx harbours no secret. It is blank all the way through. When we react to this blankness by branding the pain as a pointless outrage, the sense of outrage is an aspect of the ego, not of the pain itself.

Witnessing pain is something quite different. When we open up to pain in order to see it unobstructedly, the lowering of our defences can show us with a directness not calculated to please the ego what pain actually is, and what we are in relation to it. The pain shows itself to be an intense energy that is fully and unavoidably "there." It is nature, that aspect of nature that is unnegotiably right there right now. Received nakedly without interpretation, it is neither good nor bad: it is what it is, raw body-feeling. In identifying this inner burning as one of the aspects of the inner energy kosha, Advaita views it quite impersonally.

What we are in relation to that pain is the consciousness that takes it in – that's all. We are not the body in pain, but we can be outraged by the body in pain. To the extent that we align our vagrant sense of self with the unwavering I Am of consciousness, we will do better in dealing with a pain problem. There are effective resources – mindfulness practice in combination with an appropriate level of medication – that can enable us to get by, or do better than just get by. This is a hard road but a navigable one. As for the worst cases of pain, those that may involve terminal illness and palliative care, the sensible course is to fully accede to the opiate in the knowledge that we have done our best.

I know that people living with chronic pain sometimes try to "own" it by bestowing onto it a kind of "personal" intelligibility or significance that makes it easier to live with. I don't know that I've done that, for to me pain is an impersonal objective phenomenon. Or perhaps I've just done it in a less obvious way. In any event I concluded somewhere along the line that pain was just part of the natural array, and that it wouldn't be improved by our projecting onto it a narrowly personal significance.

In that regard I have a metaphor that I sometimes fall back on, one that represents pain in an entirely non-personal way. It identifies my gross body and attendant physical circumstances simply as the framework for a life. That body is not the self, and those circumstances are not the life. The framework is sometimes pliable and at other times as rigid as iron, but in either case it is quite distinct from the life of consciousness that goes along with it. A life centred in the light of consciousness is the one and only kind of life that can incorporate the frame and reach far beyond it. It is the only kind of life that acknowledges the pain without our becoming glued fast to it through enmity. This is life as bare lucent spaciousness, in which pain and other aversive phenomena are suspended at a distance. Because this suspension requires a certain kind of ongoing engagement, such a life is always a work in progress.

So much for the heavy issues. The third problem on my mindfulness to-do list, which you may remember if you are not as forgetful and absent-minded as I am, was my forgetfulness and absent-mindedness. This problem puzzled me because of the way I tended to frame it in words: how can one become aware of one's unawareness? This contradiction turned out to be a mere artifact of language. Once I began to explore mindfulness or at least to think about it, I saw that there really was no contradiction at all. Unmindfulness had simply become a habit, so mindfulness would have to be cultivated as a counter-habit. If inattentiveness is the disease, metaphorically speaking, then attentiveness is the obvious treatment.

For the longest time, however, I didn't avail myself of the treatment. I just kept drifting around the house thinking great thoughts and bumping into things. Once again I was ignoring the requirement of disciplined practice. But once again, as with navigating outdoors, I could resist the facts for only so long. What finally compelled me to change my ways was the cold touch of Necessity, the rather chilling realization that the degree of distractedness I was now experiencing was something more than a bad habit. I had now reached the age when I sometimes couldn't remember why I had come downstairs, or whether I had taken my pills, or who I was supposed to telephone that evening. In short, I was coming up against age-related memory loss. My capacity for mindfulness seemed to come down to this: either learn to use it, and soon, or lose it.

Eventually I did form the habit of walking around mindfully indoors. This works best when I am not trying to keep up a conversation with Pressi or whoever else is in the house when I am in transit from one room to another. Given my sensory, proprioceptive and balance deficits, the best principle seemed to be to focus on only one thing at a time – either walking or talking. As the new habit began to develop, I found that when I walk mindfully over the floors that have become so familiar to me there was always somehow a sense of freshness, of being right in the present moment. Just the simple experience of moving through space and especially of going up or down stairs was deeply engrossing. It cracked open the great voluminous expanse that was always there anyway.

To sum up, getting a handle on the pain management, mobility, and inattention problems described in these pages helped me feel more centred and smoothed out my daily round. But there had been a greater benefit, the restoration of a lost gift. This was the gradual recovery of my access to the luminous consciousness-self at a time when I was discovering its fuller iteration in the Commentaries of Shankara. I began to feel and think of it as a gathering sense of presence: the vast and nurturing self-presence of the real. I was somehow That, and yet That was immeasurably more than me.

8

The Challenge of Integration

1 FACTOR Z, AT LONG LAST

Lives as most of us live them, as distinct from lives neatly laid out on resumés or celebrated at retirement banquets, can seem from the inside to be rather jagged or less than whole, even when the externalities are hanging together well enough. There may be inner zones of dull stasis or inanition, of unfinished business, even or especially for those who are trying to open up the life of the spirit. Every little opening may be followed by the reminder that there is still stuff down inside (or even up at the surface) that needs to be worked through, and integrated into a whole life. In this chapter I will identify three areas of particular concern and aspiration that I eventually had to deal with over the past fifteen years. Each one of them represented a challenge to a truly integrated life.

To pick up where I broke off at the end of the previous chapter, I was summing up my first few years of mindfulness practice. I must add now that if my account of trying to develop mindfulness left you with the impression that I must have got especially "good" at it, you can take it from me that I hadn't. I reaped the benefits described in chapter 7 despite the fact that I have not yet developed what I would call a really deep level of practice. I think this point deserves to be emphasized, especially to those of you who may wonder if you need some kind of special talent in order to develop this art. You don't. What is required is patience or doggedness; the art of attention grows out of that. It isn't just the high adepts or heroes of meditation but ordinary students of it like me who experience its welcome effects. I was in fact an inconsistent student at first; the fruits of mindfulness became accessible to me only after an inner struggle that had more to do with my past than it did with the typical requirements of meditative practice.

Even as circumstances were pushing me to apply mindfulness to the problem of outdoor and indoor mobility and the challenge of living with pain, I was avoiding the regular practice of sitting meditation that is part and parcel of the MBSR program. This was in a sense getting things backward. It is above all else the habit of sitting mindfully with a variety of physical and emotional states that best equips the practitioner to deal flexibly with daily problems. I just couldn't seem to get down to the business of simply sitting, of being still and witnessing whatever came up in mind or body. Yet I knew from the literature that this was the best basis for establishing staying power in the art of sustained attention.

I became paradoxically less rather than more comfortable with the idea of sitting meditation when I read my way through a series of excellent books on mindfulness practice in 2000–2001. Those books made me feel somehow that I wouldn't be up to the inner challenge of a regular sitting practice, which seemed in some obscure way to be rather threatening. Of course I asked myself why this should be so – after all, I had already come to terms with the big issue of my gayness – but the answer was slow in coming. So I limited myself to following the guided meditation tapes, and even within that kind of supportive structure I had moments of real discomfort and doubt. This went on into 2002.

As it turned out, my resistance to sitting meditation (and to the far more daunting project of enlightenment) arose out of what might be called the unfinished business from 1994. In that year I faced up to my innate sexual orientation, and on that score I had never looked back. No regression, no second thoughts, no regrets. But I continued to carry within me the memory – including the living body-memory – of the early sexual and emotional abuse that I had wrongly identified as the root cause of my homosexuality. Whenever I found myself remembering those scenes I still felt the old confused mixture of revulsion and self-abnegation, blunted to some extent by time but still palpably present within me. What I succeeded in doing in 1994 was to claim the core fact of my gayness and release it from the degradation and shame that marked me from the age of eight through adolescence. That was a big step forward, but deep down the old sense of shame was manifestly not expunged. The counsellor with whom I worked in 1994 did not warn me that this layer of painful feeling might have to be opened up and reprocessed; I don't think he even recognized it as an issue.

Yet in 2002 I could not meditate, or rather try to meditate, without becoming aware of a level of tension that did not want to be looked at. It would express itself most obviously as a tightening up of the chest muscles and diaphragm, felt mainly as a constriction of my breathing. This was similar to what I had sometimes experienced when I was still in denial over my gayness, but it seemed to be coming from even deeper down. Nevertheless, with other ordinary problems involving situational or physical discomfort, I could still remain within the space-like awareness that was the principal feature and resource of the "middle ground" described in chapter 7. When those problems were enfolded and cradled in deep, edgeless awareness they lost much of their sting and urgency. But this other thing, the inner holding and tightening and near-nausea associated with the sexual abuse, could not be resolved or even engaged in that way. When I managed to "look" at it I was overtaken by a feeling of pure, adamant negation.

Over a period of days in March 2002 I did what I always do when I have to come to terms with something I have been avoiding: I went to ground. I holed myself up behind a closed door and allowed myself to feel that tightness as clearly as I could, pulling myself out of it long enough to consider all that had happened over the past half-dozen years – all those new adjustments, the experiences of visual chaos and the ocean of empty light, my work on the koshas, the occasional deeper openings into Advaita, all the ways in which I had tried to live affirmatively – and I had to admit that the layer of tension was still impregnable. It was there even when things were at their best and I judged myself happy. This was my oldest problem, my Factor Z, the last big obstacle that stood between me and my real nature. I had known for years that spiritual practice and psychotherapy were two different things; the former could not be a substitute for the latter, and given what I was facing now the former might not even prosper without a strong dose of the latter. I decided that this time I would seek out the help of a genuine expert.

For some months, when I allowed myself to consider the problem, I had a hunch about the kind of work I was going to have to do on myself in order to confront and resolve Factor Z, and it was this hunch that governed my choice of therapist. I felt I must go back into that early trauma and come as close as possible to actually

re-experiencing what happened; only in this way could I break through
my own defences and allow all the buried feeling to come to the
surface. I knew it would be awful, but I had absolutely no doubts
about the necessity of doing this. And I confirmed from my networking in the Ottawa medical community and discussions with Bill
Gayner, the social worker/psychotherapist who had introduced me
to MBSR, that there were therapeutic protocols expressly designed
for this kind of release.

I think my decision to follow this route was based on a kind of
faith. I had learned from my own experience that if we gaze into any
difficult personal experience deeply enough, it uncovers a truth that
was not apparent before. One way or the other, that truth always has
to do with some constriction or misrepresentation of self. Those old
body-echoes or memories of abuse constituted such a misrepresentation, a frozen identity in its own right that did not link up with my
wider experience. But it didn't have to be that way. I was prepared
to bet that that benumbed little "I" could be opened up and absorbed
into the rest of me, through insight and acceptance.

What I meant by insight and acceptance was pretty much what
Advaita means by discrimination and compassionate detachment
(viveka and vairagya). It boiled down to discriminating between what
is truly self and what has been arbitrarily imposed onto self, followed
by spontaneously moving back from the imposition and witnessing
it with some measure of compassion. That was the goal. But I couldn't
get there on my own. I needed a particular kind of therapist, not one
who knew Advaita Vedanta, but one who knew how to help me look
into the abuse and the abusers until there was nothing left to see.

The right man for this job turned out to be Dr George Fraser, a
psychiatrist who at that time was the director of the Ottawa Anxiety
and Trauma Clinic. He had decades of experience both as a Canadian
Armed Forces psychiatrist and a civilian therapist, and his special
field of expertise was post-traumatic stress. He had a very high reputation among referring physicians in the Ottawa area.

Earlier in this narrative I stated that I was not going to get into the
details of the childhood sexual abuse or identify its two perpetrators,
because these particulars were not relevant to the basic aims of this
book. But the way I finally came to terms with the abuse bears directly
on the subject of mindfulness and its obstacles. My work with Dr
Fraser would remove the most serious and long-standing impediment
to my future mindfulness/witnessing practice. And although the goals

and methodologies of therapy and mindfulness have evolved on separate tracks, I would find that the form of therapy employed by Dr Fraser was designed to facilitate a very intense and direct experience of "witnessing" the scenes of early trauma.

When I started with Dr Fraser in the summer of 2002 it required four or five sessions just to fill him in on what happened to me from when it all began – the age of eight, so far as I can remember – up to my teenage years. I told him what I made of it and how I thought it had affected me. Then we went to work on it, and this work continued on a weekly basis until October 2003. Once we had examined in some detail the family context for what had taken place, most of our time together was focused on the actual experiences, the specific incidents of sexual abuse.

Among the methods that Dr Fraser employed, the most dramatic was a form of sensory-facilitated intervention known as eye movement desensitization and reprocessing (EMDR), which allows the client to imaginatively re-experience a specific early traumatic scene with exceptional vividness. It involves the introduction of a repeated, left-right pattern of sensory stimuli, originally designed to be visual in nature. In my case the mode of stimulation consisted of a pulsing auditory tone that alternated between my left and right ear, continuing throughout the minute or so that the remembered scene of abuse was being inwardly witnessed. I found that this procedure very rapidly generated a powerful surge of aversive inner body-feelings, to the point of nausea, together with sharp and detailed visual images. These images seemed to spill out of my mind's eye into Dr Fraser's office, generating a strongly recalled visual scene that was much wider than the constricted ophthalmic field I was now used to. Both the feelings and the memory-images generated by this procedure confirmed the appalling resilience of a long-buried cache of horrors.

Apparently there are neurological models that purport to explain the sheer intensity and broad, multi-sensory nature of the memories that this method precipitates. But the account that made intuitive sense to me was the one that conceived of the regular pulsing tone as "anchoring" that portion of the mind that would otherwise seek to escape from the scene into a defensive reaction or frozen state. This anchoring meant that even the sensory part of the mind would remain "close" to the scene being enacted, and would therefore have to attend to it. The upshot was that I was right inside the scene both in my body-feelings and in the projected imagery.

These sharp, deep probes into the past, or rather into the lower reaches of present memory, were contextualized by Dr Fraser in a carefully structured and highly supportive way. We discussed each probe after it was over, gradually unfreezing its features and opening up to interpretation that which had always been stored as a blank to which no meaning could adhere. This was a remarkable process. Through the repetition of scenes involving one or the other abuser – first the woman, then the man, then the woman again – I could "see" more and more significance, finding associations that had never occurred to me before. I immediately shared these with the therapist.

Once I realized the full extent to which I had been not only abused but subtly manipulated and disempowered, I began to enter the scene as my adult self. In a sequence of probes that introduced moral judgment into those entrenched memories, I stepped between the boy and his abusers and confronted them. I was still in my chair, but my body-mind was vividly imagining the act of intervention. I would sometimes walk out of that office wringing wet and shaking, but with the conviction – with the knowledge – that I was systematically breaking that boy's chains. In the evenings after these sessions I would just sit quietly and allow body and mind to subside into space-like awareness.

The principal features of this therapeutic process, in the language of the clinicians who had originally devised it, were desensitization and reprocessing. Desensitization meant lowering the stress level of those key memory experiences by going back into them repeatedly and seeing them with increasing insight. Reprocessing, considered neurologically, was a particular kind of repatterning of brain function that had the effect of reinforcing desensitization, as therapy progressed. Dr Fraser summed up reprocessing by saying that the intense state of reliving a memory in this particular way allowed it to finally link up with the learning functions of the brain, including those responsible for pattern recognition and judgment. But the key to the whole process was insight – the insight that arose seemingly out of nowhere when those scenes were witnessed fully and unresistingly.

As we got further into the probes, Dr Fraser began to reiterate a consistent gloss or message. This was to the effect that every last bit of the pathology of these scenes was on the side of my abusers, none of it belonging to me, none of it detracting from my essential sound-ness. All of that should be obvious, but it was something that the young boy within me needed to hear. I did not take this gloss as an attempt on Dr Fraser's part to impose his own storyline onto the material, or even to influence my own interpretation of what was being revealed. It was obvious that we were "seeing" what was there identically, almost as though we shared a single pair of "eyes." The truth was accessible to both of us in exactly the same way, through immediate recognition. This mutuality was something quite different from what I had experienced in 1994, when I was struggling to face up to the question of my sexual orientation. At that time I would do the most important inner excavating and interpreting in solitude, explain the results to the counsellor at our next meeting, and wait for him to catch up to me.

Through the old fog of emotional blackmail I was finally able to see my two abusers as they really were, inwardly stunted and twisted. I considered the term "evil," but I found somewhat to my surprise that it was too large for their dirty littleness. At the same time I saw my younger self as one who never stopped resisting inwardly even when he couldn't control external events. I recalled and relived specific instances of staring my abusers down until they had to turn their eyes away. The result of remembering and reclaiming all this was the dissolving of my shame and the breaking of my residual attachment to them, or rather to their memory, including even the attachment of hatred. In the end I had a kind of mantra for the final result: *I'm free, and they're finished.*

What my work with Dr Fraser achieved was something more than the healing of an old wound. As I saw the experience, I had removed one more barrier or screen obscuring the Advaitic self. In this latest instance of dissolving a false identification – here it was the identification with early trauma and shame – the upshot once again was not a new substitute self defined as a this or a that. It was the further freeing-up of the inner space and ineffable inner light that seemed less and less to be merely personal. To use a metaphor that is at one level factually physical, I had as a result of this process opened up my tight chest and given the whole body/mind more amplitude. I could if necessary cradle the little boy in that protective space, but he seemed to be gone or melted into me.

It was a good collaboration, during which Dr Fraser never stopped being every inch the medical man, and I never stopped being a student of Advaita in search of a quieter and more clarified mind. The neurological processing described by Dr Fraser had as its product or sequella the emergent insight that made every session worthwhile. But underlying and observing everything that happened was the still, fully sufficient light of consciousness in which we have our being. It was within that immensity that I increasingly wanted to ground myself.

As it turned out there was an unlooked-for epilogue to my work with Dr Fraser. He had warned me that maintaining the gains won through therapeutic insight would depend on something else that had to do in a simple and direct way with the body. He explained that because the abuse I had experienced began so early and continued for so many years, it had conditioned my body into a kind of baseline state of relative tension. More importantly, it had laid down a path between the body and the panic centre of the brain – apparently there really is such a centre. What this meant is that I would always be prone to react to ordinary life-stressors with something more than the ordinary degree of physical tension. If I did not attend to that tension and deal with it, it could heighten over time into an anxiety that would seem out of proportion to the immediate circumstances. On the other hand, it was clear from the way I had handled my blindness, other physical problems, and work experience, that I should be able to deal very efficiently with ordinary daily stress by making use of certain simple techniques to relax the body.

He then introduced me to the elements of a practical and quite ingenious stress management program, which I immediately began to practice. It was designed to enable the user to recognize the beginning of a stress or anxiety state, to immediately begin to relax, and then eventually to identify the underlying problem and address it in a number of ways. Because I got involved in this self-help program during the therapeutic process itself, I had plenty of time to experiment at home, ask questions, and fine-tune the various components before we wound up our work together. The idea was to finish up by my having established a new counter-habit that would override the old habit of physically tensing up when things began to go wrong. At our last meeting together Dr Fraser referred once again to the program: "It really does work," he said emphatically, "but all the literature shows that you have to keep it up."

I didn't keep it up. I let it slide, so confident was I that I could now deal with any eventuality out of the clarified perspective I'd gained by working through Factor Z. This was one more example of my long-standing tendency to more or less overlook the body and try to live from the neck up. So I had to learn of my mistake the hard way, feeling in 2004 the slow return of physical tension and ignoring it, and then experiencing periods of unfocused anxiousness.

Yet all along I had no difficulty in keeping up a daily program of stretching and strengthening exercises tailor-made for me by my excellent physiotherapist, Daniel Gagné. This had become what it ought to be, a more or less automatic habit. In the same vein I plugged away every day on my treadmill, which was equipped with sturdy handrails to compensate for my balance problems. I finally got it through my thick head that there was a perfect parallel between my stretching and exercise program, on the one hand, and what I had to do for my body in order to reduce tension, on the other. In fact it was more than a parallel: the disc degeneration, possible fibromyalgia, advanced RP, and the other components of NARP were co-inducers of the same stress complex that was generated at first by sexual abuse. All of it involved just one indivisible body.

It was only when I saw the whole pattern of stressors in terms of a single somatic package that I finally dropped the absurd notion that I ought to be able to undo the body-brain links set up by Factor Z merely through insight and positive thinking. This was magical thinking, not positive thinking. For the first time in my life I began to look at this aging, imperfect body with something like compassion, and with a certain sense of respect for what it had endured even as it kept trying to do its best. I got back on the program.

As I became more relaxed again and physically loosened up, I also began to explore sitting meditation. I found that now I could "do" it – that is, I could begin at the beginning again and paddle around in it like anybody else with a beginner's mind. I was no longer inhibited by that inner tightness, or by the lurking feeling that there was something down below the surface of consciousness that I wouldn't care to see. Simply being with the body and mind in this way was to discover at last my natural capacity for repose. And yet I have become aware of an exasperating problem having to do with sitting meditation, which I will identify further below.

By 2005 I had four excellent, time-tested, and roadworthy programs or sets of resources that I could rely on. The first set is the stress management program I got from Dr Fraser, tailored to some degree to my specific circumstances. The second resource is the Harding method of in-turning, which when cultivated as a regular habit opens up the inner space from which stressors can be dealt with more effectively. I have a great fondness for these "experiments," and although the in-turning has become second nature to me I find myself going back to the experiments from time to time because they are charming, and always somehow a surprise.

The third resource set is M B S R with its emphasis on the basic modes of mindfulness practice. Among the books on mindfulness that I have read I would especially recommend those by Jon Kabat-Zinn, Larry Rosenberg, and Sharon Salzberg[1] It is a nice bonus that M B S R and any kind of activity-based, physical stress reduction program dovetail with each other, in the sense that you can practise many of the elements of a standard stress program mindfully.

The last of my four stress-reducing resources is of course the suite of Advaitic practices described in chapter 7 – most notably kosha work, with its cultivation of discrimination and detachment, together with the simple, calming habit of witnessing. The witness remains unentangled. In that regard I was intrigued by the two little words with which Dr Fraser characterized the stress-reduction program that he not only teaches but practises every day: "blissful neutrality." There seems to be a natural commonality between well-founded detachment techniques known to professionals such as Dr Fraser, and the basic practices of the Vedantic/Buddhist tradition: blissful neutrality indeed.

But here I must make a confession. Because of an exasperating problem or quirk, I have failed to plumb the depths of M B S R sitting meditation, one of the best resources to which I have been introduced. After my work with Dr Fraser I could indeed enter into sitting meditation without encountering the old submerged barriers, and for a time I "practised" every day. But I didn't stick with it; as embarrassing as it is to admit, I just kept "forgetting" to do my sitting when other things intervened. This was all too typical of me; I plunge enthusiastically into some program, confirm its merits, and before long wander off at an angle with my hands in my pockets, whistling, thinking great thoughts that are totally unconnected to the program. A day or so later I would "remember" with a start, and try again for a while to get on track. If you too decide to give M B S R sitting meditation a try, dear reader, I hope you can profit from my record of mistakes and chronic distractedness. Perhaps you will discover a capacity for persistent application that far outstrips my own.

2 INTERZONE, PHANTASMAGORIA, OWNERSHIP

In the next several pages I am going to attempt something quite different. Instead of showing the reader as I did in the previous chapters how the changes in my vision have been closely bound up with the other aspects of my life, I will present the end of vision and its unexpected denouement as a subject in its own right. That is, in what follows I will make only limited references to the current daily life in which I have found myself confronting new forms of pseudo-visual experience, so that those forms themselves may occupy centre stage. These phenomena make up a parallel, para-sensory domain that stands quite apart from other modes of experience.

My intent here is simply to attract and hold the reader's attention and elicit some kind of inner response, simple or complex, positive or negative. What, I wonder, will you think of what I now inwardly "see"? By the end of this section you too will have vicariously "seen" much of the stuff that has been processing through my mind's eye lately, notwithstanding my total external blindness. You will also take in my final valuation of the whole, seventy-year process of vision loss. Does that valuation strike you as an attempt to make something out of almost nothing? Or even if I seem to have created a structure of meaning that works for me, is it so foreign and so tied up with the circumstances of my atypical childhood that it is unlikely to strike a chord with most readers? Finally, is it possible to find inherent interest in those last-stage, pseudo-visual phenomena, a degree of beauty, perhaps, or a silent appeal from a world other than your own to acknowledge those forms as valid modes of inner being? If you are moved to comment on any of this, please do not hesitate to email McGill-Queen's University Press (mqup@mcgill.ca) with the request that your comments be forwarded to me.

For three years or so after my work with Dr Fraser I lived in a visual space that was for the most part restful, uneventful, and indeed almost blank. Unlike the stages of vision loss described in the previous chapters it was free of problems, apart from the simple fact that I couldn't see anything. I welcomed the relative absence of visual static or garble. This was, on the one hand, the positive side of these newly simplified circumstances. On the other hand, visual experience was still not blank enough or empty enough to satisfy me. To explain this attitude – which for most visually impaired and sighted readers alike will seem incredible – I must refer again to the powerful influence that the writings of John Hull had on my evaluation of vision loss, and to the complete and liberating disidentification from eyesight that I had experienced in New Delhi.

When I read Hull's *Touching the Rock* in 1995 I was captivated by his vivid description of a tactile-acoustic, non-visual world, which when entered into unreservedly was inseparable from a deeper

experience of consciousness. Even at that juncture, when I still had
some remnants of workable vision, I knew that if no cure for RP were
discovered I would eventually want to open myself fully to that world.
Since New Delhi I had been free of any emotional entanglement
with eyesight, and as I worked my way through the late stages of RP
I found that I was divided in my reception of the visual illusions that
were then so prominent. As phenomena they were intriguing, so much
so that I documented them as best I could on cassette tape. But in
practical terms bearing on mobility and object-recognition, the illusions were completely superfluous and sometimes obstructive. The
time finally came when I wanted to get beyond those scrambled or
empty visions – beyond pseudo-visual phenomena altogether – into
a new experience of space. Based on my engagement with Advaita
and my reading of Jacques Lusseyran, I anticipated that that space
would be indivisibly both inner and outer.

But by 2006 I found myself fully immersed in an odd reality that
I would come to think of as the Interzone, an in-between place that
was neither full-sightedness nor functional partial-sightedness nor
out-and-out blindness, neither one kind of world nor yet another. Far
behind me lay the narrow visual world of RP partial seeing; somewhere out in front was the tactile-acoustic world known to the totally
blind. The Interzone between these worlds was a kind of limbo. It
was now characterized by a presence that should have been, but was
not, a perfectly blank visual screen. There was still somehow a sense
of visual being or existence, despite the fact that except under very
particular conditions I could not even perceive light. This odd sense
of visual presence was mainly the result of a general perturbation of
the visual field, a field that contained nothing but a vague sense of
formless swirling. As I explained in chapter 7, this empty swirling first
appeared after the phenomenon that I called the ocean of empty light
had totally drained away. The swirling may have been related to my
growing dizziness and/or uncontrolled eye movements (nystagmus),
which according to Pressi and my doctors had become more marked.

The upshot of the swirling was that my attention got pulled back
repeatedly from the possibilities of sound and touch and scent to
pseudo-vision, where there was a vertiginous something that was
really nothing. When I "looked" into it I sometimes thought of the
dark, turbulent Chaos described by Milton in *Paradise Lost*, the formless potentiality that Satan detected during his epic voyage from Hell
to Eden. That was *his* epic, I thought sourly, not mine. I didn't choose

this and I didn't need it. I found that the pull of that almost-blank visual screen was strong enough and distracting enough that the other senses were simply not opening up, in the way they can for the sort of totally blinded person who is patient, observant, and non-judgmental. As a result the overall feeling-tone of my sensorium was one of muting or constriction.

In order now to invite the non-visual senses to come forward a little more, I took time every day to mindfully attend to them. But nothing much seemed to happen. Eventually I had to admit to myself that I was sulking. Because I didn't much like what was on show, I had thrown over the first rule of mindfulness practice: to take in what is actually there without resistance. It was only when I gave up the inner grumbling over these substandard "visual" offerings that my resistance softened, and I found myself taking in ordinary touch-sensations and household sounds with a degree of rediscovered pleasure. That was better. What followed was a modest re-enactment of the sensory efflorescence that I had experienced in New Delhi. All right, I thought, I can become a permanent Interzone resident if that's the way it has to be. I knew that if the experience of vague visual churning were connected with my previous meningitis, or in some way with my NARP, it could continue for as long as this body lasted.

During this transition period I listened to a great deal of music and especially to Bach, not just for pleasure or solace but for the inner depths it opened. This was a resource that could never be exhausted. When I gave myself over to the preludes and fugues of the Well-Tempered Clavier, with my eyes wide open, it was as though seeing had become sound. What I "saw" was a formless, slowly swirling visual space that served somehow as the energetic ground or raw substance for those elegant musical forms. This was of course imagination rather than a genuine synesthesia – an imagination that acted quite on its own, with me as witness or audience. All I had to do was sit back and take it all in.

In 2008 the visual screen changed in a most unexpected way: hallucinations began to appear. By degrees they became stronger and more definite, giving mock, surreal substance to the vague phenomenon of empty visual agitation. Most of the time I just tried to ignore these apparitions, but they increasingly claimed my attention. Coincidentally, it was just at this time that I wrote to the eminent New York–based neurologist and author Oliver Sacks regarding my book project, and my personal experience with RP. I had been an admirer of Dr Sacks's writing for many years, and I must own now that one of my half-acknowledged motives in writing this book was to try to depict the blind condition with at least some measure of the phenomenological exactitude and compassion that Sacks extends to his own subjects. Dr Sacks and I continued to exchange letters for several years, during which he read excerpts from my evolving book draft and warmly encouraged me to keep at it. In August 2015 he died of the cancer to which he so candidly referred in his late essays and books.

Dr Sacks's reply to my initial 2009 letter – a handwritten response together with some of his essays on blindness and visual impairment – was fascinating and buoying. It was also prescient, for in the course of his letter he rather startled me by asking in an apparently incidental way if I was experiencing any hallucinations. And that did it. I immediately began to pay close attention to the display that was already revving itself up in my visual mind, and got totally hooked on it. It was like turning up the lights.

With that I became the fascinated observer of not just one but three distinct kinds of visual hallucination, which waxed and waned according to their own laws or whims. For the first few months I just surrendered myself to the inner spectacle when a hallucination was on show, if external circumstances permitted. Before I try to describe these phenomena and explain how I dealt with them, I must make the point that they were hallucinations in the proper sense of that word, not mere illusions. The visual chaos and ocean of empty light described earlier were visual illusions. Like all sensory illusions they were caused by an incomplete, ambiguous, or garbled message to the brain transmitted by an external sensory organ, in this case the eyes. This results in a misrepresentation of what is being seen.

A visual hallucination is by contrast the work of the visual brain all on its own, without benefit of any input whatever from the eyes.[2] In my case the retinal photoreceptor cells had become almost completely non-functional, while my visual cortex remained whole and undamaged despite its new isolation from the visual world. It tried, accordingly, to keep doing what it had always done: generate visual experience. And to this day it succeeds in doing so, sometimes spectacularly, serving up a repertoire of visual forms that range from deceptively real-looking objects to the most extravagant displays of abstract expressionism. This is a completely natural activity on the part of an organ that is still robust and lively.

The brain is the province of neurologists, who in recent years have made great advances in explaining how this extraordinary sense-object "works." The intricacy of neural functioning is a remarkable process, all the more so when it is superimposed on the revelations presented by modern physics. That is, like all other objects of direct experience, the human brain as known and probed by the neurosurgeon is a complex that abides *within the sensorium* – not a thing-in-itself existing outside of consciousness. Yet it is this supernally intricate phenomenal object, the expression somehow of an underlying and baffling quantum actuality, that makes possible our thinking, imaginings, and hallucinations. We could take this state of affairs to be inexplicably odd, but we may as well regard it as a bountiful if rather uncanny gift of nature. It is precisely the kind of sly gift that seems to place us, illusorily, right at the centre of things.

When the hallucinations began to appear out of the blue, I was absolutely gobsmacked. It is no wonder that I tried at first to ignore the presence of these images, for by the standards of ordinary experience they are simply impossible. They cannot really exist, and yet there they are. And unlike visual illusions these phenomena cannot be turned off by closing one's eyes. This is the part that took me aback at first; the whole show is spread out unavoidably inside oneself, with no external source or referent and no internal "stop" button. In earlier times visual hallucinations were often attributed to evil or mischievous spirits or divine retribution, burdening the one who experiences them with both intense fear and social ostracism. In those pre-modern societies that had a strong tradition of shamanism, such visions might have been identified as uninvited, eldritch gifts that put the recipient in thrall to an unknown external power. Now that I had my own visions to deal with I could imagine what it must have been like to believe oneself possessed in this way.

When I mentioned to friends and neighbours that I had begun to experience visual hallucinations they were quite taken aback, and for some moments dumbstruck. Then when I explained how and why it was happening they all responded in pretty much the same way. If the person experiencing these visual phenomena didn't know better, they said, he would think he was going crazy. The unspoken implication was clear, of course: if I had not described the precipitating circumstances of my hallucinations, my friends and neighbours would have wondered if I had lost my grip. Ophthalmologists are very familiar with this kind of reaction, and with the hallucinations that provoke them; when I went for an eye checkup at this time I was treated to what was clearly a well-rehearsed spiel on the non-pathological nature of my visitations. They are experienced, I was told reassuringly, by many, many people after total vision loss.

My initial disbelief in the face of what was happening to me is best illustrated by the strange case of the phantom forearms, the first of the three kinds of hallucinations that I set myself to actively investigate. One evening I was washing dishes in the kitchen sink when my eyes closed of their own accord, for I was feeling sleepy. I noticed with a start that my forearms were still visibly "there," still moving laterally back and forth in a "place" that corresponded to the bottom of what used to be my visual field. As I continued to work with closed eyes I saw how the mobile image of those ghost-forearms moved in perfect concert with the movement-sensations of their physical counterparts.

I just couldn't credit it. Was it just my imagination finding a new modality to play with? Over the next few days I tested out this queer phenomenon in various settings and circumstances. One night I ended up in our windowless basement bathroom with the door firmly closed and no light turned on either in the bathroom or anywhere else in the house, a sleeping mask covering my eyes and a scarf tied over the mask so that my eyes could not even open, and voila: there again was the vision of those faithful forearms, their movements matching per-fectly the muscle-sensations of the arms that were slicing through "external" space. So there is no doubt about it, I thought. This is some sort of natural process.

It was soon after this that I was able to take in and digest the articles by Dr Sacks that he had thoughtfully included with his letter. They were recorded onto cassette tape by my ever-helpful volunteer readers, Dana Mullen and Sonia Tilson. I had already learned from the Internet that one of these articles, "The Mind's Eye – What the Blind See," had been widely received as a classic of its kind following its original publication in the *New Yorker* in 2003.[3] I found that it was exactly the right essay to pass on to people who are just beginning to come to terms with the probability of serious future vision loss. It is the one essay I wish I could have read when I was twenty-two, on the day I accepted my own prognosis.

"The Mind's Eye" explores the personal meaning, self-confirmation, and adaptive ingenuity that blinded people somehow manage to discover or create in the midst of their altered circumstances. As Sacks demonstrates with vivid, detailed examples drawn from a number of very different lives, blind people have the capacity to penetrate, explore, and ungrudgingly accept their condition in remarkably diverse ways. This essay not only reinforced my old conviction that there were many paths to positive adjustment, but conveyed something of the immediacy or "feel" of particular lives lived on those paths. I was especially interested in Sacks's portrayal of the late John Hull and Jacques Lusseyran, in whose writings I had steeped myself for years (chapter 6, section 1). It was refreshing and intriguing to see them through a different pair of eyes. I was reminded all over again that, first and foremost, Hull and Lusseyran were real, complex men, not (as they have sometimes been for me) the exemplars of alternative world views.

After reading the rest of the material Dr Sacks had sent me I got back to my tape recorder and the notes I had been dictating regarding my hallucinations. I tried now to come up with something incisive or at least coherent regarding my second form of visual abracadabra, but I felt awkward and tentative. After reading all that Sacks I just stood in awe of his intellectual breadth and literary talent: I then found that I had come down with a rather stiff dose of what literary critic Harold Bloom referred to as "the anxiety of influence."[4] It took me a couple of weeks to get through this incipient writer's block. At least the pseudo-visual anomaly I was now trying to describe was easy to name – it was light, nothing but light.

It was hard to find words for the feeling that this new experience evoked, a feeling compounded at first of incredulity and delight. It consists entirely of an upsurge of radiant light, a light that appears suddenly out of nowhere and is unlike anything I ever saw with my eyes. It is somehow at one and the same time delicate and commanding, ethereal and intense. It is clear that this light exists only within my sensory mind, as I can confirm by closing my eyes or completely covering my face when it begins to appear. It is not the light of consciousness, but a strangely beautiful pseudo-ophthalmic light that consciousness registers as other than itself.

The light appears most frequently late in the evening or at night when it is dark outdoors, as I am preparing for bed. Most of the time it contains no discernable forms but just shines in its own right. Its effect is to make me feel that I am being bathed in it. I continue to experience its beauty to this day, although with gradually reducing frequency. It usually persists for about half an hour, and when it finally fades away, always to my regret, I cannot recreate it through imagination or mindful expectant waiting, or through any form of meditation that I know.

For me this light has a spiritual quality. But I do not see it as some kind of purpose-driven revelation, a signal to break through into something new. The light is simply there, gently waxing and waning according to its own periodicity. I take the phenomenon to be a little grace, the sort of thing to which we can assign value as we please. After all, I made the point in chapter 6 that our ordinary sensory experience may be regarded as a gift – a gift of some agency that lies deeper than quantum mechanics can go. I find that I have the same attitude toward this non-sensory, entirely private but comforting radiance.

My third type of hallucination merits the title of "the undismissible," for it is a going concern that just keeps going. So far as I can gather from Oliver Sacks's 2012 book *Hallucinations*, it is an example of Charles Bonnet syndrome. This is a broad class of visual hallucinations, both figurative and abstract, that are experienced by many but not all people who go completely blind. What I "see" is a kinetic field of abstract forms, a highly unstable display that is present much of the time when I am awake. For the most part it manifests itself quite separately from the radiant light and phantom forearms. The display can look like a cockeyed, pulsing work of art, and at other times like a jumble of random pieces. When these hallucinations first began in 2008 they were occasional and rather muted, but they have gained over time in vividness, variety, and frequency. Now they seem to have settled in as long-term or possibly permanent guests. My job has been to domesticate them.

The display sometimes seems to arise out of an almost featureless rest or "reset" state, which I become aware of after having been abstracted for some minutes in a chain of thinking or a household task. This emptied-out view is more or less like the blank but subtly swirling ground-state that was typically on show until the hallucinations began. The one difference is that there is a kind of detailed puckering or frothing all over the visual field, as though on the surface of a wind-blown lake. Then forms begin slowly to appear out of the froth, and to move more or less together in a particular direction.

More frequently, though, I find that when I emerge from some mental activity and become "visually" aware, the forms are already manifest and going full tilt. In one of the more common presentations the acuity of the blob-like forms can vary over time from very vague to strikingly sharp-edged and definite. Some blobs are curved in on themselves like early-stage fetuses or plump forms from a paisley pattern. Bordering these things or sometimes standing behind them – for there is some sense of three-dimensionality, of separate planes that slide over one another – there will be a number of shattered geometric structures that are more or less rectilinear and tilted sideways at odd angles.

All the different parts of the array pulse and change, their respective boundaries sometimes melting into one another only to reformulate in a slightly different way a moment later. When the display is bright there are evident colour contrasts, the fetuses or blobs of protoplasm assuming a characteristic mauve tint or sometimes an ochre one, while the irregular geometric pieces are white or silver or more rarely a rich blue or vermilion.

In another display with a completely different set of "parts," I see a dense, closely set arrangement of cunningly detailed curvilinear objects for which I can find no name. They are bright and metallic-looking, fashioned it would seem by a pint-sized smith or jeweller. The sub-components of these objects are so complex and inter-nested that I cannot make out which are imbedded in which others. Or perhaps there are no real boundaries but just a single complex object. I have the sense that there are layers and layers of activity, of formation and reformation, and that I am seeing only the surface.

In these cases and most of the others that I experience, the entire display moves or streams across the visual field. The direction of motion seems to coincide with my nystagmic eye movements, as observed by Pressi. When she tells me that the eyes have rolled to the side, "righted" themselves and rolled back again, I find that I had just finished seeing a particular set of components retrace the same path they had followed a few moments earlier. If I should become preoccupied with this back-and-forth repetition and attend to it closely, the jerkiness tends to increase. I may feel a little light-headed. On some days the streaming motion is violent, and this is when I especially feel dizzy and unbalanced. If I am moving about I have to be very mindful of what my legs are doing, ignoring the surge of forms that seem to buffet my inner gyroscope.

Occasionally I am presented with a far simpler and almost static picture quite unlike the examples of visual streaming described above. This consists of one or two pale yellow panels that somehow give the impression of being monumental in size and far removed from the observer. They drift very slowly across a dull greenish ground. This near-stillness together with the sense of great size and distance creates an odd effect, one that is the exact opposite of the confinement or impingement I sometimes experience during episodes of violent streaming or surging. In the presence of those monumental panels I feel that I am slowly opening out or sifting or blending into the empty space that separates me from what I see. It is not an unpleasant experience – quite the contrary.

Less frequently I experience a movement of visual forms that is not lateral but seemingly straight at me, the images steadily approaching the invisible inner Eye or I that is taking the scene in. It is a little like viewing a 3-D movie in which a car is seen to be hurtling, in suspenseful slow motion, directly at the viewer. There is a "wavering" of the approaching images that may have to do, once again, with my nystagmic eye movements. The images are also shape-shiftingly unstable in themselves. Because of this instability the sense of impending collision leads not to a crisis but a peculiar muddle or indeterminacy. As the blob-like thing grows larger and larger there is a point at which it seems to be right "here," in the space that I already occupy. I have been drawn into it or it into me. I wait to see what will happen. Soon the form begins to break up; the daughter-blobs move off to either side rather than further forward, and the conventional sense of a subject looking at a set of objects is restored.

In late 2009 I began to see a new version of the jeweller's display of curvilinear objects referred to above. I watched as the familiar array broke apart into its smallest sub-components, which began to move independently in every direction at once. This multidirectional motion could not, I thought, be a simple effect of my eye movements. I was amazed at the coherence of it all – it looked almost choreographed. It was like peering down through a microscope into a world of one-celled organisms that moved as smoothly and purposefully as fishes, streaming or scooting around one another without any collisions or muddling of their boundaries.

More recently I have begun to see another innovation, a display in dull earth tones of several ill-fitting, irregularly-shaped panels whose instability or shiftings allow me to catch glimpses of other layers of material underneath. This would be enough to hold my attention, but there is another feature that is superimposed on this array and completely dominates the show: a starkly simple set of two or sometimes three horizontal black bars. These thick, misshapen bars are of the blackest black I have ever seen. It is an absolute black, a glaring black, and when it is present it draws my attention like a magnet. For some reason it fascinates me. The bars frame the display and in a presentational sense overwhelm it, for once the gaze has been drawn into this blackness it requires a little effort of will to pull it out again, and attend to the shiftings of those broken panels. Then the panels look pallid by comparison, while the horizontal black presences seem compellingly real. In radiating their own peculiar intensity they impart a rather oppressive, ominous quality.

The reader may see from these examples that the main problem with such hallucinations is their capacity to distract, to capture and hold the inner gaze when the viewer wants or needs to be engaged with something else. When I first began to pay close attention to the emergent field of abstract forms it was almost as though they were feeding themselves on my interest. As I watched them gain in clarity I was for a time unresistingly spellbound. But for obvious practical reasons I had to begin redeploying my attention.

I was pretty sure that people who find themselves in this situation eventually get used to the hallucinations and just learn to ignore them. But I wanted to quickly develop a flexible response, so I decided to return for a while to morning and afternoon sessions of formal daily mindfulness practice. This meant fully taking in the images without resistance, from that slight inner distance that confirms the images to be peripheral to one's conscious centre. This example of mindful detachment, like others I had experienced, might be described as accommodation or acceptance at arm's length. That kind of stance or attitude beats the alternatives: inwardly shrinking away from the display, feeling helplessly tied to it in anger, or rejecting it without being able to get rid of it.

When I began to dwell mindfully on the display I did not expect any problems. But I found that in one sense the hallucinations presented a novel challenge that I did not encounter with my earlier visual illusions: the constant flowing and occasional "swirling" of the visual field and everything it contained. In the face of this agitation it can be tempting to break off the mindful attending, to go off somewhere and just do something. There are good days and bad days, but overall the agitation seems slowly to be getting worse. When the flowing is turbulent and accompanied by lightheadedness or dizziness, I have to be very aware of myself as the still centre of consciousness – especially if I am up on my feet and in motion.

That centre is *not* just imagination; it is real, as the motionless core sentience that is aware of all the motion. Grounding myself in it is like being the secure hub of a revolving wheel. Indeed, there is a Harding experiment that is designed expressly to disclose this capacity for centredness while spinning in a circle.

Outside these occasions of intense visual turbulence, which coincide with a "spiking" of my dizziness and the feeling of being unbalanced, I do not find it difficult to live with my kinetic field of images. When I have to be busy with something, its natural place most of the time is that of a largely ignorable background. In that sense it is like the weather outdoors, ordinary inner body-feelings, and the sound of the furnace. Only when I really attend to it does it seem to become brighter.

Having made room for my visual hallucinations, I find that on ordinary days of minor turbulence I have a choice. I can ride the forms when I feel like taking a trip, or recede inward and witness them when I want to be especially still, or just ignore them when I have to get involved in some practical activity or mental work. Eventually I came to think of the moving forms in their most agitated state as a litter of hare-brained and exuberant young terriers, who surge through my house and tumble about me without ever quite getting under foot. If this is the worst they can get up to, it is not too bad at all. And most of the time these forms are far more novel and less demanding than your run-of-the-mill household pet.

My hallucinations have become the moveable stage set for this book project – for the meetings with friends, volunteer readers, and fellow-sojourners down the RP path; for the trips to the computer store and the sessions with Daniel, my physiotherapist; and of course for the writing and dictating here at home. The words you are reading now were recorded in the presence of restless visual forms. Right at this moment as I pause to attend to the display I see that it consists of an intricate and delicate weave of more or less vertical presences, rather like vines and tendrils or slender trunks with upraised branches. They look rather Japanese. These dark forms process in a slow, stately way from right to left against a background that looks very much like a wintry grey Ottawa sky. It is austerely beautiful.

One night after I went to bed and began the slow descent into sleep, I saw something entirely new. It began with an arrangement of dark, irregularly shaped panels that were much like others I have recently experienced. I think they were two-dimensional. But what distinguished this display from anything I had "seen" before was a set of small bright forms that appeared all at once in the lower right-hand quadrant of the display, disappearing perhaps thirty seconds later. There were three forms or perhaps only one, three folds of a continuous silver net that rippled and furled and unfurled itself like some sinuous living thing.

No ordinary creature could ever interpenetrate itself the way this one did. Its graceful movements were like those of an aquatic animal such as a jellyfish or a large-winged ray or skate, except that the thing kept curving in upon itself to flow through its own substance. In a rapid but smooth succession of these movements it maintained the appearance of having three layers, all silver and all equally bright. Through its rippling mesh I could perceive the greenish tint of the background panels. From moment to moment it gave the impression of being not just alive but joyously alive. Watching it had brought me fully awake, marvelling at the thing even as it disappeared.

I wonder if the animated silver net could have been a product of the hypnagogic or hypnopompic states, those pseudo-sensory states that often intervene, respectively, between the waking state and dreamless sleep, and between dreaming and waking up. Yet the background panels had the appearance of one of my frequent waking-state hallucinations. Wherever it came from, the silver creature was so intricate and subtle and sportive that, as I burrowed back in and pulled the blankets up, I found myself muttering something through my dental appliance: "Who was *doing* that?" Never in a million years could "I" – the "I" of this limited, familiar personality – ever summon the creative visual intelligence required to mentally project such an artifice. Of course there was nobody at all "doing" it; once again it was just the visual cortex blowing off steam, gratifyingly but impersonally. Or to put it more generally it was the nature of things or life itself that was doing it, calling forth, as it so often does, the kind of structured phenomenon in which human beings may delight.

It reminded me of something, and it was not until the next day that the memory came to light. In one of Beethoven's Razumovsky string quartets there is a very short but wonderful passage, perhaps a minute or so into the second movement, in which the voices of the instruments leap over one another in the architectonics of pure exultation. The lissome silver net, I thought, was the visual counterpart of that music. It had come out of the nowhere that lay behind the green background to gladden my heart when I just happened to be watching. It is good to have seen such a thing at so improbable a stage of my sensory life.

The hallucinations, then, are the most recent substitute for the conventional visual world to be framed by my mind's eye. They are my phantasmagoria. Like the much earlier partial functional vision, the successive stages of visual illusion and the swirling emptiness of the Interzone, the hallucinations represent one more attempt by the now isolated visual brain to conjure something out of consciousness. In common with all those predecessor phenomena, this latest innovation is quite unlike the opposites of full external vision and total, dysfunctional internal blackness, the latter being the sighted person's wrong notion of what blindness is like. With my hallucinations I once again find myself in the middle between the conventional ideas of seeing and unseeing, in a place that is hard to describe (let alone evoke) for the sighted majority.

I take this in-between, pseudo-visual space to be the natural complement of the other in-between aspects of my experience. These include the decades of sexual ambiguity, my divided orientation toward the contending attractions of spirituality and secular humanism, a division that inevitably led me to the middle ground between enlightenment and materialism, and most basically my partiality to being an unaffiliated observer. It was the satisfaction of being an observer that was the common element in my anthropological pursuits, diplomatic reporting, and philosophical explorations. Each of these pursuits was necessarily based on maintaining a certain distance from what I was taking in, in order to receive it as clearly and non-judgmentally as I could.

The strategy of distancing was the key in my practical adaptation to RP, from the age of twenty-three. It was by detaching myself from the flow of degrading visual experience and observing it from a strategic inner remove that I learned how to remain mobile, try out a series of vocational options, and accept my sensorium. So if the word "identity" as distinct from the real self or Atman has any useful meaning at all, then I suppose that my surface identity is that of a blind watcher – one who waits in expectancy and hope, and does not identify with what he observes.

The beginning of this detachment or non-clinging was of course the acceptance of my prognosis in 1965. It was then that I finally grasped the life I had been given with both hands, despite or because of the fact that it came packaged in the shrink-wrap of RP. I had found something to contend with that was hard but clean, something entirely removed from the corrupt pathology of my upbringing. The absorption of my prognosis started a process of self-exploration that I may not have been able to initiate in any other way. This would be the making of me, or at least the beginning of the unmaking of the not-me.

In retrospect it seems almost fated that this should lead to Advaita. Moving back inwardly from failing vision was the first unsuspecting step toward cultivating the inner position that Advaita calls the witness. It was from the position of the witness that I came to feel with complete certainty that selfhood and the light of consciousness were one and the same. This discovery still left plenty of room for new erroneous assumptions, or pseudo-Advaita, and as I will show in the next chapter I made my share of mistakes. But I would never again fall back into the conventional, body-grounded sense of self. How could I not value the vision loss and in-turning that made all of this possible? And how could I not value the startling projections of late-stage RP, which revealed the sensory world to be a marvellous weave of mind-stuff?

Communicating this even in part with my visually impaired friends and acquaintances has not always been easy. Twenty years ago when I told friends of my readiness to launch myself fully into the deep blindness of John Hull's tactile-acoustic world, I think some of them took this to be a kind of surrender or failure of spirit on my part. To them it would have seemed like a writing-off of the world in its fullest and most vivid sensory aspect, an inexplicable slide into blankness. They stuck to this position even when I described my eyesight as it was then, a dysfunctional scramble that left me with almost no useful vision. Some were similarly taken aback recently when I described how I live comfortably with my hallucinations. They do understand why I should wish to get on as well as I can with my oddly mixed sensory and hallucinatory experience, but they think I should be yearning for a cure.

I still marvel that people should find it so difficult to grasp how a person living with blindness may claim full ownership of the condition, opening up and saying yes to it. After all, all philosophy aside, he or she has a blazingly obvious motive for doing so. It consists simply in wanting to live as fully as possible in the present – not in some dream of future medical rescue, or in dolorous and fading memories of vision long since lost. You cannot go wrong in choosing to live as openly as possible in the present moment. In accepting your circumstances ungrudgingly and getting on with things, you free yourself from the inauthenticity of denial – and from a strange kind of irrationality or superstition. This latter is the patient's skewed, spooked-out sense that accepting his vision loss would amount not only to a perverse embrace of self-diminishment, but to a downright jinx. Some ophthalmology patients are burdened by the irrational notion that to say "yes" to their prognosis would be an act of bad faith, one that would render them black-magically ineligible for eventual medical liberation. There is of course no such jinx.

I will round off this summary valuation of blindness by telling you about a little thought-experiment I perform on myself every couple of years. It begins with the following question. If you could take a magic potion here and now that would not only restore your eyesight but give you the full-sightedness that you never experienced even as a child, would you take it or just stay the way you are? There is an alternative question, which goes like this: if there were another potion that could undo the past by giving you normal vision at birth, vision that subsequently you never would have lost, would you quaff it or reject it?

Here are my answers. First, I would not hesitate a moment in taking the first potion, the one that would give me full vision in the present. I am pretty well done exploring the stages of my RP, including most recently the post-visual hallucinations, and although I do not find myself yearning for it I would jump at the chance of experiencing what for me is the almost unimaginable novelty of full field vision. Grabbing such an opportunity would be a healthy organic response, a no-brainer. There would be great practical benefits: being able to read again, for example, and to be able to go anywhere with my new walker and – such an exotic prospect – to actually drive a car for the first time in my life. And, practicalities aside, I would be able to see Pressi and Evan and all else that pleases the eye.

Perhaps this response will seem puzzling, given my advocacy a little way above of total acceptance of one's blindness. But there is a difference between accepting something and identifying with it, and the difference is vast. After discovering visual detachment during my posting in India I no longer identified with my remaining vision, and as vision gave way to blindness I did not identify with that, either. Although I accepted the blindness, it was not necessary for me to validate it by taking it to be a "part" of myself. This I know is very different from the position adopted by many blind persons, for whom a close identification with the blind condition becomes, for good or ill, a salient feature of their identity. For my part, I am sure I would enjoy the fruits of seeing again or seeing fully for the first time, but I am equally sure that I would not identify with this new capacity. I know better now. If I should subsequently lose my vision again I would no doubt find it disappointing and poignant, but not gut-wrenching or existentially threatening. I would still be "me."

As to that other magic potion – the one that would remake me as sighted from birth – I wouldn't touch it. For the reasons I have documented at length in this memoir, I feel deeply that for me RP has been a boon – an unlikely and problematic boon, to be sure, but a boon nonetheless. It was when I parlayed my prognosis into a constructive project that my adulthood began. Later on, the intriguing phenomenality of RP helped open me to the inner light, a great discovery the price of which was the cancelling of outer ophthalmic light. If all this amounted to a gift, an uninvited and implacable gift, who or what was the giver? Or is there none, nothing but physics and genetics and unpredictable contingency? Advaita offers its own kind of response, which does not so much answer the questions as deconstruct and decommission them. What we have then is the fullness of the here and now, the real.

In this section I have given my outer blindness its due, set down a final account of what my inner or mind's eye has been concocting, and tried to explain how I have integrated these phenomena into a life. Blindness is important to the blind, but even when it is freighted with the sort of uncommon valuation I have granted to it here, it cannot and should not constitute the centre of things. For us as for the sighted, life has mainly to do with two things. The first consists of finding useful and absorbing work – work defined very broadly, so that it can include the writing/dictating of books such as this one. The second is the challenge of opening up the heart and then somehow keeping it open.

Yet there is a whole other dimension of experience. If we are lucky we may also have the chance to explore life in another way, by burrowing beneath its thin, sensory surface to find out what is really down there where the senses cannot go. Douglas Harding and Jacques Lusseyran were quite right, I find, in insisting that the blind have a potential advantage when it comes to sussing out the deep nature of things. I am referring here to the true nature of the regular, daily existence we think we already know, ordinary life with its partially veiled but extraordinary interior glow. I find that this subtle glow, which seems somehow to be both right in front of us and secreted within us, can become more apparent if we just open ourselves to its presence. More of that below.

3 ORDINARY LIFE AS I FIND IT

There was a particular aspect of spiritual practice or *sadhana* that I did not really get into until 2009. This had to do with opening up the heart. I first came across it in an Advaitic context in the late 1990s when I immersed myself in Shankara's Commentaries on the Upanishads, the Bhagavad-Gita and the Brahma Sutras, commentaries that lay out the method and basic findings of classical Advaita Vedanta. In passages dealing with spiritual practice, I found a number of references to a preliminary stage or station of life that would normally precede discrimination and detachment (viveka and vairagya). It concentrated on the development of the kind of integrity, altruism, and non-acquisitiveness that make it possible for us to live in a less selfish and grasping way.

The Shankara version emphasized the cultivation of simplicity, straight dealing, kindness, friendliness, and above all helpfulness in our interactions with others. These factors taken together were what Shankara called benevolence. According to him the meditative cultivation of benevolence is not only possible but essential: it reduces the narrow egoism that would otherwise interfere with the later consolidation of discrimination and detachment. The contrary or obstructive factors that impede benevolence are possessiveness, judgmentalism, and wrath.

It all looked very familiar. I had found similar presentations in all the other Eastern and Western spiritual traditions and moral philosophies I had surveyed. All too frequently these kinds of injunctions are dried and stored as a standard tonic for boosting personal "goodness" or "righteousness"; for that reason I tended to pay them little attention. But seeing them in Shankara really pulled me up short. It didn't take much thinking to figure out why they were there. How could you possibly see your "others" as integral to our common selfhood and not practice benevolence? This, I thought, is not something I can skip over or should even want to skip over.

Right into my fifties I had doubted that I could live in such a simple, non-ego-based way. I just wasn't a good enough person. This judgment against myself began to soften when I came out in 1994; my subsequent work with Dr Fraser completed the long, internal thawing-out process. I then discovered a deceptively simple benevolence practice as taught by the late Hari Prasad Shastri, the Advaita teacher who for many years served as director of the Shanti Sadan study centre in London.[5] It consists first of entering a state of inner stillness and silence, and then expressing in the mind and heart the wish that others might derive good from oneself, and equally that one might derive good from others. I followed this practice as best I could for a couple of years, surprising myself by staying with it and finding it worthwhile despite (or because of?) Its simplicity. But the parallel practice that I really made my own was introduced to me by Bill Gayner in 2009, and in accordance with Bill's own background it was Buddhist rather than Advaitic. It is known as the loving kindness (*maitri*) meditation, the first of the four key observances known as the Brahma Viharas. These exercises have as their objective the opening-up of a channel of fellow-feeling toward other people. I had no hesitation in taking up this Buddhist resource as a means of cultivating the benevolence advocated by Shankara. In its content and purpose it is a non-denominational exercise.

Before I tried them out experimentally I never could have guessed how powerful these simple meditations could be. I found that, practised regularly and with real intention, these affirmations can have a very positive effect on the disposition of the mind. They lift the tone of an entire day, and I am certainly more open and responsive when I include them in my regular routine. Such practices are effective because they both distill and fortify the ordinary interpersonal giving and receiving that keep us from hardening into isolated little monads.

The maitri loving kindness meditation has one feature that I found odd when Bill first described it to me. You begin by expressing the hope that you yourself will experience peace, or happiness, or equanimity in the face of pain, or whatever other kind of inner benefit is being invoked, before going on to wish the same to other individuals or classes of people. How could putting yourself first in this way not be a kind of egoism or self-indulgence? I found however that the inner effect of the meditation, as actually performed, was the exact opposite of that. It was like reaching out a hand. When you begin the meditation by expressing kindness toward the body-mind you know best, and then go on to do the same with equal concentration toward all the others, you are putting everyone on the same footing.

But perhaps more importantly, that which wishes well to this particular body-mind – "yours" – is at that moment standing apart from it. This means that it is acting as the observer of the mental or physicalized identity that makes up your usual experience of self. In this impulse of giving, which involves moving back into the kind of detachment that affords a clear view of the recipient, you are learning to recede into a reality that is as supra personal in itself as it is person-directed in its expression of sympathy. That is the key to the sense of release that this exercise can bring about. But the whole point of this undertaking is that you find yourself putting it into practice, sponta-neously, situationally, with real people. I started with Pressi, of course, and found that in a simple, natural way I was becoming more attentive and responsive.

After growing accustomed to the Brahma Viharas I found myself turning now and then to spontaneous prayer. This was not interces-sionary prayer, in the sense of a petitioner asking for a boon from some presumed entity. It was a simple acknowledgment of edgeless consciousness, a wordless expression of thanks for its clear presence, and now and then a deeper subsidence into its great space. Sometimes I prayed to find within myself the strength I needed to deal with some problem. If I could patiently sit with my request in stillness, and then forget the request itself, the waiting usually led to an easing of tension and a restoration of confidence. I never confided my prayer life to anyone until I was well into the writing of this book.

Eventually I cobbled together various practice elements into a loose program that I followed for several years. A really good, integrated day began with a rare hour of sitting meditation (why didn't I do this every day?), followed by a maitri dedication and then breakfast. After that I was good for two or three hours of study and dictation in the morning and two and a half in the afternoon, working on the material that would culminate in this book. Between these work periods or during breaks there were relaxation and stretching exercises, mindful walking on a good day when the ataxia was not too bad, my workout on the treadmill with hands firmly wrapped around the handgrips, and lunch with Pressi or with music if she had gone shopping.

Over supper we would catch up on each other's versions of the day and take in the six o'clock radio news. In the evening I normally did the little chores I could physically handle. I always tried to do them in a spirit of karma-yoga, dedicating them to the presence out of which everything arises and back into which it disappears. As the evening unfolded I would usually listen to CBC radio or a recorded book or a music CD while Pressi watched television. I might do a body scan, or pray. Later still as I became tired and a little unfocused

I would just sit still and follow the breath. Finally I took the muscle relaxant that on most days was my only pain-related prescription drug, a small dose taken at bedtime that reduced the discomfort to the point where I could sleep.

None of this felt like a regimen, but once you lay it out in so many words I guess it looks like one. It didn't always go smoothly. There could be problems with pain or fatigue that would compel me to set the writing aside so I could work on the physical problem, or just accept the exhaustion. Acceptance too is a kind of spiritual practice – sometimes the hardest kind to come by. At other times I got so wrapped up in the writing that I pushed spiritual practice out of my mind until I was too tired to remember that there was such a thing, and then found that the day was ended. But one way or the other I was never bored.

Pressi had to budget her time or pace herself because of physical problems of her own. Several years ago she too was diagnosed with fibromyalgia, and a painful arthritis has developed in her fingers, toes, and right shoulder. In her case as with mine, the "fibromyalgia" label had to do with specific trigger points, chronic muscle pain, and spasticity, which is partially offset by a regular stretching program. After retiring from teaching in 2004 she developed the habit of going to an aerobics class four times a week. At home she worked hard to develop a fine garden, where we began to feed many kinds of birds. The birds were intensely present to me through their voices, which are so ardent that I forgot about not perceiving them as images. My favourites were the goldfinches, who like golden retrievers (their perfect counterparts in the dog world) are natural-born ecstatics.

The one thing I found hard to accept about our circumstances was my not being able to help Pressi more in the garden, around the house, and with shopping. At one level my reduced capacity to lift and carry things seemed preposterous – I am so big, after all, and she is so small. Sometimes I asked our younger and sturdier neighbours to help with the heavier tasks.

This was the general shape of things up until the spring of 2011. Despite our physical limitations we were living exactly the kind of quiet life we wanted, I concentrating on my studies and writing, Pressi on her garden and flower beds and her own reading, which was, as ever, voracious. I suppose we took the apparent stability of our situation as our due, for we had created these circumstances through our own planning, parsimony, and discipline. We may even have lobbed into the ether a smug thought or two regarding our entitlement or just deserts. If so, the Fates who picked up the message as they passed over our condo must have found it presumptuous. Wherever they had been heading, they evidently altered their course to home in on our kitchen like a brace of armed drones. There at 9:15 a.m. on May 26, 2011, they clobbered Pressi.

When she began to scream with pain – and with something else that sounded worse than pain – I was in the upstairs bathroom. I rushed down the stairs, almost losing my footing, and skidded into the kitchen, where I found Pressi on the floor. "My leg is broken," she cried, and with that I knew what I had heard in that first scream. It was fear, and now I was gripped by it too. Just a few days earlier we had been appalled by a report on the TV program *60 Minutes* concerning a new medical anomaly – a cluster of catastrophic fractures of the femur or thighbone that were linked to the anti-osteoporosis drug Fosamax, which Pressi had been taking for years. In each of the cases reported by *60 Minutes* the femur had simply shattered while the woman was going about her normal activities.

These were no ordinary fractures. Unlike the typical "broken hip" experienced by many seniors, which is actually a crack in the ball at the top of the femur, this new anomaly involved a severing of the femur in mid-shaft. In these atypical cases the strange spiral form of the break revealed that the bone was completely degraded all the way through, and eventually it became clear that this damage extended right up and down the shaft. Other large bones in the body might be similarly affected. According to *60 Minutes* the only warning signs, which were not recognized as such by the affected women, were deep but initially discontinuous pains at the locus of the impending fracture. At the end of the program Pressi had turned to me and said that she was experiencing what seemed to be that same kind of pain. It had begun four or five days earlier.

As I crouched over Pressi on the kitchen floor and spoke to the emergency dispatcher on our land line, I very lightly ran the fingertips of my other hand down her left pant leg, confirming by touch what would have been a sickening sight. A third of the way down, the femur had simply snapped in two; the lower part was now angled outward at about twenty degrees. The pain must have been terrible, but it wasn't just that that had Pressi sobbing: life from now on was going to be difficult and uncertain. Fortunately the paramedics arrived within seven minutes of my dialling 911, and soon Pressi was being stabilized in an ER bed at Montfort Hospital.

Because of an unusual spike in the number of bad traffic accidents and the resulting triage in the ER, Pressi's surgery was delayed for two days. During this wait she was heavily sedated, thank goodness, and thus free of pain. The orthopaedic surgeon who finally operated on her, Dr Andrew Marshall, had to perform another emergency operation as soon as Pressi was wheeled out, and it was not until evening that I was able to speak with him by telephone. He explained that the surgery had involved the insertion of a titanium rod right up through the middle of the femur, and that the procedure had gone well – despite the fact that the bone proved to be so degraded that he had to resort to "some fancy wiring."

The doctor did his best to assure me that Pressi would regain the use of her leg. It was clear, however, that the healing process was bound to be very slow. Over the coming months I would learn of studies that documented this delay; in some cases there was no healing at all. In the event, Pressi's femur would take seventeen months to heal – heal in the sense that the spiral fracture finally, fully filled in. But the quality of the bone remained degraded, and the key to her recovery was that all-important titanium rod. During this long process we were very much aware that other major bones remained at risk.

I could write reams about Pressi's gallantry and determination during the rehabilitation process. Both while she was in care and afterwards back at home, she proved to be totally committed to recuperation. She was not merely compliant with the rehab program but determined to squeeze out of it every last drop of healing and adaptation. After her first week in the hospital I had been aware every time I visited her of a faint rhythmic swishing issuing from her damaged leg: these were the sounds of the small but crucial prescribed exercises that she seemed never to stop doing, lying in bed in those first few weeks and then later sitting in her wheelchair. In the end she would be hailed by the whole rehab team as a star.

She spent a total of three months in care, first in the hospital and then in a rehabilitation centre. When she was ready to come home, Evan flew in from Vancouver to help out for a month – a great boost for both of his parents. By this point Pressi could get about with a walker, unhealed bone and all, and climb stairs using a cane. But it was all very strenuous. There was still a long way to go before she would consolidate a new version of normalcy.

During Pressi's long absence I was able to manage well enough at home, working out new ways of doing things without screwing up my back. I got invaluable help with grocery shopping from neighbours, and friends brought in some lovely cooked meals. Best of all, I was able to deal with my pain and mobility problems well enough to visit Pressi almost every day. After the first month I finally allowed myself to break down at home and grieve for what Pressi was enduring, and for what according to a growing number of reports she might have to endure later – the shattering of the other femur, or of a shoulder, or one or more lumbar vertebrae, or a necrosis of the jaw. When Pressi returned from the rehab centre I learned that she too had done her grieving in solitude and at night, when the ward was still and she would not be interrupted.

In those critical months my exhaustion or discomfort would sometimes become so distracting that I lost the sense of the space-like consciousness that really contained the whole show, whether I was at the hospital or rehab centre or at home. But I found invariably that I could get it back again through simple remembrance. For me that all-enfolding space was the basis for everything that really counted, starting with keeping myself open and flexible. I came to feel that maintaining it was not an option but a necessity, not just for my sake but for hers.

By early spring of 2013 Pressi had made a remarkable recovery. She was able to walk and even go grocery shopping without using a cane, and her gait sounded entirely normal. She was finally feeling ready to return to her aerobics classes, although at a rather less demanding level than before. She knew that her years of aerobics, with its strengthening and daily stretching of her leg and hip muscles, had been an important factor in her recovery. We knew there could still be other problems to come, but we figured we could deal with them. We might hope that she was over the worst. After all, she was going on seventy-four and had earned a break.

Then the other shoe dropped, or very nearly dropped. In mid-April Pressi began to feel the same deep pain in her right femur that she had experienced two years earlier in the left, before the spontaneous shattering of the bone. It was the same pattern all over again, periodic pain that steadily grew worse and became more frequent. An x-ray and nuclear bone scan indicated an incipient fracture. At first it seemed that nothing could be done by way of treatment, and I was simply awed by the way Pressi dealt with this. She methodically laid in supplies for what would surely be another long absence, cooking up food that went straight into the freezer. She was consistently gentle, sad, and accepting. I helped where I could, and wished as never before that I could drive and spare her the shopping.

But there had been a communications glitch: in May we discovered that Pressi did have an option. We learned this not from our doctors in Ottawa but from a friend, Dr Martin Jerry, a retired oncologist living in Canmore, Alberta. He advised us that in circumstances such as these it was possible, if relatively rare, to have preventive surgery. In her case, this would feature the insertion into the right femur of the same kind of titanium rod that was now supporting the left. That was apparently the only means of effectively forestalling another catastrophic break. So Pressi was booked into the first surgery slot Dr Marshall had available, and was also placed on his cancellation list. She immediately and understandably began to feel tense and anxious – would the bone hold out over the intervening days?

On June 14, 2013, twenty-five months after the previous operation, Dr Marshall performed the second surgery that made Pressi bilaterally bionic. When she woke up after the operation we were able to share a long, trilateral (three-person, six-legged) sigh of relief. The third party present was Evan, who once again had flown in to support us. According to Dr Marshall the surgery had gone extremely well, and in contrast to the three-month institutionalization Pressi had endured in 2011, this time she was back home in three days. All this came about because of our wonderful friend Martin Jerry, a committed practitioner of a spiritual path known as the Himalayan Tradition. Over the next several months Pressi was able to walk mostly without a cane. Of course it was going to take time for the right leg to get used to its foreign occupant. Unfortunately, Pressi has been unable to return to her aerobics program because its jumping components are now beyond her capacity.

Pressi and I both feel that these trials have brought us closer together, strengthening our faith in and love for each other. We found during those months in 2011 when she was at the rehab centre that we could sit in her room for long companionable visits even when there wasn't much to say. Although Pressi is naturally quiet, this comfortable, shared silence was something new to me. At these times I just held the sense of her presence lightly within consciousness, and perhaps this helped to make me seem more present and accessible to her, in a non-verbal way. Both of us found it curious that we should come closer by being pulled down into the dark or wounding side of ordinary life, the disabling side, the side you would wish to deny. Somewhere in the Eastern or Western spiritual literature there must be a pithy epigraph that perfectly expresses this unlikely discovery, this bonus, but I can't think of one. In the meantime there are lines from a popular song by Leonard Cohen that will do just fine:

> Ring the bells that still can ring
> Forget your perfect offering
> There is a crack, a crack in everything
> That's how the light gets in.[6]

Throughout late 2013 we settled into the new normal, which in most regards was agreeably similar to the old normal. When Pressi broke her left leg my book project was put on ice for six months, and the daily round of spiritual practices described earlier simply stopped. It did not start up again in any organized way, but from time to time I revisited one or more of those observances out of affection. They remained evergreen, like old favourite songs. What largely took their place was a steadier sense of that great edgeless consciousness, and sometimes a related experience that I will try to describe a little way below.

For a time I became more involved in housework, until a resurgence of spinal and sciatic pain and a worsening of my ataxia and neuropathy got in the way. The grab bars that I had installed in the upstairs bathroom were intended for Pressi, but I began to use them too. In late 2013 I had two falls, and after that I began to experiment indoors with a pair of Nordic walking poles. I also tried them outdoors but found that I was too shaky (and too emphatically blind) to proceed safely. So I made the transition to a walker, under the urging of my doctor and physiotherapist, but I found even then that I needed a sighted companion. I lacked the double-jointed, chest-mounted third arm that would have enabled me to keep wielding my white cane while holding on to both of the walker's handgrips. Rats! Anyway, inside the condo I could still clump about Nordically on my own.

The four paragraphs that follow below are taken from my tape-recorded diary of December 6, 2013. They describe our ordinary daily round and my obsession with the latest draft of my writing project.

There would be many other drafts to follow. My diary was generated in exactly the same compulsive way as my drafts for this book: I would record an entry on one tape recorder, then listen to it critically and dictate a revised version onto another. Occasionally a diary entry such as the one below would end up in the book draft itself.

Moving about the house on our respective rounds during the day, Pressi and I are like fish in an aquarium that is big enough for us to be apart and together at the same time. When we pass each other in the hall, Pressi sees the hall, its walls decorated with the small animal prints that we brought back from India. I see all kinds of things, for the visual hallucinations continue to run full-tilt. A few minutes ago as I moved gingerly out of the living room to enter the hallway, clutching both walking poles, I saw what looked like a cross-section of geological strata torn open by a massive earthquake. There were alternating bands of light and dark, all in subdued earth-tones, the whole lot plunging dizzily downward and to the left.

Of course there was also the seemingly solid floor on which my seemingly solid body walked, and the sound of my tread, and the complete absence of rending or ripping noises. Whenever this sort of thing happens now while I am in the act of perambulating from A to B, I am always aware of the great consciousness that effortlessly cradles the hallucinations within its subtle presence. This sense of vast extension in no way detracts from my tactile and aural attention, as I keep on walking.

I said "Hi" to Pressi as we brushed by each other in the hall and she said "Hi" back to me. The neighbours' dogs are quiet, so this will be a good morning for writing. And the act of writing is performed, happily enough, in a perfectly stable sitting position.

Pressi never asks me how the writing is going; she knows that I am too abstracted by it to respond very coherently. I have never been involved in anything so obsessive as the making of this book. I feel that the time available to me now is the best and possibly the last opportunity I will ever have to get what I want to say down on paper, before my physical circumstances become too distracting. When I am not actually dictating text I am often thinking about it, groping for the right words and mumbling, aware sometimes that this is the exact opposite of the

mindfulness that would be happy to rest lightly on whatever is in
the mind even if it were only a blank. How will my day go after
the book is finished? Do I really have it in me to write the second
book that I have in mind, a work on Advaitic philosophy?

When in 2013 I recorded the diary entry set out above we were
making plans for a simple Christmas that would not include Evan,
as he was deeply buried in his work in Vancouver. At university Evan
got interested in Canadian aboriginal issues, prompted perhaps to
some extent by the fact that our blurry, complex lines of familial
descent apparently included Crees and/or Ojibways a few generations
back. After graduation Evan worked for several years for a federal
government department, Indigenous and Northern Affairs Canada,
in British Columbia. This work was punctuated by periodic assignments to other government departments that were wrestling with
politically sensitive aboriginal issues. For much of the time Evan served
as an economic programming officer operating out of the Vancouver
office: from that base he was responsible for a big chunk of territory
in north-central British Columbia. During this same period he also
assisted a First Nation in the Yukon to develop and implement various laws under their self-government powers, an experience that
reinforced his commitment to frank and flexible consultations with
indigenous communities.

It is Evan more than his father who turned out to be the family's
natural anthropologist or practical diplomat. When I think of his
work with aboriginal organizations I remember that even in high
school he had become essentially what he remains today: a young
man who wants to do something of practical value and has a knack
for reaching across racial and cultural lines. Unfortunately the public
service was once again in the throes of downsizing, and the additional
cuts would be the deepest ever. Morale throughout the service would
prove to be even lower, if that were possible, than in 1990 when I
was medically retired. Evan managed to hang on to his job in
Indigenous and Northern Affairs, where morale was exceptionally
low, but in 2016 he would voluntarily resign from that department
and take up a one-year appointment as aboriginal consultant to the
Port of Vancouver.

In 2017 he would finally secure a permanent position in a highly
professional setting where morale was buoyant: the federal Department of Transport. At Transport, as with the Port of Vancouver, his

focus was to be on west coast deep sea terminals. He would have to assess the potential impact of increased vessel traffic – container ships, oil tankers, LNG vessels – on aboriginal rights and practices. This was complex work that involved high stakes – economically, politically, and above all else inter-communally.

For Evan and his parents the changes described in this section, together with the slender continuities that run through them, make up the stuff of ordinary life. It is the life of time passing, with its sense of gain and sometimes wrenching loss. It is the outer life of maintaining the body and getting things done, the inner subtle life of relationships and inner solitude, and the dimensionless light of awareness in which all this is contained. For me, at least, it adds up to a pared-down sufficiency in which anything I really need may be within reach, either inside this cluttered condo or built right into the nature of things.

I must now try to say a word or two about a mode of experience regarding which I have as yet remained silent. It has been this discovery more than anything else that supported me over the past several years. At some point prior to Pressi's accident in 2011 – it may have been as much as a year earlier – I began to follow the simple and direct advice of Rama Tirtha on how to live in the ontological truth. This was at first as an adjunct to my regular daily meditation. You may recall Rama as the Bengali sage who identified the Cross of Jesus and the Trishula of Shiva as the two great symbols of human suffering (chapter 4, section 1).

Rama insisted that you can best attain to Advaita, the undivided reality that underlies all individual appearances, by opening yourself completely to its immediate phenomenal expression. This means experiencing world and life as a single field of being – an actual, single presence. It is within this whole and given over to the whole that one's unmet needs and periodic entanglement with affliction gradually lose their sense of overweening importance. And it is during this process that one may discover something entirely new.

I had had a sense of that presence for several years, beginning with the Rideau Centre incident and then spreading out into the space-like awareness that seemed to enfold and illumine the sensory world. That awareness or light also seemed to contain and support my daily spiritual observances. But I had to acknowledge that in the last few years I began to take for granted the field of all-inclusive consciousness, which at first I had found so revelatory. It no longer declared itself in quite so vivid a way. After reviewing the key passages in Rama

Tirtha, I concluded that the reason for this change was a degree of falling-off in my own attention or receptiveness.

So at times when I was just sitting quietly I began to surrender myself to that presence, that sense of a supra-personal consciousness, to whatever extent I could. I didn't really know how to "do" this, but I did know that I wanted to drop the remaining sense of a strictly personal centre. These were not heroic, marathon meditation sessions, but a simple turning toward that greater alternative whenever it occurred to me to do so. At these times I allowed the contents of consciousness to come and go and just stayed with the light of con- sciousness itself, somehow remaining inwardly still and (I don't know how else to put this) undefended.

On these occasions I did not look for anything new in the flow of phenomena. There were the usual sorts of ambient sounds and body- feelings, and the particular kinds of visual hallucinations that were then on show. But so far as I can recall there was little in the way of my usual mind-chatter. Over a period of weeks and months the con- sciousness that contained all this came to feel more subtle but at the same time more intensely present, and most significantly far more whole, in a way that completely subsumed all sense-phenomena with- out in any way dimming them down. I was somehow in there too, within that consciousness or presence, although I took it in from what seemed to be my own side. This meant that I as an individual was somehow contained within the presence instead of being dissolved into it. In that sense it was something like my experience at Mahabalipuram temple in 1970, but without the guardedness on my part. By degrees this came to feel natural and familiar. It was just the way things were.

But there was another element as well. As I look back on this time I think that I must have been posing some kind of half-conscious wordless question and waiting for a response. Whether or not "ques- tioning" is the right word for what I was about, the "answer" that eventually came to light was not one I ever would have predicted. Over a period of several days the presence opened up – just a little at first, and then definitively – into love. In the end there was just love, all-enfolding and all-pervasive, with only a vestigial sense of the usual subject-object polarity. It was not a matter of the presence loving me, or the other way around. It was love as an inherent aspect of the presence, fully offered front and centre. Though I retained a subtle sense of experiencing the presence from my own side, the love that was grounded in that presence permeated everything without distinction – including the nominal "me." One simply dissolved into love.

This was love without an object, love that would welcome but did not require the presence of lover and beloved. I am quite sure that I had not been consciously looking for this, and when it came it was like nothing I had ever known before. It was not a peak experience followed by a descent or crash, and in fact not an emotional state at all. What it amounted to was an incredibly simple and direct confirmation that, in the general scheme of things, love was real. Love was at the heart of the daily flux, profound and inexpressibly tender.

I would find from that day on that the love was sometimes joyous and at other times serene and subtle, conveying in the latter case a sense of completion and peace as much as of love. But what really struck me was that it seemed in some basic way to be always "there," although it could be lost from view through stress or fatigue or distractedness. Even then it could sometimes be re-entered through surrender, by which I mean the giving up of all prerogatives, including especially the prerogative of entitlement to the love itself. These two – the love and the egocentric sense of entitlement to it – were mutually excluding. The love was apparently a grace, a gift without an objective giver. And in a gratifyingly confusing way it was everywhere, spread both "before" and "within."

It was because of this undivided doubleness, the sense of its being both within and without, that I began to see why love was sometimes identified by Advaita as the heart's affirmation of non-duality. I recall now that it was only after my third or fourth concentrated reading of the *Forty Verses* of Ramana Maharshi – the master Advaitist introduced in chapter 5, section 2 – that I finally grasped that the text was absolutely permeated with love. Perhaps my experience of the presence and the love that emanated from it was a direct confirmation of what the *Forty Verses* subtly conveys. I was finding that even when the experience of the presence was joyous and streaming it contained within itself a stillness, silence, and peace that had the taste of immutability. Above all else, the love had a subtlety and fineness and clarity that beggar description.

When I am especially open to this love, I have sometimes had a sense of the natural non-duality of self and other – not as a bilateral flow of special feeling between myself and the other person, but as a simple sense of undivided presence. This does not involve any mystical access of one mind, with its stream of private thoughts, to that other mind. It has to do with the basic fact that love may be felt as coextensive with the light of consciousness, a consciousness that is apparently not merely individual. In 2011 I would sometimes feel the love and peace of this light during my daily visits to Pressi at the rehab facility, and I still experience it now. These are times when Pressi too finds that she feels closer to me.

But I do not impose on her my Advaitic interpretation of what is going on, for she has her own spirituality. She is a non-church Protestant with an intensely private prayer life, and an adamant disinclination to be catechized or preached to by anyone. Her innate resources for dealing with affliction are closely bound, I am sure, to her religious beliefs. That is reason enough for my not trying to question or meddle with them.

For my part, I just do what I can to stay within the Advaitic perspective as I understand it, in order to deal with my own challenges. These have to do with the imperative of integration and acceptance presented in this chapter. Above all else, it has been the wide-open "space" of the Advaitic perspective that has made it possible for me to absorb those experiences that seemed at first to reach far beyond me. This was still very much a work in progress. During the years documented above I would wake up every morning looking for something new – a further confirmation, perhaps, or better still a corrective.

9

Opening Up

1 A HUMANE TRANSITION

In this final chapter I am going to gesture toward our problematic collective future and look again at the perennial human dilemma against which the teachings on a universal self might be seen as a corrective, rather than a metaphysical abstraction. The dilemma I refer to here is the defensive narrowness of our ego-based individualism. I will offer a few observations that may give the reader some sense of how a transition from egoism to something approaching non-duality (Advaita) could be enacted, at least for those few who have considered such a possibility.

In section 1 we will look more closely at certain aspects of Western secular humanism that can actually serve as bridges to an exploration of our commonal selfhood. The possibility of a life less dominated by egoism and naive materialism can be addressed in general terms that apply to humankind as a species, and in intimately personal terms that bear upon the ultimate concerns sometimes referred to as "last things." These have to do with one's inevitable demise, as anticipated and pondered over when one attains to a certain age.

In section 2, I will describe how a recent, intense, long-overdue re-examination of my own world view revealed that I would have to abandon it. This sharp corrective brought my immediate experience of common sensory objects into line with Advaitic insight. The upshot of this change, following its initial destabilizing jolt, was a deeper and more affirmative experience of the present moment. I hope that this unexpected reorientation will eventually open up the prospect of living consistently in non-duality, instead of just writing about it.

I want to start off here by identifying a problem that rises implicitly from our examination of the conventional sense of self. Up to this point I have been presenting non-duality in its Vedantic version as an optional alternative to the status quo, an aspiration that might be either taken up or allowed to lie fallow. But, to be frank, I have come to feel more and more that the conventional mode of ego-based life may for our species be unsustainable over the long term. That is because it is not only divisive but is based on a sense of self that does not stand up to analysis. I have already described some of the difficulties that the standard construction of self can lead to under certain circumstances – under the fear and doubt generated by RP vision loss, for example. In what follows we will look briefly at the tensions generated by the ego-based sense of self as presented on a far larger canvas, and identify the kind of insight and release that can be brought to bear upon them.

The Western intellectual tradition has developed to the point where conventional assumptions of selfhood can now be seen to be conventions and not much else, received ideas that can be considered objectively. All we have to do is look; in fact we have already done much of that looking. We have considered those particular findings of modern physics that radically call into question our perennial notion of a free-standing, more or less solid, conventional physical selfhood. There is in fact no such "thing." The other Western disciplines that offer complementary accounts bearing on the question of the human self are, as we have seen, developmental psychology and evolutionary biology. Evolutionary analysis now extends not only to biological structure, function, variation and adaptation, but to thinking as well – to all our beliefs, superstitions, and ideologies. It is within this context that we can reconsider the ideology, the construct, of what a self supposedly is.

When our ancient human self-construct is considered objectively, it is revealed to be as contingent and experimental as any other interim product of the evolutionary process. This self-construct is an operational program for placing an assumed identity – that is, a putative individual or "I" – within a sensory world, and for living a more or less secure life. Apart from its complexity, the most remarkable feature of the evolved self-construct is the unquestioned sense of being that it bestows on the putative "I" – i.e., on the ego. This creative/protective evolutionary strategy, which is also an ideology of egocentrism, is under most circumstances extremely resilient. And so it must be, to the extent that it has developed to ward off harm and destruction to the assumed (but questionable) individual self.

Like other evolutionary strategies, the human self-construct is in many ways very adaptive, but it imposes some significant opportunity costs. The most consequential of these is the obscuring and de-legitimizing of any deeper or novel means for sussing out our fundamental nature. This limitation or taboo is imposed by the ego in its most atavistic mode, when it is reinforced by defensive body-feelings. The mental/physical sense of presence is what we think of as our basic self. But seen in broader evolutionary terms this complex – defensive, territorial, aggressive – is as much primate as human and in all probability is much older even than that. Such a line of descent, it might be assumed, does not lend itself to much self-reflection.

Apart from this limitation, the other major problem with the human self-construct – and this involves both opportunity costs for the species and energy costs for the individual – is the way in which the evolutionary process has closely intertwined the drives and rationales of several distinct life-strategies. These include cooperation, competition, charismatic leadership, stubbornly independent individualism, negotiation, treachery, open conflict, conquest leading to bondage and exploitation, and short as opposed to long-term thinking. Each of these strategies on its own has adaptive value under certain circumstances.

But, as complexly entangled, their product is the human world as we know it, with its turbulence, tribalism, dangerous ideologies, religious hatreds, dysfunctionally complicated and opaque economic structures, weapons of mass destruction, greenhouse gasses and environmental toxins, all of which presage an ominous future. We are perhaps more aware than ever before that "we"– the conventional egocentric self writ large – are an evolutionary experiment that may, like so many others, end in extinction. A distinct shift toward broader cooperation, fellow-feeling, and long-term planning would seem to be in order, to put it mildly. I don't know if we can achieve that without reconsidering what we fundamentally are, especially with reference to one another. What we *seem* to be is dyed-in-the-wool, self-seeking individuals: in short, egos.

Yet the ego is not a reality in itself. As we have seen, Jean Piaget showed the nascent ego to be a slowly emergent mental program rather than an entity (chapter 6, section 2). The ego does not exist outside the ego-based mode of mind, let alone outside of consciousness. And, as Advaita and Buddhism emphasize, it does not exist in dreamless sleep. As for the more sophisticated accounts of the ego developed by leading psychological theorists, these too are mental constructs – and fully acknowledged as such. No matter what heuristic power they might command, these individualizing constructs are not entities. Sigmund Freud intended his brilliant account of the emergent mature ego as a clarification of intra-psychic processes, most particularly of a coalescing sense of agency. However, he did not claim that the ego is a real, continuous being that somehow makes its home within a psyche.

Throughout this book I have tried in various ways to introduce the idea of a consciousness-based, non-ego-based, universalist understanding of our essential nature or selfhood. So, is there anything in the Western intellectual tradition that can be applied to a more fruitful and less convention-bound understanding of what we essentially are? Is there some idea or representation that would allow us to move, without too much initial discomfort, beyond the problematical concept of the egocentric self? What we need is a usable bridge concept, the kind that can ease us from one ontology into another. And as it turns out, the Western secular humanism that acknowledges the intriguing findings of modern science, and more to the point those of psychology, does offer a humane and surprisingly resilient bridge concept for reconsidering the question of our basic nature.

This bridge is the idea (and apparent presence) of the persona, which in the flow of daily life presents itself as something more or other than the bare ego-sense. Effectively it manifests as a person or self. The term "persona" is sometimes used, as I deployed it in chapter 2, to designate a fabricated (e.g., professional) identity, or a constricted identity based on a handicap such as blindness. But, employed more broadly in accordance with humanist values, the persona is a full and rich identity that seems to have a life of its own.

The persona consists of the intricate skein of memories, convictions, ambitions, fears, quirks, loves, hates, and external expressive style that add up to give the sense of a unique individuality. This is far more elaborate than the basic, defensive, bottom-line ego-sense that is much the same for all of us. The persona constantly shifts in the small details of its expressivity, but just as constantly projects the picture of the same old recognizable person. What the persona adds to the general human self-construct is its person-specific and indeed person-specifying uniqueness and vividness. As its completion and crowning feature, it makes of the human self-construct a very particular individual.

And it is worth noting for newcomers to Advaita, who may be rather uncomfortable at first with its transpersonal perspective, that the persona is too securely established and used to its own company, too functionally adaptive (at least in fits and starts), and perhaps too damned ornery, to just disappear in response to Advaitic teaching. And yet, as we shall see, the persona can "soften" and open up to those teachings that confirm it to be the most fully developed expression of the objectively human. As such it is distinct from the inner subject or true self that registers its existence.

Of course, this persona exists only in the presence of, and never apart from, consciousness. After all, how else than through consciousness – the inner self – could the persona appear and its self-expression be conveyed? Just like all the other self-representations and self-expressions that we experience, the persona does not constitute a continuously existent entity. It gives way every night to the muted or fantastical personae of dreams, and like the ego it disappears completely into the featureless condition of dreamless sleep, these two states adding up to what amounts to one-third of one's lifelong personal career. Nevertheless, we take the waking-state persona to be that which makes us most fully and expansively human. It is what we especially love, and hate, in others. Yet the most significant thing about the persona for our project here – that of realizing a deeper and more authentic sense of self – is that, according to reports from the Advaitic path of discovery, its unique characteristics remain pretty much the same throughout the process of clarifying the nature of things.

In fact, not even the most assiduous and serious-minded student or practitioner of Advaita "loses" her persona. It is simply her valuation of it that changes, and the change is significant. She eventually drops the habit of secretly endowing the persona with an absolute reality that no set of phenomena could ever possess, and finds that she no longer regards it as "I." At the same time, she is likely to view that virtual entity with an affection and tolerance that was not possible before. It is only she who knows all that the persona has been through, and there is no reason why she would not get around to extending to it the same sort of sympathy and understanding that she freely offers to its immediate counterparts – that is, to her close friends.

What brings these changes about is a fuller, broader practice of witnessing, which as presented in chapter 7 was applied mainly to

the management of specific problems such as pain and sensory degradation. When you develop the general habit of seeing things and
occurrences from the position of the witness, you become more
detached or disentangled, more settled and non-judgmental, more
laissez-faire. This just seems to happen in an unplanned, non–goal-
oriented way. Under these circumstances the cluster of elements making up the persona can be affirmed in all their actuality simply as
"personalized" phenomena, which up to now have obscured the
deeper self.

It is in this context that the persona eventually seems to lose some
of its self-affirming sense of indispensability or, conversely, its self-
deprecating sense of inadequacy. That is because its elements are being
witnessed both objectively and in full acceptance. As noted earlier, it
is natural at a certain stage of witnessing to become very interested
in the phenomenological expressivity of the whole sensory body-mind,
kosha by kosha (chapter 7, sections 2 and 3). Each kosha is an intricate
web of phenomenality worthy of our curiosity and closer attention.
Yet none of them is the real self, just as the persona that is threaded
throughout the physical and mental koshas is not the self, and one
not only knows this but inwardly comes to *see* it. At the same time,
even when one has developed the habit of viewing the persona objectively, it may take on the mildly positive valuation of a biographical
memento, an old uniform that still retains its shape after retirement.
I must own that after all my inner reprocessing I have become rather
fond of my well-worn and now off-centre persona, who just sort of
hangs around. He doesn't "do" much, but then again he doesn't have
to. Things simply get done.

What, amidst these changes, becomes of the bare ego-sense? When
the consciousness-based view of reality is discovered and then by
degrees consolidated, the inherently defensive ego-sense begins to
relax and move away from centre stage. The practical competencies
that originally developed as attributes of the ego, or so it seemed, are
seen now to operate very nicely on their own. The feeling or sense of
self has opened up, or rather opened inward, as the self-contained
witness of these changes. Over time the witness feels less and less like
a discrete centre of reference and more like all-inclusive space, as
described in chapter 7. When this expansiveness is lost as a result of
stress, it can always be regained through simple remembrance.

None of this is metaphysical rocket science. The implicit de-
egoization that is involved in the consecutive processes of reversing

the arrow of attention, receding inward, quietly observing whatever comes up, and learning to let go and remain disentangled, is common to many meditative traditions. It is described and taught in many different ways. But whatever the particular circumstances and degree of relative de-egoization, the residual ego-sense and the more elaborated persona just continue to manifest, the latter fully recognizable in one's own mind and in the minds of others. The one change that your intimates and associates may notice is that this person, the friend or colleague whom they know so well, is perhaps less subject now to those little occasions of assertiveness, defensiveness, or apparent self-doubt.

The changing disposition of the persona described above is a key aspect of the notional "middle ground" described in chapter 7. At the same time, this gradual softening and eventual backgrounding or sidelining of the persona will necessarily be of a modest and preliminary nature when viewed from the vastness of full Advaitic enlightenment. This gradualism hasn't bothered me, although I know there are others who progress far more quickly and effectively. In any event this book is intended simply as a primer. I can say that the kind of reorientation sketched here did "me" – whatever that pronoun may ultimately prove experientially to designate – a world of good. Many people have experienced this sort of settling-down or settling-in. If few go on to write about the experience it is in part because the act of writing seems to be so "personal," even when the implicit, emergent self is essentially transpersonal.

And yet the Western secular humanism that continues to influence our very sense of being, despite the fact that we may have occasional glimpses into a transpersonal commonality, involves a seemingly unresolvable conundrum. This has to do with the fate of the individual. One of the most positive aspects of humanism is quite simply its humaneness – its valuation of the human person or persona. At the same time, however, it compassionately acknowledges the inevitabilities of the human journey, the final stroke of which is death. This is the conundrum: the knowledge that those we love are destined to die. What do we find, then, when this unnegotiable fact of life is refracted through the prism of Advaita Vedanta? A Shankara or a Ramana Maharshi or a Rama Tirtha would respond that Advaita recognizes the real self as transpersonal consciousness and reality as essentially whole, not fragmented, and this perspective has its own way of receiving and absorbing the tragedy that seems to be built right into the fabric of human life.

To begin with things as distinct from people, it is possible within the non-dual perspective to love the works of nature and of human-kind in the full knowledge that they are impermanent sensory-mental appearances, destined eventually to dissipate and disappear, and even to watch them disappear without being reduced to bitterness or depression. One can acknowledge the fact of loss without the sense of loss being irremediable. The basis for this self-possession is the recognition that all phenomena without exception are non-self-existent, wholly dependent upon a fundamental, non-material, luminous reality that does not change. Here I refer once again to a maxim from the non-dual Islamic teachings of Ibn Araby, quoted earlier in this text: "Love the forms and let them go." This means living with sense forms non-clingingly but open-heartedly. Such a view is based on an awareness or partial awareness of the luminous ground that makes those forms possible.

As with "things," then, so too with people. People as we experience them are like all other phenomena: contingent upon the real, slated inevitably for dissolution. Those clusters of lively characteristics that we call the persona, including the intimately known persona of the beloved, were never self-existent in the first place, never possessed of permanence. They are like projections, the dramatis personae of a multisensory, empirically structured waking dream. I have no problem in viewing my seeming individuality, my apparent existence in space and time, in the terms provided by this metaphor. But it is different when I try to view in the same way those to whom I am closest – Pressi and Evan, and a few special friends.

The events of the last five years and the continuing process of aging have for both Pressi and me conjured up some sense that we will soon be entering the final stage of life, the stage of last things, in which inevitably one of us must die first and leave the other behind. And Evan could take the chop on any one of the climbing expeditions he has enjoyed over the years. It is most especially with respect to this kind of knowledge, and my gut-level resistance to it, that I know myself to be far from enlightened. The enlightened grieve, but not as I would do. If Pressi were to go first, I would grieve her loss out of the full, obdurate, physical-sensory-mental creatureliness into which I was born and within which I grew up. It is still available and always will be, just offstage, waiting for a cue.

Yet I know, and there is a sense of unfairness about this, that my privileged access to the presence described earlier would at least to some extent buffer the experience of loss and give it a meaning it would otherwise lack. But why the sense of unfairness? Because of Pressi – because I wish I could just give her the presence too, ushering her into it before she has to go. But at times I have the powerful feeling that she has long known of the supra-personal love that I discovered only three years ago. If that is true, it is something she has found in the apparent nowhere that she chose to enter when she unchurched herself and turned her back on organized religion. The precipitating factor for her was the absence in church of the presence of God: apparently God was within us, instead. In any case she would never talk about the presence, for as she once told me talking just dissipates the real thing.

2 A FINAL AFFIRMATION OF THE SENSORY WORLD

There is one more subject, identified at the beginning of this chapter, that I must address here. It bears directly on the kind of spiritual experience referred to just above, that of the subtle presence, on spiritual undertakings in general, and on the whole question of how we are to understand and receive the world we live in. I am going to address once again the question of the sensory world's putative reality, a question that stands quite apart from the joys, challenges, and travails of ordinary worldly life. This will cast an unsparing light on a certain attitude that may have been inculcated into us early in our lives, a thought or feeling or judgment that the world as we perceive it should without doubt be affirmed as absolutely real, celebrated as such, and even loved. This inculcation may be the result of a conventional religious upbringing, or a happy and adventuresome family life exploring the beauties of nature, or both. Such experiences and attitudes may predispose the young person to fiercely resist any argument that challenges the conventional sense of material reality.

My upbringing did not include these affirmative elements, but once I struck out on my own I was able to cobble together a more or less positive view of a conventionally material world – a view that I was compelled to re-examine in later life. You can perhaps best take in the re-examination described below by receiving it not as a philosophical interpretation but as a kind of story – and it is certainly that, among other things, the last choppy phase of a narrative that has stretched itself out all through this book. Aside from a couple of explanatory passages, this account has both the immediacy and the

limitations of straight autobiography. It is the record of a "trip" that
I found myself taking almost against my will.

· Is the world as we experience it real in itself, or real-ish in the qualified sense of borrowing or partaking of the reality of something deeper
than itself, or is it downright unreal? This is a more nuanced version
of the question that we grappled with when we looked into modern
physics in chapter 6, section 2. With this more flexible and accom-
modating question in mind, we are now going to see whether the
implicit answer offered by Advaita Vedanta and modern science allows
for any variation – for individual interpretation and wiggle room. In
order to get to the bottom of things we may be prompted to reconsider
some of our deepest conditioning and strongest convictions, as I was
compelled to do quite recently. For me the review process took me
back, first of all, to the absolute primacy of consciousness. The large
and tricky question that followed from that had to do with the "relationship" between consciousness and the objects of consciousness –
i.e., the things of the world.

In the Rideau Centre in 1995 the consciousness-grounded identity
that suddenly opened up for me had the authority of direct, unam-
biguous experience. It affirmed that our true being or bottom-line
selfhood is of the nature of pure, unalloyed consciousness, as described
in chapter 6, section 3. Furthermore, I found that the disclosure of a
deep, more-than personal sense of consciousness was the natural
complement to the accompanying realization that all the objects on
show were physically unreal. You could *see* that, or feel it, grasp
directly what Berkeley had to work out through phenomenological
intuition and hard thinking. That is, the objects illumined by consciousness prove to be sensory-mental projections rather than
things-in-themselves.

The problem was what happened next, when my empirical mind
fumbled for a way of harmonizing two realizations – i.e., the disclosure of seemingly edgeless, lucent consciousness, and, within that
consciousness, the startling but liberating de-materialization of the
objects of common experience. What the mind came up with immediately was the notion of "containment" or "inclusiveness." According
to this idea, the objects of common experience not only exist within
consciousness and nowhere else, but actually partake of the very
nature of consciousness. This was a seemingly novel view that took
me entirely by surprise, although as I was to realize years later it had
been instilled by an implicit personal agenda.

At any rate, following the Rideau Centre incident I began to think of the contents of our experience as "expressions" or "instantiations" of consciousness. Despite the fact that these objects were in one sense illusory, the complementary fact that they appeared at all must be due, one might conjecture, to the representational power of consciousness. Those "objects" were certainly associated with neurological activity, but as sheer presences they seemed to be part and parcel of the luminosity of consciousness itself. From moment to moment the shifting array of objects (or rather sense-forms) presented themselves as temporary formations of consciousness, a consciousness that had declared its reality in the most unequivocal way.

And because consciousness seemed so clearly to be more than personal, both in its immensity and through its presentation of objects experienced by multiple people all at once, I found myself drawn increasingly to the transpersonal teachings of Advaita Vedanta. It must be Brahman, the foundation of us all, that projects and eventually dissolves all phenomena. Finally, I arrived at a simple ontological formula: common objects were illusory as appearances, but *in their essence* they shared completely in the reality of the universal consciousness that projected them. This coupling of the limpid nature of consciousness and its form-making capacity had for me the taste of a new, pantheistic spirituality – as distinct from the more conventional religions, both Eastern and Western.

I had "saved" the world – the manifest world or sensorium that I had slowly learned to love – from being nothing but an empty appearance. My private agenda was to pull this off by indulging half-aware in a bit of double-think. I conceived of sense-forms in two contradictory ways: they were simultaneously illusory, as things that seemed misleadingly to exist in their own right, and real, as expressions of the indivisible consciousness in whose protective enfoldment they dwell for as long as they are manifest. To express this doubleness, I tried for a time to come up with illustrative metaphors. At one point I likened the objects of common experience to ice shards floating on a vast reach of cold water; they were fashioned out of the water, which metaphorically stood for consciousness or Brahman, and they would eventually melt back into it. It was all really a oneness. But eventually I gave up on metaphors – none of them were really satisfactory – while continuing in my conviction that the objects of consciousness were actually aspects of consciousness. That meant that in a borrowed, indirect, or proxy-like way the world was real or at least real-ish. It just had to be: didn't the Upanishads say that all was Brahman?

By slow degrees I would come to vaguely imagine Brahman as the meta-intelligence that stood behind the laws of science, and also as the implicit agency that expressed and supported the empirical world. Within such an overarching context, modern physics was free to demonstrate that the objects of common experience did not exist in and as themselves. This puncturing of naive materialism was salutary, I thought, for I knew the other half of the story: in the end Brahman rescued everything from nothingness. It was this Brahman, my Brahman, that endowed the world with intelligible significance and legitimacy. Such a mindset was at once both comforting and discomfiting. Every now and then I got a whiff or taste of my categorical inconsistencies, which to my puzzlement reminded me of my inner war over sexual identity. That had been all about denial. Now there was, in a sense, far more at stake, a form of denial that tried stealthily to preserve empirical identities and the whole empirical world that went with them.

As I proceeded through my review of Advaita Vedanta I became more and more aware that, in its most explicit and logically rigorous mode, Advaitic teaching seemed to call my private ontology into question. In 2012–13 I discovered and seized upon the teachings of Baruch Spinoza (1632–1677), one of the great illuminati of the Western enlightenment. His vision of an ultimate and all-inclusive reality was expressed through his formulation, "God or nature" (*deus sive natura*).[1] This would seem to be a kind of pantheism, wherein God is not only the fount of scientific law but is inseparable in his being from the manifest forms of nature. To my mind this seemed to echo what I was attributing to (or imposing upon) Advaitic teaching. I found myself thinking of the vision of Krishna re-engorging his projected world, as depicted in the theophanic eleventh chapter of the Bhagavad-Gita. This was admittedly a bit of a stretch from Spinoza's serene *deus sive natura*.

Considered in retrospect, I was grasping at straws. It was only in early 2014 that all my doubts and discomfort finally came to the surface. The timing was probably significant. During the period 2011–13 I was preoccupied with Pressi's consecutive medical crises and rehabilitation: the big questions regarding the nature of reality moved accordingly to the back of my mind. But eventually they re-occupied the front and became unavoidable. Looking back on this now, I am chagrined to recall how in 2012, when I drafted an early version of chapter 6, I described with some smugness how shocking it can be to discover through modern physics that the world we actually experience is illusory. By way of just desserts, I suppose, I was about to experience my own, long-delayed version of that shock.

Fortunately I received some timely support and counsel from a friend, one of several Ontario-based Indian scholars and medical doctors I had come to know over the years. This particular friend is a retired professor who is steeped in both the Vedic and Buddhist traditions, and I had been sharing my successive drafts with her. She prefers not to be named here because, as she expresses it, our discussions are a mutual search for meaning in which egos, names, and titles are best set aside. So I must concur and in these pages render her anonymous. It was in the spring of 2014 that this friend began gently but firmly to express concern regarding the basic contradiction of acknowledging pro forma that the world is an illusion, while at the same time investing it with what amounted to a metaphysically based reality.

She explained that the position I had taken – that of virtually incorporating the sensory world into the indivisibility of Upanishadic consciousness, even while insisting that the objects that comprised the world were individually "real" as expressions of consciousness – could not be a feature of Advaita. Advaita, she emphasized, is a philosophy of absolute Oneness that denies and refutes all individualities without exception. You can argue for a multiplicity of real things (the conventional world view), or for a single reality that is indivisible (Advaita), but you cannot argue for both at once. The two views negate each other. I was irrationally conflating them, the better to have my cake and eat it too. I wanted to have the world whole, and yet take it in piece by piece.

My friend observed that what I had fallen into resembled to some extent an alternative rendition of Vedanta known as "Visishtadvaita" (qualified non-duality). This designation or label is at once a technical philosophical term and a kind of euphemism: the word "qualified" is meant to soften or abridge the absolute non-duality of Advaita, so that some kind of individuality or multiplicity can be preserved. By resorting to this inconsistent, contradictory perspective one preserves (or seems to preserve) both the variegated world and the indivisible Brahman. This compromised approach downplays or ignores the fact that Brahman is strictly defined by the Upanishads as the One without a second, i.e., the only possible reality. As it turned out, my "private" ontology wasn't so private after all. It was similar in some respects to a spiritual world view that offered a dubious half-way house between Advaitic oneness and theistic dualism.

I was really taken aback by all this. In my years of reading Advaita I had never thought to look into the alternative of "qualified" non-duality, though I had come upon references to it. Now that I scrutinize this construct, the very idea of a diluted or softened non-dualism struck me as patently self-contradictory. And I had no desire to end up trammelled, so to speak, within the tugging and hauling of a contradiction.

Yet I had sometimes felt over the years that I was being drawn sideways into an un-Brahmanic, Berkeleyan sort of theism. George Berkeley eventually arrived at the position that God contains the universe – all things and all persons – within Himself. This leaves unresolved the status of the individual: in Berkeley as in Visishtadvaita Vedanta, the devotee takes himself to be subsumed within – but not Advaitically merged into – God. And what would that be like? A permanently protected individuality, I supposed, protected through a divine, compassionate engulfment. This conclusion conjured up a cartoonish mind's-eye image of an undigested Jonah waiting it out in the belly of the whale.

On the positive side, I was aware that some contemporary accounts of Berkeley portrayed him as a kindly and radiantly happy man. In the same vein, Spinoza's immersion into a logical and beatific panthe-ism (if that is the appropriate word) led his friends to describe him as the very picture of serene equanimity. Could I, should I, become like these two excellent men by sharing in their perspective?

I soon saw that I would have to work things out on my own, by coming to terms with Advaitic teaching rather than modelling myself on anyone. Although my friend was not herself an Advaitin, she was during this period at pains to keep reiterating, for my sake, that in Advaita the world was an unqualified ontological illusion. There were no ifs, ands, or buts on that score. I still temporized, trying to preserve a distinction between an object's form and its essence. Yet when I finally got down to it and grappled with the Advaitic demonstration that the sensory world was sheer illusion, I found that demonstration to be absolutely bullet-proof, and consonant with the findings of modern physics. And I had actually known all this, years earlier, known it and waffled before it and tried to negotiate around it.

Before I describe what all of this led me to as the inevitable consequence, I think I should pause to let the reader who anticipates what
is coming next to shout out the obvious question: Why were you
doing this to yourself? Why on earth (if that's where we still are)
would you subject yourself to the experience of taking in the physical
array as utter illusion, without anything to dilute the effect? It must
be utterly horrible. Yet my circumstances had predisposed me to
eventually get down to the bottom of things. Specifically, in the Rideau
Centre, my experience with vision loss finally revealed the "material"
world to be a sense-show. On top of that, from adolescence onwards
I had felt a sense of separation from the world because of the recurrent, immobilizing, and isolating experience of acute sciatic pain. I
was also quite helpless when it came to building or fixing things with
my hands: this made me feel that the world was over there while I
was right here, separated and unhandy. I do not mean to suggest that
I was deeply alienated from the world as I fuzzily perceived it. But I
often found myself to be in the position of just observing the show
– and speculating about it, or waiting for something to happen.

This is the background that led me to the inner struggle of 2015.
What held me back from experientially plunging into the depths of
Advaita was the feeling, acknowledged in the previous chapters, that
I just wasn't ready for such a journey. Nevertheless, the course of
developments outlined here had an impetus that wiped away fear,
aspiration, and choice. On a particular day in 2015 that did not seem
to be different from any other, I finally went over the edge and found
myself in free fall.

So, then, what was it like to unguardedly "fall" into the immaterial,
illusory sensorium? I must confess that when I finally took in the
stripped-down emptiness of the sense-world, with every shred of my
old hedging and rationalization torn away, I found the experience
downright wrenching at first. But it was not horrible. In those first
few days, during which I hid my inner reactions even from Pressi, I
simply felt that everything around me had subtly but utterly changed.
The world was still fully present with all its familiar features, but it
was newly and awesomely voided, rendered dream-like. Although my
four remaining external senses were operating normally, everything
I perceived was manifestly insubstantial.

What I felt was not so much an emotional alienation toward this
display as the simple experience of being stunned, gobsmacked, by a
pervasive sense of sheer unreality. The things I touched were simply

the experience of touching. So this, I thought, is what it is like to be disabused of ontological illusion. This is what it feels like to open up to those evolution-based, adaptive sensory projections described by biologists such as Richard Dawkins. What can one possibly say about this? It is simply astounding, and feels astounding.

It occurred to me that this state of affairs was a little like a lucid dream: over the years I have had a few of those. But in this case my "dream" did not include the feeling, the certainty, that I was about to wake up. The only truth or reality into which I could wake up now was enlightenment, as understood and taught by Advaita, and just then I was feeling light-years removed from such a fulfillment. Yet before long I became intrigued, and then rather pleased, with the way everything still continued to "work." All the old sequences and patterns were still there, together with all the basic laws that still had me walking on the floor rather than the ceiling, but it was as though the whole business was being enacted somewhere up on a cloud. This cloud was rather cluttered, had recognizable rooms and a backyard complete with goldfinches, and it was still serviced by garbage collection on Monday mornings.

Those first two months were interestingly, uniquely strange. The sense of being in a lucid dream persisted in the most obvious sense, as my awareness of the objects on display continued to be coupled with the knowledge that they did not and could not exist in their own right. One could register that fact in a completely unfiltered way. As the weeks passed and those "objects" continued to defy conventional materialist expectations, it was as though they had taken on a tone of pure self-contradiction. They were entirely ordinary and actual-factual, and yet uncanny. The things were just plain "there," somehow, simply given and yet complexly evolved, our totally insubstantial but undismissible stage-set. Towards the end of this transition and without my worrying or fuming over it (and the absence of worry was somehow not surprising), I found myself wondering where my gut-level acknowledgment of the ontological facts had landed me. Where is "here," and what am I to "do" with it?

Before I could even begin to frame an answer I became aware of a novel and growing feeling of freedom and release. It did not come all at once but seeped into me over a period of about two weeks. The reader may find such a shift surprising, for that sense of freedom would seem to be utterly incompatible with our defensive materialist conditioning. I think it was my slow absorption of positive Advaitic teaching over the years that predisposed me to look upon this quintessentially negative experience – the experience of being literally unworlded – with a growing curiosity and quickening interest.

Just as the initial shock at recognizing the world as illusion had given way to a bemused acceptance, acceptance now opened up in turn into a gratified amazement, even a kind of mirth. The world – our world – was a marvellous, mind-bending artifice, a seeming impossibility, and yet it was blaringly on show. What can you do but admire it? It all fits together, and it goes like hell and never stops. This world/sensorium may be taken as a gift, all right, the gift of an evolutionary process that blithely and blindly ignores the fact that none of these things could possibly exist in themselves. It's enough to make you shake your head. Or laugh out loud, as now and then I found myself doing.

As I got used to the new dispensation, the new "feel" of things – or rather of unthings – I found myself reconsidering all those affirmative experiences that over a period of two decades I had grouped together under the rubric of "space-like consciousness." They had included my first introduction to the voluminous space-like realm opened up by the Harding experiments, my occupation of that realm through the practices of mindfulness and witnessing, the discovery that this realm could be a strategic inner redoubt from which I could apply mindfulness-based stress reduction (MBSR) to the problems of pain management and white cane mobility, and most fundamentally the accompanying sense of the sheer, simple, limpid luminosity that is consciousness itself.

Of course I had fallen into the mistake of mixing the reality of that consciousness with the objective features of the sensory world: now I had to ask myself if that mistake had somehow compromised or inhibited my attempts to make use of MBSR and those other practical meditative resources. It had not, I concluded, not in the least. It turns out that it is possible to live innocently with the kind of ontological error I have described here, to live with it for twenty years, while still reaping benefits from the vocation of giving oneself over to the light of consciousness. It was this simple recession into self-aware consciousness that allowed me to enter into mindfulness and witnessing.

So far so good, I thought. But where, exactly, was I heading? I had gone through an intense process of re-examination, totally accepted the results, and experienced the accompanying sense of existential dislocation, and then the emergent, unexpected feeling of relief. Yet the process had left me with no fixed address, so to speak, and no sense of material ties. This was in one sense satisfying. But I was becoming aware of a certain poignancy or nostalgia, the nostalgia of once having been able to draw sustenance from those special individual things-in-the-world – this rare possession, that piece of property – as other people do. I did not want to sink back into the old materialistic enmeshment, but the nostalgia was there nonetheless.

It never occurred to me at this point that the new process was finished. However, I found myself wondering a little despondently if my book – this book – was all but finished, with nothing more of significance to add. I decided to just wait and see. By that I mean that over the next month or so I took time at intervals to be still, both physically and mentally, and remain open. It was during one of these occasions that something entirely new and transformational occurred. The setting was the quiet hour that I habitually set aside early every morning before getting into the day's first writing session. As I sat and nursed my coffee, I found myself trying to remember the exact words with which Eliot Deutsch concludes the final chapter of *Advaita Vedanta – A Philosophical Reconstruction*. This was the most valuable and inspiring contemporary study of classical Advaita that I had come across. The cassettes on which my friend and volunteer reader Dana Mullen had fluently recorded the entire text were always within reach.

Eventually I was moved to go to my desk and load the final cassette into the machine, fast forwarding it to the aural beep tone that marks the end of the main text. I then pressed rewind to locate that small final paragraph, and this is what I heard: "To the jivan mukta, to the man who is free while living, Brahman is everywhere seen. Mokta or mukti, freedom or liberation, as realized through jnana yoga, is just this power of being and seeing that excludes nothing, that includes everything. Brahman is one. Everything has its being in spirit. Everything in its true being is Brahman."[2]

Everything? The manifest world too? And then at last I got it, *really* got it. I finally registered the hugely incomplete nature of that stark, seer realization that had come to me several months earlier, the correct but limited realization that the world of multiplicity is an illusion. For the first time I "saw" straight through that world-illusion and took in what had really been there all along. Before I try to find the words for this experience, and I might as well state right here that they are bound to be inadequate, I must say something about how and why this happened to me when it did. The key, it seems, was a certain strain of thought or intuition that had been obscurely working itself out within me for several years.

You may recall that in my account of the events of 2011 in chapter 8, section 3, I referred to a particular teaching of Rama Tirtha that afforded me an unexpected solace and inner opening. I came upon it during the months of Pressi's slow recovery in the rehabilitation centre. This teaching of Rama was in the technical sense of the term a positive one – that is, a teaching on the reality and indivisibility of Brahman – as distinct from the preparatory and negative teaching that exposes the illusory nature of the manifest world. Rama's basic and very simple injunction was to take the reality that is obscured by the sensory world as a single field of being. It was my experimental, uncertain attempts to put this injunction into effect that eventually resulted in my first experience of the presence. That affirmative experience would return, waxing and waning, over the subsequent years. Then in 2014 the presence withdrew, temporarily, in the wake of that stark, dismaying revelation of the world's emptiness.

So I tried once again now to take up Rama Tirtha's basic injunction. The trouble was that I had become so fixated on all those non-self-existent sense-forms that I couldn't rediscover the simplicity of the presence. I certainly tried. I "looked" for it only to find myself derailed by – and obsessed with – the unreal but actual-factual side-show. After that I sort of pulled myself together and began to consider an alternative rendition of Rama Tirtha's message that might address my problem. It went like this: the way of getting from the negative (the illusory world-show) to the positive (the reality) must surely be to somehow "subtract" the former from the latter.

The act of "subtraction" is based on the key truth underscored both by Advaita and contemporary science, to the effect that the sensory world is not real in itself. So, one imaginatively and determinedly deletes from the world-show all those apparent individualities, variations, and divisions that had seemed to confirm a real manifold or multiplicity. What would remain, then, would be an intimation of the indivisibly real that underlies all multiplicity. Or so one could hope. But I found it surprisingly hard to "do" this – to perform the act of erasure. How do you bring off this act in a way that is more immediate, more intense, than to just mentally rehearse once again the familiar old Advaitic teaching? Is it all a matter of will power, or some kind of technique – or an inner ripening that cannot be hurried?

What actually occurred in 2015 during the early morning session referred to above answered these questions in a breathtakingly simple way. Deutsch's crowning summation of the Oneness of Brahman, presented to me by a recorded voice, suddenly impressed itself as a single pulse of being that was both within me and all around me. This was the necessary "subtraction" of all that multiplicity, occurring instantly and automatically and all at once. The precipitating factor for this experience was simply my intense engagement with the text. And what the experience gave rise to was equally simple: an unqualified, exultant, silent *Yes!*

All of this happened while my fingertips were still poised over the function buttons of my tape recorder. There it was, *here* it was, the relief and absolute wonder of it. I let out a long sigh as the egocentric envelope of "I am I and none other" opened up, or just forgot about itself. This was a glimpse of the reality that is glossed by Advaita as "non-duality." Such was the end of poignancy and nostalgia and the beginning of something new, a deep, affirmative, remarkably simple sense of borderlessness.

The field of being now ran straight through me; I recognized it as the presence, but with a significant difference. The former feeling of separateness had dissolved. It was as though the presence had come to invite and then absorb me, rather than stand apart from me as it had done before. This transformation from dividedness to an apparent borderlessness was categorical but not in the least threatening – the change was astonishing, yet gentle. I revelled in it.

Not surprisingly the experience began to fade away when I had to get up and do something with Pressi, for after all this opening was by no means the final and definitive realization known as enlightenment. I understood this even during the alteration of perspective, an alteration that might be described as a temporary figure-ground fusion. For that brief interval I was both foreground and background, indistinguishable from the presence.

Since then I have found that I can return to that revelation through remembrance. I bring to mind the preparatory condition of complete philosophical conviction, or alternatively the sheer openness of the full subsequent experience. In either case I find myself re-entering the original openness, with its total lack of distinction between the inner "seer" and that which is "seen." It is always the same, a simple, beatific apperception of wholeness. Whatever physical tension may be present begins immediately to release itself, and I have the thought or feeling that what is happening is miraculous and yet at the same time blaz-ingly obvious. But I am keenly aware that over time I could begin to lose this opening through distraction or stress, through forgetting to remember. Remembering must become a habit, just as the practical, adaptive forms of witnessing had become a habit. Eventually I took up a particular Advaitic practice, or sadhana, that reinforces remem-brance. This classical sadhana – *adhyatma* yoga as taught by Shankara – directly addresses the fact that I have not yet broken through into full realization.

In the wake of my new, intermittent opening into a sense of border-less being – the late but welcome fruit of recognizing the empirical world as an illusion – my "relationship" with that world is sorting itself out in an unforced, natural-seeming way. It is already clear that my long-standing interest in the physical and social sciences, and my sometimes dour preoccupation with geopolitical trends, are unlikely to disappear. This interest and involvement helps me to consider and understand something of the intricate, churning, endlessly fascinating and sometimes appalling show that Advaita calls "appearance."

As for ordinary empirical life, this just goes on and things somehow just get done. And when I consider a single, "solid," empirical object – take for example the smooth stone that my friend Sonia Tilson brought back for me from her holiday in Turkey – I find that it can be experienced in a number of different ways. In its shapeliness and tide-washed smoothness it is pleasant to the touch. Sometimes the stone conjures up my fading, mind's-eye memories of particular Mediterranean beaches: nothing wrong with that, and no sense of loss or inaccessibility. But best of all I can palm the stone and return to the remembrance that does not deny tactile or any other kind of sensory experience, but puts that experience in its proper "place" – the vast unbroken field of being, against which all sense-objects manifest only as contingent appearances. For me, this flexible, Advaitically informed perspective is still new enough that I feel I am starting over again, starting afresh.

The stages of doubt, dissonance, resistance, acceptance, and partial revelation described here have led me to a greater appreciation of the alternative paths available within the broad Vedanta tradition, even as this unfolding revealed once and for all that it is Advaitic Vedanta that fits my purposes and aspirations. The greatest gift of my private, year-long ontological revolution – a gift that was insepa-rable from the new experience of borderlessness – was to finally recognize the genuine human value of the world-show. For Advaita there is no contradiction involved in taking to heart the illusory nature of the objects of common experience, while affirming at the same time that those "objects" are not only practical necessities but grist for the mill of clarification.

It is natural that the refutation of the conventional world view should be uncomfortable at first. For readers who would like to find out more about how Advaita addresses and sublimates this discomfort, I would strongly recommend the Eliot Deutsch book referred to above. Over the past four decades, *Advaita Vedanta – A Philosophical Reconstruction* has been a source of illumination, support and encouragement for new students of Advaita, especially those who are in the throes of digesting the demonstrable but gritty fact that the empirical world is not what it appears to be.

Eliot Deutsch's account of the beauty and unitive potential that is inherent in the deepest aspects of sensory-mental life encapsulates much that I have slowly come to feel, but have never before articulated. Deutsch shows how the illusory world-show can serve as a kind of stage-set, the only one to which we will ever have direct access. It is the immediate setting in which we can learn how to value those aspects of life that foreshadow the deeper realization. These aspects include rational metaphysical enquiry, intense aesthetic experiences that prove to have abiding value, and above all else the love and fellow-feeling we discover with our "others." Deutsch's treatment of Advaitic spiritual vision and practice is the necessary complement to the evolutionary perspective on phenomenality and adaptivity that we looked at earlier in this chapter. The two kinds of presentation, taken together, offer a multi-dimensional view of human development and transcendent potential.

It is the fully argued claim of Advaita that the transcendent is already present, though not recognized by most of us. As for me, these days I just stay with what I know or "see." What I see increasingly is that the presence is a harbinger of undivided reality. According to Advaita this reality is self-knowing and self-sufficient, manifest both within us and beyond us, and boundless in a way that has nothing to do with spatial extension. It is absolutely still yet charged with love and life. If I were enlightened I would feel it fully and consistently as "I". If I were a theist, I would probably call it the work of the Lord. Sometimes this presence appears together with the newly amplified nerve root pain brought about by further degenerative changes to the spine, the pain interposed like a branding iron between body and presence. When I am especially pulled down by pain or burdened with worry the presence may be apparent only for moments at a time, but even then those moments are definitive. They offer a glimpse into our real nature – the being that is indistinguishable from consciousness – as seen from the edge of a thin boundary that does not really exist.

It doesn't seem right even to try to say much more about this, except for the following. It is this presence, and nothing else, that serves as the great but incomparably simple sufficiency against which the inconvenience of not being able to see or avoid pain assumes its right proportion. It is this presence that gets me through the bad patches. It is this presence, if I can remain faithful and open to it, that will help me receive and accept this body non-judgmentally, even as it continues to decline. And it may indeed be this presence, one and the same everywhere, that is helping Pressi to get through sleepless nights of arthritic pain.

I know very well that the view of reality I have tried to present stage by stage in these pages is not generally understood. That is why I usually remain silent regarding Advaita in my ordinary dealings with the people around me. It is perhaps not surprising that it should be difficult to communicate from one person to another that which is patently immaterial and transpersonal. Or one can communicate some sense of it through shared fellow-feeling or practical help, but not easily through words. Sometimes I have the fond illusion that if we were back in India all I would have to do is say, "Look – there is nothing but the one, all appearances to the contrary." But few of the Indians I knew in Delhi, or at least in official Delhi, would be interested. It is right here that I have the few special friends with whom I can share this kind of exploration.

And that, I find, is all I have to say about my life experience up to now, and the various ways through which I have tried to make sense of it. I was a slow learner; it has taken more than seven decades for the contending forces that have shaped this life to work themselves out, a process that is still going on. It has been quite a show to behold. It is what they call karma, which means something like action and its consequences, cause and effect, the bonds of contingency. This term never applies to the essential self but only to the ego-sense and the incidental attributes, physical and mental, to which it clings.

According to Advaita, the true self or Atman that is one and the same for all of us remains unbound and untouched by the vicissitudes of karma. This is not a claim to be accepted on mere faith, or in acquiescence to a broader doctrine. The way to affirm first-hand that we are not the object of karma but rather the observer of it is to attain to the position of the witness, the clear consciousness that takes everything in while remaining calmly detached from it. This experience of inner autonomy is certainly attainable.

As to our collective, gross material, geopolitical future, I don't know any more than you do what it holds in store for us. Every Friday morning for more years than we can count, my old friend Mary Van Buskirk and I get together to read the *Economist* – always absorbing, but seldom revealing of obvious solutions. And yet it is sometimes possible for citizens to push for public policies and private initiatives that are actually sane and constructive, rather than the opposite. Even if they prove to be insufficient to turn things around they can affirm what is to be really valued, both in the world-show and implicitly within ourselves. That is reason enough to support them.

Now: with what carefully chosen words should I sign off on my ontological autobiography? I have found myself hesitating over this, and not just because the story-line is not yet extinguished. So I have decided to leave the last word to someone else, a venerable, consummate word-artist and humanist. Here in this final section I have tried once again to open a little through-way from secular humanism to a non-theistic spiritual perspective, Advaita. As we have seen, Advaita has two aspects or stages, those of refutation and substitution, or if you will refutation and revelation. It is becoming more and more apparent that when secular humanism in its current, science-dominated form is examined with real dispassion, it proves itself to be very adept at the business of refuting some of our most cherished ego-based assumptions regarding the nature of things. It isn't set up to do "revelation," but for us here that doesn't matter. In its most uncompromising iterations secular humanism not only scuttles false views but exposes what it feels like to be what we conceive of as nakedly human, isolatingly individual, contingent. And with that, we may find that we are ready to begin "seeing" in a different way.

Instead of falling back on some Upanishad, then, we will conclude with lines from the poet and playwright who remains to this day our most evocative and unsparing portrayer of the human condition. Some of his work contains carefully coded references to the "new" science, particularly astronomy; all of it reflects a disinclination to refer human conflict and suffering to the prescriptions of conventional religion. In the quotation set out below, our poet speaks through the imagined persona of Prospero, a sage and wizard. As he begins to speak, his referent is a band of players in a particular theatre, but it soon becomes evident that his real subject is the world, and our apparent selves, as we know them or think we know them. The resulting portrayal of insubstantiality is breathtaking, but it is not dark or despairing. What struck me when I first read these lines in my freshman year at university was their tone of calm acceptance and even tenderness, and their manifest authority. It is all true, I thought.

> Our revels now are ended. These our actors,
> As I foretold you, were all spirits and
> Are melted into air, into thin air:
> And, like the baseless fabric of this vision
> The cloud-capp'd towers, the gorgeous palaces,
> The solemn temples, the great globe itself,
> Yea, all which it inherit, shall dissolve
> And, like this insubstantial pageant faded,
> Leave not a rack behind. We are such stuff
> As dreams are made on, and our little life
> Is rounded with a sleep.
>   William Shakespeare
>   *The Tempest*, Act IV, Scene I, lines 148–58

Notes

INTRODUCTION

1 Marla Runyan, *No Finish Line – My Life as I See It* (New York: Putnam, 2001). Also available from Brilliance Audio on MP3-CD, MP3 Una edition, read by Emily Schirner, 2004.

CHAPTER ONE

1 Saul Bellow, *The Adventures of Augie March* (New York: Viking Press, 1953).

CHAPTER TWO

1 For reasons of discretion (these fictions drew indirectly upon the lives of real people without explicitly identifying them) I adopted a pen name, Evan Green. For the short story and novella respectively, see Evan Green, "Peters in Shinjuku," in *New Press Anthology #1: Best Canadian Short Fiction*, ed. John Metcalf and Leon Rooke (Toronto: General Publishing Co., 1984) and Evan Green, "Marginals," in *New Press Anthology #2: Best Canadian Stories*, ed. John Metcalf and Leon Rooke (Toronto: General Publishing, 1985).

CHAPTER THREE

1 Hindutva – an aggressive, politicized form of "Hinduization" – can lead not just to confrontation but to whole cycles of violence. Since 1990 a major focal point of Hindutva-fuelled tension has been the city of

Ayodhya in Uttar Pradesh, where in 1992 a decommissioned Moslem
mosque was destroyed by rioting Hindu nationalists. These militants
claimed the site to be the birthplace of the god Rama. In 1992–93 a
campaign to build a Hindu temple on this site involved widespread inter-
communal violence. Related outbreaks of rioting in Mumbai left an
estimated 900 people dead, including 275 Hindus, 575 Muslims, and
50 unidentified. In subsequent years Islamic fundamentalists in Pakistan
and Bangladesh retaliated against their small Hindu populations, leading
finally to revenge attacks within India itself. The most outrageous of these
was the 2008 Mumbai bombing and assault-rifle attack that killed more
than 250 people, an atrocity that was planned and expedited by Pakistan-
based Islamic terrorists. Meanwhile, Muslim community leaders in north
India tried desperately to restrain embittered young men who had been
targeted and humiliated by Hindutva nationalists.

2　Alistair Shearer, *The Traveler's Key to Northern India* (New York: Knopf,
1983).

3　Jorge Juis Borges, "The Immortal," in *Collected Fictions*, trans. Andrew
Hurley (New York: Penguin Books, 1998), 183–95.

CHAPTER FOUR

1　Stephen Mitchell, introduction to his translation of *The Book of Job*,
repr. ed. (New York: HarperPerennial, 1992). Stephen Mitchell is a highly
articulate, multilingual spiritual seeker whose work spans the breadth
of the Western and Eastern traditions. His subjects have included his own
Jewish tradition (the Job book and a translation of selected Psalms), the
Gospels of Jesus, the Gilgamesh epic, the Tao Te Ching, and the Bhagavad-
Gita. Mitchell's study of the Book of Job is a classic; it is iconoclastic,
tough-minded, and profoundly insightful. Mitchell argues effectively
that the "Hollywood ending" of Job is a late afterthought, one that is
completely at odds with the hard but liberating lesson conveyed by the
Voice in the Whirlwind.

2　Swami Rama Tirtha, *In Woods of God-Realization*. Available free at
www.ramatirtha.org/

3　Rob McRae would eventually write *Resistance and Revolution: Václav
Havel's Czechoslovakia* (Ottawa: Carleton University Press, 1997). It is an
authoritative and engrossing account of the Velvet Revolution, the essentially non-violent political movement that transformed Czechoslovakia in
the late 1980s. In his book, Rob includes an account of a visit that he and
I made to future president Václav Havel, while he was still under house

arrest in his apartment in Prague. This meeting gave me a once-in-a-lifetime opportunity to tell Havel how deeply I had been moved over the years by his courageous essays and plays. Thanks again, Rob.

CHAPTER FIVE

1 Dennis Lee, *Body Music* (Toronto: House of Anansi Press, 1988).
2 In both the Western and Eastern versions of the transcultural negative way, the student or seeker examines the attributes conventionally assigned to "God," in order to see that such attributes are inherently self-contradictory. This refutation does not take the form of an abstract philosophical proof; it is instead an intense mental enactment that opens up the mind in an uncommonly direct way. What may then be intuited by the seeker is the reality that lies "beneath" the presumed but refutable deity. This reality is the singularity referred to in the Western negative way as "godhead" as distinct from "God," or as the Absolute or Ground of Being.
3 As to the perennial question of cultural fertilization between the Western and Eastern wings of the negative way, there is very little evidence of specific teachings by Western masters percolating into the Eastern tradition, or vice versa. What we do find, intriguingly, is that the basic strategies and intuitions that characterize these two traditions are to a large extent identical. The Western Neoplatonic tradition that informs the Jewish, Christian, and Islamic iterations of the Negative Way is summed up by the single word *apophasis*: the corresponding term in Advaita Vedanta is *apavada*. It turns out that the Greek term apophasis and the Sanskrit term apavada are derived from the same Indo-European root. Both may be translated as revelatory negation or deconstruction, the unsaying of that which obscures the truth.
4 Michael A. Sells, *Mystical Languages of Unsaying* (Chicago: University of Chicago Press, 1994).
5 Raymond B. Blakney, trans., *Meister Eckhart, A Modern Translation* (New York: Harper Torchbooks, 1941).
6 Arthur Osborne, *Ramana Maharshi and the Path of Self-Knowledge* (New York: Weiser, 1970 [1954]); Arthur Osborne, ed., *The Collected Works of Ramana Maharshi* (New York: Red Wheel/Weiser, 1997 [c. 1959]).
7 George Orwell, *Nineteen Eighty-Four* (London: Secker & Warburg, 1949).
8 Christopher Hitchens, *God Is Not Great – How Religion Poisons Everything* (Toronto: McClelland and Stewart, 2007), 196. American author Frances Fitzgerald devotes a full chapter to the ethos and problems of Rajneesh's Oregon ashram in her book *Cities on a Hill* (New York: Simon & Schuster, 1987).

CHAPTER SIX

1 The peculiar title of this book – *On Having No Head* – had its origins in a startling experience that came to Douglas Harding one day out of the blue. Prompted by the remembrance of something he had read years before, Harding looked purposefully down at his feet and slowly ran his gaze up his legs, midsection, and chest, and then tried to "look" at what was all the way up, above his chest and shoulders. That would have been his head, of course, if his eyes could have shot out from their sockets and turned around to look back at it. What Douglas actually "saw" (or rather, vividly experienced) was the space-like consciousness that had registered the existence of everything from his feet up. It was as though consciousness, the bottom-line inner perceiver, had abruptly displaced the meatball that contains the eye, nose, ears, and tongue, all those second-order perceivers. Apparently, it was astonishing to discover in this way the intimate presence of the consciousness-self. That experience would give rise to the ingenious thought experiments that were a conspicuous feature of Douglas's later writings.

2 Jacques Lusseyran, trans. Elizabeth R. Cameron, *And There Was Light*, 2nd rev. ed. (Sandpoint, ID: Morning Light Press, (2006 [1963]).

3 Jacques Lusseyran, *Against the Pollution of the I: Selected Writings*, 2nd ed. (Sandpoint, ID: Morning Light Press, 2006 [1999]).

4 John Hull, *Touching the Rock: An Experience of Blindness* (New York: Pantheon, 1991).

5 George Berkeley, *An Essay towards a New Theory of Vision*, 1709. Available online through Wikisource at https://en.wikisource.org/wiki/An_Essay_Towards_a_New_Theory_of_Vision and http://psychclassics.yorku.ca/Berkeley/vision.htm. Also George Berkeley, *A Treatise Concerning the Principles of Human Knowledge*, 1710. Both of these seminal works are collected in *George Berkeley: Philosophical Writings*, ed. Desmond M. Clarke (Cambridge: Cambridge University Press, 2008).

6 The counterintuitive but unavoidable implications of the new physics were summed up frankly by Sir Arthur Eddington as far back as the 1920s. "We have dismissed the metaphysical conception of substance ... The balance placed on permanence creates the world of apparent substance ... The solid substance of things is another illusion. It too is a fancy projected by the mind into the external world." These comments by Eddington appear in Ken Wilber's *Quantum Questions*, rev. ed. (Boulder, CO: Shambhala, 2001). Their original source is Arthur Eddington, *The Nature of the Physical World*, 1929, chapters 12 through 15.

7 The seemingly impossible features of quantum physics include single particles that can be in two different places at the same time, and phenomena that take the form of either particles or waves, depending on the circumstances. An excellent history and overview of this arcane field of inquiry is *Quantum Reality: Beyond the New Physics*, by science journalist Nick Herbert (New York: Anchor, 1985). Herbert provides detailed descriptions of the ingenious experiments through which quantum physicists illustrate a whole range of phenomena that violate the laws of pre-quantum physics, and the laws of common sense as well.

8 Erwin Schrödinger, *My View of the World* (Cambridge: Cambridge University Press, 1951).

9 Richard Dawkins, *Queerer than We Can Suppose – The Strangeness of Science*, 2006 Beatty Memorial Lecture, McGill University, Montreal. A key feature of this lecture was Dawkins's account of how a painful collision between two conventional objects, for example a human foot and a rock, can powerfully but erroneously convey the impression that both objects are absolutely solid. What actually happens is that the atomic forces associated with the virtually empty foot interact with those associated with the virtually empty rock, in such a way as to keep the two near-emptinesses from interpenetrating. It is upon this strangely immaterial but actual external environment that our adaptively evolved senses project illusory objects, which seem to have unbroken surfaces and inner density. There are in fact no such objects.

10 W.B. Yeats, "Sailing to Byzantium," *The Tower* (1928). Available at www.csun.edu/~hceng029/yeats/collectedpoems.html

11 See, for example, Howard E. Gruber and J. Jacques Vonèche, eds., *The Essential Piaget: An Interpretative Reference and Guide* (Lanham, MD: Jason Aronson, 1995). Other relevant titles by Piaget include *The Psychology of the Child, The Child's Conception of the World, The Origins of Intelligence in Children*, and *The Structure of Reality in the Child*.

12 Thomas Traherne, *Centuries, Poems, and Thanksgivings*, vol. 1, ed. H.M. Margoliouth (Oxford: The Clarendon Press, 1958).

13 Paul Monette, *Borrowed Time: An AIDS Memoir* (San Diego: Harcourt Brace Jovanovich, 1988).

CHAPTER SEVEN

1 For a rich, challenging, but entirely accessible account of how the Mahavakyas reveal the underlying identicality of self and Brahman, see R. Krishnaswami Aiyar, *The Great Equation – A Logical Presentation of*

Advaita Vedanta. This modern classic is a valuable complement to the
writings of Shankara. The basic works of Shankara are collected and
annotated in an excellent multi-volume set referenced in note 3 below.

2 Allan Jones, "Walking Through the Interzone: Excerpts From a Vision
Loss Diary," *Ars Medica* 6, no. 2 (Spring 2010): 2–9.

3 *Shankara SourceBook*, complete set in six volumes, paperback, compiled
by A.J. Alston (London, UK: Shanti Sadan, 2004). The volumes are
1. Shankara on the Absolute; 2. Shankara on the Creation; 3. Shankara
on the Soul; 4. Shankara on Rival Views; 5. Shankara on Discipleship;
6. Shankara on Enlightenment.

4 To learn more about MBSR, see the website of the Center for Mindfulness
in Medicine, Health Care, and Society, University of Massachusetts
Medical School, at www.umassmed.edu/cfm/. See also note 6 below.

5 Jon Kabat-Zinn, *Coming to Our Senses: Healing Ourselves and the World
through Mindfulness* (New York: Hyperion, 2005), 88.

CHAPTER EIGHT

1 Suggested reading on mindfulness practice: Jon Kabat-Zinn, *Full
Catastrophe Living* (1996), *Wherever You Go There You Are* (1994), and
Coming to Our Senses (2005); Larry Rosenberg, *Breath by Breath – The
Liberating Practice of Insight Meditation* (2004); and Sharon Salzberg's
Voices of Insight (2001), *Faith* (2002), and *Loving Kindness* (1995). For
reasons of my own I was especially impressed and moved by Salzberg's
little book *Faith*, in which the author vividly documents how she applied
mindfulness practice to the resolution of childhood trauma.

Visually impaired Americans interested in mindfulness practice may
check with Learning Ally (formerly Recording for the Blind and Dyslexic)
at 1-800-221-4792. For copyright reasons Canadians with reading disabilities are excluded from this service. They can try CELA, the Centre
for Equitable Library Access at 1-855-655-2273. CELA has in effect taken
over the acquisitions of the CNIB library. This new organization has a few
titles bearing on mindfulness practice, including Kabat-Zinn's *Full Catastrophe Living*. But, as noted above, the quickest way for anyone to begin
exploring mindfulness teaching is to access the MBSR website, which
contains information on courses you can take and instructional materials
available in audio format. Go to www.umassmed.edu/cfm/index.aspx.

2 Oliver Sacks, "What Hallucinations Reveal About Our Minds," TED Talk
of February 2009, available at www.ted.com/talks/oliver_sacks_what_
hallucination_reveals_about_our_minds

3 Eventually Oliver Sacks' essay "The Mind's Eye" was collected into a book bearing the same title, together with other pieces that explore the startling vicissitudes of vision loss. Sacks graphically portrays the visual phenomena experienced by his subjects while explaining the neurological anomalies on which they are based. The emphasis throughout is on the ingenuity and tenacity of the men and women who occupy these "parallel" visual worlds. See Oliver Sacks, *The Mind's Eye* (New York: Vintage, 2010).

4 Harold Bloom, *The Anxiety of Influence*, 2nd ed. (Oxford: Oxford University Press, 1997).

5 The Shanti Sadan web site (www.shantisadan.org) includes a list of currently available publications. In addition to the Shankara Sourcebook and other classics by the Advaitic masters, the catalogue includes contemporary works (e.g., meditation guides) by Hari Prasad Shastri and Marjorie Waterhouse.

6 Leonard Cohen, "Anthem" (1992), from the album *The Future*, copyright 2013 Sony Music Entertainment.

CHAPTER NINE

1 The metaphysical religion of Baruch Spinoza is presented (or rather implied, gestured toward, partially worked through) in his masterwork, the *Ethics* (1677). The account of the deity, or Absolute, or natural order presented in the *Ethics* is not easy to assimilate; Spinoza's argument may rest upon a direct intuition or realization that is not fully unpacked on the page. To some readers he will appear to be a pantheist. Spinoza's depiction of fundamental reality has elements in common with some renditions of Vedanta.

2 Eliot Deutsch, *Advaita Vedanta: A Philosophical Reconstruction* (Honolulu: University of Hawaii Press, 1980). I would also recommend *The Essential Vedanta: A New Source Book of Advaita Vedanta*, edited by Eliot Deutsch and Rohit Dalvi (Bloomington, IN: World Wisdom, 2004). This volume includes key selections from the Upanishads, Bhagavad-Gita, Brahma Sutras, and other foundational texts, together with extensive commentaries by Shankara, his contemporaries, and successors.